CHANGES IN LAW AND SOCIETY DURING THE
CIVIL WAR AND RECONSTRUCTION

A LEGAL HISTORY DOCUMENTARY READER

Changes in Law and Society during the Civil War and Reconstruction

EDITED BY
CHRISTIAN G. SAMITO

SOUTHERN ILLINOIS UNIVERSITY PRESS
CARBONDALE

12 11 10 09   4 3 2 1

Library of Congress Cataloging-in-Publication Data
Changes in law and society during the Civil War and
Reconstruction : a legal history documentary reader
/ edited by Christian G. Samito.
     p. cm.
  Includes bibliographical references and index.
  ISBN-13: 978-0-8093-2889-5 (alk. paper)
  ISBN-10: 0-8093-2889-5 (alk. paper)
  1. African Americans—Legal status, laws, etc.—His-
tory—19th century. 2. African Americans—Civil
rights—History—19th century. 3. United States—
Armed Forces—African Americans—History—19th
century. I. Samito, Christian G.
  KF4757.C48 2009
  342.7308'73—dc22   2008043099

Printed on recycled paper. ♻
The paper used in this publication meets the minimum
requirements of American National Standard for Information Sciences—Permanence of Paper for Printed
Library Materials, ANSI Z39.48-1992. ∞

To two outstanding professors and friends, David Quigley and Alan Rogers

Contents

CHAPTER 2: THE EXPANSION OF GOVERNMENTAL POWER AND THE NATIONALIZATION OF THE UNION · 59

CHAPTER 3: AFRICAN AMERICANS, EMANCIPATION, AND MILITARY SERVICE · 100

ILLUSTRATIONS

Changes in Law and Society during the Civil War and Reconstruction

Introduction

During the era of the Civil War and Reconstruction, the government and people of the United States undertook the most comprehensive reconsideration of issues since the original constitutional convention in 1787. As New Yorker Daniel Morris announced in 1864 to his fellow congressmen, they faced a "moment of greater responsibility than has devolved upon a like body since the year 1776. The events of an entire century transpire in a year. The United States have made more history in the three years last past than can be written out in an ordinary lifetime."[1] Americans confronted the contours of governmental power and considered the boundaries of civil liberties during wartime. Legislation fueled national development, furthered the centralization and expansion of the federal government, revolutionized and nationalized the monetary and banking systems, and promoted both the coercive power of government (taxation and conscription) as well as its role in taking care of citizens (pensions for Civil War veterans).

For African Americans, military service shattered the old order, necessitated the end of slavery, and fueled demands and expectations for equal citizenship rights and inclusion. African Americans sought more than emancipation in name only: they called for broad changes so as to secure for themselves an enduring freedom, including equality before the law, voting rights, and economic self-sufficiency. During the 1860s, the law of slavery gave way to the hard-fought struggle for black equality, and, in the process, Americans debated how to restore the egalitarian ideals of the Declaration of Independence to actual practices.

National citizenship existed as a vague concept prior to the Civil War, with most rights now associated with citizenship handled on a state or local level and governed by race. We hold a different understanding of citizenship today, emphasizing its national character and the idea of civil, political, and social rights bundled together to form a larger whole. This modern vision of national citizenship did not manifest itself in America in 1787 but developed as a result of the tumult of the era of the Civil War and Reconstruction. Citizenship's rapid centralization, nationalization, heightened importance, and emergence to give rise to claims for rights all represent a major break with prior history. Amid the tempest of the Civil War, statesmen, soldiers, and ordinary people forged a more robust definition of American citizenship, one that eventually integrated national rights and duties along with the embrace of American ideals.

The crisis of the antebellum constitutional system, culminating in the Civil War, both necessitated and enabled the large-scale rethinking of American constitutionalism that occurred. As early as April 21, 1861, abolitionist Wendell Phillips roused an audience of four thousand Bostonians when he announced that the Civil War would allow the people of the United States to reclaim the Revolutionary ideals proclaimed by the Declaration of Independence, and he added his own egalitarian vision of America's future: "[W]hen the smoke of this conflict clears away, the world will see under our banner all tongues, all creeds, all races,—one brotherhood,—and on the banks of the Potomac, the Genius of Liberty, robed in light, four and thirty stars for her diadem, broken chains under feet, and an olive branch in her right hand."[2] Those who advocated reordering society based on a more expansive view of civil rights recognized that the United States could never return to the antebellum status quo. As Maryland Unionist congressman Henry Winter Davis argued, "Call the dead to life . . . restore the soul to the soulless eyes of the thousands that have fallen martyrs upon the battle-field, and then you can restore the Union as it was."[3] Yet, for Davis and other advocates of reform, the changes they proposed did not mean breaking with the Founders, and they instead equated change with a restoration and reclaiming of the Constitution as it came from the Founders. Reformers of the Reconstruction generation came to realize that amending the Constitution did not mean destroying it and that the polity could correct the error of allowing slavery to persist while continuing to respect the Constitution's fundamental legitimacy and the Founders' basic vision.

On the other hand, the potential of this reformative moment eroded in the face of violence in the South conducted by white supremacists and because of judicial limitation of the Civil War Amendments and associated legislation. The legal history of the United States in the last third of the nineteenth century demonstrates that legal change is not always one of linear progression, and the evolution of American citizenship did not end with the ratification of the Civil War Amendments. Yet, even where initial expansions of citizenship and accompanying rights contracted for African Americans beginning in the 1870s, painful but temporary defeat sowed the seeds for long-term success. Theoretical arguments and practical changes regarding citizenship and civil rights in the 1860s set valuable precedents, influencing future struggle and arguments over these same issues, until a new corrective moment in the twentieth century again brought constitutional doctrine in line with the ideals of the Founders of 1776 as well as those of the 1860s.

The selections in this book highlight the fluidity and contingency during the era of the Civil War and Reconstruction, wherein law, society, and politics inextricably mixed and set American constitutionalism and legal development on particular paths that were not predetermined. Things now taken for granted—black citizenship, for example—could have had a far different outcome. The United States that ratified the Civil War Amendments in 1865–70 stood in marked contrast to the United States of 1861. Whereas on March 2, 1861, Congress approved and sent to the states a proposed thirteenth amendment that would have protected slavery from federal interference in the states where it existed, Congress on January 31, 1865, sent the nation a far different version that abolished slavery. The materials in this book also illuminate how idealism and pragmatism converged to change the law. For example, blacks shrewdly and persuasively connected their loyalty and military service to deliberations over suffrage, the fate of the Union, and the success of the Republican agenda at a time when even many Republicans remained unenthusiastic at best about giving the vote to the black man.

As others have recognized, American constitutionalism encompasses more than judicial interpretation; it also relies on unofficial commitments by the people and their acceptance and support of official pronouncements that they deem legitimate and appropriate. The people hold power to criticize, challenge, and oppose official practice, as well as move that practice into conformity with their vision, often by use of moral suasion and the ballot (for example, see the Republican Party's growth in response to *Dred Scott*). Episodes of public disagreement can resolve to create new accords on constitutional issues, and public deliberation makes up a critical, non-governmental aspect of constitutional development. The Reconstruction years also provide an example of how public reaction can affect legal change as a practical matter: the extralegal means and racist violence by which white supremacists in the South deprived blacks from practical enjoyment of the rights granted them in theory.

The era of the Civil War and Reconstruction is a particularly rich and especially important one for students of American legal history. This book offers only a fraction of the vast store of source material that exists, but I hope I have provided readers with a starting point for further exploration, a better understanding of how American law evolved during the second half of the nineteenth century, and a greater appreciation for the personal, individual impact the law has on those living under it.

Several people assisted me in this work, and I would like to acknowledge their help. At Boston College, Professors David Quigley and Alan Rogers provided me with valuable ideas and, along with Professor James O'Toole, have been true mentors. For years, the Interlibrary Loan Staff at Boston College's O'Neill Library has cheerfully obtained for me a variety of obscure documents, and they still surprise me as to how they do it so quickly and effectively. Sylvia Frank Rodrigue showed friendship and great enthusiasm for this project from the start and, along with John Rodrigue and the readers and staff at Southern Illinois University Press, provided valuable suggestions for improving the manuscript. I would also like to thank all my friends, whose fellowship is more important to me than they might know, and my family for their continuous love and support.

This book provides verbatim excerpts of selected documents, and I have preserved capitalization, spelling, and grammar as they appear in the originals. In some areas, I have placed bracketed additions and, in a few instances, standardized indentations for the sake of clarity. In some cases, slightly differing versions of the same document exist. In general, the materials are reprinted in chronological order, except where it made sense to deviate from that order so that documents related to certain topics remained together.

CHAPTER 1

THE STATUS OF AFRICAN AMERICANS
BEFORE THE CIVIL WAR

From 1787 until the ratification of the Thirteenth Amendment, slavery was a central cause of tension between the North and South and was the focus of debates about the relationship between the states and the federal government. While states in the North early on passed gradual emancipation acts or abolished slavery outright, and some Northern jurists rejected human bondage as repugnant to natural law, Southern states upheld the institution of slavery. By 1860, fifteen slave-holding states contained 3,950,000 slaves who were considered property to be bought, sold, and largely treated as their masters wished. Another 251,000 free blacks lived in the slave-holding states, but few had the rights that whites did.

The North contained almost 240,000 free blacks by 1860. African Americans in the North did not enjoy uniform rights, and according to historian Leon Litwack, they remained "largely disenfranchised, segregated and economically oppressed."[1] At the time of the Civil War, only Maine, New Hampshire, Vermont, Rhode Island, and Massachusetts permitted black men to vote on the same terms as white men. During the period 1848–57, Illinois, Indiana, and Iowa passed measures to prevent migration of free blacks into their states. As of 1860, blacks could not testify against whites in Indiana, Illinois, California, and Oregon (Oregon removed this stricture in 1862, and California did so by 1863). According to legal historian Paul Finkelman, Iowa's 1851 law fining blacks who remained in the state two dollars a day after three days went largely unenforced. Indiana, on the other hand, did enforce its 1851 prohibition against black migration, and the state's black population remained almost identical from 1850 to 1860. Illinois also enforced, albeit much less strictly than did Indiana, its comparable 1853 legislation mandating expelling and fining black immigrants (as well as a provision permitting sale at auction of blacks unable to pay the fine to someone who would pay it in exchange for the black's unpaid labor). Nonetheless, Illinois's black population grew in the 1850s by almost 2,200 people.[2]

Finkelman's research illuminates the complexity of Northern race relations and demonstrates that attitudes toward blacks varied across the states and even within states. Racism in Cincinnati contrasted with the tolerance manifested by the existence of Ohio's Oberlin College, which began to admit black students in 1835; integrated schools in Syracuse, New York, differed from segregated schools in Buffalo and Albany in the 1840s and 1850s. Older and more northern states tended to provide more rights, while newer states and those closer to the South proved less egalitarian. In contrast to bondage in the South, in the North blacks at least enjoyed basic legal rights such as the ability to purchase and sell property, educate themselves, make contracts, sue, and convene in public meetings or conventions; in most states they could testify against whites, and in some they could vote. Yet, Chief Justice Roger Taney of the Supreme Court chillingly declared in his *Dred Scott* ruling (1857) that blacks held no rights that whites had to respect. Any rights that African Americans possessed were at the whim of state legislatures, and they continued to suffer curtailment of equal rights in both official (for example, blacks could not obtain patents) and unofficial ways.

White abolitionists vehemently attacked both the morality and legality of slavery in the decades leading up to the Civil War. The 1833 Declaration of the American Anti-Slavery Society contrasted slavery with the principles of the Declaration of Independence: "that all men are created equal, that they are endowed by their Creator with certain unalienable Rights, that among these are Life, Liberty and the pursuit of Happiness." The Society condemned that slaves were instead "recognized by the law, and treated by their fellow beings, as marketable commodities, as goods and chattels, as brute beasts," and "plundered daily of the fruits of their toil without redress; really enjoying no constitutional nor legal protection from licentious and murderous outrages upon their persons; are ruthlessly torn asunder—the tender babe from the arms of its frantic mother—the heart-broken wife from her weeping husband—at the caprice or pleasure of irresponsible tyrants. For the crime of having a dark complexion, they suffer the pangs of hunger, the infliction of stripes, and the ignominy of brutal servitude." These abolitionists maintained that "no man has a right to enslave or imbrute his brother . . . or to brutalize his mind by denying him the means of intellectual, social, and moral improvement," affirmed that the "right to enjoy liberty is inalienable," called for slaves "instantly to be set free, and brought under the protection of law," and declared that "all persons of color who possess the qualifications which are demanded of others, ought to be admitted forthwith to the enjoyment of the same privileges, and the exercise of the same prerogatives, as others; and that the paths of preferment, of wealth, and of intelligence, should be opened as widely to them as to persons of a white complexion."[3]

Free blacks in the North, meanwhile, argued not only for abolition but also for their place in "the people" of the United States, even where they faced discrimination. These African Americans called for equal political rights as a weapon with which to kill slavery, believing that improving rights for themselves would also hasten emancipation in the South. Boston-born black historian William Cooper Nell and other African Americans in the mid-nineteenth-century North repeatedly cited black military participation in the American Founding to bolster their claims to equal rights. For blacks, the Revolution also exemplified a bitter paradox of antebellum American freedom: African Americans participated only to find the memory of their service subsumed by continued racial prejudice and ignored by those who defined the United States as a white republic. In his *Services of Colored Americans, in the Wars of 1776 and 1812* (1851), later expanded into *The Colored Patriots of the American Revolution* (1855), Nell sought to recover the history of black involvement in the American Founding and restore it to the record of the early Republic. Nell and others decried injustice against a group that contributed to the Founding, and they argued that blacks' active service in the Revolution warranted their inclusion in the American people. Black antebellum state conventions made similar arguments, and some whites also took up Nell's historical point: Justice Benjamin Curtis relied on an analysis of black rights during the early history of the Republic to bolster his dissent refuting Chief Justice Taney's opinion in *Dred Scott*.

Integrationists such as Nell, Frederick Douglass, and others focused on blacks' American identity, and while they called for self-help within the United States, they also claimed automatic inclusion as part of the American people as a result of their American birth, heritage, and historical contributions and civic participation. On the other hand, other blacks, such as Martin Delaney, responded to exclusion by seeking to form a separate black state. They urged emigration in order to create a successful, luminous black nation and undermine prejudice by proving black genius and productivity.

In the South, slaves sometimes tried to resist slavery by running away. Fugitive slaves greatly exacerbated sectional tensions. Southerners contended that the Constitution allowed them to reclaim their slave property, while many Northerners countered that a "higher law" required them to assist those seeking freedom. Some Northern states passed personal liberty laws, but the Supreme Court ruled in *Prigg v. Pennsylvania* (1842) that under the Constitution, federal legislation on this point preempted any contradictory state legislation.

A stricter Fugitive Slave Act, passed by Congress as part of the Compromise of 1850, brought home to Northerners the issue of slavery in a very personal way. The requirement that they help return fugitive slaves to bondage made Northerners feel like slave-catchers. Riots, such as one concerning the case of a fugitive slave recaptured in Boston, Anthony Burns, heightened sectional tension over slavery to the breaking point in the years shortly before the Civil War. The 1854 Kansas-Nebraska Act, which allowed people in the Kansas and Nebraska territories to decide for themselves whether or not to allow slavery within their borders, generated open guerrilla warfare and two opposing state legislatures in "Bleeding Kansas" and moved the nation closer to war as Northerners perceived the expansion of the slave power. In the 1850s, increasingly radical positions—both among Northern abolitionists and defenders of the Southern way of life—began to take stage in an era of greater sectional polarization. In the end, Chief Justice Taney sought to end divisive political debate about slavery with his *Dred Scott* ruling, but the opinion he drafted only hastened the Civil War. Dissatisfaction with the 1850 Fugitive Slave Act, the Kansas-Nebraska Act, and the *Dred Scott* ruling strengthened the new

Republican Party in the North. Abolitionists and Republicans rejected the logic and practical effect of the *Dred Scott* ruling and vowed to overturn the Supreme Court's holding at the ballot box. Northerners who formerly tolerated slavery for the sake of maintaining sectional balance increasingly saw that balance destroyed and refused to accept it any longer.

1. *THE STATE v. JOHN MANN*, 13 N.C. 263 (SUPREME COURT OF NORTH CAROLINA, 1829)

Elizabeth Jones rented her slave Lydia to John Mann, and when Mann tried to "chastise" Lydia for a "small offence," she ran off to avoid punishment. Mann shot Lydia in the back and appealed his subsequent conviction for battery. The North Carolina Supreme Court overturned Mann's conviction on the basis that the hirer or possessor of a slave must be treated at that time as the owner and that the "power of the master must be absolute to render the submission of the slave perfect."

The defendant was indicted for an assault and battery upon Lydia, the slave of one Elizabeth Jones.

On the trial it appeared that the defendant had hired the slave for a year; that during the term the slave had committed some small offence, for which the defendant undertook to chastise her; that while in the act of so doing the slave ran off, whereupon the defendant called upon her to stop, which being refused, he shot at and wounded her.

His Honor Judge DANIEL, charged the jury that if they believed the punishment inflicted by the defendant was cruel and unwarrantable, and disproportionate to the offence committed by the slave, that in law the defendant was guilty, as he had only a special property in the slave.

A verdict was returned for the State, and the defendant appealed.

RUFFIN, Judge [Thomas].—A judge cannot but lament when such cases as the present are brought into judgment. . . . The struggle, too, in the Judge's own breast between the feelings of the man and the duty of the magistrate is a severe one, presenting strong temptation to put aside such questions, if it be possible. It is useless, however, to complain of things inherent in our political state. And it is criminal in a Court to avoid any responsibility which the laws impose. With whatever reluctance, therefore, it is done, the Court is compelled to express an opinion upon the extent of the dominion of the master over the slave in North Carolina.

The indictment charges a battery on Lydia, a slave of Elizabeth Jones. . . . The inquiry here is whether a cruel and unreasonable battery on a slave by the hirer is indictable. The judge below instructed the jury that it is. He seems to have put it on the ground that the defendant had but a special property. Our laws uniformly treat the master or other person having the possession and command of the slave as entitled to the same extent of authority. The object is the same—the services of the slave; and the same powers must be confided. In a criminal proceeding, and indeed in reference to all other persons but the general owner, the hirer and possessor of a slave, in relation to both rights and duties, is, for the time being, the owner. . . . [U]pon the general question whether the owner is answerable *criminaliter* for a battery upon his own slave, or other exercise of authority or force not forbidden by statute, the Court entertains but little doubt. That he is so liable has never yet been decided; nor, as far as is known, been hitherto contended. There have been no prosecutions of the sort. The established habits and uniform practice of the country in this respect is the best evidence of the portion of power deemed by the whole community requisite to the preservation of the master's dominion. If we thought differently we could not set our notions in array against the judgment of ev[e]rybody else, and say that this or that authority may be safely lopped off. This had indeed been as-similated at the bar to the other domestic relations; and arguments drawn from the well-established principles which confer and restrain the authority of the parent over the child, the tutor over the pupil, the master over the apprentice, have been pressed on us. The Court does not recognize their application. There is no likeness between the cases. They are in opposition to each other, and there is an impassable gulf between them. The difference is that which exists between freedom and slavery—and a greater cannot be imagined. In the one, the end in view is the happiness of the youth, born to equal rights with that governor, on whom the duty devolves of training the young to usefulness in a station which he is afterwards to assume among freemen. To such an end, and with such a subject, moral and intellectual instruction seem the natural means; and for the most part they are found to suffice. Moderate force is superadded only to make the others effectual. If that fail it is better to leave the party to his own headstrong passions and the ultimate correction of the law than to allow it to be immoderately inflicted by a private person. With slavery it is far otherwise. The end is the profit of the master, his security and the public safety; the subject, one doomed in his own person and his posterity, to live without knowledge and without the capacity to make anything his own, and to toil that another may reap the fruits. What moral considerations shall be addressed to such a being to convince him what it is impossible but that the most stupid must feel and know can never be true—that he is thus to labor upon a principle of natural duty, or for the sake of his own personal happiness, such services can only be expected from one who has no will of his own; who surrenders his will in im-plicit obedience to that of another. Such obedience is the consequence only of uncontrolled authority over the body. There is nothing else which can operate to produce the effect. The power of the master must be absolute to render the submission of the slave perfect. I most freely confess my sense of the harsh-ness of this proposition; I feel it as deeply as any man can; and as a principle of moral right every person in his retirement must repudiate it. But in the actual condition of things it must be so. There is no remedy. This discipline belongs to the state of slavery. They cannot be disunited without abrogating at once the rights of the master and absolving the slave from his subjection. It constitutes the curse of slavery to both the bond and free portion of our population. But it is inherent in the relation of master and slave.

That there may be particular instances of cruelty and deliberate barbarity where, in conscience, the law might properly interfere, is most probable. The difficulty is to determine where a Court may properly begin. Merely in the abstract it may well be asked, which power of the master accords with right? The answer will probably sweep away all of them. But we cannot look at the matter in that light. The truth is that we are forbidden to enter upon a train of general reasoning on the subject. We cannot allow the right of the master to be brought into discussion in the courts of justice. The slave, to remain a slave, must be made sensible that there is no appeal from his master; that his power is in no instance usurped; but is conferred by the laws of man at least, if not by the law of God. The danger would be great, indeed, if the tribunals of justice should be called on to graduate the punishment appropriate to every temper and every dereliction of menial duty. No man can anticipate the many and aggravated provocations of the master which the slave would be constantly stimulated by his own passions or the instigation of others to give; or the consequent wrath of the master, prompting him to bloody vengeance upon the turbulent traitor—a vengeance generally practiced with impunity by reason of its privacy. The Court, therefore, disclaims the power of changing the relation in which these parts of our people stand to each other.

We are happy to see that there is daily less and less occasion for the interposition of the Courts. The protection already afforded by several statutes, that all-powerful motive, the private interest of the owner, the benevolences towards each other, seated in the hearts of those who have been born and bred together, the frowns and deep execrations of the community upon the barbarian who is guilty of excessive and brutal cruelty to his unprotected slave, all combined, have produced a mildness of treatment and attention to the comforts of the unfortunate class of slaves, greatly mitigating the rigors of servitude and ameliorating the condition of the slaves. The same causes are operating and will continue to operate with increased action until the disparity in numbers between the whites and blacks shall have rendered the latter in no degree dangerous to the former, when the police now existing may be further relaxed. This result, greatly to be desired, may be much more rationally expected from the events above alluded to, and now in progress, than from any rash expositions of abstract truths by a judiciary tainted with a false and fanatical philanthropy, seeking to redress an acknowledged evil by means still more wicked and appalling than even that evil.

I repeat that I would gladly have avoided this ungrateful question. But being brought to it the Court is compelled to declare that while slavery exists amongst us in its present state, or until it shall seem fit to the legislature to interpose express enactments to the contrary, it will be the imperative duty of the judges to recognize the full dominion of the owner over the slave, except where the exercise of it is forbidden by statute. And this we do upon the ground that this dominion is essential to the value of slaves as property, to the security of the master, and the public tranquillity, greatly dependent upon their subordination; and, in fine, as most effectually securing the general protection and comfort of the slaves themselves.

Per Curiam.—Let the judgment below be reversed, and judgment entered for the defendant.

2. *COMMONWEALTH V. THOMAS AVES*, 35 MASS. 193
(MASSACHUSETTS SUPREME JUDICIAL COURT, 1836)

A six-year-old black child, Med, and her mother were the slaves of Samuel Slater, a citizen of Louisiana who lived in New Orleans. Slater's wife, Mary, brought Med with her on a visit to her father, Thomas Aves, in Boston. Mary intended to return to New Orleans with Med, but when Mary fell ill, she asked Aves to take care of Med for a few days. At an abolitionist's petition, the court issued a writ of habeas corpus and summoned Aves to show the cause of Med's detention. Chief Justice Lemuael Shaw of the Massachusetts Supreme Judicial Court ruled that a non-fugitive slave voluntarily brought into Massachusetts became free and that slavery was so "odious" and contrary to natural law and justice that it could exist only locally and by force of positive law (statute).

. . . In showing cause Aves states upon his oath, that he has the child in his custody; that in 1833, Samuel Slater, a citizen of the State of Louisiana . . . purchased the child and its mother as and for his slaves, the mother and child being then and there, and long before that time, slaves by the laws of that State; that from the time of the purchase until about the first day of May, 1836, the mother and child remained the slaves of Slater in New Orleans, and by force of the laws of Louisiana; that on or about that day Mary Slater, the wife of S. Slater and the daughter of Aves, left New Orleans for the purpose of coming to Boston and visiting her father, intending to return to New Orleans and to her husband, (who remained in that city,) after an absence of four or five months for the purpose above mentioned; that the mother of the child remained in New Orleans, in slavery . . . ; that Mary Slater brought the child with her from New Orleans to Boston, having and retaining the child in her custody as the agent and representative of her husband, her object, intent, and purpose being to have the child accompany her and remain in her custody and under her care during her temporary absence from New Orleans, and that the child should return with her to New Orleans, their legal domicil; that the child was confided to the custody and care of Aves by Mary Slater, to be by him kept and nurtured during the absence of Mary Slater from Boston for a few days on account of ill health; that by the laws of Louisiana the marriage of a slave is void; that this child is the daughter of a slave, born in a state of slavery, and is by force of the laws of Louisiana a natural child; that by the same laws the mother of a natural child is its legal guardian, and that such right of guardianship over the infant children of a slave, where such children are not themselves slaves, devolves upon the owner of their mother; that if this child is, by force of the laws of Massachusetts, now emancipated and a free person, S. Slater, as the owner of the mother of this natural child, is entitled to the custody of the person of the child as its legal guardian, and that Aves is the agent and legally authorized representative of S. Slater in this behalf; that the child is about six years of age and wholly incapable of taking care of itself; that it is absolutely necessary that some person should have the custody of the person of the child and the right to restrain it of its liberty; that no private person nor magistrate has, by the laws of Massachusetts, any right to take the child out of the possession of Aves while he continues to use that possession and custody only for the purpose of benefiting the child, and only restraining it of its liberty so far as is necessary for its safety and health; and that he does not now and has not at any time restrained it of its liberty in any other way, or to any greater extent, than is necessary for its health and safety. . . .

SHAW C. J. delivered the opinion of the Court. The question now before the Court arises upon a return to a *habeas corpus* . . . for the purpose of bringing up the person of a colored child named Med, and instituting a legal inquiry into the fact of her detention, and the causes for which she was detained. . . .

The precise question presented by the claim of the respondent is, whether a citizen of any one of the United States, where negro slavery is established by law, coming into this State, for any temporary purpose of business or pleasure, staying some time, but not acquiring a domicil here, who brings a slave with him as a personal attendant, may restrain such slave of his liberty during his continuance here, and convey him out of this State on his return, against his consent. It is not contended that a master can exercise here any other of the rights of a slave owner, than such as may be necessary to retain the custody of the slave during his residence, and to remove him on his return. . . .

. . .[I]t is sufficient for the purposes of the case before us, that by the [Massachusetts state] constitution adopted in 1780, slavery was abolished in Massachusetts, upon the ground that it is contrary to natural right and the plain principles of justice. The terms of the first article of the declaration of rights are plain and explicit. "All men are born free and equal, and have certain natural, essential, and unalienable rights, which are, the right of enjoying and defending their lives and liberties, that of acquiring, possessing, and protecting property."

It would be difficult to select words more precisely adapted to the abolition of negro slavery. According to the laws prevailing in all the States, where slavery is upheld, the child of a slave is not deemed to be born free, a slave has no right to enjoy and defend his own liberty, or to acquire, possess, or protect property. That the description was broad enough in its terms to embrace negroes, and that it was intended by the framers of the constitution to embrace them, is proved by the earliest contemporaneous construction, by an unbroken series of judicial decisions, and by a uniform practice from the adoption of the constitution to the present time. . . .

Such being the general rule of law, it becomes necessary to inquire how far it is modified or controlled in its operation; either,

1. By the law of other nations and states, as admitted by the comity of nations to have a limited operation within a particular state; or

2. By the constitution and laws of the United States.

In considering the first, we may assume that the law of this State is analogous to the law of England, in this respect; that while slavery is considered as unlawful and inadmissible in both, and this because contrary to natural right and to laws designed for the security of personal liberty, yet in both, the existence of slavery in other countries is recognized, and the claims of foreigners, growing out of that condition, are, to a certain extent, respected. Almost the only reason assigned by Lord *Mansfield* in Sommersett's case was, that slavery is of such a nature, that it is incapable of being introduced on any reasons moral or political, but only by positive law; and, it is so odious, that nothing can be suffered to support it but positive law. . . .

But although slavery and the slave trade are deemed contrary to natural right, yet it is settled by the judicial decisions of this country and of England, that it is not contrary to the law of nations. . . . The consequence is, that each independent community, in its intercourse with every other, is bound to act on the principle, that such other country has a full and perfect authority to make such laws for the government of its own subjects, as its own judgment shall dictate and its own conscience approve, provided the same are consistent with the law of nations; and no independent community has any right to interfere with the acts or conduct of another state, within the territories of such state, or on the high seas, which each has an equal right to use and occupy; and that each sovereign state, governed by its own laws, although competent and well authorized to make such laws as it may think most expedient to the extent of its own territorial limits, and for the government of its own subjects, yet beyond those limits, and over those who are not her own subjects, has no authority to enforce her own laws, or to treat the laws of other states as void, although contrary to its own views of morality.

This view seems consistent with most of the leading cases on the subject.

Sommersett's case . . . decides that slavery, being odious and against natural right, cannot exist, except by force of positive law. But it clearly admits, that it may exist by force of positive law. . . . [P]ositive law . . . may be as well understood customary law as the enactment of a statute; and the word is used to designate rules established by tacit acquiescence or by the legislative act of any state, and which derive their force and authority from such acquiescence or enactment, and not because they are the dictates of natural justice, and as such of universal obligation. . . .

. . . [T]hough slavery is contrary to natural right, to the principles of justice, humanity and sound policy, as we adopt them and found our own laws upon them, yet not being contrary to the laws of nations, if any other state or community see fit to establish and continue slavery by law, so far as the legislative power of that country extends, we are bound to take notice of the existence of those laws, and we are not at liberty to declare and hold an act done within those limits, unlawful and void, upon our views of morality and policy, which the sovereign and legislative power of the place has pronounced to be lawful. . . .

. . . But it is not speaking with strict accuracy to say, that a property can be acquired in human beings, by local laws. Each state may, for its own convenience, declare that slaves shall be deemed property, and that the relations and laws of personal chattels shall be deemed to apply to them; as, for instance, that they may be bought and sold, delivered, attached, levied upon, that trespass will lie for an injury done to them, or trover for converting them. But it would be a perversion of terms to say, that such local laws do in fact make them personal property generally; they can only determine, that the same rules of law shall apply to them as are applicable to property. . . .

The conclusion to which we come from this view of the law is this:

That by the general and now well established law of this Commonwealth, bond slavery cannot exist, because it is contrary to natural right, and repugnant to numerous provisions of the constitution and laws, designed to secure the liberty and personal rights of all persons within its limits and entitled to the protection of the laws.

That though by the laws of a foreign state, meaning by "foreign," in this connection, a state governed by its own laws, and between which and our own there is no dependence one upon the other, but which in this respect are as independent as foreign states, a person may acquire a property in a slave, such acquisition, being contrary to natural right, and effected by the local law, is dependent upon such local law for its existence and efficacy, and being contrary to the fundamental laws of this State, such general right of property cannot be exercised or recognized here.

That, as a general rule, all persons coming within the limits of a state, become subject to all its municipal laws, civil and criminal, and entitled to the privileges which those laws confer; that this rule applies as well to blacks as whites, except in the case of fugitives, to be afterwards considered; that if such persons have been slaves, they become free, not so much because any alteration is made in their *status*, or condition, as because there is no law which will warrant, but there are laws, if they choose to avail themselves of them, which prohibit, their forcible detention or forcible removal.

That the law arising from the comity of nations cannot apply; because if it did, it would follow as a necessary consequence, that all those persons, who, by force of local laws, and within all foreign places where slavery is permitted, have acquired slaves as property, might bring their slaves here, and exercise over them the rights and power which an owner of property might exercise, and for any length of time short of acquiring a domicil; that such an application of the law would be wholly repugnant to our laws, entirely inconsistent with our policy and our fundamental principles, and is therefore inadmissible.

Whether, if a slave, voluntarily brought here and with his own consent returning with his master, would resume his condition as a slave, is a question which was incidentally raised in the argument, but is one on which we are not called on to give an opinion in this case, and we give none. From the principle above stated, on which a slave brought here becomes free, to wit, that he becomes entitled to the protection of our laws, and there is no law to warrant his forcible arrest and removal, it would seem to follow as a necessary conclusion, that if the slave waives the protection of those laws, and returns to the state where he is held as a slave, his condition is not changed. . . .

The question has thus far been considered as a general one, and applicable to cases of slaves brought from any foreign state or country; and it now becomes necessary to consider how far this result differs, where the person is claimed as a slave by a citizen of another State of this Union. As the several States, in all matters of local and domestic jurisdiction are sovereign, and independent of each other, and regulate their own policy by their own laws, the same rule of comity applies to them on these subjects as to foreign states, except so far as the respective rights and duties of the several States, and their respective citizens, are affected and modified by the constitution and laws of the United States.

In *art.* 4, § 2, the constitution declares that no person held to service or labor in one State, under the laws thereof, escaping into another, shall in consequence of any law or regulation therein, be discharged from such service or labor, but shall be delivered up on claim of the party to whom such service or labor may be due.

The law of congress made in pursuance of this article provides, that when any person held to labor in any of the United States, &c. shall escape into any other of the said States or Territories, the person entitled, &c. is empowered to arrest the fugitive, and upon proof made that the person so seized, under the law of the State from which he or she fled, owes service, &c. Act of February 12, 1793, c. 7, § 3.

In regard to these provisions, the Court are of opinion, that as by the general law of this Commonwealth, slavery cannot exist, and the rights and powers of slave owners cannot be exercised therein; the effect of this provision in the constitution and laws of the United States, is to limit and restrain the operation of this general rule, so far as it is done by the plain meaning and obvious intent and import of the language used, and no further. The constitution and law manifestly refer to the case of a slave escaping from a State where he owes service or labor, into another State or Territory. He is termed a fugitive from labor; the proof to be made is, that he owed service or labor, under the laws of the State or Territory *from which he fled*, and the authority is given to remove such fugitive to the State *from which he fled*. This language can, by no reasonable construction, be applied to the case of a slave who has not fled from the State, but who has been brought into the State by his master. . . .

. . . The States have a plenary power to make all laws necessary for the regulation of slavery and the rights of the slave owners, whilst the slaves remain within their territorial limits; and it is only when they escape, without the consent of their owners, into other States, that they require the aid of other States, to enable them to regain their dominion over the fugitives. . . .

. . . It is upon these grounds we are of opinion, that an owner of a slave in another State where slavery is warranted by law, voluntarily bringing such slave into this State, has no authority to detain him against his will, or to carry him out of the State against his consent, for the purpose of being held in slavery.

This opinion is not to be considered as extending to a case where the owner of a fugitive slave, having produced a certificate according to the law of the United States, is *bonâ fide* removing such slave to his own domicil, and in so doing passes through a free State; where the law confers a right or favor, by necessary implication it gives the means of enjoying it. Nor do we give any opinion upon the case, where an owner of a slave in one State is *bonâ fide* removing to another State where slavery is allowed, and in so doing necessarily passes through a free State, or where by accident or necessity he is compelled to touch or land therein, remaining no longer than necessary. Our geographical position exempts us from the probable necessity of considering such a case, and we give no opinion respecting it.

The child who is the subject of this *habeas corpus*, being of too tender years to have any will or give any consent to be removed, and her mother being a slave and having no will of her own and no power to act for her child, she is necessarily left in the custody of the law. The respondent having claimed the custody of the child, in behalf of Mr. and Mrs. Slater, who claim the right to carry her back to Louisiana, to be held in a state of slavery, we are of opinion that his custody is not to [be] deemed by the Court a proper and lawful custody.

Under a suggestion made in the outset of this inquiry, that a probate guardian would probably be appointed, we shall for the present order the child into temporary custody, to give time for an application to be made to the judge of probate.

3. *PRIGG V. PENNSYLVANIA*, 41 U.S. 539 (1842)

A Pennsylvania court convicted a slave-catcher of kidnapping a runaway slave and her children, in violation of that state's 1826 personal liberty law. The Supreme Court affirmed the constitutionality of the federal Fugitive Slave Act of 1793 and held that, pursuant to the Constitution, federal legislation that enforced a slave owner's right to recapture fugitive slaves preempted any contradictory state legislation.

The defendant in error, Edward Prigg, with [three other men] were indicted by the Grand Jury of York county, Pennsylvania, for that, on the first day of April, 1837, upon a certain negro woman named Margaret Morgan, with force and violence they made an assault, and with force and violence feloniously did take and carry her away from the county of York, within the Commonwealth of Pennsylvania, to the state of Maryland, with a design and intention there to sell and dispose of the said Margaret Morgan, as and for a slave and servant for life. . . .

. . . [T]he jurors further found, that the negro woman, Margaret Morgan . . . came into the state of Pennsylvania from the state of Maryland, some time in the year eighteen hundred and thirty-two; that at that time, and for a long period before that time, she was a slave for life, held to labour, and owing service or labour for, under, and according to the laws of the said state of Maryland . . . to a certain Margaret Ashmore, a citizen of the state of Maryland . . . ; and that the said negro woman, Margaret Morgan, escaped and fled from the state of Maryland without the knowledge and consent of the said Margaret Ashmore; that in the month of February, eighteen hundred and thirty-seven, the within named defendant, Edward Prigg, was duly and legally constituted and appointed by the said Margaret Ashmore, her agent or attorney, to seize and arrest the said negro woman, Margaret Morgan, as a fugitive from labour, and to remove, take, and carry her from this state into the state of Maryland, and there deliver her to the said Margaret Ashmore, that as such agent or attorney the said Edward Prigg afterwards, and in the same month of February, eighteen hundred and thirty-seven, before a certain Thomas Henderson, Esquire, then being a justice of the peace in and for the county of York, in this state, made oath that the said negro woman, Margaret Morgan, had fled and escaped from the state of Maryland, owing service or labour for life, under the laws thereof, to the said Margaret Ashmore; that the said Thomas Henderson . . . thereupon issued his warrant, directed to one William McCleary, then and there being a regularly appointed constable in and for York county, commanding him to take the said negro woman, Margaret Morgan, and her children, and bring them before the said Thomas Henderson, or some other justice of the peace for said county; that the said McCleary, in obedience to said warrant, did accordingly take and apprehend the said negro woman, Margaret Morgan, and her children, in York county aforesaid, and did bring her and them before the said Thomas Henderson; that the said Henderson thereupon refused to take further cognisance of said case, and that the said Prigg afterwards, and without complying with the provisions of the said act of the General Assembly of the Commonwealth of Pennsylvania, passed the 25th of March, 1826, entitled "An act to give effect to the provisions of the Constitution of the United States relative to fugitives from labour, for the protection of free people of colour, and to prevent kidnapping," did take, remove and carry away the said negro woman, Margaret Morgan, and her children, mentioned in said warrant, out of this state into the state of Maryland, and did there deliver the said woman and children into the custody and possession of the said Margaret Ashmore.

And further say, that one of the said children so taken, removed and carried away, was born in this state more than one year after the said negro woman, Margaret Morgan, had fled and escaped from the state of Maryland as aforesaid. . . .

Mr. Justice [Joseph] STORY delivered the opinion of the Court.

. . . There are two clauses in the Constitution upon the subject of fugitives, which stand in juxtaposition with each other, and have been thought mutually to illustrate each other. They are both contained in the second section of the fourth article, and are in the following words: "A person charged in any state with treason, felony, or other crime, who shall flee from justice, and be found in another state, shall, on demand of the executive authority of the state from which he fled, be delivered up, to be removed to the state having jurisdiction of the crime."

"No person held to service or labour in one state under the laws thereof, escaping into another, shall in consequence of any law or regulation therein, be discharged from such service or labour; but shall be delivered up, on claim of the party to whom such service or labour may be due."

The last clause is that, the true interpretation whereof is directly in judgment before us. Historically, it is well known, that the object of this clause was to secure to the citizens of the slaveholding states the complete right and title of ownership in their slaves, as property, in every state in the Union into which they might escape from the state where they were held in servitude. The full recognition of this right and title was indispensable to the security of this species of property in all the slaveholding states; and, indeed, was so vital to the preservation of their domestic interests and institutions, that it cannot be doubted that it constituted a fundamental article, without the adoption of which the Union could not have been formed. Its true design was to guard against the doctrines and principles prevalent in the non-slaveholding states, by preventing them from intermeddling with, or obstructing, or abolishing the rights of the owners of slaves.

By the general law of nations, no nation is bound to recognise the state of slavery, as to foreign slaves found within its territorial dominions, when it is in opposition to its own policy and institutions, in favour of the subjects of other nations where slavery is recognised. If it does it, it is as a matter of comity, and not as a matter of international right. The state of slavery is deemed to be a mere municipal regulation, founded upon and limited to the range of the territorial laws. . . . It is manifest from this consideration, that if the Constitution had not contained this clause, every non-slaveholding state in the Union would have been at liberty to have declared free all runaway slaves coming within its limits, and to have given them entire immunity and protection against the claims of their masters; a course which would have created the most bitter animosities, and engendered perpetual strife between the different states. The clause was, therefore, of the last importance to the safety and security of the southern states; and could not have been surrendered by them without endangering their whole property in slaves. The clause was accordingly adopted into the Constitution by the unanimous consent of the framers of it; a proof at once of its intrinsic and practical necessity. . . .

The clause manifestly contemplates the existence of a positive, unqualified right on the part of the owner of the slave, which no state law or regulation can in any way qualify, regulate, control, or restrain. . . .

. . . If this be so, then all the incidents to that right attach also; the owner must, therefore, have the right to seize and repossess the slave, which the local laws of his own state confer upon him as property; and we all know that this right of seizure and recaption is universally acknowledged in all the slaveholding states. . . . Upon this ground we have not the slightest hesitation in holding, that, under and in virtue of the Constitution, the owner of a slave is clothed with entire authority, in every state in the Union, to seize and recapture his slave, whenever he can do it without any breach of the peace, or any illegal violence. In this sense, and to this extent this clause of the Constitution may properly be said to execute itself, and to require no aid from legislation, state or national.

. . . [T]his leads us to the consideration of the other part of the clause, which implies at once a guaranty and duty. It says, "But he (the slave) shall be delivered up on claim of the party to whom such service or labour may be due." Now, we think it exceedingly difficult, if not impracticable, to read this language and not to feel that it contemplated some farther remedial redress than that which might be administered at the hands of the owner himself. A claim is to be made. What is a claim? It is, in a just juridical sense, a demand of some matter as of right made by one person upon another, to do or to forbear to do some act or thing as a matter of duty. . . . The slave is to be delivered up on the claim. By whom to be delivered up? In what mode to be delivered up? How, if a refusal takes place, is the right of delivery to be enforced? Upon what proofs? What shall be the evidence of a rightful recaption or delivery? When and under what circumstances shall the possession of the owner, after it is obtained, be conclusive of his right, so as to preclude any further inquiry or examination into it by local tribunals or otherwise, while the slave, in possession of the owner, is in transitu to the state from which he fled?

These, and many other questions, will readily occur upon the slightest attention to the clause; and it is obvious that they can receive but one satisfactory answer. They require the aid of legislation to protect the right, to enforce the delivery, and to secure the subsequent possession of the slave. If, indeed, the Constitution guarantees the right, and if it requires the delivery upon the claim of the owner, (as cannot well be doubted,) the natural inference certainly is, that the national government is clothed with the appropriate authority and functions to enforce it. The fundamental principle applicable to all cases of this sort, would seem to be, that where the end is required, the means are given; and where the duty is enjoined, the ability to perform it is contemplated to exist on the part of the functionaries to whom it is entrusted. The clause is found in the national Constitution, and not in that of any state. It does not point out any state functionaries, or any state action to carry its provisions into effect. The states cannot, therefore, be compelled to enforce them; and it might well be deemed an unconstitutional exercise of the power of interpretation, to insist that the states are bound to provide means to carry into effect the duties of the national government, nowhere delegated or intrusted to them by the Constitution. On the contrary, the natural, if not the necessary conclusion is, that the national government, in the absence of all positive provisions to the contrary, is bound, through its own proper departments, legislative, judicial, or executive, as the case may require, to carry into effect all the rights and duties imposed upon it by the Constitution. . . .

The very [federal Fugitive Slave Act] of 1793, now under consideration, affords the most conclusive proof that Congress . . . has supposed that the right as well as the duty of legislation on the subject of fugitives from justice, and fugitive slaves was within the scope of the constitutional authority conferred on the national legislature. . . .

Upon these grounds, we are of opinion that the act of Pennsylvania upon which this indictment is founded, is unconstitutional and void. It purports to punish as a public offence against that state, the very act of seizing and removing a slave by his master, which the Constitution of the United States was designed to justify and uphold. . . .

4. *Sarah C. Roberts v. The City of Boston*, 59 Mass. 198 (Massachusetts Supreme Judicial Court, 1850)

Regulations of Boston's primary school committee required all students to obtain a ticket of admission from a member of the committee, who "shall admit . . . all applicants, of suitable age and qualifications, residing nearest to the school under his charge, (excepting those for whom special provision has been made)."[4] The regulations also held that applicants for admission to the schools were "especially entitled to enter the schools nearest to their places of residence." At the same time, Boston maintained two primary schools for the exclusive use of black children. According to the court, "The colored population of Boston constitute less than one sixty-second part of the entire population of the city. For half a century, separate schools have been kept in Boston for colored children, and the primary school for colored children in Belknap street was established in 1820, and has been kept there ever since. The teachers of this school have the same compensation and qualifications as in other like schools in the city. Schools for colored children were originally established at the request of colored citizens, whose children could not attend the public schools, on account of the prejudice then existing against them."

Local black leader Benjamin F. Roberts challenged Boston's regulations that required his five-year-old daughter, Sarah, to travel an extra distance and go past a school for whites to attend an all-black school. Roberts applied to a member of the school committee to admit Sarah to the primary school nearest her residence. After the member refused the application, Roberts applied to the committee, which likewise refused the application on account of Sarah's color. On February 15, 1848, Sarah Roberts "went into the primary school nearest her residence, but without any ticket of admission or other leave granted, and was on that day ejected from the school by the teacher." Future Massachusetts senator Charles Sumner and black attorney Robert Morris Jr. argued this case for plaintiff Roberts, in which the Massachusetts Supreme Judicial Court ruled that segregated schools did not violate the equal rights secured for blacks by the constitution of the state. In 1855, Boston desegregated its public schools, but the doctrine of "separate but equal" would live on well into the twentieth century.

SHAW, C. J. [Lemuel] The plaintiff, a colored child of five years of age, has commenced this action, by her father and next friend, against the city of Boston, upon the statute of 1845, c. 214, which provides, that any child unlawfully excluded from public school instruction, in this commonwealth, shall recover damages therefor, in an action against the city or town, by which such public school instruction is supported. The question therefore is, whether, upon the facts agreed, the plaintiff has been unlawfully excluded from such instruction.

By the agreed statement of facts, it appears, that the defendants support a class of schools called primary schools, to the number of about one hundred and sixty, designed for the instruction of children of both sexes, who are between the ages of four and seven years. Two of these schools are appropriated by the primary school committee, having charge of that class of schools, to the exclusive instruction of colored children, and the residue to the exclusive instruction of white children.

The plaintiff, by her father, took proper measures to obtain admission into one of these schools appropriated to white children, but pursuant to the regulations of the committee, and in conformity therewith, she was not admitted. Either of the schools appropriated to colored children was open to her; the nearest of which was about a fifth of a mile or seventy rods more distant from her father's house than the nearest primary school. It further appears, by the facts agreed, that the committee having charge of that class of schools had, a short time previously to the plaintiff's application, adopted a resolution, upon a report of a committee, that in the opinion of that board, the continuance of the separate schools for colored children, and the regular attendance of all such children upon the schools, is not only legal and just, but is best adapted to promote the instruction of that class of the population. . . .

. . . The plaintiff had access to a school, set apart for colored children, as well conducted in all respects, and as well fitted, in point of capacity and qualification of the instructors, to advance the education of children under seven years old, as the other primary schools; the objection is, that the schools thus open to the plaintiff are exclusively appropriated to colored children, and are at a greater distance from her home. Under these circumstances, has the plaintiff been unlawfully excluded from public school instruction? Upon the best consideration we have been able to give the subject, the court are all of opinion that she has not. . . .

The great principle, advanced by the learned and eloquent advocate of the plaintiff, is, that by the constitution and laws of Massachusetts, all persons without distinction of age or sex, birth or color, origin or condition, are equal before the law. This, as a broad general principle, such as ought to appear in a declaration of rights, is perfectly sound; it is not only expressed in terms, but pervades and animates the whole spirit of our constitution of free government. But, when this great principle comes to be applied to the actual and various conditions of persons in society, it will not warrant the assertion, that men and women are legally clothed with the same civil and political powers, and that children and adults are legally to have the same functions and be subject to the same treatment; but only that the rights of all, as they are settled and regulated by law, are equally entitled to the paternal consideration and protection of the law, for their maintenance and security. What those rights are, to which individuals, in the infinite variety of circumstances by which they are surrounded in society, are entitled, must depend on laws adapted to their respective relations and conditions.

Conceding, therefore, in the fullest manner, that colored persons, the descendants of Africans, are entitled by law, in this commonwealth, to equal rights, constitutional and political, civil and social, the question then arises, whether the regulation in question, which provides separate schools for colored children, is a violation of any of these rights. . . .

We must then resort to the law, to ascertain what are the rights of individuals, in regard to the schools. By the Rev. Sts. *c.* 23, the general system is provided for. This chapter directs what money shall be raised in different towns, according to their population; provides for a power of dividing towns into school districts, leaving it however at the option of the inhabitants to divide the towns into districts, or to administer the system and provide schools, without such division. The latter course has, it is believed, been constantly adopted in Boston, without forming the territory into districts.

The statute . . . provides (§ 10) that the inhabitants shall annually choose, by ballot, a school committee, who shall have the general charge and superintendence of all the public schools in such towns. There being no specific direction how schools shall be organized; how many schools shall be kept; what shall be the qualifications for admission to the schools; the age at which children may enter; the age to which they may continue; these must all be regulated by the committee, under their power of general superintendence. . . .

The power of general superintendence vests a plenary authority in the committee to arrange, classify, and distribute pupils, in such a manner as they think best adapted to their general proficiency and welfare. If it is thought expedient to provide for very young children, it may be, that such schools may be kept exclusively by female teachers, quite adequate to their instruction, and yet whose services may be obtained at a cost much lower than that of more highly-qualified male instructors. So if they should judge it expedient to have a grade of schools for children from seven to ten, and another for those from ten to fourteen, it would seem to be within their authority to establish such schools. So to separate male and female pupils into different schools. It has been found necessary, that is to say, highly expedient, at times, to establish special schools for poor and neglected children, who have passed the age of seven, and have become too old to attend the primary school, and yet have not acquired the rudiments of learning, to enable them to enter the ordinary schools. If a class of youth, of one or both sexes, is found in that condition, and it is expedient to organize them into a separate school, to receive the special training, adapted to their condition, it seems to be within the power of the superintending committee, to provide for the organization of such special school.

A somewhat more specific rule, perhaps, on these subjects, might be beneficially provided by the legislature; but yet, it would probably be quite impracticable to make full and precise laws for this purpose, on account of the different condition of society in different towns. In towns of a large territory, over which the inhabitants are thinly settled, an arrangement or classification going far into detail, providing different schools for pupils of different ages, of each sex, and the like, would require the pupils to go such long distance from their homes to the schools, that it would be quite unreasonable. But in Boston, where more than one hundred thousand inhabitants live within a space so small, that it would be scarcely an inconvenience to require a boy of good health to traverse daily the whole extent of it, a system of distribution and classification may be adopted and carried into effect, which may be useful and beneficial in its influence on the character of the schools, and in its adaptation to the improvement and advancement of the great purpose of education, and at the same time practicable and reasonable in its operation.

In the absence of special legislation on this subject, the law has vested the power in the committee to regulate the system of distribution and classification; and when this power is reasonably exercised, without being abused or perverted by colorable pretences, the decision of the committee must be deemed conclusive. The committee, apparently upon great deliberation, have come to the conclusion, that the good of both classes of schools will be best promoted, by maintaining the separate primary schools for colored and for white children, and we can perceive no ground to doubt, that this is the honest result of their experience and judgment.

It is urged, that this maintenance of separate schools tends to deepen and perpetuate the odious distinction of caste, founded in a deep-rooted prejudice in public opinion. This prejudice, if it exists, is not created by law, and probably cannot be changed by law. Whether this distinction and prejudice, existing in the opinion and feelings of the community, would not be as effectually fostered by compelling colored and white children to associate together in the same schools, may well be doubted; at all events, it is a fair and proper question for the committee to consider and decide upon, having in view the best interests of both classes of children placed under their superintendence, and we cannot say, that their decision upon it is not founded on just grounds of reason and experience, and in the result of a discriminating and honest judgment.

The increased distance, to which the plaintiff was obliged to go to school from her father's house, is not such, in our opinion, as to render the regulation in question unreasonable, still less illegal.

On the whole the court are of opinion, that upon the facts stated, the action cannot be maintained.

5. An Act to amend, and supplementary to, the Act entitled, "An Act respecting Fugitives from Justice, and Persons escaping from the Service of their Masters," approved February twelfth, one thousand seven hundred and ninety-three, 9 Stat. 462 (September 18, 1850) (Fugitive Slave Act of 1850)

As a part of the Compromise of 1850, Congress passed a stronger Fugitive Slave Act that sought to circumvent resistance in the North to returning escaped slaves into bondage.

. . . SEC. 6. *And be it further enacted*, That when a person held to service or labor in any State or Territory of the United States, has heretofore or shall hereafter escape into another State or Territory of the United States, the person or persons to whom such service or labor may be due, or his, her, or their agent or attorney . . . may pursue and reclaim such fugitive person, either by procuring a warrant from some one of the courts, judges, or commissioners aforesaid, of the proper circuit, district, or county, for the apprehension of such fugitive from service or labor, or by seizing and arresting such fugitive, where the same can be done without process, and by taking, or causing such person to be taken, forthwith before such court, judge, or commissioner, whose duty it shall be to hear and determine the case of such claimant in a summary manner; and upon satisfactory proof being made . . . make out and deliver to such claimant, his or her agent or attorney, a certificate setting forth the substantial facts . . . with authority . . . to use such reasonable force and restraint as may be necessary, under the circumstances of the case, to take and remove such fugitive person back to the State or Territory whence he or she may have escaped as aforesaid. In no trial or hearing under this act shall the testimony of such alleged fugitive be admitted in evidence; and the certificates in this and the first [fourth][5] section mentioned, shall be conclusive of the right of the person or persons in whose favor granted, to remove such fugitive to the State or Territory from which he escaped, and shall prevent all molestation of such person or persons by any process issued by any court, judge, magistrate, or other person whomsoever.

SEC. 7. *And be it further enacted*, That any person who shall knowingly and willingly obstruct, hinder, or prevent such claimant, his agent or attorney, or any person or persons lawfully assisting him, her, or them, from arresting such a fugitive from service or labor, either with or without process as aforesaid, or shall rescue, or attempt to rescue, such fugitive from service or labor, from the custody of such claimant, his or her agent or attorney, or other person or persons lawfully assisting as aforesaid, when so arrested, pursuant to the authority herein given and declared; or shall aid, abet, or assist such person so owing service or labor as aforesaid, directly or indirectly, to escape from such claimant, his agent or attorney, or other person or persons legally authorized as aforesaid; or shall harbor or conceal such fugitive, so as to prevent the discovery and arrest of such person, after notice or knowledge of the fact that such person was a fugitive from service or labor as aforesaid, shall, for either of said offences, be subject to a fine not exceeding one thousand dollars, and imprisonment not exceeding six months, by indictment and conviction before the District Court of the United States for the district in which such offence may have been committed, or before the proper court of criminal jurisdiction, if committed within any one of the organized Territories of the United States; and shall moreover forfeit and pay, by way of civil damages to the party injured by such illegal conduct, the sum of one thousand dollars, for each fugitive so lost as aforesaid, to be recovered by action of debt, in any of the District or Territorial Courts aforesaid, within whose jurisdiction the said offence may have been committed.

SEC. 8. *And be it further enacted*, That the marshals, their deputies, and the clerks of the said District and Territorial Courts, shall be paid, for their services, the like fees as may be allowed for similar services in other cases; and where such services are rendered exclusively in the arrest, custody, and delivery of the fugitive to the claimant, his or her agent or attorney, or where such supposed fugitive may be discharged out of custody for the want of sufficient proof as aforesaid, then such fees are to be paid in whole by such claimant, his agent or attorney; and in all cases where the proceedings are before a commissioner, he shall be entitled to a fee of ten dollars in full for his services in each case, upon the delivery of the said certificate to the claimant, his or her agent or attorney; or a fee of five dollars in cases where the proof shall not, in the opinion of such commissioner, warrant such certificate and delivery, inclusive of all services incident to such arrest and examination, to be paid, in either case, by the claimant, his or her agent or attorney. The person or persons authorized to execute the process to be issued by such commissioners for the arrest and detention of fugitives from service or labor as aforesaid, shall also be entitled to a fee of five dollars each for each person he or they may arrest . . . with such other fees as may be deemed reasonable by such commissioner for such other additional services as may be necessarily performed by him or them[.] . . .

SEC. 9. *And be it further enacted*, That, upon affidavit made by the claimant of such fugitive, his agent or attorney, after such certificate has been issued, that he has reason to apprehend that such fugitive will be rescued by force from his or their possession before he can be taken beyond the limits of the State in which the arrest is made, it shall be the duty of the officer making the arrest to retain such fugitive in his custody, and to remove him to the State whence he fled, and there to deliver him to said claimant, his agent, or attorney. And to this end, the officer aforesaid is hereby authorized and required to employ so many persons as he may deem necessary to overcome such force, and to retain them in his service so long as circumstances may require. The said officer and his assistants, while so employed, to receive the same compensation, and to be allowed the same expenses, as are now allowed by law for transportation of criminals, to be certified by the judge of the district within which the arrest is made, and paid out of the treasury of the United States. . . .

6. SOLOMON NORTHUP, *TWELVE YEARS A SLAVE. NARRATIVE OF SOLOMON NORTHUP, A CITIZEN OF NEW-YORK, KIDNAPPED IN WASHINGTON CITY IN 1841 AND RESCUED IN 1853, FROM A COTTON PLANTATION NEAR THE RED RIVER IN LOUISIANA* (AUBURN: DERBY AND MILLER; BUFFALO: DERBY, ORTON AND MULLIGAN; LONDON: SAMPSON LOW, SON & COMPANY, 1853)

Born into a free black family in upstate New York, Solomon Northup married in 1829 and had several children. In 1841, two white men overheard Northup playing the violin in Saratoga Springs, New York, approached him with a lucrative offer to play for a circus, and persuaded him to travel to Washington, D.C., to take the job. Once there, Northup was likely drugged, and after several days where he slipped in and out of consciousness, he found himself chained in the slave pen of James H. Burch. Burch beat Northup, told him to assume the identity of a runaway slave from

Fig. 1. "Effects of the Fugitive-Slave-Law." This stinging critique of the Fugitive Slave Act quotes from the Bible and the Declaration of Independence and depicts a slave patrol shooting at several slaves as they try in vain to escape to freedom. (Th. Kaufmann, 1850; Library of Congress)

Georgia, threatened that Northup would be killed if he ever revealed his true identity and free birth, and sent him to New Orleans. In Louisiana, Northup experienced both benevolent and cruel masters as well as life on a cotton plantation. In 1852, Northup met a white man named Bass who was on the plantation to do some building. Bass, who disliked slavery, agreed to send a letter to Northup's wife, who immediately began working for his freedom. Northup's wife obtained assistance from a lawyer, Henry Northup, who was a member of the family that had once owned Solomon Northup's father. On the basis of an 1840 New York law requiring the recovery of any free black resident unlawfully captured and made a slave, Northup obtained his freedom in 1853. He afterward wrote of his experiences in *Twelve Years a Slave* and lectured to abolitionist audiences. In the excerpt that follows, Northup describes a slave auction in which he was put up for sale.

. . . In the first place we were required to wash thoroughly, and those with beards, to shave. We were then furnished with a new suit each, cheap, but clean. The men had hat, coat, shirt, pants and shoes; the women frocks of calico, and handkerchiefs to bind about their heads. We were now conducted into a large room in the front part of the building to which the yard was attached, in order to be properly trained, before the admission of customers. The men were arranged on one side of the room, the women on the other. The tallest was placed at the head of the row, then the next tallest, and so on in the order of their respective heights. Emily was at the foot of the line of women. Freeman [the owner of the slave pen] charged us to remember our places; exhorted us to appear smart and lively,—sometimes threatening, and again, holding out various inducements. During the day he exercised us in the art of "looking smart," and of moving to our places with exact precision.

After being fed, in the afternoon, we were again paraded and made to dance. Bob, a colored boy, who had some time belonged to Freeman, played on the violin. Standing near him, I made bold to inquire if he could play the "Virginia Reel." He answered he could not, and asked me if I could play. Replying in the affirmative, he handed me the violin. I struck up a tune, and finished it. Freeman ordered me to continue playing, and seemed well pleased, telling Bob that I far excelled him—a remark that seemed to grieve my musical companion very much.

Next day many customers called to examine Freeman's "new lot." The latter gentleman was very loquacious, dwelling at much length upon our several good points and qualities. He would make us hold up our heads, walk briskly back and forth, while customers would feel of our hands and arms and bodies, turn us about, ask us what we could do, make us open our mouths and show our teeth, precisely as a jockey examines a horse which he is about to barter for or purchase. Sometimes a man or woman was taken back to the small house in the yard, stripped, and inspected more minutely. Scars upon a slave's back were considered evidence of a rebellious or unruly spirit, and hurt his sale.

One old gentleman, who said he wanted a coachman, appeared to take a fancy to me. From his conversation with Freeman, I learned he was a resident in the city. I very much desired that he would buy me, because I conceived it would not be difficult to make my escape from New-Orleans on some northern vessel. Freeman asked him fifteen hundred dollars for me. The old gentleman insisted it was too much, as times were very hard. Freeman, however, declared that I was sound and healthy, of a good constitution, and intelligent. He made it a point to enlarge upon my musical attainments. The old gentleman argued quite adroitly that there was nothing extraordinary about the nigger, and finally, to my regret, went out, saying he would call again. During the day, however, a number of sales were made. David and Caroline were purchased together by a Natchez planter. They left us, grinning broadly, and in the most happy state of mind, caused by the fact of their not being separated. Lethe was sold to a planter of Baton Rouge, her eyes flashing with anger as she was led away.

The same man also purchased Randall. The little fellow was made to jump, and run across the floor, and perform many other feats, exhibiting his activity and condition. All the time the trade was going on, Eliza was crying aloud, and wringing her hands. She besought the man not to buy him, unless he also bought herself and Emily. She promised, in that case, to be the most faithful slave that ever lived. The man answered that he could not afford it, and then Eliza burst into a paroxysm of grief, weeping plaintively. Freeman turned round to her, savagely, with his whip in his uplifted hand, ordering her to stop her noise, or he would flog her. He would not have such work—such snivelling; and unless she ceased that minute, he would take her to the yard and give her a hundred lashes. Yes, he would take the nonsense out of her pretty quick—if he didn't, might he be d——d. Eliza shrunk before him, and tried to wipe away her tears, but it was all in vain. She wanted to be with her children, she said, the little time she had to live. All the frowns and threats of Freeman, could not wholly silence the afflicted mother. She kept on begging and beseeching them, most piteously not to separate the three. Over and over again she told them how she loved her boy. A great many times she repeated her former promises—how very faithful and obedient she would be; how hard she would labor day and night, to the last moment of her life, if he would only buy them all together. But it was of no avail; the man could not afford it. The bargain was agreed upon, and Randall must go alone. Then Eliza ran to him; embraced him passionately; kissed him again and again; told him to remember her—all the while her tears falling in the boy's face like rain.

Freeman damned her, calling her a blubbering, bawling wench, and ordered her to go to her place, and behave herself, and be somebody. He swore he wouldn't stand such stuff but a little longer. He would soon give her something to cry about, if she was not mighty careful, and that she might depend upon.

The planter from Baton Rouge, with his new purchases, was ready to depart.

"Don't cry, mama. I will be a good boy. Don't cry," said Randall, looking back, as they passed out of the door.

What has become of the lad, God knows. It was a mournful scene indeed. I would have cried myself if I had dared.

7. WILLIAM J. WATKINS, *OUR RIGHTS AS MEN. AN ADDRESS DELIVERED IN BOSTON, BEFORE THE LEGISLATIVE COMMITTEE ON THE MILITIA, FEBRUARY 24, 1853* (BOSTON: BENJAMIN F. ROBERTS, 1853)

In 1852, several African Americans sought a charter to form a black militia company in Boston. In addressing the Massachusetts legislature's militia committee, William J. Watkins challenged Massachusetts to carry out the principles of the Declaration of Independence and argued that participation in the American Founding and birth in the United States warranted black inclusion as part of "the people." Despite the state's progressive reputation on racial issues, however, the committee took no further action on the petition. By 1855, in the wake of the Anthony Burns incident, African Americans in Boston formed the Massasoit Guard without state approval.

... We merely ask for a Charter to form an Independent Military Company; such a one as has been granted to a company of white citizens. We ask, Sir, that the Old Bay State will throw around us its protecting arm. We know that by wishing to be treated as men, we shall elicit the vindictive anathemas of a few, who live daily and hourly on the pap of American prejudice; but none of these things move us, if Massachusetts but gather us together as a hen gathereth her brood under her wings. We might, with propriety, have petitioned your honorable body, that we be enrolled among the General Militia; that the same immunities be extended towards us, that are extended towards other citizens of Massachusetts, irrespective of complexional distinction and physical peculiarities. . . .

Having briefly noticed the nature of the Petition, and shown that there is nothing particularly dreadful and alarming about it, we will, in accordance with our arrangement, INQUIRE INTO THE CHARACTER OF THE PETITIONERS.

And who are they, Mr. Chairman? What is their character, gentlemen? In a word, they are among the most respectable men in the community. They are law-abiding, tax-paying, liberty-loving, NATIVE-BORN, AMERICAN CITIZENS; men who love their country, despite its heinous iniquities; iniquities piled up in dreadful agony to the heavens. I see arrayed in the List of Signers, men of affluence and education, of respectability and moral worth; men, in possession of those great and good qualities, the development of which, exerts a healthy influence throughout the varied ramifications of society. They are men, Sir, that do honor to the State; as respectable in every point of view, as any list ever appended to a Petition, since "the morning stars sang together, and all the sons of God shouted for joy." And more than this, some of them are the descendants of revolution sires, and revolution mothers; the descendants of those, who, in those times that tried men's souls, counted not their lives dear unto them, but their blood flowed freely in defence of their country; they fought, they bled, they conquered; aye, they died, that we might live as FREEMEN. And shall we be excluded from the pale of humanity, denied those rights, left to us as a legacy by our fathers? . . .

In the third place, Gentlemen, WHY SHOULD THIS PETITION BE GRANTED?

It should be granted because the request is a reasonable one, and one emanating from a body of men who have an absolute right to demand it. We proceed, then, upon the assertion that we have an unrestricted right to the enjoyment of full civil privileges; a right to demand and receive every thing which Massachusetts by her Bill of Rights, grants to her citizens, irrespective of any accidental or fortuitous circumstance, the contingency of birth, education, fortune, or complexion. We are men, and we wish to be treated, as men in the land of the Pilgrims should be treated. Mr. Chairman, the laws of this Commonwealth know no man by the color of his skin, the texture of his hair, or the symmetrical development of his physical organism. It is too true, sir, that even here, American Prejudice, the inseparable concomitant of American Slavery, stands out in bold relief, the embodiment of Death, Hell, and the Grave; the incarnation of a principle which had its origin in the council chamber of the lost, and one which is fostered only by those affiliated with the Prince of darkness. But, thank God, in the eye of the Law, we all, sir, stand upon one common platform. What have the colored people of this country done, that we should be treated as a hissing and a by-word, a pest and a nuisance, the off-scouring of the earth?

When we cast our eyes abroad this vast Republic, a singular anomaly, a living paradox presents itself. Once, every year, in this land of the free, on Freedom's Natal day, the people assemble in public convocations, and in intonations loud and long, proclaim to the despotism of the world, "We hold these truths to be self-evident; that all men are born free and created equal, and are endowed by their Creator, with certain inalienable rights, and among these are life, liberty, and the pursuit of Happiness." Yes. Our jubilatic anthems roll over the wide waste of waters, o'er hills and valleys, rivers, woods, and plains; and the burden of our song is, "We are free, We are free."

But hark! For amid the rapturous symphonies of Freedom's song, I hear a low sepulchral voice; the voice of agony, of Rachel weeping for her children, and refusing to be comforted; I also hear the voice of the nominally free; of men, women, and children, whose Freedom (?) gives the lie to your song of Jubilee. . . .

Your laws are founded in caste, conceived in caste, born in caste. Caste is the God whom this great Nation delights to honor. Caste is in your singing, your preaching, your praying; your *beau-ideal* of Heaven is a place of unfading joy, and resplendent magnificence, where you shall play for ever upon your golden

31

harps, and the colored people, if they, like Uncle Tom, submit to your indignities with Christian meekness and becoming resignation, shall be permitted, from the Negro pew, to *peep into* the glory of your third heaven to all eternity!

Gentlemen, only look at the picture. Your schools, and colleges, and stores, and pulpits, are all closed against us; every avenue to honor and renown is piled up with mountains to obstruct our progress, and if we ever stand forth, a disenthralled people, we must burst a chain as long and broad as the ever grasping arm of this great country, and ten thousand times more solid than the compact which binds you together. . . .

We ask no favors, Mr. Chairman, at the hands of our country; all we demand, is, the unrestricted right to breathe unmolested, the pure, unadulterated atmosphere of Heaven. We are told we cannot rise! Take the millstone from off our necks. We are inferior to the white man! *Give us our rights.* We can't be elevated in the land of our birth! Give us our rights, we ask no more. Treat us like men; carry out the principles of your immortal declaration, "all men are born free, and created equal, and are endowed by their Creator with certain inalienable rights, and among these are life, liberty, and the pursuit of happiness," and *then*, if we do not equal you in every respect, let us be the recipients of your intensified hate, your vituperative anathemas; *then* let your ponderous Juggernaut roll on, or, like Nebuchadnezzar, let us be driven beyond the pale of Humanity, to herd with the beasts of the field. But do not blame us for occupying a position in which *you* have placed us. And all this Petition demands, is, that you place us in a position that we may command respect. . . .

But, Sir, if colored men helped achieved *your* liberty as well as mine, if *your* fathers and my fathers found one common revolutionary grave, we ask you in the name of crushed and bleeding humanity, why should you, in point of privileges . . . be elevated to heaven, and we be cast down to Hell? No wonder Jefferson "trembled for his country, when he reflected that God is just, and his justice sleeps not forever." Why should *you* be a chosen people more than *we*? The great poniard of British tyranny, which was plunged in the heart of *your* Fathers, and caused their noble blood to flow so freely, brought the purple flood from *our* hearts also. We have referred to the fact of our Fathers' having fought to achieve this country's Independence. Allow me to quote in this connection, the eloquent words of a talented Reverend gentleman of Color, of the City of New York:—"We are NATIVES of this country: we ask only to be treated as well as FOREIGNERS. Not a few of our Fathers suffered and bled to purchase its Independence; we ask only to be treated as well as those who fought against it. We have toiled to cultivate it, and to raise it to its present prosperous condition; we ask only to share equal privileges with those who come from distant lands to enjoy the fruits of our labor." Yes! all we ask is, that you treat us as well as you do the Irish, German, Hungarian; aye, the whole host of them. . . .

. . . It cannot be denied, that if we are men, we are entitled to all the rights of men every where; and no one has a right gentlemen, morally speaking, either natural or acquired, to dehumanize and segregate us from the rest of mankind. You may withhold our right, but you can't annihilate it. . . .

. . . Our fathers were not able-bodied white male citizens; but they were able enough to face British cannon, in 1776 and 1812.

So, gentlemen, you perceive that we base our petition upon the grand, fundamental, eternal, Heaven-approving, principle of RIGHT; OUR ABSOLUTE RIGHT TO ENJOY FULL CIVIL PRIVILEGES. If it can be proved we are not able-bodied MEN; if it can be proved we are incapable of performing every honorable duty, you should consider our petition as a gross insult to your body, but if not, there is no alternative but to treat us as citizens of this Commonwealth should be treated; as able-bodied, honorable men. . . .

8. *THE BOSTON SLAVE RIOT, AND TRIAL OF ANTHONY BURNS, CONTAINING THE REPORT OF THE FANEUIL HALL MEETING; THE MURDER OF BATCHELDER; THEODORE PARKER'S LESSON FOR THE DAY; SPEECHES OF COUNSEL ON BOTH SIDES, CORRECTED BY THEMSELVES; VERBATIM REPORT OF JUDGE LORING'S DECISION; AND A DETAILED ACCOUNT OF THE EMBARKATION* (BOSTON: FETRIDGE AND COMPANY, 1854)

A Virginia slave, Anthony Burns, escaped in early 1854 by stowing away aboard a ship bound for Boston. Burns's owner pursued him, and on May 24, Burns was arrested and held as a fugitive slave. On May 26, thousands of Bostonians packed into Faneuil Hall to discuss action to liberate Burns when word arrived that a group of blacks and whites were at that moment marching on the courthouse where Burns was held. As participants of the Faneuil Hall meeting arrived, a group of blacks led by white abolitionist minister Thomas Wentworth Higginson battered down the courthouse door before being beaten back.

. . . On taking the chair, Judge Russell said, he had once thought that a fugitive could never be taken from Boston. But he had been mistaken! One had been taken from among us, and another lies in peril of his liberty. The boast of the slave holder is that he will catch his slaves under the shadow of Bunker Hill. We have made compromises until we find that compromise is concession, and concession is degradation. (Applause.)

The question has come at last whether the North will still consent to do what it is held base to do at the South. Why, when Henry Clay was asked whether it was expected that Northern men would catch slaves for the slave holders, he replied, "No! of course not! We will never expect you to do what we hold it base to do." *Now*, the very men who had acquiesced with Mr. Clay, demand of us that we catch their slaves. It seems that the Constitution has nothing for us to do but to help catch fugitive slaves!

When we get Cuba and Mexico as slave States—when the foreign slave trade is reëstablished, with all the appalling horrors of the Middle Passage, and the Atlantic is again filled with the bodies of dead Africans, then we may think it time to waken to our duty! God grant that we may do so soon! The time *will* come when Slavery will pass away, and our children shall have only its hideous memory to make them wonder at the deeds of their fathers. For one I hope to *die* in a land of liberty—in a land which no slave hunter shall dare pollute with his presence. . . .

Mr. [Theodore] Parker then proposed that when the meeting adjourn it adjourn to meet in Court Square to-morrow morning at 9 o'clock. A hundred voices cried out, "no, to-night," "let us take him out," "let us go now," "come on," and one man rushed frantically from the platform, crying "come on," but none seemed disposed to follow him. Mr. Parker—"Those in favor of going to-night will raise their hands." About half the audience raised their hands. Much confusion ensued, and the persons on the platform seemed bewildered and in hesitancy how to control the excitement they had raised. The audience were shouting and cheering—a voice was heard saying "the slave shall not go out, but the men that came here to get him shall not stay in: let us visit the slave catchers at the Revere House to-night." . . .

. . . At last Wendell Phillips again took the platform, and said:

Let us remember where we are and what we are going to do. You have said to-night you will vindicate the fair fame of Boston. Let me tell you you won't do it groaning at the slave-catchers at the Revere House . . . in attempting the impossible feat of insulting a slave-catcher. If there is a man here who has an arm and a heart ready to sacrifice any thing for the freedom of an oppressed man, let him do it to-morrow. (Cries of to-night.)

If I thought it could be done to-night I would go first. I don't profess courage, but I do profess this: when there is a possibility of saving a slave from the hands of those who are called officers of the law, I am ready to trample any statute or any man under my feet to do it, and am ready to help any one hundred men to do it. He urged the audience to wait until the day time: said that he knew the vaults of the banks in State street sympathized with them; that the Whigs who had been kicked once too often sympathized with them. He told them that it was in their power so to block up every avenue that the man could not be car-ried off. He urged them not to balk the effort of to-morrow by foolish conduct to-night, giving the enemy the alarm. You that are ready to do the real work, be not carried away by indiscretion which may make shipwreck of our hopes.

The zeal that won't keep till to-morrow will never free a slave. (Cries of "No!")

Mr. Phillips seemed to have partially carried the feelings of the audience with him, when a man at the lower end of the hall cried out—"Mr. Chairman. I am just informed that a mob of negroes is in Court square, attempting to rescue Burns. I move we adjourn to Court square."

The audience immediately began rapidly to leave the hall, and most of them wended their way to Court square.

The Attempted Rescue And Loss Of Life

The crowd moved from Faneuil Hall to the Court House, and halting on the East side endeavored to force the door on that part of the building, but failing in their attempt they ran round to the door on the West side opposite the Railroad Exchange, with loud cries that the fugitive was in that wing of the building, and there proceeded with a long plank, which they used as a battering-ram, and two axes to break in and force an entrance, which they did, and two of their number entered the building, but were quickly ejected by those inside. The battering-ram was manned by a dozen or fourteen men, white and colored, who plunged it against the door, until it was stove in. Meantime, several brickbats had been thrown at the windows, and the glass rattled in all directions. The leaders, or those who appeared to act as ringleaders in the melee, continually shouted: "Rescue him!" "Bring him out!" "Where is he!" &c. &c. The Court House bell rung an alarm at half past nine o'clock. At this point reports of pistols were heard in the crowd, and firearms, we understand, were used by those within the building, but whether loaded with ball or not we cannot say. During this struggle some thirty shots were fired by rioters, and the most intense excitement prevailed. The whole square was thronged with people. The Chief of Police, Taylor, was upon the ground with a full force of the Police, to stay the proceedings of the mob, now pressing still more reckless and threatening. Mr. Taylor pressed through the excited multitude, and, with great heroism, seized several men with axes in their hands, while breaking down the Court House door.

At the time the mob beat down the westerly door of the Court House, several men, employed as United States officers, were in the passage-way, using their endeavors to prevent the ingress of the crowd, and among the number was Mr. James Batchelder . . . who . . . received a pistol shot, (evidently a very heavy charge,) in the abdomen. Mr. Batchelder uttered the exclamation, "I'm stabbed," and falling backwards into the arms of watchman Isaac Jones, expired almost immediately. The unfortunate man resided in Charlestown, where he leaves a wife and one or two children to mourn his untimely fate.

At the time of forcing the door, and just as the fatal shot was fired, one of the rioters who was standing on the upper step, exclaimed to the crowd, "You cowards, will you desert us now!" At this moment, the exclamation of Mr. Batchelder, "I'm stabbed!" was heard, and the rioters retreated to the opposite side of the street. . . .

9. THEODORE PARKER, *THE NEW CRIME AGAINST HUMANITY.*
A SERMON, PREACHED AT THE MUSIC HALL, IN BOSTON, ON
SUNDAY, JUNE 4, 1854 (BOSTON: B. B. MUSSEY, 1854)

On June 2, 1854, a probate court judge declared Anthony Burns to be a fugitive slave. That same day, militia deployed to maintain order in the city as fifty thousand Bostonians somberly lined the streets and watched from rooftops and windows as Burns, in shackles, marched to the wharf and a ship there waiting to take him against his will back to bondage in Virginia. Black bunting dressed windows along the route, and an oversized coffin, painted black and inscribed with the word "Liberty," hung suspended from ropes over State Street. Theodore Parker, an abolitionist minister, delivered the following address, which reveals the increasing frustration in the North with the slave power as well as with any further compromise for the sake of keeping the peace. A black church later raised money to purchase Burns's freedom, and he afterward studied at Oberlin College, became a minister, and died in 1862 at the age of twenty-eight.

... Since last we came together, there has been a MAN STOLEN in this city of our fathers. It is not the first, it may not be the last. He is now in the great slave pen in the city of Boston. He is there against the law of the Commonwealth, which, if I am rightly informed, in such cases prohibits the use of State edifices as United States jails. I may be mistaken. Any forcible attempt to take him from that BARRACOON of Boston, would be wholly without use. For, besides the holiday soldiers who belong to the city of Boston, and are ready to shoot down their brothers in a just or an unjust cause, any day when the city government gives them its command and its liquor, I understand that there are one hundred and eighty-four United States marines lodged in the Court House, every man of them furnished with a musket and a bayonet, with his side-arms, and twenty-four ball cartridges. They are stationed, also, in a very strong building, and where five men, in a passage-way half the width of this pulpit, can defend it against five-and-twenty, or a hundred. To keep the peace, the Mayor, who, the other day, regretted the arrest of our brother, Anthony Burns, and declared that his sympathies were *wholly* with the alleged fugitive—and of course wholly *against* the claimant and the Marshal—in order to keep the peace of the city, the Mayor must become corporal of the guard for kidnappers from Virginia. He must keep the peace of our city, and defend these guests of Boston over the graves, the unmonumented graves, of John Hancock and Samuel Adams. . . .

The Fugitive Slave Bill was presented to us, and Boston rose up to welcome it. The greatest man in all the North came here, and in this city told Massachusetts she must obey the Fugitive Slave Bill with alacrity—that we must all conquer our prejudices in favor of justice and the rights of man. Boston conquered her prejudices in favor of justice and the unalienable rights of man. Do you not remember the meeting that was held in Faneuil Hall, when a political soldier of fortune, sometimes called the "Democratic Prince of the Devils," howled at the idea that there was a law of God higher than the Fugitive Slave Bill? He sneered, and asked, "Will you have the 'Higher Law of God' to rule over you?" and the multitude that occupied the floor, and the multitude that crowded the galleries, howled down the higher law of God! They treated the higher law to a laugh and a howl! That was Tuesday night. It was the Tuesday before Thanksgiving day. On that Thanksgiving day, I told the congregation that the men who howled down the higher law of Almighty God, had got Almighty God to settle with; that they had sown the wind, and would reap the whirlwind. At that meeting, Mr. Choate told the people—"**REMEMBER!** REMEMBER! *Remember!*" Then nobody knew what to "remember." Now you know. That is the state of that case.

Then you "remember" the kidnappers came here to seize Thomas Sims. Thomas Sims *was* seized. Nine days he was on trial for more than his life, and never saw a judge—never saw a jury. He was sent back into bondage from the city of Boston. You remember the chains that were put around the Court House; you remember the judges of Massachusetts stooping, crouching, creeping, crawling, under the chain of Slavery, in order to get to their own courts. All these things you "remember." Boston was non-resistant. She gave her "back to the smiters"—from the South; she "withheld not her cheek"—from the scorn of South Carolina, and welcomed the "spitting" of kidnappers from Georgia and Virginia. To-day we have our pay for that conduct. . . .

The Nebraska Bill has just now been passed. Who pressed it? The fifteen hundred "gentlemen of property and standing" in Boston, who, in 1851, volunteered to carry Thomas Sims into Slavery by force of arms. *They* passed the Nebraska Bill. If Boston had punished the kidnapping of 1845, there would have been no Fugitive Slave Bill in 1850. If Massachusetts, in 1850, had declared the bill should not be executed, the kidnapper would never have shown his face in the streets of Boston. If, failing in this, Boston had said, in 1851, "Thomas Sims shall not be carried off," and forcibly or peacefully, by the majesty of the great mass of men, had resisted it, no kidnapper would have come here again. There would have been no Nebraska Bill. But to every demand of the Slave power, Massachusetts has said "Yes, yes!—we grant it all!" "Agitation must cease!" "Save the Union!"

Southern Slavery is an institution which is in earnest. Northern Freedom is an institution that is not in earnest. It was in earnest in '76 and '83. It has not been much in earnest since. The Compromises are but provisional. Slavery is the only finality. Now, since the Nebraska Bill is passed, an attempt is made to add insult to insult, injury to injury. . . . Behold the consequences of the doctrine that there is no "higher law." Look at Boston, to-day. There are no chains around your Court House—there are *ropes* around it. A hundred and eighty-four United States soldiers are there. They are, I am told, mostly foreigners—the scum of the earth—none but such enter into armies as common soldiers, in a country like ours. I say it with pity—they are not to blame for having been born where they were and what they are. I pity the scum as well as I pity the mass of men. The soldiers are there, I say, and their trade is to kill. Why is this so?

You remember the meeting at Faneuil Hall, last Friday, when even the words of my friend Wendell Phillips, the most eloquent words that get spoken in America, in this century, hardly restrained the multitude from going, and by violence attempting to storm the Court House. What stirred them up? It was the spirit of our fathers—the spirit of justice and liberty in your heart, and in my heart, and in the heart of us all. Sometimes it gets the better of a man's

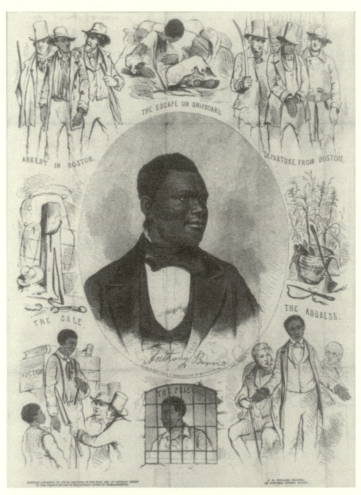

Fig. 2. An 1855 broadside depicting scenes from Anthony Burns's escape, arrest in Boston, and return to bondage under the Fugitive Slave Law. (Library of Congress)

prudence, especially on occasions like this; and so excited was that assembly of four or five thousand men, that even the words of eloquent Wendell Phillips could hardly restrain them from going at once rashly to the Court House, and tearing it to the ground.

Boston is the most peaceful of cities. Why? Because we have commonly had a peace that was worth keeping. No city respects laws so much. Because the laws have been made by the people, for the people, and are laws which respect justice. Here is a law which the people will not keep. It is a law of our Southern masters, a law not fit to keep. . . .

10. George Fitzhugh, *Sociology for the South; or, the Failure of Free Society* (Richmond, Va.: A. Morris, 1854) and *Cannibals All! or, Slaves Without Masters* (Richmond, Va.: A. Morris, 1857)

George Fitzhugh, a Virginia lawyer and author, is a Southern exemplar of how thought became increasingly radicalized on both sides in the 1850s. Fitzhugh went beyond identifying slavery as an institution to be tolerated. Instead, he defended slavery in patriarchal terms as a positive good, and he claimed that blacks were inferior to whites and benefited from slavery. Fitzhugh also critiqued Northern capitalism as the true evil.

Sociology for the South; or, the Failure of Free Society

. . . He [the Negro] is but a grown up child, and must be governed as a child, not as a lunatic or criminal. The master occupies toward him the place of parent or guardian. We shall not dwell on this view, for no one will differ with us who thinks as we do of the negro's capacity, and we might argue till dooms-day, in vain, with those who have a high opinion of the negro's moral and intellectual capacity.

Secondly. The negro is improvident; will not lay up in summer for the wants of winter; will not accumulate in youth for the exigencies of age. He would become an insufferable burden to society. Society has the right to prevent this, and can only do so by subjecting him to domestic slavery.

In the last place, the negro race is inferior to the white race, and living in their midst, they would be far outstripped or outwitted in the chase of free competition. Gradual but certain extermination would be their fate. We presume the maddest abolitionist does not think the negro's providence of habits and money-making capacity at all to compare to those of the whites. This defect of character would alone justify enslaving him, if he is to remain here. In Africa or the West Indies, he would become idolatrous, savage and cannibal, or be devoured by savages and cannibals. At the North he would freeze or starve.

We would remind those who deprecate and sympathize with negro slavery, that his slavery here relieves him from a far more cruel slavery in Africa, or from idolatry and cannibalism, and every brutal vice and crime that can disgrace humanity; and that it christianizes, protects, supports and civilizes him; that it governs him far better than free laborers at the North are governed. There, wife-murder has become a mere holiday pastime; and where so many wives are murdered, almost all must be brutally treated. Nay, more: men who kill their wives or treat them brutally, must be ready for all kinds of crime, and the calendar of crime at the North proves the inference to be correct. Negroes never kill their wives. If it be objected that legally they have no wives, then we reply, that in an experience of more than forty years, we never yet heard of a negro man killing a negro woman. Our negroes are not only better off as to physical comfort than free laborers, but their moral condition is better.

Cannibals All! or, Slaves Without Masters

The negro slaves of the South are the happiest, and, in some sense, the freest people in the world. The children and the aged and infirm work not at all, and yet have all the comforts and necessaries of life provided for them. They enjoy liberty, because they are oppressed neither by care nor labor. The women do little hard work, and are protected from the despotism of their husbands by their masters. The negro men and stout boys work, on the average, in good weather, not more than nine hours a day. The balance of their time is spent in perfect abandon. Besides: they have their Sabbaths and holidays. White men, with so much of license and liberty, would die of ennui; but negroes luxuriate in corporeal and mental repose. With their faces upturned to the sun, they can sleep at any hour; and quiet sleep is the greatest of human enjoyments. "Blessed be the man who invented sleep." 'Tis happiness in itself—and results from contentment with the present, and confident assurance of the future. . . .

A common charge preferred against slavery is, that it induces idleness with the masters. The trouble, care, and labor of providing for wife, children, and slaves, and of properly governing and administering the whole affairs of the farm is usually borne on small estates by the master. On larger ones, he is aided by an overseer or manager. If they do their duty, their time is fully occupied. If they do not, the estate goes to ruin. The mistress, on Southern farms, is usually more busily, usefully and benevolently occupied than any one on the farm. She unites in her person, the offices of wife, mother, mistress, housekeeper, and sister of charity. And she fulfills all these offices admirably well. The rich men, in free society, may, if they please, lounge about town, visit clubs, attend the theatre, and have no other trouble than that of collecting rents, interest and dividends of stock. In a well constituted slave society, there should be no idlers. But we cannot divine how the capitalists in free society are to put to work. The master labors for the slave, they exchange industrial value. But the capitalist, living on his income, gives nothing to his subjects. He lives by mere exploitation. . . .

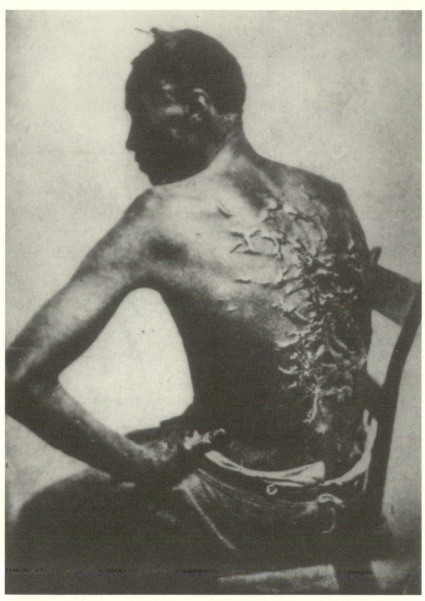

Fig. 3. "Overseer Artayou Carrier whipped me. I was two months in bed sore from the whipping. My master come after I was whipped; he discharged the overseer. The very words of poor Peter, taken as he sat for his picture." (Baton Rouge, Louisiana, 1863; National Archives)

11. *DRED SCOTT V. SANDFORD*, 60 U.S. 393 (1857) (OPINION OF
CHIEF JUSTICE TANEY, DISSENT OF JUSTICE CURTIS)

**Dred Scott, a slave, belonged to Dr. John Emerson of the United States Army. In
1834, Emerson took Scott from Missouri to the military post at Rock Island, Illinois,
and held him there as a slave until spring 1836. Emerson then moved with Scott to
the military post at Fort Snelling in present-day Minnesota, an area that was free
pursuant to the Missouri Compromise, and there held Scott in slavery. In 1836,
Emerson purchased another slave, Harriet, from a fellow officer at the post. Scott
married Harriet with Emerson's consent, and the couple had several daughters.
The Scotts moved to Missouri in 1840, while Emerson served in Florida during the
Seminole War. Emerson died in 1843.**

**In 1846, Scott began this suit for his freedom based on the principle that if a master
took a slave into free territory, the slave became free. In 1850, a St. Louis court held
that Scott had become free while living in free territory, but the Missouri Supreme
Court reversed the holding in 1852. By this time, Emerson's widow no longer owned
Scott and his family; Emerson's widow's brother, John Sanford, was their new owner.[6]
Because Sanford was a New Yorker, Scott now sued for his freedom in federal court
under diversity jurisdiction, and the case worked its way up to the Supreme Court.
In the context of growing sectionalism, Chief Justice Roger Taney sought to resolve
whether blacks could be citizens of the United States, as well as the scope of Congress's
power to regulate slavery in the territories.**

Mr. Chief Justice [Roger] TANEY delivered the Opinion of the Court.

. . . The question is simply this: Can a negro, whose ancestors were imported
into this country, and sold as slaves, become a member of the political community formed and brought into existence by the Constitution of the United States,
and as such become entitled to all the rights, and privileges, and immunities,
guarantied by that instrument to the citizen? . . .

The words "people of the United States" and "citizens" are synonymous terms,
and mean the same thing. They both describe the political body who, according
to our republican institutions, form the sovereignty, and who hold the power and
conduct the Government through their representatives. . . . The question before
us is, whether the class of persons described in the plea in abatement compose
a portion of this people, and are constituent members of this sovereignty? We
think they are not, and that they are not included, and were not intended to be
included, under the word "citizens" in the Constitution, and can therefore claim
none of the rights and privileges which that instrument provides for and secures
to citizens of the United States. On the contrary, they were at that time considered
as a subordinate and inferior class of beings, who had been subjugated by the
dominant race, and, whether emancipated or not, yet remained subject to their
authority, and had no rights or privileges but such as those who held the power
and the Government might choose to grant them. . . .

In discussing this question, we must not confound the rights of citizenship which a State may confer within its own limits, and the rights of citizenship as a member of the Union. It does not by any means follow, because he has all the rights and privileges of a citizen of a State, that he must be a citizen of the United States. He may have all of the rights and privileges of the citizen of a State, and yet not be entitled to the rights and privileges of a citizen in any other State. For, previous to the adoption of the Constitution of the United States, every State had the undoubted right to confer on whomsoever it pleased the character of citizen, and to endow him with all its rights. But this character of course was confined to the boundaries of the State, and gave him no rights or privileges in other States beyond those secured to him by the laws of nations and the comity of States. Nor have the several States surrendered the power of conferring these rights and privileges by adopting the Constitution of the United States. Each State may still confer them upon an alien, or any one it thinks proper, or upon any class or description of persons; yet he would not be a citizen in the sense in which that word is used in the Constitution of the United States, nor entitled to sue as such in one of its courts, nor to the privileges and immunities of a citizen in the other States. The rights which he would acquire would be restricted to the State which gave them. . . .

It is very clear, therefore, that no State can, by any act or law of its own, passed since the adoption of the Constitution, introduce a new member into the political community created by the Constitution of the United States. It cannot make him a member of this community by making him a member of its own. . . .

The question then arises, whether the provisions of the Constitution, in relation to the personal rights and privileges to which the citizen of a State should be entitled, embraced the negro African race, at that time in this country, or who might afterwards be imported, who had then or should afterwards be made free in any State; and to put it in the power of a single State to make him a citizen of the United States, and endue him with the full rights of citizenship in every other State without their consent? Does the Constitution of the United States act upon him whenever he shall be made free under the laws of a State, and raised there to the rank of a citizen, and immediately clothe him with all the privileges of a citizen in every other State, and in its own courts?

The court think the affirmative of these propositions cannot be maintained. . . .

. . . [T]he legislation and histories of the times, and the language used in the Declaration of Independence, show, that neither the class of persons who had been imported as slaves, nor their descendants, whether they had become free or not, were then acknowledged as a part of the people, nor intended to be included in the general words used in that memorable instrument. . . .

They had for more than a century before been regarded as beings of an inferior order, and altogether unfit to associate with the white race, either in social or political relations; and so far inferior, that they had no rights which the white man was bound to respect; and that the negro might justly and lawfully be reduced to slavery for his benefit. He was bought and sold, and treated as an ordinary article of merchandise and traffic, whenever a profit could be made by it. This opinion was at that time fixed and universal in the civilized portion of the white race. . . . The legislation of the different colonies furnishes positive and indisputable proof of this fact. . . .

. . . [T]hese laws . . . show, too plainly to be misunderstood, the degraded condition of this unhappy race. They were still in force when the Revolution began, and are a faithful index to the state of feeling towards the class of persons of whom they speak, and of the position they occupied throughout the thirteen colonies, in the eyes and thoughts of the men who framed the Declaration of Independence and established the State Constitutions and Governments. They show that a perpetual and impassable barrier was intended to be erected between the white race and the one which they had reduced to slavery, and governed as subjects with absolute and despotic power, and which they then looked upon as so far below them in the scale of created beings, that intermarriages between white persons and negroes or mulattoes were regarded as unnatural and immoral, and punished as crimes, not only in the parties, but in the person who joined them in marriage. And no distinction in this respect was made between the free negro or mulatto and the slave, but this stigma, of the deepest degradation, was fixed upon the whole race. . . .

The language of the Declaration of Independence is equally conclusive: . . .

. . . "We hold these truths to be self-evident: that all men are created equal; that they are endowed by their Creator with certain unalienable rights; that among them is life, liberty, and the pursuit of happiness; that to secure these rights, Governments are instituted, deriving their just powers from the consent of the governed."

The general words above quoted would seem to embrace the whole human family, and if they were used in a similar instrument at this day would be so understood. But it is too clear for dispute, that the enslaved African race were not intended to be included, and formed no part of the people who framed and adopted this declaration; for if the language, as understood in that day, would embrace them, the conduct of the distinguished men who framed the Declaration of Independence would have been utterly and flagrantly inconsistent with the principles they asserted; and instead of the sympathy of mankind, to which they so confidently appealed, they would have deserved and received universal rebuke and reprobation.

Yet the men who framed this declaration were great men—high in literary acquirements—high in their sense of honor, and incapable of asserting principles inconsistent with those on which they were acting. They perfectly understood the meaning of the language they used, and how it would be understood by others; and they knew that it would not in any part of the civilized world be supposed to embrace the negro race, which, by common consent, had been excluded from civilized Governments and the family of nations, and doomed to slavery. They spoke and acted according to the then established doctrines and principles, and in the ordinary language of the day, and no one misunderstood them. The unhappy black race were separated from the white by indelible marks, and laws long before established, and were never thought of or spoken of except as property, and when the claims of the owner or the profit of the trader were supposed to need protection.

This state of public opinion had undergone no change when the Constitution was adopted, as is equally evident from its provisions and language. . . .

. . . [T]here are two clauses in the Constitution which point directly and specifically to the negro race as a separate class of persons, and show clearly that they were not regarded as a portion of the people or citizens of the Government then formed.

One of these clauses reserves to each of the thirteen States the right to import slaves until the year 1808, if it thinks proper. . . . And by the other provision the States pledge themselves to each other to maintain the right of property of the master, by delivering up to him any slave who may have escaped from his service, and be found within their respective territories. . . . And these two provisions show, conclusively, that neither the description of persons therein referred to, nor their descendants, were embraced in any of the other provisions of the Constitution; for certainly these two clauses were not intended to confer on them or their posterity the blessings of liberty, or any of the personal rights so carefully provided for the citizen.

No one of that race had ever migrated to the United States voluntarily; all of them had been brought here as articles of merchandise. The number that had been emancipated at that time were but few in comparison with those held in slavery; and they were identified in the public mind with the race to which they belonged, and regarded as a part of the slave population rather than the free. It is obvious that they were not even in the minds of the framers of the Constitution when they were conferring special rights and privileges upon the citizens of a State in every other part of the Union.

Indeed, when we look to the condition of this race in the several States at the time, it is impossible to believe that these rights and privileges were intended to be extended to them.

It is very true, that in that portion of the Union where the labor of the negro race was found to be unsuited to the climate and unprofitable to the master, but few slaves were held at the time of the Declaration of Independence; and when the Constitution was adopted, it had entirely worn out in one of them, and measures had been taken for its gradual abolition in several others. But this change had not been produced by any change of opinion in relation to this race[.] . . .

... [The slave-holding states] have continued to treat them as an inferior class, and to subject them to strict police regulations, drawing a broad line of distinction between the citizen and the slave races, and legislating in relation to them upon the same principle which prevailed at the time of the Declaration of Independence. As relates to these States, it is too plain for argument, that they have never been regarded as a part of the people or citizens of the State, nor supposed to possess any political rights which the dominant race might not withhold or grant at their pleasure. ...

And if we turn to the legislation of the States where slavery had worn out, or measures taken for its speedy abolition, we shall find the same opinions and principles equally fixed and equally acted upon. [Taney here summarizes a 1786 Massachusetts law prohibiting "marriage of any white person with any negro, Indian, or mulatto," strictures against blacks in Connecticut, and an 1815 New Hampshire law closing the militia to all "but free white citizens."]

The legislation of the States therefore shows, in a manner not to be mistaken, the inferior and subject condition of that race at the time the Constitution was adopted, and long afterwards ... and it is hardly consistent with the respect due to these States, to suppose that they regarded at that time, as fellow-citizens and members of the sovereignty, a class of beings whom they had thus stigmatized ... and upon whom they had impressed such deep and enduring marks of inferiority and degradation; or, that, when they met in convention to form the Constitution, they looked upon them as a portion of their constituents, or designed to include them in the provisions so carefully inserted for the security and protection of the liberties and rights of their citizens. It cannot be supposed that they intended to secure to them rights, and privileges, and rank, in the new political body throughout the Union, which every one of them denied within the limits of its own dominion. More especially, it cannot be believed that the large slaveholding States regarded them as included in the word citizens, or would have consented to a Constitution which might compel them to receive them in that character from another State. For if they were so received, and entitled to the privileges and immunities of citizens, it would exempt them from the operation of the special laws and from the police regulations which they considered to be necessary for their own safety. It would give to persons of the negro race, who were recognised as citizens in any one State of the Union, the right to enter every other State whenever they pleased, singly or in companies, without pass or passport, and without obstruction, to sojourn there as long as they pleased, to go where they pleased at every hour of the day or night without molestation, unless they committed some violation of law for which a white man would be punished; and it would give them the full liberty of speech in public and in private upon all subjects upon which its own citizens might speak; to hold public meetings upon political affairs, and to keep and carry arms wherever they went. And all of this would be done in the face of the subject race of the same color, both free and slaves, and inevitably producing discontent and insubordination among them, and endangering the peace and safety of the State. . . .

And, upon a full and careful consideration of the subject, the court is of opinion, that . . . Dred Scott was not a citizen of Missouri within the meaning of the Constitution of the United States, and not entitled as such to sue in its courts; and, consequently, that the Circuit Court had no jurisdiction of the case, and that the judgment on the plea in abatement is erroneous. . . .

The principle of law is too well settled to be disputed, that a court can give no judgment for either party, where it has no jurisdiction; and if, upon the showing of Scott himself, it appeared that he was still a slave, the case ought to have been dismissed, and the judgment against him and in favor of the defendant for costs, is, like that on the plea in abatement, erroneous, and the suit ought to have been dismissed by the Circuit Court for want of jurisdiction in that court.

But, before we proceed to examine this part of the case, it may be proper to notice an objection taken to the judicial authority of this court to decide it; and it has been said, that as this court has decided against the jurisdiction of the Circuit Court on the plea in abatement, it has no right to examine any question presented by the exception; and that anything it may say upon that part of the case will be extra-judicial, and mere obiter dicta.

This is a manifest mistake; there can be no doubt as to the jurisdiction of this court to revise the judgment of a Circuit Court, and to reverse it for any error apparent on the record, whether it be the error of giving judgment in a case over which it had no jurisdiction, or any other material error; and this, too, whether there is a plea in abatement or not. . . .

. . . [I]t appears affirmatively on the record that he is not a citizen, and consequently his suit against Sandford was not a suit between citizens of different States, and the court had no authority to pass any judgment between the parties. The suit ought, in this view of it, to have been dismissed by the Circuit Court, and its judgment in favor of Sandford is erroneous, and must be reversed.

It is true that the result either way, by dismissal or by a judgment for the defendant, makes very little, if any, difference in a pecuniary or personal point of view to either party. But the fact that the result would be very nearly the same to the parties in either form of judgment, would not justify this court in sanctioning an error in the judgment which is patent on the record, and which, if sanctioned, might be drawn into precedent, and lead to serious mischief and injustice in some future suit.

We proceed, therefore, to inquire whether the facts relied on by the plaintiff entitled him to his freedom. . . .

In considering this part of the controversy, two questions arise: 1. Was he, together with his family, free in Missouri by reason of the stay in the territory of the United States hereinbefore mentioned? And 2. If they were not, is Scott himself free by reason of his removal to Rock Island, in the State of Illinois, as stated in the above admissions?

We proceed to examine the first question.

The act of Congress upon which the plaintiff relies, declares that slavery and involuntary servitude, except as a punishment for crime, shall be forever prohibited in all that part of the territory ceded by France, under the name of Louisiana, which lies north of thirty-six degrees thirty minutes north latitude, and not included within the limits of Missouri. And the difficulty which meets us at the threshold of this part of the inquiry is, whether Congress was authorized to pass this law under any of the powers granted to it by the Constitution; for if the authority is not given by that instrument, it is the duty of this court to declare it void and inoperative, and incapable of conferring freedom upon any one who is held as a slave under the laws of any one of the States.

The counsel for the plaintiff has laid much stress upon that article in the Constitution which confers on Congress the power "to dispose of and make all needful rules and regulations respecting the territory or other property belonging to the United States," but, in the judgment of the court, that provision has no bearing on the present controversy, and the power there given, whatever it may be, is confined, and was intended to be confined, to the territory which at that time belonged to, or was claimed by, the United States, and was within their boundaries as settled by the treaty with Great Britain, and can have no influence upon a territory afterwards acquired from a foreign Government. It was a special provision for a known and particular territory, and to meet a present emergency, and nothing more. . . .

. . . Consequently, the power which Congress may have lawfully exercised in this Territory, while it remained under a Territorial Government, and which may have been sanctioned by judicial decision, can furnish no justification and no argument to support a similar exercise of power over territory afterwards acquired by the Federal Government. . . .

But there is another point in the case which depends on State power and State law. And it is contended, on the part of the plaintiff, that he is made free by being taken to Rock Island, in the State of Illinois, independently of his residence in the territory of the United States; and being so made free, he was not again reduced to a state of slavery by being brought back to Missouri. . . .

. . . As Scott was a slave when taken into the State of Illinois by his owner, and was there held as such, and brought back in that character, his *status* as free or slave, depended on the laws of Missouri, and not of Illinois. . . .

Upon the whole, therefore, it is the judgment of this court, that it appears by the record before us that the plaintiff in error is not a citizen of Missouri, in the sense in which that word is used in the Constitution; and that the Circuit Court of the United States, for that reason, had no jurisdiction in the case, and could give no judgment in it. Its judgment for the defendant must, consequently, be reversed, and a mandate issued, directing the suit to be dismissed for want of jurisdiction.

Mr. Justice [Benjamin] CURTIS dissenting.

... To determine whether any free persons, descended from Africans held in slavery, were citizens of the United States under the Confederation, and consequently at the time of the adoption of the Constitution of the United States, it is only necessary to know whether any such persons were citizens of either of the States under the Confederation, at the time of the adoption of the Constitution.

Of this there can be no doubt. At the time of the ratification of the Articles of Confederation, all free native-born inhabitants of the States of New Hampshire, Massachusetts, New York, New Jersey, and North Carolina, though descended from African slaves, were not only citizens of those States, but such of them as had the other necessary qualifications possessed the franchise of electors, on equal terms with other citizens. . . .

. . . [N]o argument can obscure, that in some of the original thirteen States, free colored persons, before and at the time of the formation of the Constitution, were citizens of those States. . . .

Did the Constitution of the United States deprive [free colored persons] or their descendants of citizenship?

That Constitution was ordained and established by the people of the United States, through the action, in each State, of those persons who were qualified by its laws to act thereon in behalf of themselves and all other citizens of that State. In some of the States, as we have seen, colored persons were among those qualified by law to act on this subject. These colored persons were not only included in the body of "the people of the United States," by whom the Constitution was ordained and established, but, in at least five of the States they had the power to act, and doubtless did act, by their suffrages, upon the question of its adoption. It would be strange if we were to find in that instrument anything which deprived of their citizenship any part of the people of the United States who were among those by whom it was established.

I can find nothing in the Constitution which . . . deprives of their citizenship any class of persons who were citizens of the United States at the time of its adoption, or who should be native-born citizens of any State after its adoption; nor any power enabling Congress to disfranchise persons born on the soil of any State, and entitled to citizenship of such State by its Constitution and laws. And my opinion is, that, under the Constitution of the United States, every free person born on the soil of a State, who is a citizen of that State by force of its Constitution or laws, is also a citizen of the United States. . . .

But, further: though . . . I do not think the enjoyment of the elective franchise essential to citizenship, there can be no doubt it is one of the chiefest attributes of citizenship under the American Constitutions; and the just and constitutional possession of this right is decisive evidence of citizenship. The provisions made by a Constitution on this subject must therefore be looked to as bearing directly on the question what persons are citizens under that Constitution; and as being decisive, to this extent, that all such persons as are allowed by the Constitution to exercise the elective franchise, and thus to participate in the Government of the United States, must be deemed citizens of the United States. . . .

It has been often asserted that the Constitution was made exclusively by and for the white race. It has already been shown that in five of the thirteen original States, colored persons then possessed the elective franchise, and were among those by whom the Constitution was ordained and established. If so, it is not true, in point of fact, that the Constitution was made exclusively by the white race. And that it was made exclusively for the white race is, in my opinion, not only an assumption not warranted by anything in the Constitution, but contradicted by its opening declaration, that it was ordained and established by the people of the United States, for themselves and their posterity. And as free colored persons were then citizens of at least five States, and so in every sense part of the people of the United States, they were among those for whom and whose posterity the Constitution was ordained and established. . . .

It has been further objected, that if free colored persons, born within a particular State, and made citizens of that State by its Constitution and laws, are thereby made citizens of the United States, then, under the second section of the fourth article of the Constitution, such persons would be entitled to all the privileges and immunities of citizens in the several States; and if so, then colored persons could vote, and be eligible to not only Federal offices, but offices even in those States whose Constitutions and laws disqualify colored persons from voting or being elected to office. . . .

A naturalized citizen cannot be President of the United States, nor a Senator till after the lapse of nine years, nor a Representative till after the lapse of seven years, from his naturalization. Yet, as soon as naturalized, he is certainly a citizen of the United States. . . . [I]n all the States, numerous persons, though citizens, cannot vote, or cannot hold office, either on account of their age, or sex, or the want of the necessary legal qualifications. The truth is, that citizenship, under the Constitution of the United States, is not dependent on the possession of any particular political or even of all civil rights; and any attempt so to define it must lead to error. To what citizens the elective franchise shall be confided, is a question to be determined by each State, in accordance with its own views of the necessities or expediencies of its condition. What civil rights shall be enjoyed by its citizens, and whether all shall enjoy the same, or how they may be gained or lost, are to be determined in the same way. . . .

The conclusions at which I have arrived on this part of the case are:

First. That the free native-born citizens of each State are citizens of the United States.

Second. That as free colored persons born within some of the States are citizens of those States, such persons are also citizens of the United States.

Third. That every such citizen, residing in any State, has the right to sue and is liable to be sued in the Federal courts, as a citizen of that State in which he resides.

Fourth. That as the plea to the jurisdiction in this case shows no facts, except that the plaintiff was of African descent, and his ancestors were sold as slaves, and as these facts are not inconsistent with his citizenship of the United States, and his residence in the State of Missouri, the plea to the jurisdiction was bad, and the judgment of the Circuit Court overruling it was correct.

I dissent, therefore, from that part of the opinion of the majority of the court, in which it is held that a person of African descent cannot be a citizen of the United States; and I regret I must go further, and dissent both from what I deem their assumption of authority to examine the constitutionality of the act of Congress commonly called the Missouri compromise act[.] . . .

The general question may be stated to be, whether the plaintiff's *status*, as a slave, was so changed by his residence within that territory that he was not a slave in the State of Missouri, at the time this action was brought. . . .

. . . [I]f the acts of Congress on this subject are valid, the law of the Territory of Wisconsin, within whose limits the residence of the plaintiff and his wife, and their marriage and the birth of one or both of their children, took place . . . is a law operating directly on the *status* of the slave. . . . [The Missouri Compromise] enacted that, within this Territory, "slavery and involuntary servitude, otherwise than in the punishment of crimes, whereof the parties shall have been duly convicted, shall be, and is hereby, forever prohibited: *Provided, always,* that any person escaping into the same, from whom labor or service is lawfully claimed in any State or Territory of the United States, such fugitive may be lawfully reclaimed, and conveyed to the person claiming his or her labor or service, as aforesaid." . . .

On what ground can it be denied that all valid laws of the United States, constitutionally enacted by Congress for the government of the Territory, rightfully extended over an officer of the United States and his servant who went into the Territory to remain there for an indefinite length of time, to take part in its civil or military affairs?

What, then, shall we say of the consent of the master, that the slave may contract a lawful marriage, attended with all the civil rights and duties which belong to that relation; that he may enter into a relation which none but a free man can assume—a relation which involves not only the rights and duties of the slave, but those of the other party to the contract, and of their descendants to the remotest generation? In my judgment, there can be no more effectual abandonment of the legal rights of a master over his slave, than by the consent of the master that the slave should enter into a contract of marriage, in a free State, attended by all the civil rights and obligations which belong to that condition. . . .

51

To avoid misapprehension on this important and difficult subject, I will state, distinctly, the conclusions at which I have arrived. They are:

First. The rules of international law respecting the emancipation of slaves, by the rightful operation of the laws of another State or country upon the *status* of the slave, while resident in such foreign State or country, are part of the common law of Missouri, and have not been abrogated by any statute law of that State.

Second. The laws of the United States, constitutionally enacted, which operated directly on and changed the *status* of a slave coming into the Territory of Wisconsin with his master, who went thither to reside for an indefinite length of time, in the performance of his duties as an officer of the United States, had a rightful operation on the *status* of the slave[.] . . .

Third. The laws of the United States, in operation in the Territory of Wisconsin at the time of the plaintiff's residence there, did act directly on the *status* of the plaintiff, and change his *status* to that of a free man.

Fourth. The plaintiff and his wife were capable of contracting, and, with the consent of Dr. Emerson, did contract a marriage in that Territory, valid under its laws; and the validity of this marriage cannot be questioned in Missouri, save by showing that it was in fraud of the laws of that State, or of some right derived from them; which cannot be shown in this case, because the master consented to it.

Fifth. That the consent of the master that his slave, residing in a country which does not tolerate slavery, may enter into a lawful contract of marriage, attended with the civil rights and duties which being to that condition, is an effectual act of emancipation. And the law does not enable Dr. Emerson, or any one claiming under him, to assert a title to the married persons as slaves, and thus destroy the obligation of the contract of marriage, and bastardize their issue, and reduce them to slavery. . . .

I have thus far assumed, merely for the purpose of the argument, that the laws of the United States, respecting slavery in this Territory, were constitutionally enacted by Congress. It remains to inquire whether they are constitutional and binding laws. [Curtis finds that the Missouri Compromise was, in fact, constitutional and that Congress had the right to enact legislation governing slavery in the territories.]

In my opinion, the judgment of the Circuit Court should be reversed, and the cause remanded for a new trial.

12. Speech of James Henry Hammond to the U.S. Senate (March 4, 1858) (*Congressional Globe*, 35th Congress, 1st Session)

A wealthy plantation owner, James Henry Hammond represented South Carolina in the U.S. Senate from 1857 to 1860. Hammond delivered this speech in the context of increasing sectional tension, and in it, he declared that no nation in the world

could dare to make war on the South because "cotton is king," integral to the world economy. "But," Hammond continued, "the greatest strength of the South arises from the harmony of her political and social institutions." George Fitzhugh's arguments percolated through Hammond's speech to the Senate, as Hammond compared the conditions of slavery in the South with what he identified as the worse off wage-slaves of the industrializing North. Hammond also justified slavery in blatantly racist terms, and he identified black slaves as the mudsill that enabled Southern whites to participate in politics and other endeavors.

. . . In all social systems there must be a class to do the mean duties, to perform the drudgery of life. That is, a class requiring but a low order of intellect and but little skill. Its requisites are vigor, docility, fidelity. Such a class you must have, or you would not have that other class which leads progress, refinement, and civilization. It constitutes the very mud-sills of society and of political government; and you might as well attempt to build a house in the air, as to build either the one or the other, except on the mud-sills. Fortunately for the South, she found a race adapted to that purpose to her hand. A race inferior to herself, but eminently qualified in temper, in vigor, in docility, in capacity to stand the climate, to answer all her purposes. We use them for the purpose, and call them slaves. We are old-fashioned at the South yet; it [slave] is a word discarded now by ears polite; but I will not characterize that class at the North with that term; but you have it; it is there; it is everywhere; it is eternal.

The Senator from New York [William H. Seward] said yesterday that the whole world had abolished slavery. Ay, the name, but not the thing; and all the powers of the earth cannot abolish it. God only can do it when he repeals the *fiat*, "the poor ye always have with you;" for the man who lives by daily labor, and scarcely lives at that, and who has to put out his labor in the market and take the best he can get for it; in short, your whole class of manual laborers and operatives, as you call them, are slaves. The difference between us is, that our slaves are hired for life and well compensated; there is no starvation, no begging, no want of employment among our people, and not too much employment either. Yours are hired by the day, not cared for, and scantily compensated, which may be proved in the most deplorable manner, at any hour, in any street in any of your large towns. Why, sir, you meet more beggars in one day, in any single street of the city of New York, than you would meet in a lifetime in the whole South. Our slaves are black, of another, inferior race. The status in which we have placed them is an elevation. They are elevated from the condition in which God first created them, by being made our slaves. None of that race on the whole face of the globe can be compared with the slaves of the South, and they know it. They are happy, content, unaspiring, and utterly incapable, from intellectual degradation, ever to give us any trouble by their aspirations.

Your slaves are white, of your own race; you are brothers of one blood. They are your equals in natural endowment of intellect, and they feel galled by their degradation. Our slaves do not vote. We give them no political power. Yours do vote, and being the majority, they are the depositories of all your political power. If they knew the tremendous secret, that the ballot-box is stronger than an army with bayonets, and could combine, where would you be? Your society would be reconstructed, your government reconstructed, your property divided, not as they have mistakenly attempted to initiate such proceedings by meeting in parks, with arms in their hands, but by the quiet process of the ballot-box. You have been making war upon us to our very hearthstones. How would you like for us to send lecturers or agitators North, to teach these people this, to aid and assist in combining, and to lead them?

13. ABRAHAM LINCOLN'S SPEECH AT CHICAGO, ILLINOIS (JULY 10, 1858)

Northern fears about slavery's expansion and hostility to the Supreme Court's *Dred Scott* ruling helped energize the growth of the Republican Party. In this speech during his campaign to represent Illinois in the U.S. Senate, Abraham Lincoln attacked both the logic and the validity of *Dred Scott*.[7]

A little now on the other point—the Dred Scott Decision. Another one of the issues [Stephen Douglas] says that is to be made with me, is upon his devotion to the Dred Scott Decision, and my opposition to it.

I have expressed heretofore, and I now repeat, my opposition to the Dred Scott Decision, but I should be allowed to state the nature of that opposition, and I ask your indulgence while I do so. What is fairly implied by the term Judge Douglas has used "resistance to the Decision"? I do not resist it. If I wanted to take Dred Scott from his master, I would be interfering with property, and that terrible difficulty that Judge Douglas speaks of, of interfering with property, would arise. But I am doing no such thing as that, but all that I am doing is refusing to obey it as a political rule. If I were in Congress, and a vote should come up on a question whether slavery should be prohibited in a new territory, in spite of that Dred Scott decision, I would vote that it should. . . .

That is what I would do. . . . Judge Douglas said last night, that before the decision he might advance his opinion, and it might be contrary to the decision when it was made; but after it was made he would abide by it until it was reversed. Just so! We let this property abide by the decision, but we will try to reverse that decision. . . . We will try to put it where Judge Douglas would not object, for he says he will obey it until it is reversed. Somebody has to reverse that decision, since it is made, and we mean to reverse it, and we mean to do it peaceably.

What are the uses of decisions of courts? They have two uses. As rules of property they have two uses. First—they decide upon the question before the court. They decide in this case that Dred Scott is a slave. Nobody resists that. Not only that, but they say to everybody else, that persons standing just as Dred Scott stands is [*sic*] as he is. That is, they say that when a question comes up upon another person it will be so decided again, unless the court decides in another way . . . unless the court overrules its decision. . . . Well, we mean to do what we can to have the court decide the other way. That is one thing we mean to try to do.

The sacredness that Judge Douglas throws around this decision, is a degree of sacredness that has never been before thrown around any other decision. I have never heard of such a thing. Why, decisions apparently contrary to that decision, or that good lawyers thought were contrary to that decision, have been made by that very court before. It is the first of its kind; it is an astonisher in legal history. . . . It is based upon falsehood in the main as to the facts—allegations of facts upon which it stands are not facts at all in many instances, and no decision made on any question—the first instance of a decision made under so many unfavorable circumstances—thus placed has ever been held by the profession as law, and it has always needed confirmation before the lawyers regarded it as settled law. But Judge Douglas will have it that all hands must take this extraordinary decision, made under these extraordinary circumstances, and give their vote in Congress in accordance with it, yield to it and obey it in every possible sense. Circumstances alter cases. Do not gentlemen here remember the case of that same Supreme Court, some twenty-five or thirty years ago, deciding that a National Bank was constitutional? I ask, if somebody does not remember that a National Bank was declared to be constitutional? . . . Such is the truth, whether it be remembered or not. The Bank charter ran out, and a re-charter was granted by Congress. That re-charter was laid before General Jackson. It was urged upon him, when he denied the constitutionality of the bank, that the Supreme Court had decided that it was constitutional; and that General Jackson then said that the Supreme Court had no right to lay down a rule to govern a co-ordinate branch of the government, the members of which had sworn to support the Constitution—that each member had sworn to support that Constitution as he understood it. I will venture here to say, that I have heard Judge Douglas say that he approved of General Jackson for that act. What has now become of all his tirade about "resistance to the Supreme Court"? . . .

We were often—more than once at least—in the course of Judge Douglas' speech last night, reminded that this government was made for white men—that he believed it was made for white men. Well, that is putting it into a shape in which no one wants to deny it, but the Judge then goes into his passion for drawing inferences that are not warranted. I protest, now and forever, against that counterfeit logic which presumes that because I do not want a negro woman for a slave, I do necessarily want her for a wife. . . . My understanding is that I need not have her for either, but as God made us separate, we can leave one another alone and do one another much good thereby. There are white men enough to marry all the white women, and enough black men to marry all the black women, and in God's name let them be so married. The Judge regales us with the terrible enormities that take place by the mixture of races; that the inferior race bears the superior down. Why, Judge, if we do not let them get together in the Territories they won't mix there. . . .

Now, it happens that we meet together once every year, sometime about the 4th of July, for some reason or other. These 4th of July gatherings I suppose have their uses. If you will indulge me, I will state what I suppose to be some of them.

We are now a mighty nation, we are thirty—or about thirty millions of people, and we own and inhabit about one-fifteenth part of the dry land of the whole earth. We run our memory back over the pages of history for about eighty-two years and we discover that we were then a very small people in point of numbers, vastly inferior to what we are now, with a vastly less extent of country,—with vastly less of everything we deem desirable among men,—we look upon the change as exceedingly advantageous to us and to our posterity, and we fix upon something that happened away back, as in some way or other being connected with this rise of prosperity. We find a race of men living in that day whom we claim as our fathers and grandfathers; they were iron men, they fought for the principle that they were contending for; and we understood that by what they then did it has followed that the degree of prosperity that we now enjoy has come to us. We hold this annual celebration to remind ourselves of all the good done in this process of time of how it was done and who did it, and how we are historically connected with it; and we go from these meetings in better humor with ourselves—we feel more attached the one to the other, and more firmly bound to the country we inhabit. In every way we are better men in the age, and race, and country in which we live for these celebrations. But after we have done all this we have not yet reached the whole. There is something else connected with it. We have besides these men—descended by blood from our ancestors—among us perhaps half our people who are not descendants at all of these men, they are men who have come from Europe—German, Irish, French and Scandinavian—men that have come from Europe themselves, or whose ancestors have come hither and settled here, finding themselves our equals in all things. If they look back through this history to trace their connection with those days by blood, they find they have none, they cannot carry themselves back into that glorious epoch and make themselves feel that they are part of us, but when they look through that old Declaration of Independence they find that those old men say that "We hold these truths to be self-evident, that all men are created equal," and then they feel that that moral sentiment taught in that day evidences their relation to those men, that it is the father of all moral principle in them, and that they have a right to claim it as though they were blood of the blood, and flesh of the flesh of the men who wrote that Declaration . . . and so they are. That is the electric cord in that Declaration that links the hearts of patriotic and liberty-loving men together, that will link those patriotic hearts as long as the love of freedom exists in the minds of men throughout the world. . . .

Now, sirs, for the purpose of squaring things with this idea of "don't care if slavery is voted up or voted down," for sustaining the Dred Scott decision . . . for holding that the Declaration of Independence did not mean anything at all, we have Judge Douglas giving his exposition of what the Declaration of Independence means, and we have him saying that the people of America are equal to the people of England. According to his construction, you Germans are not connected with it. Now I ask you in all soberness, if all these things, if indulged in, if ratified, if confirmed and endorsed, if taught to our children, and repeated to them, do not tend to rub out the sentiment of liberty in the country, and to transform this Government into a government of some other form. Those arguments that are made, that the inferior race are to be treated with as much allowance as they are capable of enjoying; that as much is to be done for them as their condition will allow. What are these arguments? They are the arguments that kings have made for enslaving the people in all ages of the world. You will find that all the arguments in favor of king-craft were of this class; they always bestrode the necks of the people, not that they wanted to do it, but because the people were better off for being ridden. That is their argument, and this argument of the Judge is the same old serpent that says you work and I eat, you toil and I will enjoy the fruits of it. Turn in[8] whatever way you will—whether it come from the mouth of a King, an excuse for enslaving the people of his country, or from the mouth of men of one race as a reason for enslaving the men of another race, it is all the same old serpent, and I hold if that course of argumentation that is made for the purpose of convincing the public mind that we should not care about this, should be granted, it does not stop with the negro. I should like to know if taking this old Declaration of Independence, which declares that all men are equal upon principle and making exceptions to it where will it stop. If one man says it does not mean a negro, why not another say it does not mean some other man? If that declaration is not the truth, let us get the Statute book, in which we find it and tear it out! Who is so bold as to do It! . . . If it is not true let us tear it out! [cries of "no, no,"] let us stick to it then, [cheers] let us stand firmly by it then. [Applause.][9]

It may be argued that there are certain conditions that make necessities and impose them upon us, and to the extent that a necessity is imposed upon a man he must submit to it. I think that was the condition in which we found ourselves when we established this government. We had slavery among us, we could not get our constitution unless we permitted them to remain in slavery, we could not secure the good we did secure if we grasped for more, and having by necessity submitted to that much, it does not destroy the principle that is the charter of our liberties. Let that charter stand as our standard.

. . . So I say in relation to the principle that all men are created equal, let it be as nearly reached as we can. If we cannot give freedom to every creature, let us do nothing that will impose slavery upon any other creature. [Applause.] Let us then turn this government back into the channel in which the framers of the Constitution originally placed it. Let us stand firmly by each other. If we do so we are turning in the contrary direction, that our friend Judge Douglas proposes—not intentionally—as working in the traces tend to make this one universal slave nation. . . . He is one that runs in that direction, and as such I resist him.

My friends, I have detained you about as long as I desired to do, and I have only to say, let us discard all this quibbling about this man and the other man—this race and that race and the other race being inferior, and therefore they must be placed in an inferior position—discarding our standard that we have left us. Let us discard all these things, and unite as one people throughout this land, until we shall once more stand up declaring that all men are created equal.

My friends, I could not, without launching off upon some new topic, which would detain you too long, continue to-night. . . . I thank you for this most extensive audience that you have furnished me to-night. I leave you, hoping that the lamp of liberty will burn in your bosoms until there shall no longer be a doubt that all men are created free and equal.

Fig. 4. Five generations on Smith's Plantation, Beaufort, South Carolina. (1862; Library of Congress)

CHAPTER 2

THE EXPANSION OF GOVERNMENTAL POWER
AND THE NATIONALIZATION OF THE UNION

After the bombardment of Fort Sumter, a Virginia convention passed an ordinance of secession on April 17, 1861, and many Unionists and secessionists alike anticipated that Maryland would quickly follow suit. Two days later, a Baltimore mob attacked a Massachusetts regiment as it passed through that city en route to undefended Washington, D.C., leaving four soldiers and nine civilians dead. That night, as the weary regiment took up quarters in the U.S. Senate chamber, hostile local authorities and Confederate sympathizers burned key railroad bridges and slashed telegraph lines around Baltimore and Washington, isolating the capital and its terrified residents from the rest of the North. Although a special session of the Maryland legislature declined to consider a secession ordinance when it convened on April 26, Washington remained vulnerable to attack. The next day, amid fear for the security of railroad lines leading into Pennsylvania, and with Congress not scheduled to convene until July 4, Abraham Lincoln authorized Major General Winfield Scott to suspend the writ of habeas corpus in the vicinity of the military line used between Philadelphia and Washington.

Lincoln's decision to suspend the writ of habeas corpus (an order issued by a court directing that a prisoner be brought before it for determination as to whether confinement is legally justified) rather than wait for Congress to do so sparked intense debate about not only the legality of his action but also the character and interrelationship of the three branches of the federal government. Opponents of Lincoln's administration bitterly attacked suspension of the writ and later measures taken to prosecute the war, such as conscription, which expanded the power of the federal government.

This debate also played out in the courts. On May 25, 1861, U.S. authorities arrested John Merryman, a Marylander who aided in the destruction of some of the bridges around Baltimore. Supreme Court chief justice Roger Taney, sitting as judge of the U.S. Circuit Court for the District of Maryland, swiftly ruled in *Ex parte Merryman* (1861) that only Congress had the authority to suspend the writ under the Constitution. Lincoln and his administration countered by defending the constitutional validity of the suspension and justifying the necessity of the measure. Disregarding Taney's ruling, Lincoln on July 2, 1861, expanded the suspension to include "any point, on or in the vicinity of any military line which is now, or which shall be used, between the City of New York and the City of Washington," and he defended this action in his July 4 speech to Congress.[1] Through the summer of 1861, federal authorities imprisoned Baltimore's mayor, police chief, and several members of Maryland's legislature, among others, and in mid-October 1861, Lincoln expanded the "military line" so that the writ could be suspended from Washington, D.C., to Bangor, Maine. Lincoln suspended the writ nationwide in September 1862. Congress validated Lincoln's actions in 1863 with legislation authorizing presidential suspension "throughout the United States" during the rebellion, along with mandating certain safeguards for those imprisoned.[2]

During the war, the Supreme Court largely deferred to Lincoln's administration, allowing it wide latitude to prosecute the war and confirming the constitutionality of the blockade that Lincoln ordered against Southern ports in the Prize Cases (1862). The matter of wartime dissent came before the Supreme Court in the case of *Ex parte Vallandingham* (1863), after Clement L. Vallandingham's arrest and trial by a military commission. In April 1863, the military commander of the Department of Ohio issued an order that any persons who committed acts for the benefit of the enemies of the United States, including declaring their sympathy for the Confederacy, would be tried as spies or traitors and face possible death or banishment beyond the Union lines. In May 1863, Vallandingham delivered a searing speech that charged Lincoln with seeking to establish a dictatorship, prosecuting a war for the purpose of freeing blacks and enslaving whites, and depriving the people of their liberties, rights, and privileges. Although the military commission afforded Vallandingham the right to counsel and the opportunity to call and cross-examine witnesses, Vallandingham challenged the military court's jurisdiction and asserted his entitlement to a jury trial in a civil court. The military commission found Vallandingham guilty and sentenced him to imprisonment for the duration of the war. Lincoln intervened and had Vallandingham banished to the Confederate States by the end of May 1863. In reviewing Vallandingham's case, the Supreme Court upheld military jurisdiction during "a rebellion, when a part of a country wages war against its legitimate government, seeking to throw off all allegiance to it, to set up a government of its own."[3] The Court also ruled that it had no jurisdiction to issue a writ of habeas corpus or revise the military commission's proceedings, because military courts stood outside of its appellate jurisdiction as created by Article III of the Constitution and by the Judiciary Act of 1789. After the Union secured victory, the Supreme Court in *Ex parte Milligan* (1866) retracted from its expansive position in the Vallandingham case and ruled that military tribunals could not try civilians where civil courts operated.

In the defeat of the Southern/states' rights justification for secession, and in the victory of Unionists who asserted the ultimate sovereignty of the national political community, the Civil War also definitively resolved the nature of the Union. Lincoln argued the indestructibility of the national Union in his July 4, 1861, speech to Congress, and U.S. troops secured that vision by winning the war. Afterward, in *Texas v. White* (1869), Chief Justice Salmon P. Chase wrote a majority opinion for the Supreme Court that considered the question of what constituted a state and what rights it held. The Court rejected secession in ruling that the "Constitution, in all its provisions, looks to an indestructible Union, composed of indestructible States."

The Civil War not only resulted in the destruction of secessionism but also allowed the Republican Party to construct a more cohesive, nationalized industrial republic. Congress approved a wealth of groundbreaking legislation during the Civil War, the effects of which are still felt today. Republicans in Congress crafted an economic program mandated by wartime necessity but also guided by ideology, including creation of a national bank system chartered and regulated by the federal government (National Bank Acts of 1863, 1864, and 1865), placing into circulation a stable currency of greenbacks (Legal Tender Act of 1862), and establishing the first national income tax as well as the bureaucracy—the forerunner of the Internal Revenue Service—to collect it (Revenue Acts of 1861 and 1862). The Republican-controlled Congress also approved legislation promoting internal improvements, such as construction of a transcontinental railroad (the Pacific Railway Act of 1862).

To encourage development of land west of the Mississippi, as well as to promote free labor principles such as individual self-improvement and self-sufficiency, the Homestead Act of 1862 gave citizens, or intended citizens who never bore arms against the United States, title to 160 acres of public land, so long as they lived on and cultivated the tract for five years. Similarly advancing opportunities for individual self-improvement, the Morrill Act of 1862 granted for sale to each state (while not in the rebellion) 30,000 acres of public land for each senator and representative, with all proceeds designated for "the endowment, support, and maintenance of at least one college where the leading object shall be, without excluding other scientific and classical studies, and including military tactics, to teach such branches of learning as are related to agriculture and the mechanic arts . . . in order to promote the liberal and practical education of the industrial classes in the several pursuits and professions in life."[4] The fruits of the Morrill Act live on today in universities such as the University of Kentucky and Ohio State University, to name a few. After the war, Republican civil rights legislation, such as the Civil Rights Act of 1866, sought to assist freedpeople in entering the economy based on free labor principles.

In addition to wartime experiences and Republican economic legislation, conscripting soldiers and appropriating pension funds to care for these soldiers and their dependents after injury or death strengthened the ties between the federal government and its citizens during and after the war. In unofficial ways, organizations such as the Union League both created a cult of nationality and afforded citizens another way to participate in the national state. The movement swiftly grew from its founding in the fall of 1862 to induct nearly a million members by the fall of 1864.

Local leagues organized rallies promoting loyalty to the United States, distributed millions of pamphlets, which often had a Republican bent, and sought to bolster a war-weary public. These pamphlets defended the federal government's expansion; urged support for income taxes, conscription, emancipation, and the arming of blacks; and praised the nation and the opportunities generated for citizens by its democratic and free labor characteristics.

1. LINCOLN'S PROCLAMATION CALLING FORTH THE MILITIA
AND CONVENING CONGRESS (APRIL 15, 1861)

Whereas the laws of the United States have been for some time past, and now are opposed, and the execution thereof obstructed, in the States of South Carolina, Georgia, Alabama, Florida, Mississippi, Louisiana, and Texas, by combinations too powerful to be suppressed by the ordinary course of judicial proceedings, or by the powers vested in the Marshals by law,[5]

Now therefore, I, Abraham Lincoln, President of the United States, in virtue of the power in me vested by the Constitution, and the laws, have thought fit to call forth, and hereby do call forth, the militia of the several States of the Union, to the aggregate number of seventy-five thousand, in order to suppress said combinations, and to cause the laws to be duly executed. The details, for this object, will be immediately communicated to the State authorities, through the War Department.

I appeal to all loyal citizens to favor, facilitate, and aid this effort to maintain the honor, the integrity, and the existence of our National Union, and the perpetuity of popular government; and to redress wrongs already long enough endured.

I deem it proper to say that the first service assigned to the forces hereby called forth will probably be to re-possess the forts, places, and property which have been seized from the Union; and, in every event, the utmost care will be observed, consistently with the objects aforesaid, to avoid any devastation, any destruction of, or interference with, property, or any disturbance of peaceful citizens in any part of the country.

And I hereby command the persons composing the combinations aforesaid to disperse, and retire peaceably to their respective abodes within twenty days from this date.

Deeming that the present condition of public affairs presents an extraordinary occasion, I do hereby, in virtue of the power in me vested by the constitution, convene both Houses of Congress. Senators and Representatives are therefore summoned to assemble at their respective chambers, at 12 o'clock, noon, on Thursday, the fourth day of July, next, then and there to consider, and determine, such measures, as, in their wisdom, the public safety, and interest may seem to demand. . . .

2. LINCOLN'S SUSPENSION OF HABEAS CORPUS (APRIL 27, 1861)

To the Commanding General of the Army of the United States [Winfield Scott]:

You are engaged in repressing an insurrection against the laws of the United States. If at any point on or in the vicinity of any military line which is now or which shall be used between the city of Philadelphia and the city of Washington you find resistance which renders it necessary to suspend the writ of habeas corpus for the public safety, you personally or through the officer in command at the point where resistance occurs are authorized to suspend that writ.

3. *EX PARTE MERRYMAN*, 17 F. CAS. 144 (CIRCUIT COURT, D. MARYLAND, 1861)

Sitting as judge of the U.S. Circuit Court for the District of Maryland, Supreme Court chief justice Roger Taney ruled in *Ex parte Merryman* that only Congress had the power constitutionally to suspend the writ of habeas corpus and that Lincoln thus overstepped his constitutional authority.

[Roger] TANEY, Circuit Justice.

... The petitioner resides in Maryland, in Baltimore county; while peaceably in his own house, with his family, it was at two o'clock on the morning of the 25th of May 1861, entered by an armed force, professing to act under military orders; he was then compelled to rise from his bed, taken into custody, and conveyed to Fort McHenry, where he is imprisoned by the commanding officer, without warrant from any lawful authority.

... [I]t is not alleged in the return, that any specific act, constituting any offence against the laws of the United States, has been charged against him upon oath, but he appears to have been arrested upon general charges of treason and rebellion, without proof, and without giving the names of the witnesses, or specifying the acts which, in the judgment of the military officer, constituted these crimes. ...

The case, then, is simply this: a military officer ... issues an order to arrest a citizen of Maryland, upon vague and indefinite charges, without any proof ...; under this order, his house is entered in the night, he is seized as a prisoner, and conveyed to Fort McHenry, and there kept in close confinement; and when a habeas corpus is served on the commanding officer, requiring him to produce the prisoner before a justice of the supreme court, in order that he may examine into the legality of the imprisonment, the answer of the officer, is that he is authorized by the president to suspend the writ of habeas corpus at his discretion ... and on that ground refuses obedience to the writ.

... I understand that the president not only claims the right to suspend the writ of habeas corpus himself, at his discretion, but to delegate that discretionary power to a military officer, and to leave it to him to determine whether he will or will not obey judicial process that may be served upon him. No official notice has been given to the courts of justice, or to the public, by proclamation or otherwise, that the president claimed this power, and had exercised it in the manner stated in the return. And I certainly listened to it with some surprise, for I had supposed it to be one of those points of constitutional law upon which there was no difference of opinion, and that it was admitted on all hands, that the privilege of the writ could not be suspended, except by act of congress. . . .

The clause of the constitution, which authorizes the suspension of the privilege of the writ of habeas corpus, is in the 9th section of the first article. This article is devoted to the legislative department of the United States, and has not the slightest reference to the executive department. . . . [A]fter prescribing the manner in which these two branches of the legislative department shall be chosen, it proceeds to enumerate specifically the legislative powers which it thereby grants (and legislative powers which it expressly prohibits); and at the conclusion of this specification, a clause is inserted giving congress "the power to make all laws which shall be necessary and proper for carrying into execution the foregoing powers, and all other powers vested by this constitution in the government of the United States, or in any department or officer thereof."

The power of legislation granted by this latter clause is, by its words, carefully confined to the specific objects before enumerated. But as this limitation was unavoidably somewhat indefinite, it was deemed necessary to guard more effectually certain great cardinal principles, essential to the liberty of the citizen, and to the rights and equality of the states, by denying to congress, in express terms, any power of legislation over them. . . . [A]ccordingly, this clause is immediately followed by an enumeration of certain subjects, to which the powers of legislation shall not extend. The great importance which the framers of the constitution attached to the privilege of the writ of habeas corpus, to protect the liberty of the citizen, is proved by the fact, that its suspension, except in cases of invasion or rebellion, is first in the list of prohibited powers; . . . and its exercise prohibited, unless the public safety shall require it.

. . . [C]ongress is . . . the judge of whether the public safety does or does not require it; and their judgment is conclusive. But the introduction of these words is a standing admonition to the legislative body of the danger of suspending it, and of the extreme caution they should exercise, before they give the government of the United States such power over the liberty of a citizen.

It is the second article of the constitution that provides for the organization of the executive department, enumerates the powers conferred on it, and prescribes its duties. And if the high power over the liberty of the citizen now claimed, was intended to be conferred on the president, it would undoubtedly be found in plain words in this article; but there is not a word in it that can furnish the slightest ground to justify the exercise of the power.

... The short term for which he [the president] is elected, and the narrow limits to which his power is confined, show the jealousy and apprehension of future danger which the framers of the constitution felt in relation to that department of the government, and how carefully they withheld from it many of the powers belonging to the executive branch of the English government which were considered as dangerous to the liberty of the subject[.] ...

Even if the privilege of the writ of habeas corpus were suspended by act of congress, and a party not subject to the rules and articles of war were afterwards arrested and imprisoned by regular judicial process, he could not be detained in prison, or brought to trial before a military tribunal, for the [Sixth Amendment] ... provides, that "in all criminal prosecutions, the accused shall enjoy the right to a speedy and public trial by an impartial jury of the state and district wherein the crime shall have been committed, which district shall have been previously ascertained by law; and to be informed of the nature and cause of the accusation; to be confronted with the witnesses against him; to have compulsory process for obtaining witnesses in his favor; and to have the assistance of counsel for his defence."

The only power, therefore, which the president possesses, where the "life, liberty or property" of a private citizen is concerned, is the power and duty prescribed in the third section of the second article, which requires "that he shall take care that the laws shall be faithfully executed." He is not authorized to execute them himself, or through agents or officers, civil or military, appointed by himself, but he is to take care that they be faithfully carried into execution, as they are expounded and adjudged by the co-ordinate branch of the government to which that duty is assigned by the constitution. It is thus made his duty to come in aid of the judicial authority, if it shall be resisted by a force too strong to be overcome without the assistance of the executive arm; but in exercising this power he acts in subordination to judicial authority, assisting it to execute its process and enforce its judgments.

With such provisions in the constitution, expressed in language too clear to be misunderstood by any one, I can see no ground whatever for supposing that the president, in any emergency, or in any state of things, can authorize the suspension of the privilege of the writ of habeas corpus, or the arrest of a citizen, except in aid of the judicial power. He certainly does not faithfully execute the laws, if he takes upon himself legislative power, by suspending the writ of habeas corpus, and the judicial power also, by arresting and imprisoning a person without due process of law. ...

... [N]o power in England short of that of parliament can suspend or authorize the suspension of the writ of habeas corpus. ... If the president of the United States may suspend the writ, then the constitution of the United States has conferred upon him more regal and absolute power over the liberty of the citizen, than the people of England have thought it safe to entrust to the crown[.] ...

. . . [T]he military authority in this case has gone far beyond the mere suspension of the privilege of the writ of habeas corpus. It has, by force of arms, thrust aside the judicial authorities and officers to whom the constitution has confided the power and duty of interpreting and administering the laws, and substituted a military government in its place, to be administered and executed by military officers. For, at the time these proceedings were had against John Merryman, the district judge of Maryland, the commissioner appointed under the act of congress, the district attorney and the marshal, all resided in the city of Baltimore, a few miles only from the home of the prisoner. Up to that time, there had never been the slightest resistance or obstruction to the process of any court or judicial officer of the United States, in Maryland, except by the military authority. And if a military officer, or any other person, had reason to believe that the prisoner had committed any offence against the laws of the United States, it was his duty to give information of the fact and the evidence to support it, to the district attorney . . . and if there was sufficient legal evidence to justify his arrest, the judge or commissioner would have issued his warrant to the marshal to arrest him; and upon the hearing of the case, would have held him to bail, or committed him for trial, according to the character of the offence . . . or would have discharged him immediately, if there was not sufficient evidence to support the accusation. . . .

The constitution provides, as I have before said, that "no person shall be deprived of life, liberty or property, without due process of law." It declares that "the right of the people to be secure in their persons, houses, papers and effects, against unreasonable searches and seizures, shall not be violated; and no warrant shall issue, but upon probable cause, supported by oath or affirmation, and particularly describing the place to be searched, and the persons or things to be seized." It provides that the party accused shall be entitled to a speedy trial in a court of justice.

These great and fundamental laws, which congress itself could not suspend, have been disregarded and suspended, like the writ of habeas corpus, by a military order, supported by force of arms. Such is the case now before me, and I can only say that if the authority which the constitution has confided to the judiciary department and judicial officers, may thus, upon any pretext or under any circumstances, be usurped by the military power, at its discretion, the people of the United States are no longer living under a government of laws, but every citizen holds life, liberty and property at the will and pleasure of the army officer in whose military district he may happen to be found. . . .

. . . It is possible that the officer who has incurred this grave responsibility may have misunderstood his instructions, and exceeded the authority intended to be given him; I shall, therefore, order . . . my opinion, to be filed and recorded . . . and direct the clerk to transmit a copy, under seal, to the president of the United States. It will then remain for that high officer, in fulfilment of his constitutional obligation to "take care that the laws be faithfully executed," to determine what measures he will take to cause the civil process of the United States to be respected and enforced.

4. LINCOLN'S MESSAGE TO CONGRESS (JULY 4, 1861) (LIBRARY OF CONGRESS)

In his speech to a specially convened joint session of Congress, Lincoln rejected secessionism, articulated the theory that the Union was perpetual and indestructible, and responded to Taney and other critics of his suspension of the writ of habeas corpus.

. . . At the beginning of the present presidential term, four months ago, the functions of the federal government were found to be generally suspended within the several States of South Carolina, Georgia, Alabama, Mississippi, Louisiana, and Florida, excepting only those of the Post Office Department.

[Lincoln here describes the events leading up to and including the bombardment and surrender of Fort Sumter.]

. . . [T]his issue embraces more than the fate of these United States. It presents to the whole family of man the question, whether a constitutional republic, or a democracy—a government of the people, by the same people—can, or cannot, maintain its territorial integrity, against its own domestic foes. It presents the question, whether discontented individuals, too few in numbers to control administration . . . can . . . break up their government, and thus practically put an end to free government upon the earth. It forces us to ask: "Is there, in all republics, this inherent, and fatal weakness?" "Must a government, of necessity, be too *strong* for the liberties of its own people, or too *weak* to maintain its own existence?"

So viewing the issue, no choice was left but to call out the war power of the government; and so to resist force, employed for its destruction, by force, for its preservation.

The call was made, and the response of the country was most gratifying; surpassing in unanimity, and spirit, the most sanguine expectation. Yet none of the States commonly called slave States, except Delaware, gave a regiment through regular State organization. . . .

Recurring to the action of the government, it may be stated that, at first, a call was made for seventy-five thousand militia; and rapidly following this, a proclamation was issued for closing the ports of the insurrectionary districts by proceedings in the nature of blockade. So far all was believed to be strictly legal. At this point the insurrectionists announced their purpose to enter upon the practice of privateering.

Other calls were made for volunteers to serve three years, unless sooner discharged; and also for large additions to the regular army and navy. These measures, whether strictly legal or not, were ventured upon, under what appeared to be a popular demand, and a public necessity; trusting then, as now, that Congress would readily ratify them. It is believed that nothing has been done beyond the constitutional competency of Congress.

Soon after the first call for militia, it was considered a duty to authorize the commanding general, in proper cases, according to his discretion, to suspend the privilege of the writ of habeas corpus; or, in other words, to arrest and detain, without resort to the ordinary processes and forms of law, such individuals as he might deem dangerous to the public safety. This authority has purposely been exercised but very sparingly. Nevertheless, the legality and propriety of what has been done under it are questioned, and the attention of the country has been called to the proposition that one who is sworn to "take care that the laws be faithfully executed," should not himself violate them. Of course some consideration was given to the questions of power, and propriety, before this matter was acted upon. The whole of the laws which were required to be faithfully executed, were being resisted, and failing of execution in nearly one-third of the States. Must they be allowed to finally fail of execution, even had it been perfectly clear, that by the use of the means necessary to their execution, some single law, made in such extreme tenderness of the citizen's liberty, that practically, it relieves more of the guilty, than of the innocent, should, to a very limited extent, be violated? To state the question more directly, are all the laws, *but one*, to go unexecuted, and the government itself go to pieces, lest that one be violated? Even in such a case, would not the official oath be broken, if the government should be overthrown, when it was believed that disregarding the single law, would tend to preserve it? But it was not believed that this question was presented. It was not believed that any law was violated. The provision of the Constitution that "the privilege of the writ of habeas corpus shall not be suspended unless when, in cases of rebellion or invasion, the public safety may require it," is equivalent to a provision—is a provision—that such privilege may be suspended when, in cases of rebellion or invasion, the public safety *does* require it. It was decided that we have a case of rebellion, and that the public safety does require the qualified suspension of the privilege of the writ which was authorized to be made. Now it is insisted that Congress, and not the Executive, is vested with this power. But the Constitution itself is silent as to which, or who, is to exercise the power; and as the provision was plainly made for a dangerous emergency, it cannot be believed the framers of the instrument intended, that in every case, the danger should run its course, until Congress could be called together; the very assembling of which might be prevented, as was intended in this case, by the rebellion.

... Whether there shall be any legislation upon the subject, and if any, what, is submitted entirely to the better judgment of Congress. ...

It is now recommended that you give the legal means for making this contest a short, and a decisive one; that you place at the control of the government, for the work, at least four hundred thousand men, and four hundred millions of dollars.... A debt of six hundred millions of dollars *now*, is a less sum per head, than was the debt of our revolution when we came out of that struggle; and the money value in the country now, bears even a greater proportion to what it was *then*, than does the population. Surely each man has as strong a motive *now*, to *preserve* our liberties, as each had *then*, to *establish* them.

A right result, at this time, will be worth more to the world than ten times the men, and ten times the money. The evidence reaching us from the country, leaves no doubt, that the material for the work is abundant; and that it needs only the hand of legislation to give it legal sanction, and the hand of the Executive to give it practical shape and efficiency. One of the greatest perplexities of the government is to avoid receiving troops faster than it can provide for them. In a word, the people will save their government, if the government itself, will do its part, only indifferently well.

It might seem, at first thought, to be of little difference whether the present movement at the South be called "secession" or "rebellion." The movers, however, well understand the difference. At the beginning, they knew they could never raise their treason to any respectable magnitude by any name which implies *violation* of law. They knew their people possessed as much of moral sense, as much of devotion to law and order, and as much pride in, and reverence for, the history and government of their common country, as any other civilized and patriotic people. They knew they could make no advancement directly in the teeth of these strong and noble sentiments. Accordingly they commenced by an insidious debauching of the public mind. They invented an ingenious sophism, which, if conceded, was followed by perfectly logical steps ... to the complete destruction of the Union. The sophism itself is, that any State of the Union may, *consistently* with the national Constitution, and therefore *lawfully*, and *peacefully*, withdraw from the Union, without the consent of the Union, or of any other State. The little disguise that the supposed right is to be exercised only for just cause, themselves to be the sole judge of its justice, is too thin to merit any notice.

With rebellion thus sugar-coated, they have been drugging the public mind of their section for more than thirty years; and until at length they have brought many good men to a willingness to take up arms against the government the day *after* some assemblage of men have enacted the farcical pretence of taking their State out of the Union, who could have been brought to no such thing the day *before*.

This sophism derives much, perhaps the whole, of its currency from the assumption that there is some omnipotent and sacred supremacy pertaining to a *State*—to each State of our Federal Union. Our States have neither more, nor less power, than that reserved to them, in the Union, by the Constitution—no one of them ever having been a State *out* of the Union. The original ones passed into the Union even *before* they cast off their British colonial dependence; and the new ones each came into the Union directly from a condition of dependence, excepting Texas. And even Texas, in its temporary independence, was never designated a State. . . . Having never been States, either in substance or in name, *outside* of the Union, whence this magical omnipotence of "State rights," asserting a claim of power to lawfully destroy the Union itself? Much is said about the "sovereignty" of the States; but the word, even, is not in the national Constitution; nor, as is believed, in any of the State constitutions. What is a "sovereignty," in the political sense of the term? Would it be far wrong to define it "A political community, without a political superior"? Tested by this, no one of our States, except Texas, ever was a sovereignty. And even Texas gave up the character on coming into the Union; by which act, she acknowledged the Constitution of the United States, and the laws and treaties of the United States made in pursuance of the Constitution, to be, for her, the supreme law of the land. The States have their *status* IN the Union, and they have no other legal *status*. If they break from this, they can only do so against law, and by revolution. The Union, and not themselves separately, procured their independence and their liberty. By conquest, or purchase, the Union gave each of them, whatever of independence and liberty it has. The Union is older than any of the States, and, in fact, it created them as States. . . .

Unquestionably the States have the powers and rights reserved to them in and by the national Constitution; but among these, surely, are not included all conceivable powers, however mischievous or destructive; but, at most, such only as were known in the world . . . as governmental powers; and certainly a power to destroy the government itself had never been known as a governmental—as a merely administrative power. . . . Whatever concerns the whole, should be confided to the whole—to the general government; while, whatever concerns *only* the State, should be left exclusively to the State. . . .

The seceders insist that our Constitution admits of secession. They have assumed to make a national constitution of their own, in which, of necessity, they have either *discarded* or *retained* the right of secession, as, they insist, it exists in ours. If they have discarded it, they thereby admit that, on principle, it ought not to be in ours. If they have retained it, by their own construction of ours they show that to be consistent they must secede from one another, whenever they shall find it the easiest way of settling their debts, or effecting any other selfish or unjust object. The principle itself is one of disintegration, and upon which no government can possibly endure.

If all the States, save one, should assert the power to *drive* that one out of the Union, it is presumed the whole class of seceder politicians would at once deny the power, and denounce the act as the greatest outrage upon State rights. But suppose that precisely the same act, instead of being called "driving the one out," should be called "the seceding of the others from that one," it would be exactly what the seceders claim to do[.] . . .

It may be affirmed, without extravagance, that the free institutions we enjoy have developed the powers, and improved the condition, of our whole people, beyond any example in the world. Of this we now have a striking, and an impressive illustration. So large an army as the government has now on foot, was never before known, without a soldier in it, but who had taken his place there, of his own free choice. But more than this: there are many single regiments whose members, one and another, possess full practical knowledge of all the arts, sciences, professions, and whatever else, whether useful or elegant, is known in the world; and there is scarcely one, from which there could not be selected, a President, a Cabinet, a Congress, and perhaps a Court, abundantly competent to administer the government itself! Nor do I say this is not true, also, in the army of our late friends, now adversaries, in this contest; but if it is, so much better the reason why the government, which has conferred such benefits on both them and us, should not be broken up. Whoever, in any section, proposes to abandon such a government, would do well to consider, in deference to what principle it is that he does it—what better he is likely to get in its stead—whether the substitute will give, or be intended to give, so much of good to the people. There are some foreshadowings on this subject. Our adversaries have adopted some declarations of independence; in which, unlike the good old one, penned by Jefferson, they omit the words "all men are created equal." Why? They have adopted a temporary national constitution, in the preamble of which, unlike our good old one, signed by Washington, they omit "We, the people," and substitute "We, the deputies of the sovereign and independent States." Why? Why this deliberate pressing out of view, the rights of men, and the authority of the people?

This is essentially a People's contest. On the side of the Union, it is a struggle for maintaining in the world, that form and substance of government, whose leading object is, to elevate the condition of men—to lift artificial weights from all shoulders; to clear the paths of laudable pursuit for all; to afford all, an unfettered start, and a fair chance, in the race of life. Yielding to partial and temporary departures, from necessity, this is the leading object of the government for whose existence we contend. . . .

Our popular government has often been called an experiment. Two points in it our people have already settled—the successful *establishing* and the successful *administering* of it. One still remains—its successful *maintenance* against a formidable attempt to overthrow it. It is now for them to demonstrate to the world, that those who can fairly carry an election, can also suppress a rebellion; that ballots are the rightful, and peaceful, successors of bullets; and that when ballots have fairly, and constitutionally decided, there can be no successful appeal back to bullets; that there can be no successful appeal except to ballots themselves, at succeeding elections. Such will be a great lesson of peace; teaching men that what they cannot take by an election, neither can they take it by a war; teaching all, the folly of being the beginners of a war. . . .

It was with the deepest regret that the Executive found the duty of employing the war-power, in defence of the government, forced upon him. He could but perform this duty, or surrender the existence of the government. . . .

As a private citizen, the Executive could not have consented that these institutions shall perish; much less could he, in betrayal of so vast, and so sacred a trust, as these free people had confided to him. He felt that he had no moral right to shrink; nor even to count the chances of his own life, in what might follow. In full view of his great responsibility, he has, so far, done what he has deemed his duty. You will now, according to your own judgment, perform yours. He sincerely hopes that your views, and your action, may so accord with his, as to assure all faithful citizens, who have been disturbed in their rights, of a certain, and speedy restoration to them, under the Constitution and the laws.

And having thus chosen our course, without guile, and with pure purpose, let us renew our trust in God, and go forward without fear, and with manly hearts.

5. Opinion of Attorney General Bates on Suspension of
Habeas Corpus, 10 Op. Att'y Gen. 74 (July 5, 1861)

The day after Lincoln's speech, Attorney General Edward Bates issued this official opinion supporting the constitutionality and the necessity of Lincoln's suspension of the writ of habeas corpus, offering his perspective on the proper roles and relations of the executive and judicial branches.

. . . In the formation of our national government, our fathers were surrounded with peculiar difficulties arising out of their novel, I may say unexampled, condition. In resolving to break the ties which had bound them to the British empire, their complaints were levelled chiefly at the King, not the Parliament nor the people. They seem to have been actuated by a special dread of the unity of power, and hence, in framing the Constitution, they preferred to take the risk of leaving some good undone, for lack of power in the agent, rather than arm any governmental officer with such great powers for evil as are implied in the dictatorial charge to "see that no damage comes to the commonwealth."

Hence . . . they adopted the plan of "checks and balances," forming separate departments of Government, and giving to each department separate and limited powers. These departments are co-ordinate and coequal—that is, neither being sovereign, each is independent in its sphere, and not subordinate to the others, either of them or both of them together. We have three of these co-ordinate departments. Now, if we allow one of the three to determine the extent of its own powers, and also the extent of the powers of the other two, that one can control the whole government, and has in fact achieved the sovereignty.

We ought not to say that our system is perfect, for its defects (perhaps inevitable in all human things) are obvious. Our fathers, having divided the government into co-ordinate departments, did not even try (and if they had tried would probably have failed) to create an arbiter among them to adjudge their conflicts and keep them within their respective bounds. They were left, by design, I suppose, each independent and free, to act out its own granted powers, without any ordained or legal superior possessing the power to revise and reverse its action. And this with the hope that the three departments, mutually coequal and independent, would keep each other within their proper spheres by their mutual antagonism—that is, by the system of checks and balances, to which our fathers were driven at the beginning by their fear of the unity or power.

In this view of the subject it is quite possible for the same identical *question* (not *case*) to come up legitimately before each one of the three departments, and be determined in three different ways, and each decision stand irrevocable, binding upon the parties to each case[.] . . .

To say that the departments of our government are co-ordinate, is to say that the judgment of one of them is not binding upon the other two, as to the arguments and principles involved in the judgment. It binds only the parties to the case decided. But if, admitting that the departments of government are co-ordinate, it be still contended that the principles adopted by one department, in deciding a case properly before it, are binding upon another department, that obligation must of necessity be reciprocal—that is, if the President be bound by the principles laid down by the judiciary, so also is the judiciary bound by the principles laid down by the President. And thus we shall have a theory of constitutional government flatly contradicting itself. Departments co-ordinate and coequal, and yet reciprocally subordinate to each other! That cannot be. The several departments, though far from sovereign, are free and independent, in the exercise of the limited powers granted to them respectively by the Constitution. Our government indeed, as a whole, is not vested with the sovereignty, and does not possess all the powers of the nation. It has no powers but such as are granted by the Constitution; and many powers are expressly withheld. The nation certainly is coequal with all other nations, and has equal powers, but it has not chosen to delegate all its powers to this Government, in any or all of its departments.

The government, as a whole, is limited, and limited in all its departments. It is the especial function of the judiciary to hear and determine *cases*, not to "establish principles" nor "settle questions," so as to conclude any person but the parties and privies to the cases adjudged. Its powers are specially granted and defined by the Constitution. (Art. 3, sec. 2.)

"The judicial power shall extend to all *cases* in law and equity arising under this Constitution, the laws of the United States, and treaties made, and which shall be made, under their authority; to all *cases* affecting ambassadors, other ministers, and consuls; to all *cases* of admiralty and maritime jurisdiction; to controversies to which the United States shall be a party; to controversies between two or more States; between States and citizens of other States; between citizens of different States; between citizens of the same State claiming lands under grants of different States, and between a State, or the citizens thereof, and foreign States, citizens, or subjects." And that is the sum of its powers, ample and efficient for all the purposes of distributive justice among individual parties, but powerless to impose rules of action and of judgment upon the other departments. Indeed, it is not itself bound by its own decisions, for it can and often does overrule and disregard them, as, in common honesty, it ought to do, whenever it finds, by its after and better lights, that its former judgments were wrong.

Of all the departments of the government, the President is the most active, and the most constant in action. He is called "the Executive," and so, in fact, he is, and much more also, for the Constitution has imposed upon him many important duties, and granted to him great powers which are in their nature *not executive*—such as the veto power; the power to send and receive ambassadors; the power to make treaties, and the power to appoint officers. This last is not more an *executive* power when used by the President than it is when exercised by either house of Congress, by the courts of justice, or by the people at large.

The President is a department of the government; and, although the only department which consists of a single man, he is charged with a greater range and variety of powers and duties than any other department. He is a *civil magistrate*, not a *military chief*; and in this regard we see a striking proof of the generality of the sentiment prevailing in this country at the time of the formation of our government, to the effect that the *military* ought to be held in strict subordination to the *civil* power. For the Constitution, while it grants to Congress the unrestricted power to declare war, to raise and support armies, and to provide and maintain a navy, at the same time guards carefully against the abuse of that power, by withholding from Congress and from the army itself the authority to appoint the chief commander of a force so potent for good or for evil to the State. The Constitution provides that "the President shall be commander-in-chief of the army and navy of the United States, and of the militia of the several States when called into the actual service of the United States." And why is this? Surely not because the President is supposed to be, or commonly is, in fact, a military man, a man skilled in the art of war and qualified to marshal a host in the field of battle. No, it is for quite a different reason; it is that whatever skilful soldier may lead our armies to victory against a foreign foe, or may quell a domestic insurrection; however high he may raise his professional renown, and whatever martial glory he may win, still he is subject to the orders of the *civil magistrate*, and he and his army are always "subordinate to the civil power."

And hence it follows, that whenever the President . . . in the discharge of his constitutional duty to "take care that the laws be faithfully executed," has occasion to use the army to aid him in the performance of that duty, he does not thereby lose his civil character and become a soldier, subject to military law and liable to be tried by a court-martial, any more than does a civil court lose its legal and pacific nature and become military and belligerent, by calling out the power of the country to enforce its decrees. The civil magistrates, whether judicial or executive, must of necessity employ physical power to aid them in enforcing the laws, whenever they have to deal with disobedient or refractory subjects; and their legal power and right to do so is unquestionable. The right of the courts to call out the whole power of the county to enforce their judgments, is as old as the common law; and the right of the President to use force in the performance of his legal duties is not only inherent in his office, but has been frequently recognized and aided by Congress. One striking example of this is the act of Congress of March 3, 1807, (2 Stats., 445,) which empowered the President, without the intervention of any court, to use the marshal, and, if he be insufficient, to use the army summarily to expel intruders and squatters upon the public lands. And that power has been frequently exercised, without, as far as I know, a question of its legality. . . .

While the judiciary and the President, as departments of the general government, are co-ordinate, equal in dignity and power, and equally trusted by the law, in their respective spheres, there is, nevertheless, a marked diversity in the character of their functions and their modes of action. The judiciary is, for the most part, passive. It rarely, if ever, takes the initiative; it seldom or never begins an operation. Its great function is *judgment*, and, in the exercise of that function, it is confined almost exclusively to cases not selected by itself, but made and submitted by others. The President, on the contrary, by the very nature of his office, is active; he must often take the initiative; he must begin operations. His great function is *execution*, for he is required by the Constitution, (and he is the only department that is so required,) to "take care that the laws (all the laws) be faithfully executed;" and in the exercise of that function, his duties are coextensive with the laws of the land. . . .

. . . I am clearly of opinion that, in a time like the present, when the very existence of the nation is assailed, by a great and dangerous insurrection, the President has the lawful discretionary power to arrest and hold in custody persons known to have criminal intercourse with the insurgents, or persons against whom there is probable cause for suspicion of such criminal complicity. And I think this position can be maintained, in view of the principles already laid down, by a very plain argument.

The Constitution requires the President, before he enters upon the execution of his office, to take an oath that he "will faithfully execute the office of President of the United States, and will, to the best of his ability, preserve, protect and defend the Constitution of the United States."

The duties of the office comprehend all the *executive power* of the nation, which is expressly vested in the President by the Constitution, (article 2, sec. 1,) and, also, all the powers which are specially delegated to the President, and yet are not, in their nature, *executive* powers. For example, the veto power; the treaty making power; the appointing power; the pardoning power. These belong to that class which, in England, are called prerogative powers, inherent in the crown. And yet the framers of our Constitution thought proper to preserve them, and to vest them in the President, as necessary to the good government of the country.... And all these are embraced within the duties of the President, and are clearly within that clause of his oath which requires him to "faithfully execute the office of President."

... All the other officers of the Government are required to swear only "to *support* this Constitution;" while the President must swear to "*preserve, protect, and defend*" it, which implies the power to perform what he is required in so solemn a manner to undertake. And then follows the broad and compendious injunction to "take care that the laws be faithfully executed." And this injunction, embracing as it does all the laws—Constitution, treaties, statutes—is addressed to the President alone, and not to any other department or officer of the Government. And this constitutes him, in a peculiar manner, and above all other officers, the guardian of the Constitution—its *preserver, protector, and defender.*

It is the plain duty of the President (and his peculiar duty, above and beyond all other departments of the Government) to preserve the Constitution and execute the laws all over the nation; and it is plainly impossible for him to perform this duty without putting down rebellion, insurrection, and all unlawful combinations to resist the General Government. The duty to suppress the insurrection being obvious and imperative, the two acts of Congress, of 1795 and 1807, come to his aid, and furnish the physical force which he needs, to suppress the insurrection and execute the laws. Those two acts authorize the President to employ for that purpose, the militia, the army, and the navy.

... It is the President's bounden duty to put down the insurrection, as (in the language of the act of 1795) the "combinations are too powerful to be suppressed by the ordinary course of judicial proceedings, or by the powers vested in the marshals." And this duty is imposed upon the President for the very reason that the courts and the marshals are too weak to perform it. The manner in which he shall perform that duty is not prescribed by any law, but the means of performing it are given, in the plain language of the statutes, and they are all means of force—the militia, the army, and the navy. The end, the suppression of the insurrection, is required of him; the means and instruments to suppress it are lawfully in his hands; but the manner in which he shall use them is not prescribed, and could not be prescribed, without a foreknowledge of all the future changes and contingencies of the insurrection. He is, therefore, necessarily, thrown upon his discretion, as to the manner in which he will use his means to meet the varying exigencies as they rise. If the insurgents assail the nation with an army, he may find it best to meet them with an army, and suppress the insurrection in the field of battle. If they seek to prolong the rebellion, and gather strength by intercourse with foreign nations, he may choose to guard the coast and close the ports with a navy, as one of the most efficient means to suppress the insurrection. And if they employ spies and emissaries, to gather information, to forward rebellion, he may find it both prudent and humane to arrest and imprison them. And this may be done, either for the purpose of bringing them to trial and condign punishment for their crimes, or they may be held in custody for the milder end of rendering them powerless for mischief, until the exigency is past. . . .

This is a great power in the hands of the chief magistrate; and because it is great, and is capable of being perverted to evil ends, its existence has been doubted and denied. It is said to be dangerous, in the hands of an ambitious and wicked President, because he may use it for the purposes of oppression and tyranny. Yes, certainly it is dangerous—all power is dangerous—and for the all-pervading reason that all power is liable to abuse; all the recipients of human power are men, not absolutely virtuous and wise. Still it is a power necessary to the peace and safety of the country, and undeniably belongs to the Government, and therefore must be exercised by some department or officer thereof.

Why should this power be denied to the President, on the ground of its liability to abuse, and not denied to the other departments on the *same grounds*? Are they more exempt than he is from the frailties and vices of humanity? Or are they more trusted by the law than he is trusted, in their several spheres of action? . . .

Having assumed . . . that the President has the legal discretionary power to arrest and imprison persons who are guilty of holding criminal intercourse with men engaged in a great and dangerous insurrection, or persons suspected, with "probable cause," of such criminal complicity, it might seem unnecessary to go into any prolonged argument to prove that, in such a case, the President is fully justified in refusing to obey a writ of *habeas corpus* issued by a court or judge[.] . . .

If it be true, as I have assumed, that the President and the judiciary are co-ordinate departments of government, and the one not subordinate to the other, I do not understand how it can be legally possible for a judge to issue a command to the President to come before him . . . to submit implicitly to his judgment—and, in case of disobedience, treat him as a criminal, in contempt of a superior authority, and punish him as for a misdemeanor, by fine and imprisonment. It is no answer to say, as has sometimes been said, that although the writ of *habeas corpus* cannot be issued and enforced against the President himself, yet that it can be against any of his subordinates, for that abandons the principle assumed, of giving relief in "all cases" of imprisonment by color of authority of the United States, and attempts to take an untenable distinction between the person of the President and his office and legal power. The law takes no such distinction, for it is no respecter of persons. The President, in the arrest and imprisonment of men, must, almost always, act by subordinate agents, and yet the thing done is no less his act than if done by his own hand. . . . As the political chief of the nation, the Constitution charges him with its preservation, protection, and defence, and requires him to take care that the laws be faithfully executed. And in that character, and by the aid of the acts of Congress of 1795 and 1807, he wages open war against armed rebellion, and arrests and holds in safe custody those whom, in the exercise of his political discretion, he believes to be friends of, and accomplices in, the armed insurrection, which it is his especial political duty to suppress. He has no judicial powers. And the judiciary department has no political powers, and claims none, and therefore (as well as for other reasons already assigned) no court or judge can take cognizance of the political acts of the President, or undertake to revise and reverse his political decisions. . . .

There is but one sentence in the Constitution which mentions the writ of *habeas corpus*, (article 1, section 9, clause 2) which is in these words: "The privilege of the writ of *habeas corpus* shall not be suspended, unless when, in cases of rebellion or invasion, the public safety may require it." . . .

. . . [W]e must try to construe the words, vague and indeterminate as they are, as we find them. "The *privilege* of the writ of *habeas corpus* shall not be *suspended*," &c. Does that mean that the writ itself shall not be issued, or, that being issued, the party shall derive no benefit from it? *Suspended*—does that mean delayed, hung up for a time, or altogether denied? The *writ of habeas corpus*—which writ? In England there were many writs called by that name, and used by the courts for the more convenient exercise of their various powers; and our own courts now, by acts of Congress (the judiciary act of 1789, section 14, and the act of March 2, 1833, section 7,) have, I believe, equivalent powers. . . .

If by the phrase *the suspension of the privilege of the writ of habeas corpus*, we must understand a repeal of all power to issue the writ, then I freely admit that none but Congress can do it. But if we are at liberty to understand the phrase to mean, that, in case of a great and dangerous rebellion, like the present, the public safety requires the arrest and confinement of persons implicated in that rebellion, I as freely declare the opinion, that the President has lawful power to *suspend the privilege* of persons arrested under such circumstances. For he is especially charged by the Constitution with the "public safety," and he is the sole judge of the emergency which requires his prompt action.

This power in the President is no part of his ordinary duty in time of peace; it is temporary and exceptional, and was intended only to meet a pressing emergency, when the judiciary is found to be too weak to insure the public safety—when—(in the language of the act of Congress,) there are "combinations too powerful to be suppressed by the ordinary course of judicial proceedings, or by the powers vested in the marshals." Then, and not till then, has he the lawful authority to call to his aid the military power of the nation, and with that power perform his great legal and constitutional duty to suppress the insurrection. And shall it be said that when he has fought and captured the insurgent army, and has seized their secret spies and emissaries, he is bound to bring their bodies before any judge who may send him a writ of *habeas corpus*, "to do, submit to, and receive whatever the said judge shall consider in that behalf?"

I deny that he is under any obligation to obey such a writ, issued under such circumstances. . . .

Whatever I have said about the suspension of the privilege of the writ of *habeas corpus*, has been said in deference to the opinions of others, and not because I myself thought it necessary to treat of that subject at all in reference to the present posture of our national affairs. For, not doubting the power of the President to capture and hold by force insurgents in open arms against the Government, and to arrest and imprison their suspected accomplices, I never thought of first suspending the writ of *habeas corpus*, any more than I thought of first suspending the writ of *replevin*, before seizing arms and munitions destined for the enemy.

The power to do these things is in the hand of the President, placed there by the Constitution and the statute law, as a sacred trust, to be used by him, in his best discretion, in the performance of his great first duty—to preserve, protect, and defend the Constitution. And for any breach of that trust he is responsible before the high court of impeachment, and before no other human tribunal. . . .

6. AN ACT TO PROVIDE INTERNAL REVENUE TO SUPPORT
THE GOVERNMENT AND TO PAY INTEREST ON THE PUBLIC
DEBT, 12 STAT. 432 (JUNE 19, 1862) (REVENUE ACT)

Be it enacted . . . That, for the purpose of superintending the collection of internal duties, stamp duties, licenses, or taxes imposed by this act, or which may be hereafter imposed, and of assessing the same, an office is hereby created in the Treasury Department to be called the office of the Commissioner of Internal Revenue; and the President of the United States is hereby authorized to nominate, and, with the advice and consent of the Senate, to appoint, a Commissioner of Internal Revenue . . . and the Secretary of the Treasury may assign to the office of the Commissioner of Internal Revenue such number of clerks as he may deem necessary, or the exigencies of the public service may require[.] . . .

SEC. 19. *And be it further enacted*, . . . all persons who shall neglect to pay the duties and taxes so as aforesaid assessed upon them to the collector within the time specified, shall be liable to pay ten per centum additional upon the amount thereof[.] . . .

SEC. 21. *And be it further enacted*, That in any case where goods, chattels, or effects sufficient to satisfy the duties imposed by this act upon any person liable to pay the same, shall not be found by the collector or deputy collector . . . he is hereby authorized to collect the same by seizure and sale of real estate; and the officer making such seizure and sale shall give notice to the person whose estate is proposed to be sold[.] . . .

SEC. 90. *And be it further enacted*, That there shall be levied, collected, and paid annually, upon the annual gains, profits, or income of every person residing in the United States, . . . except as hereinafter mentioned, if such annual gains, profits, or income exceed the sum of six hundred dollars, and do not exceed the sum of ten thousand dollars, a duty of three per centum on the amount of such annual gains, profits, or income over and above the said sum of six hundred dollars; if said income exceeds the sum of ten thousand dollars, a duty of five per centum upon the amount thereof exceeding six hundred dollars[.] . . .

7. LINCOLN'S SUSPENSION OF HABEAS CORPUS (SEPTEMBER 24, 1862)

By this proclamation, Lincoln suspended the writ of habeas corpus nationwide.[6]

Whereas, it has become necessary to call into service not only volunteers but also portions of the militia of the States by draft in order to suppress the insurrection existing in the United States, and disloyal persons are not adequately restrained by the ordinary processes of law from hindering this measure and from giving aid and comfort in various ways to the insurrection;

Now, therefore, be it ordered, first, that during the existing insurrection and as a necessary measure for suppressing the same, all Rebels and Insurgents, their aiders and abettors within the United States, and all persons discouraging volunteer enlistments, resisting militia drafts, or guilty of any disloyal practice, affording aid and comfort to Rebels against the authority of the United States, shall be subject to martial law and liable to trial and punishment by Courts Martial or Military Commission:

Second. That the Writ of Habeas Corpus is suspended in respect to all persons arrested, or who are now, or hereafter during the rebellion shall be, imprisoned in any fort, camp, arsenal, military prison, or other place of confinement by any military authority or by the sentence of any Court Martial or Military Commission. . . .

8. AN ACT RELATING TO HABEAS CORPUS, AND REGULATING JUDICIAL
PROCEEDINGS IN CERTAIN CASES, 12 STAT. 755 (MARCH 3, 1863)

With this act, Congress validated Lincoln's suspension of the writ of habeas corpus nationwide and mandated certain procedural safeguards for those imprisoned. While debate would continue as to the legality of Lincoln's actions, as of the date of this act, no one could question the constitutionality of the suspension itself.

Be it enacted . . . That, during the present rebellion, the President of the United States, whenever, in his judgment, the public safety may require it, is authorized to suspend the privilege of the writ of habeas corpus in any case throughout the United States, or any part thereof. And whenever and wherever the said privilege shall be suspended, as aforesaid, no military or other officer shall be compelled, in answer to any writ of habeas corpus, to return the body of any person or persons detained by him by authority of the President; but upon the certificate, under oath, of the officer having charge of any one so detained that such person is detained by him as a prisoner under authority of the President, further proceedings under the writ of habeas corpus shall be suspended by the judge or court having issued the said writ, so long as said suspension by the President shall remain in force, and said rebellion continue.

SEC. 2. *And be it further enacted,* . . . [The act directs the secretary of state and the secretary of war to furnish to judges of the circuit and district courts "a list of the names of all persons, citizens of states in which the administration of the laws has continued unimpaired in the said Federal courts, who are now, or may hereafter be, held . . . as state or political prisoners, or otherwise than as prisoners of war; the said list to contain the names of all those who reside in the respective jurisdictions of said judges."] And in all cases where a grand jury, having attended any of said courts having jurisdiction in the premises, after the passage of this act, and after the furnishing of said list, as aforesaid, has terminated its session without finding an indictment or presentment, or other proceeding against any such person, it shall be the duty of the judge of said court forthwith to make an order that any such prisoner desiring a discharge from said imprisonment be brought before him to be discharged; and every officer of the United States having custody of such prisoner is hereby directed immediately to obey and execute said judge's order; and in case he shall delay or refuse so to do, he shall be subject to indictment for a misdemeanor, and be punished by a fine of not less than five hundred dollars and imprisonment in the common jail for a period not less than six months, in the discretion of the court: *Provided, however,* That no person shall be discharged by virtue of the provisions of this act until after he or she shall have taken an oath of allegiance to the Government of the United States, and to support the Constitution thereof; and that he or she will not hereafter in any way encourage or give aid and comfort to the present rebellion, or the supporters thereof: *And provided, also*, That the judge or court before whom such person may be brought, before discharging him or her from imprisonment, shall have power, on examination of the case, and, if the public safety shall require it, shall be required to cause him or her to enter into recognizance, with or without surety, in a sum to be fixed by said judge or court, to keep the peace and be of good behavior towards the United States and its citizens, and from time to time, and at such times as such judge or court may direct, appear before said judge or court to be further dealt with, according to law, as the circumstances may require. And it shall be the duty of the district attorney of the United States to attend such examination before the judge.

SEC. 3. *And be it further enacted*, That in case any of such prisoners shall be under indictment or presentment for any offence against the laws of the United States, and by existing laws bail or a recognizance may be taken for the appearance for trial of such person, it shall be the duty of said judge at once to discharge such person upon bail or recognizance for trial as aforesaid. And in case the said Secretaries of State and War shall for any reason refuse or omit to furnish the said list of persons held as prisoners as aforesaid at the time of the passage of this act within twenty days thereafter, and of such persons as hereafter may be arrested within twenty days from the time of the arrest, any citizen may, after a grand jury shall have terminated its session without finding an indictment or presentment, as provided in the second section of this act, by a petition alleging the facts aforesaid touching any of the persons so as aforesaid imprisoned, supported by the oath of such petitioner or any other credible person, obtain and be entitled to have the said judge's order to discharge such prisoner on the same terms and conditions prescribed in the second section of this act: *Provided, however*, That the said judge shall be satisfied such allegations are true. . . .

9. AN ACT FOR ENROLLING AND CALLING OUT THE NATIONAL FORCES, AND FOR OTHER PURPOSES, 12 STAT. 731 (MARCH 3, 1863) (CONSCRIPTION ACT)

. . . *Be it enacted* . . . That all able-bodied male citizens of the United States, and persons of foreign birth who shall have declared on oath their intention to become citizens under and in pursuance of the laws thereof, between the ages of twenty and forty-five years . . . are hereby declared to constitute the national forces, and shall be liable to perform military duty in the service of the United States when called out by the President for that purpose.

SEC. 2. *And be it further enacted*, That the following persons be, and they are hereby, excepted and exempt from the provisions of this act, and shall not be liable to military duty under the same, to wit: Such as are rejected as physically or mentally unfit for the service; also, First the Vice-President of the United States, the judges of the various courts of the United States, the heads of the various executive departments of the government, and the governors of the several States.

Second, the only son liable to military duty of a widow dependent upon his labor for support. Third, the only son of aged or infirm parent or parents dependent upon his labor for support. Fourth, where there are two or more sons of aged or infirm parents subject to draft, the father, or, if he be dead, the mother, may elect which son shall be exempt. Fifth, the only brother of children not twelve years old, having neither father nor mother dependent upon his labor for support. Sixth, the father of motherless children under twelve years of age dependent upon his labor for support. Seventh, where there are a father and sons in the same family and household, and two of them are in the military service of the United States as non-commissioned officers, musicians, or privates, the residue of such family and household, not exceeding two, shall be exempt[.] . . .

SEC. 12. *And be it further enacted*, That whenever it may be necessary to call out the national forces for military services, the President is hereby authorized to assign to each district the number of men to be furnished by said district; and thereupon the enrolling board shall . . . make a draft of the required number, and fifty per cent. in addition, and shall make an exact and complete roll of the names of the persons so drawn, and of the order in which they were drawn, so that the first drawn may stand first upon the said roll, and the second may stand second, and so on; and the persons so drawn shall be notified of the same within ten days thereafter, by a written or printed notice, to be served personally or by leaving a copy at the last place of residence, requiring them to appear at a des-ignated rendezvous to report for duty. In assigning to the districts the number of men to be furnished therefrom, the President shall take into consideration the number of volunteers and militia furnished by and from the several states in which said districts are situated, and the period of their service since the commencement of the present rebellion, and shall so make said assignment as to equalize the numbers among the districts[.] . . .

SEC. 13. *And be it further enacted*, That any person drafted and notified to appear as aforesaid, may, on or before the day fixed for his appearance, furnish an acceptable substitute to take his place in the draft; or he may pay to such person as the Secretary of War may authorize to receive it, such sum, not exceeding three hundred dollars, as the Secretary may determine, for the procuration of such substitute [ ]   And any person failing to report after due service of notice . . . shall be deemed a deserter, and shall be arrested . . . for trial by court-martial, unless, upon proper showing that he is not liable to do military duty, the board of enrolment shall relieve him from the draft. . . .

10. ABRAHAM LINCOLN TO ERASTUS CORNING
(JUNE 1863) (LIBRARY OF CONGRESS)

In this letter, Lincoln further justifies his actions in suspending the writ of habeas corpus.

... Prior to my installation here it had been inculcated that any state had a lawful right to secede from the National Union; and that it would be expedient to exercise the right whenever the devotees of the doctrine should fail to elect a President to their own liking. I was elected contrary to their liking; and accordingly, so far as it was legally possible, they had taken seven states out of the Union, had seized many of the United States Forts, and had fired upon the United States flag,—all before I was inaugurated; and, of course, before I had done any official act whatever. The rebellion thus begun soon ran into the present civil war; and in certain respects it began on very unequal terms between the parties. The insurgents had been preparing for it more than thirty years, while the Government had taken no steps to resist them. The former had carefully considered all the means which could be turned to their account. It undoubtedly was a well pondered reliance with them that in their own unrestricted effort to destroy Union, Constitution and Law, all together, the Government would in great degree be restrained by the same Constitution and Law from arresting their progress. . . . From this material, under cover of "Liberty of speech," "Liberty of the Press" and "*Habeas Corpus*," they hoped to keep on foot amongst us a most efficient corps of spies, informers, suppliers, and aiders and abettors of their cause in a thousand ways. They knew that in times such as they were inaugurating, by the Constitution itself, the "Habeas Corpus" might be suspended; but they also knew they had friends who would make a question as to *who* was to suspend it; meanwhile their spies and others might remain at large to help on their cause. Or if, as has happened, the Executive should suspend the writ without ruinous waste of time, instances of arresting innocent persons might occur, as are always likely to occur in such cases; and then a clamor could be raised in regard to this, which might be, at least of some service to the insurgent cause. It needed no very keen perception to discover this part of the enemies' programme, so soon as by open hostilities their machinery was fairly put in motion. Yet thoroughly imbued with a reverence for the guarantied rights of individuals, I was slow to adopt the strong measures which by degrees I have been forced to regard as being within the exceptions of the Constitution, and as indispensable to the public safety. Nothing is better known to history than that Courts of justice are utterly incompetent to such cases. Civil Courts are organized chiefly for trials of individuals or at most a few individuals acting in concert; and this in quiet times, and on charges of crimes well defined in the law. Even in times of peace, bands of horse thieves and robbers frequently grow too numerous and powerful for the ordinary Courts of justice. But what comparison in numbers, have such bands ever borne to the insurgent sympathizers, even in many of the loyal States? Again a jury too frequently have at least one member, more ready to hang the panel than to hang the traitor. And yet again, he who dissuades one man from volunteering or induces one soldier to desert, weakens the Union cause as much as he who kills a Union Soldier in battle. Yet this dissuasion or inducement may be so conducted as to be no defined crime of which any civil court would take cognizance.

Ours is a case of Rebellion—so called by the resolutions before me—in fact a clear, flagrant and gigantic case of Rebellion; and the provision of the Constitution that "The privilege of the writ of Habeas Corpus shall not be suspended, unless when in cases of Rebellion or Invasion, the public safety may require it," is *the* provision which specially applies to our present case. This provision plainly attests the understanding of those who made the Constitution, that ordinary Courts of justice are inadequate to "cases of Rebellion"—attests their purpose that in such cases, men may be held in custody whom the Courts, acting on ordinary rules would discharge. Habeas Corpus does not discharge men who are proved to be guilty of defined crime; and its suspension is allowed by the Constitution on purpose that men may be arrested and held, who cannot be proved to be guilty of defined crime, "when in cases of Rebellion or invasion the public safety may require it." This is precisely our present case, a case of Rebellion, wherein the public safety does require the suspension. Indeed, arrests by process of Courts, and arrests in cases of rebellion, do not proceed altogether upon the same basis. The former is directed at the small percentage of ordinary and continuous perpetration of crime; while the latter is directed at sudden and extensive uprisings against the government, which, at most, will succeed or fail, in no great length of time. In the latter case, arrests are made, not so much for what has been done, as for what probably would be done. The latter is more for the preventive, and less for the vindictive, than the former. In such cases the purposes of men are much more easily understood than in cases of ordinary crime. The man who stands by and says nothing, when the peril of his government is discussed, can not be misunderstood. If not hindered, he is sure to help the enemy. Much more, if he talks ambiguously—talks for his country with "buts" and "ifs" and "ands." Of how little value the constitutional provision I have quoted will be rendered, if arrests shall never be made until defined crimes shall have been committed, may be illustrated by a few notable examples. General John C. Breckinridge, General Robert E. Lee, General Joseph E. Johnston, General John B. Magruder, General William B. Preston, General Simon B. Buckner, and Commodore Franklin Buchanan, now occupying the very highest places in the rebel war service, were all within the power of the government since the rebellion began, and were nearly as well known to be traitors then as now: Unquestionably if we had seized and held them, the insurgent cause would be much weaker. But no one of them had then committed any crime defined in the law. Every one of them, if arrested, would have been discharged on Habeas Corpus were the writ allowed to operate. In view of these and similar cases, I think the time not unlikely to come when I shall be blamed for having made too few arrests rather than too many.

11. *EX PARTE MILLIGAN*, 71 U.S. 2 (1866)

Despite Roger Taney's ruling, in his capacity as a circuit judge, in *Ex parte Merryman*, the Supreme Court avoided addressing the legality of Lincoln's suspension of habeas corpus. The matter of wartime dissent came before the Supreme Court in the case of *Ex parte Vallandingham*, after Clement L. Vallandingham's arrest and trial by a military commission for delivering a speech against the Lincoln administration and against local military orders prohibiting declarations of sympathy for the Confederacy. Vallandingham challenged the military court's jurisdiction and asserted his entitlement to a jury trial in a civil court, while the military commission found Vallandingham guilty. In reviewing Vallandingham's case, the Supreme Court upheld military jurisdiction during a rebellion and also ruled that it had no jurisdiction to issue a writ of habeas corpus or revise the military commission's proceedings, because military courts stood outside of its appellate jurisdiction. After the crisis of the Civil War had passed, however, and with the Union's victory secured, the Supreme Court in *Ex parte Milligan* retracted from its expansive position in the Vallandingham case and ruled that military tribunals could not try civilians where civil courts operated.

. . . An act of Congress—the Judiciary Act of 1789, section 14—enacts that the Circuit Courts of the United States

> "Shall have power to issue writs of *habeas corpus.* And that either of the justices of the Supreme Court, as well as judges of the District Courts, shall have power to grant writs of *habeas corpus* for the purpose of an inquiry into the cause of commitment. *Provided*," &c.

Another act—that of March 3d, 1863, "relating to *habeas corpus*, and regulating judicial proceedings in certain cases"—an act passed in the midst of the Rebellion—makes various provisions in regard to the subject of it. . . .

By proclamation, dated the 15th September following, the President reciting this statute suspended the privilege of the writ in the cases where, by his authority, military, naval, and civil officers of the United States "hold persons in their custody either as prisoners of war, spies, or aiders and abettors of the enemy, . . . or belonging to the land or naval forces of the United States, or otherwise amenable to military law, or the rules and articles of war, or the rules or regulations prescribed for the military or naval services, by authority of the President, or for resisting a draft, or for any other offence against the military or naval service."

. . . Lamdin P. Milligan, a citizen of the United States, and a resident and citizen of the State of Indiana, was arrested on the 5th day of October, 1864, at his home in the said State, by the order of . . . [the] military commandant of the District of Indiana, and by the same authority confined in a military prison, at or near Indianapolis, the capital of the State. On the 21st day of the same month, he was placed on trial before a "military commission," convened at Indianapolis, by order of the said General, upon the following charges . . . namely:

1. "Conspiracy against the Government of the United States;"
2. "Affording aid and comfort to rebels against the authority of the United States;"
3. "Inciting insurrection;"
4. "Disloyal practices;" and
5. "Violation of the laws of war."

Under each of these charges there were various specifications. The substance of them was, joining and aiding, at different times, between October, 1863, and August, 1864, a secret society known as the Order of American Knights or Sons of Liberty, for the purpose of overthrowing the Government and duly constituted authorities of the United States; holding communication with the enemy; conspiring to seize munitions of war stored in the arsenals; to liberate prisoners of war, &c.; resisting the draft, &c.; . . . "at a period of war and armed rebellion against the authority of the United States, at or near Indianapolis, (and various other places specified) in Indiana, a State within the military lines of the army of the United States, and the theatre of military operations, and which had been and was constantly threatened to be invaded by the enemy." . . .

Mr. Justice [David] DAVIS delivered the opinion of the court.

On the 10th day of May, 1865, Lambdin P. Milligan presented a petition . . . to be discharged from an alleged unlawful imprisonment.[7] The case made by the petition is this: Milligan is a citizen of the United States; has lived for twenty years in Indiana; and, at the time of the grievances complained of, was not, and never had been in the military or naval service of the United States. On the 5th day of October, 1864, while at home, he was arrested by order of General Alvin P. Hovey, commanding the military district of Indiana; and has ever since been kept in close confinement.

On the 21st day of October, 1864, he was brought before a military commission, convened at Indianapolis, . . . tried on certain charges and specifications; found guilty, and sentenced to be hanged; and the sentence ordered to be executed on Friday, the 19th day of May, 1865.

On the 2d day of January, 1865, after the proceedings of the military commission were at an end, the Circuit Court of the United States for Indiana met at Indianapolis and empanelled a grand jury, who were charged to inquire whether the laws of the United States had been violated; and, if so, to make presentments. The court adjourned on the 27th day of January, having, prior thereto, discharged from further service the grand jury, who did not find any bill of indictment or make any presentment against Milligan for any offence whatever;

and, in fact, since his imprisonment, no bill of indictment has been found or presentment made against him by any grand jury of the United States.

Milligan insists that said military commission had no jurisdiction to try him upon the charges preferred, or upon any charges whatever; because he was a citizen of the United States and the State of Indiana, and had not been, since the commencement of the late Rebellion, a resident of any of the States whose citizens were arrayed against the government, and that the right of trial by jury was guaranteed to him by the Constitution of the United States.

The prayer of the petition was, that under the act of Congress, approved March 3d, 1863, . . . he may be brought before the court, and either turned over to the proper civil tribunal to be proceeded against according to the law of the land or discharged from custody altogether. . . .

. . . The opinions of the judges of the Circuit Court were opposed on three questions, which are certified to the Supreme Court:

1st. "On the facts stated in said petition and exhibits, ought a writ of *habeas corpus* to be issued?"
2d. "On the facts stated in said petition and exhibits, ought the said Lambdin P. Milligan to be discharged from custody as in said petition prayed?"
3d. "Whether, upon the facts stated in said petition and exhibits, the military commission mentioned therein had jurisdiction legally to try and sentence said Milligan in manner and form as in said petition and exhibits is stated?" . . .

During the late wicked Rebellion, the temper of the times did not allow that calmness in deliberation and discussion so necessary to a correct conclusion of a purely judicial question. *Then*, considerations of safety were mingled with the exercise of power; and feelings and interests prevailed which are happily terminated. *Now* that the public safety is assured, this question, as well as all others, can be discussed and decided without passion or the admixture of any element not required to form a legal judgment. . . .

In interpreting a law, the motives which must have operated with the legislature in passing it are proper to be considered. This law was passed in a time of great national peril, when our heritage of free government was in danger. An armed rebellion against the national authority, of greater proportions than history affords an example of, was raging; and the public safety required that the privilege of the writ of *habeas corpus* should be suspended. . . . It was under these circumstances . . . that this law was passed. The President was authorized by it to suspend the privilege of the writ of *habeas corpus*, whenever, in his judgment, the public safety required; and he did, by proclamation, bearing date the 15th of September, 1863, reciting, among other things, the authority of this statute, suspend it. The suspension of the writ does not authorize the arrest of any one, but simply denies to one arrested the privilege of this writ in order to obtain his liberty.

It is proper, therefore, to inquire under what circumstances the courts could rightfully refuse to grant this writ, and when the citizen was at liberty to invoke its aid.

The second and third sections of the law are explicit on these points. The language used is plain and direct, and the meaning of the Congress cannot be mistaken. The public safety demanded, if the President thought proper to arrest a suspected person, that he should not be required to give the cause of his detention on return to a writ of *habeas corpus*. But it was not contemplated that such person should be detained in custody beyond a certain fixed period, unless certain judicial proceedings . . . were commenced against him. . . .

Milligan, in his application to be released from imprisonment, averred the existence of every fact necessary under the terms of this law to give the Circuit Court of Indiana jurisdiction. If he was detained in custody by the order of the President, otherwise than as a prisoner of war; if he was a citizen of Indiana and had never been in the military or naval service, and the grand jury of the district had met, after he had been arrested, for a period of twenty days, and adjourned without taking any proceedings against him, *then* the court had the right to entertain his petition and determine the lawfulness of his imprisonment. . . .

The controlling question in the case is this: Upon the *facts* stated in Milligan's petition, and the exhibits filed, had the military commission mentioned in it *jurisdiction*, legally, to try and sentence him? Milligan, not a resident of one of the rebellious states, or a prisoner of war, but a citizen of Indiana for twenty years past, and never in the military or naval service, is, while at his home, arrested by the military power of the United States, imprisoned, and, on certain criminal charges preferred against him, tried, convicted, and sentenced to be hanged by a military commission, organized under the direction of the military commander of the military district of Indiana. Had this tribunal the *legal* power and authority to try and punish this man?

No graver question was ever considered by this court, nor one which more nearly concerns the rights of the whole people; for it is the birthright of every American citizen when charged with crime, to be tried and punished according to law. . . . The provisions of [the Constitution] on the administration of criminal justice are too plain and direct, to leave room for misconstruction or doubt of their true meaning. Those applicable to this case are found in that clause of the original Constitution which says, "That the trial of all crimes, except in case of impeachment, shall be by jury;" and in the fourth, fifth, and sixth articles of the amendments. . . . These securities for personal liberty thus embodied, were such as wisdom and experience had demonstrated to be necessary for the protection of those accused of crime. And so strong was the sense of the country of their importance, and so jealous were the people that these rights, highly prized, might be denied them by implication, that when the original Constitution was proposed for adoption it encountered severe opposition; and, but for the belief that it would be so amended as to embrace them, it would never have been ratified.

Time has proven the discernment of our ancestors. . . . Those great and good men foresaw that troublous times would arise, when rulers and people would become restive under restraint, and seek by sharp and decisive measures to accomplish ends deemed just and proper; and that the principles of constitutional liberty would be in peril, unless established by irrepealable law. The history of the world had taught them that what was done in the past might be attempted in the future. The Constitution of the United States is a law for rulers and people, equally in war and in peace, and covers with the shield of its protection all classes of men, at all times, and under all circumstances. No doctrine, involving more pernicious consequences, was ever invented by the wit of man than that any of its provisions can be suspended during any of the great exigencies of government. Such a doctrine leads directly to anarchy or despotism, but the theory of necessity on which it is based is false; for the government, within the Constitution, has all the powers granted to it, which are necessary to preserve its existence; as has been happily proved by the result of the great effort to throw off its just authority.

Have any of the rights guaranteed by the Constitution been violated in the case of Milligan? and if so, what are they?

Every trial involves the exercise of judicial power; and from what source did the military commission that tried him derive their authority? Certainly no part of the judicial power of the country was conferred on them; because the Constitution expressly vests it "in one supreme court and such inferior courts as the Congress may from time to time ordain and establish," and it is not pretended that the commission was a court ordained and established by Congress. They cannot justify on the mandate of the President; because he is controlled by law, and has his appropriate sphere of duty, which is to execute, not to make, the laws; and there is "no unwritten criminal code to which resort can be had as a source of jurisdiction."

But it is said that the jurisdiction is complete under the "laws and usages of war."

It can serve no useful purpose to inquire what those laws and usages are, whence they originated, where found, and on whom they operate; they can never be applied to citizens in states which have upheld the authority of the government, and where the courts are open and their process unobstructed. This court has judicial knowledge that in Indiana the Federal authority was always unopposed, and its courts always open to hear criminal accusations and redress grievances; and no usage of war could sanction a military trial there for any offence whatever of a citizen in civil life, in nowise connected with the military service. Congress could grant no such power; and to the honor of our national legislature be it said, it has never been provoked by the state of the country even to attempt its exercise. One of the plainest constitutional provisions was, therefore, infringed when Milligan was tried by a court not ordained and established by Congress, and not composed of judges appointed during good behavior.

Why was he not delivered to the Circuit Court of Indiana to be proceeded against according to law? No reason of necessity could be urged against it; because Congress had declared penalties against the offences charged, provided for their punishment, and directed that court to hear and determine them. And soon after this military tribunal was ended, the Circuit Court met, peacefully transacted its business, and adjourned. It needed no bayonets to protect it, and required no military aid to execute its judgments. It was held in a state, eminently distinguished for patriotism, by judges commissioned during the Rebellion, who were provided with juries, upright, intelligent, and selected by a marshal appointed by the President. The government had no right to conclude that Milligan, if guilty, would not receive in that court merited punishment; for its records disclose that it was constantly engaged in the trial of similar offences, and was never interrupted in its administration of criminal justice. If it was dangerous, in the distracted condition of affairs, to leave Milligan unrestrained of his liberty, because he "conspired against the government, afforded aid and comfort to rebels, and incited the people to insurrection," the *law* said arrest him, confine him closely, render him powerless to do further mischief; and then present his case to the grand jury of the district, with proofs of his guilt, and, if indicted, try him according to the course of the common law. If this had been done, the Constitution would have been vindicated, the law of 1863 enforced, and the securities for personal liberty preserved and defended. . . .

The discipline necessary to the efficiency of the army and navy, required other and swifter modes of trial than are furnished by the common law courts; and, in pursuance of the power conferred by the Constitution, Congress has declared the kinds of trial, and the manner in which they shall be conducted, for offences committed while the party is in the military or naval service. Every one connected with these branches of the public service is amenable to the jurisdiction which Congress has created for their government, and, while thus serving, surrenders his right to be tried by the civil courts. *All other persons*, citizens of states where the courts are open, if charged with crime, are guaranteed the inestimable privilege of trial by jury. This privilege is a vital principle, underlying the whole administration of criminal justice; it is not held by sufferance, and cannot be frittered away on any plea of state or political necessity. When peace prevails, and the authority of the government is undisputed, there is no difficulty of preserving the safeguards of liberty; for the ordinary modes of trial are never neglected, and no one wishes it otherwise; but if society is disturbed by civil commotion—if the passions of men are aroused and the restraints of law weakened, if not disregarded—these safeguards need, and should receive, the watchful care of those intrusted with the guardianship of the Constitution and laws. In no other way can we transmit to posterity unimpaired the blessings of liberty, consecrated by the sacrifices of the Revolution.

It is claimed that martial law covers with its broad mantle the proceedings of this military commission. The proposition is this: that in a time of war the commander of an armed force (if in his opinion the exigencies of the country demand it, and of which he is to judge), has the power, within the lines of his military district, to suspend all civil rights and their remedies, and subject citizens as well as soldiers to the rule of *his will*; and in the exercise of his lawful authority cannot be restrained, except by his superior officer or the President of the United States. If this position is sound to the extent claimed, then when war exists, foreign or domestic, and the country is subdivided into military departments for mere convenience, the commander of one of them can, if he chooses, within his limits, on the plea of necessity, with the approval of the Executive, substitute military force for and to the exclusion of the laws, and punish all persons, as he thinks right and proper, without fixed or certain rules.

The statement of this proposition shows its importance; for, if true, republican government is a failure, and there is an end of liberty regulated by law. Martial law, established on such a basis, destroys every guarantee of the Constitution, and effectually renders the "military independent of and superior to the civil power"—the attempt to do which by the King of Great Britain was deemed by our fathers such an offence, that they assigned it to the world as one of the causes which impelled them to declare their independence. Civil liberty and this kind of martial law cannot endure together; the antagonism is irreconcilable; and, in the conflict, one or the other must perish.

This nation . . . cannot always remain at peace, and has no right to expect that it will always have wise and humane rulers, sincerely attached to the principles of the Constitution. Wicked men, ambitious of power, with hatred of liberty and contempt of law, may fill the place once occupied by Washington and Lincoln; and if this right is conceded, and the calamities of war again befall us, the dangers to human liberty are frightful to contemplate. If our fathers had failed to provide for just such a contingency, they would have been false to the trust reposed in them. They knew—the history of the world told them—the nation they were founding, be its existence short or long, would be involved in war; how often or how long continued, human foresight could not tell; and that unlimited power, wherever lodged at such a time, was especially hazardous to freemen. For this, and other equally weighty reasons, they secured the inheritance they had fought to maintain, by incorporating in a written constitution the safeguards which *time* had proved were essential to its preservation. Not one of these safeguards can the President, or Congress, or the Judiciary disturb, except the one concerning the writ of *habeas corpus*.

It is essential to the safety of every government that, in a great crisis, like the one we have just passed through, there should be a power somewhere of suspending the writ of *habeas corpus*. In every war, there are men of previously good character, wicked enough to counsel their fellow-citizens to resist the measures deemed necessary by a good government to sustain its just authority and overthrow its enemies; and their influence may lead to dangerous combinations. In the emergency of the times, an immediate public investigation according to law may not be possible; and yet, the peril to the country may be too imminent to suffer such persons to go at large. Unquestionably, there is then an exigency which demands that the government, if it should see fit in the exercise of a proper discretion to make arrests, should not be required to produce the persons arrested in answer to a writ of *habeas corpus*. The Constitution goes no further. It does not say after a writ of *habeas corpus* is denied a citizen, that he shall be tried otherwise than by the course of the common law; if it had intended this result, it was easy by the use of direct words to have accomplished it. The illustrious men who framed that instrument were guarding the foundations of civil liberty against the abuses of unlimited power; they were full of wisdom, and the lessons of history informed them that a trial by an established court, assisted by an impartial jury, was the only sure way of protecting the citizen against oppression and wrong. Knowing this, they limited the suspension to one great right, and left the rest to remain forever inviolable. But, it is insisted that the safety of the country in time of war demands that this broad claim for martial law shall be sustained. If this were true, it could be well said that a country, preserved at the sacrifice of all the cardinal principles of liberty, is not worth the cost of preservation. Happily, it is not so.

It will be borne in mind that this is not a question of the power to proclaim martial law, when war exists in a community and the courts and civil authorities are overthrown. Nor is it a question what rule a military commander, at the head of his army, can impose on states in rebellion to cripple their resources and quell the insurrection. The jurisdiction claimed is much more extensive. The necessities of the service, during the late Rebellion, required that the loyal states should be placed within the limits of certain military districts and commanders appointed in them; and, it is urged, that this, in a military sense, constituted them the theatre of military operations; and, as in this case, Indiana had been and was again threatened with invasion by the enemy, the occasion was furnished to establish martial law. The conclusion does not follow from the premises. If armies were collected in Indiana, they were to be employed in another locality, where the laws were obstructed and the national authority disputed. On *her* soil there was no hostile foot; if once invaded, that invasion was at an end, and with it all pretext for martial law. Martial law cannot arise from a *threatened* invasion. The necessity must be actual and present; the invasion real, such as effectually closes the courts and deposes the civil administration. . . .

It follows, from what has been said on this subject, that there are occasions when martial rule can be properly applied. If, in foreign invasion or civil war, the courts are actually closed, and it is impossible to administer criminal justice according to law, *then*, on the theatre of active military operations, where war really prevails, there is a necessity to furnish a substitute for the civil authority, thus overthrown, to preserve the safety of the army and society; and as no power is left but the military, it is allowed to govern by martial rule until the laws can have their free course. As necessity creates the rule, so it limits its duration; for, if this government is continued *after* the courts are reinstated, it is a gross usurpation of power. Martial rule can never exist where the courts are open, and in the proper and unobstructed exercise of their jurisdiction. It is also confined to the locality of actual war. Because, during the late Rebellion it could have been enforced in Virginia, where the national authority was overturned and the courts driven out, it does not follow that it should obtain in Indiana, where that authority was never disputed, and justice was always administered. And so in the case of a foreign invasion, martial rule may become a necessity in one state, when, in another, it would be "mere lawless violence." . . .

To the third question, then, on which the judges below were opposed in opinion, an answer in the negative must be returned.

It is proper to say, although Milligan's trial and conviction by a military commission was illegal, yet, if guilty of the crimes imputed to him, and his guilt had been ascertained by an established court and impartial jury, he deserved severe punishment. Open resistance to the measures deemed necessary to subdue a great rebellion, by those who enjoy the protection of government, and have not the excuse even of prejudice of section to plead in their favor, is wicked; but that resistance becomes an *enormous crime* when it assumes the form of a secret political organization, armed to oppose the laws, and seeks by stealthy means to introduce the enemies of the country into peaceful communities, there to light the torch of civil war, and thus overthrow the power of the United States. Conspiracies like these, at such a juncture, are extremely perilous; and those concerned in them are dangerous enemies to their country, and should receive the heaviest penalties of the law, as an example to deter others from similar criminal conduct. It is said the severity of the laws caused them; but Congress was obliged to enact severe laws to meet the crisis; and as our highest civil duty is to serve our country when in danger, the late war has proved that rigorous laws, when necessary, will be cheerfully obeyed by a patriotic people, struggling to preserve the rich blessings of a free government. . . .

If the military trial of Milligan was contrary to law, then he was entitled, on the facts stated in his petition, to be discharged from custody by the terms of the act of Congress of March 3d, 1863. . . .

But it is insisted that Milligan was a prisoner of war, and, therefore, excluded from the privileges of the statute. It is not easy to see how he can be treated as a prisoner of war, when he lived in Indiana for the past twenty years, was arrested there, and had not been, during the late troubles, a resident of any of the states in rebellion. If in Indiana he conspired with bad men to assist the enemy, he is punishable for it in the courts of Indiana; but, when tried for the offence, he cannot plead the rights of war; for he was not engaged in legal acts of hostility against the government, and only such persons, when captured, are prisoners of war. If he cannot enjoy the immunities attaching to the character of a prisoner of war, how can he be subject to their pains and penalties? . . .

The CHIEF JUSTICE [Salmon P. Chase] delivered the following [dissenting] opinion.

. . . The crimes with which Milligan was charged were of the gravest character, and the petition and exhibits in the record, which must here be taken as true, admit his guilt. But whatever his desert of punishment may be, it is more important to the country and to every citizen that he should not be punished under an illegal sentence, sanctioned by this court of last resort, than that he should be punished at all. The laws which protect the liberties of the whole people must not be violated or set aside in order to inflict, even upon the guilty, unauthorized though merited justice. . . .

[Chase here agrees with the majority that the writ of habeas corpus ought to issue, that Milligan was entitled to discharge, and that the military commission in Indiana did not have jurisdiction to try and sentence Milligan under the facts stated.]

But the opinion which has just been read goes further; and as we understand it, asserts not only that the military commission held in Indiana was not authorized by Congress, but that it was not in the power of Congress to authorize it. . . .

We cannot agree to this. . . .

Congress has the power not only to raise and support and govern armies but to declare war. It has, therefore, the power to provide by law for carrying on war. This power necessarily extends to all legislation essential to the prosecution of war with vigor and success, except such as interferes with the command of the forces and the conduct of campaigns. That power and duty belong to the President as commander-in-chief. Both these powers are derived from the Constitution, but neither is defined by that instrument. Their extent must be determined by their nature, and by the principles of our institutions. . . .

Where peace exists the laws of peace must prevail. What we do maintain is, that when the nation is involved in war, and some portions of the country are invaded, and all are exposed to invasion, it is within the power of Congress to determine in what states or districts such great and imminent public danger exists as justifies the authorization of military tribunals for the trial of crimes and offences against the discipline or security of the army or against the public safety.

In Indiana, for example, at the time of the arrest of Milligan and his co-conspirators, it is established by the papers in the record, that the state was a military district, was the theatre of military operations, had been actually invaded, and was constantly threatened with invasion. It appears, also, that a powerful secret association, composed of citizens and others, existed within the state, under military organization, conspiring against the draft, and plotting insurrection, the liberation of the prisoners of war at various depots, the seizure of the state and national arsenals, armed cooperation with the enemy, and war against the national government.

We cannot doubt that, in such a time of public danger, Congress had power, under the Constitution, to provide for the organization of a military commission, and for trial by that commission of persons engaged in this conspiracy. The fact that the Federal courts were open was regarded by Congress as a sufficient reason for not exercising the power; but that fact could not deprive Congress of the right to exercise it. Those courts might be open and undisturbed in the execution of their functions, and yet wholly incompetent to avert threatened danger, or to punish, with adequate promptitude and certainty, the guilty conspirators. . . .

. . . It was for Congress to determine the question of expediency. And Congress did determine it. That body did not see fit to authorize trials by military commission in Indiana, but by the strongest implication prohibited them. With that prohibition we are satisfied, and should have remained silent if the answers to the questions certified had been put on that ground, without denial of the existence of a power which we believe to be constitutional and important to the public safety[.] . . .

We think that the power of Congress, in such times and in such localities, to authorize trials for crimes against the security and safety of the national forces, may be derived from its constitutional authority to raise and support armies and to declare war, if not from its constitutional authority to provide for governing the national forces.

We have no apprehension that this power, under our American system of government, in which all official authority is derived from the people, and exercised under direct responsibility to the people, is more likely to be abused than the power to regulate commerce, or the power to borrow money. And we are unwilling to give our assent by silence to expressions of opinion which seem to us calculated, though not intended, to cripple the constitutional powers of the government, and to augment the public dangers in times of invasion and rebellion.

Mr. Justice WAYNE, Mr. Justice SWAYNE, and Mr. Justice MILLER concur with me in these views.

12. TEXAS V. WHITE ET AL., 74 U.S. 700 (1869)

In 1851, the United States delivered to Texas $10,000,000 in bonds redeemable in 1864 and payable to the state or bearer. In 1862, Texas's legislature repealed a requirement that the state governor endorse the bonds before they could be redeemed and also created a military board to provide for the defense of the state and authorized its use of the bonds to purchase war supplies. After the war, Texas's Reconstruction government sought to recover bonds that had been transferred to George White and several others. The state of Texas, claiming these bonds as its property, sought an injunction to restrain the defendants from receiving payment from the national government and to compel the surrender of the bonds to the state.

The CHIEF JUSTICE [Salmon P. Chase] delivered the opinion of the Court:

. . . It is not to be questioned that this court has original jurisdiction of suits by States against citizens of other States, or that the States entitled to invoke this jurisdiction must be States of the Union. But, it is equally clear that no such jurisdiction has been conferred upon this court of suits by any other political communities than such States.

If, therefore, it is true that the State of Texas was not at the time of filing this bill, or is not now, one of the United States, we have no jurisdiction of this suit, and it is our duty to dismiss it. . . .

The Republic of Texas was admitted into the Union, as a State, on the 27th of December, 1845. By this act the new State, and the people of the new State, were invested with all the rights, and became subject to all the responsibilities and duties of the original States under the Constitution.

From the date of admission, until 1861, the State was represented in the Congress of the United States by her senators and representatives, and her relations as a member of the Union remained unimpaired. In that year, acting upon the theory that the rights of a State under the Constitution might be renounced, and her obligations thrown off at pleasure, Texas undertook to sever the bond thus formed, and to break up her constitutional relations with the United States. . . .

In all respects, so far as the object could be accomplished by ordinances of the convention, by acts of the legislature, and by votes of the citizens, the relations of Texas to the Union were broken up, and new relations to a new government were established for them. . . .

Did Texas, in consequence of these acts, cease to be a State? Or, if not, did the State cease to be a member of the Union? . . .

The Union of the States never was a purely artificial and arbitrary relation. It began among the Colonies, and grew out of common origin, mutual sympathies, kindred principles, similar interests, and geographical relations. It was confirmed and strengthened by the necessities of war, and received definite form, and character, and sanction from the Articles of Confederation. By these

97

the Union was solemnly declared to "be perpetual." And when these Articles were found to be inadequate to the exigencies of the country, the Constitution was ordained "to form a more perfect Union." It is difficult to convey the idea of indissoluble unity more clearly than by these words. What can be indissoluble if a perpetual Union, made more perfect, is not?

But the perpetuity and indissolubility of the Union, by no means implies the loss of distinct and individual existence, or of the right of self-government by the States. . . . Under the Constitution, though the powers of the States were much restricted, still, all powers not delegated to the United States, nor prohibited to the States, are reserved to the States respectively, or to the people. . . . Not only, therefore, can there be no loss of separate and independent autonomy to the States, through their union under the Constitution, but it may be not unreasonably said that the preservation of the States, and the maintenance of their governments, are as much within the design and care of the Constitution as the preservation of the Union and the maintenance of the National government. The Constitution, in all its provisions, looks to an indestructible Union, composed of indestructible States.

When, therefore, Texas became one of the United States, she entered into an indissoluble relation. All the obligations of perpetual union, and all the guaranties of republican government in the Union, attached at once to the State. The act which consummated her admission into the Union was something more than a compact; it was the incorporation of a new member into the political body. And it was final. The union between Texas and the other States was as complete, as perpetual, and as indissoluble as the union between the original States. There was no place for reconsideration, or revocation, except through revolution, or through consent of the States.

Considered therefore as transactions under the Constitution, the ordinance of secession, adopted by the convention and ratified by a majority of the citizens of Texas, and all the acts of her legislature intended to give effect to that ordinance, were absolutely null. They were utterly without operation in law. The obligations of the State, as a member of the Union, and of every citizen of the State, as a citizen of the United States, remained perfect and unimpaired. It certainly follows that the State did not cease to be a State, nor her citizens to be citizens of the Union. If this were otherwise, the State must have become foreign, and her citizens foreigners. The war must have ceased to be a war for the suppression of rebellion, and must have become a war for conquest and subjugation.

Our conclusion therefore is, that Texas continued to be a State, and a State of the Union, notwithstanding the transactions to which we have referred. . . .

. . . [I]t is said that the restriction imposed by the act of 1851 was repealed by the act of 1862. And this is true if the act of 1862 can be regarded as valid. But, was it valid?

The legislature of Texas, at the time of the repeal, constituted one of the departments of a State government, established in hostility to the Constitution of the United States. It cannot be regarded, therefore, in the courts of the United States, as a lawful legislature, or its acts as lawful acts. And, yet, it is an historical fact that the government of Texas, then in full control of the State, was its only actual government; and certainly if Texas had been a separate State, and not one of the United States, the new government, having displaced the regular authority, and having established itself in the customary seats of power, and in the exercise of the ordinary functions of administration, would have constituted, in the strictest sense of the words, a *de facto* government, and its acts, during the period of its existence as such, would be effectual, and, in almost all respects, valid. And, to some extent, this is true of the actual government of Texas, though unlawful and revolutionary, as to the United States.

. . . It may be said, perhaps with sufficient accuracy, that acts necessary to peace and good order among citizens, such for example, as acts sanctioning and protecting marriage and the domestic relations, governing the course of descents, regulating the conveyance and transfer of property, real and personal, and providing remedies for injuries to person and estate, and other similar acts, which would be valid if emanating from a lawful government, must be regarded in general as valid when proceeding from an actual, though unlawful government; and that acts in furtherance or support of rebellion against the United States, or intended to defeat the just rights of citizens, and other acts of like nature, must, in general, be regarded as invalid and void. . . .

That board . . . was organized, not for the defence of the State against a foreign invasion, or for its protection against domestic violence . . . but for the purpose . . . of levying war against the United States. This purpose was, undoubtedly, unlawful, for the acts which it contemplated are, within the express definition of the Constitution, treasonable.

. . . [T]he enlarged powers of the board appear to us to have been conferred in furtherance of its main purpose, of war against the United States, and that the contract, under consideration, even if made in the execution of these enlarged powers, was still a contract in aid of the rebellion, and, therefore, void. . . .

It follows that the title of the State was not divested by the act of the insurgent government in entering into this contract. . . .

On the whole case, therefore, our conclusion is that the State of Texas is entitled to the relief sought by her bill, and a decree must be made accordingly.

CHAPTER 3

AFRICAN AMERICANS, EMANCIPATION, AND MILITARY SERVICE

In contrast to slavery and the doctrine of the *Dred Scott* case that blacks "had no rights which the white man was bound to respect," federal law began to acknowledge the personhood and rights of African Americans during the Civil War. The Confiscation Acts and Emancipation Proclamation sought to remove slaves from their Confederate owners, and the Union armed forces began to enlist African American soldiers in the army. On one hand, blacks saw this as a great moment of hope—as Frederick Douglass pronounced, "Once let the black man get upon his person the brass letters U. S.; let him get an eagle on his button, and a musket on his shoulder, and bullets in his pocket, and there is no power on the earth or under the earth which can deny that he has earned the right of citizenship in the United States."[1] On the other hand, prejudice persisted in the army. Inequality in pay led to low morale and protests among the black troops, but their ultimate success on this issue proved to be one of the first civil rights victories borne by African American action. Due process under the same military code applied to white soldiers marked general courts-martial of black soldiers, creating a model for future equal treatment. In the end, the service of nearly 200,000 black troops created a corps of civil rights leaders.

The following documents are exceptional not only in how they show that black military service affected legal history and constitutional law but because they emphasize the profoundly personal effects of these legal changes. Moreover, the choice to enlist in the armed forces compelled soldiers, families, and communities to consider, often for the first time, the issues of individual allegiance and identity. Few slaves, for example, likely considered before the war whether they owed allegiance to any nation—and if they did, to what nation they owed it. Even free-born blacks in the North found themselves excluded, by Chief Justice Roger Taney's decision in *Dred Scott*, from national citizenship. The choices involved in deciding whether to volunteer for the federal armed forces, or to support the Union in other ways, forced blacks to confront and determine the issue of their personal allegiance.

The black military experience in the Civil War was, in the words of Ira Berlin, a "complex, ambiguous experience," one that included pervasive racism at the same time it advanced black claims to the rights and privileges of citizenship.[2] Moreover, military success or failure defined public support on Republican policies, including emancipation, so that by helping advance the Union cause, blacks also fueled acceptance for an agenda they supported.

For blacks, military service shattered the old order, necessitated the end of slavery, and fueled demands and expectations for rights and inclusion. A process of change and validation took place in the camps of African American soldiers, and blacks asserted their belief that serving in the military affirmed their admission to equality and citizenship. While some blacks may have enlisted for financial motivations or because of conscription by federal agents, many others joined the army for political reasons or grew to understand that their service had broader significance and meaning. Moments that instilled in blacks pride or symbolized their admittedly incomplete integration into the fabric of American society—from flag presentation ceremonies to proving valor on the battlefield, from exchanging slave garb for the soldier's uniform to the exhilaration of helping strike slavery's death blow—generated confidence within African American soldiers that manifested itself in political ways.

By the war's conclusion, a little over 178,000 blacks served in the Union army and between 10,000 and 18,000 more in the Union navy. Success as to some issues, such as the struggle for equal pay, awarded black soldiers with self-affirming victories that acknowledged their change in status and sharpened developing leadership qualities, something that carried forward into a reenergized black convention movement during and after the war. While racism in the army undeniably persisted throughout the Civil War era, this period also presented an opportunity for change upon which blacks eagerly seized. Black military service during the Civil War bore a long-lasting and positive impact. In the 1860s, African American leaders and tens of thousands of black soldiers in blue built on the theme that their service to the Republic affirmed and guaranteed their citizenship. The erosion during Reconstruction and beyond of some of the civil rights victories gained during the Civil War era does not diminish the successes won at that point and the template for future action and argument that blacks molded.

1. An Act to suppress Insurrection, to punish Treason and Rebellion, to seize and confiscate the Property of Rebels, and for other Purposes, 12 Stat. 589 (July 17, 1862) (Second Confiscation Act)

Congress passed the First Confiscation Act during the special summer session of 1861, authorizing seizure of property used to aid the rebellion and permitting discharge of certain slaves on those grounds. Congress recognized Southern blacks as valuable but passive assets of which the Confederacy should be deprived: they did not hold rifles, but they released white men for service by performing the labor necessary for the South's sustenance. While Republicans sought by the Confiscation Act to nudge the identity of slaves from chattel property to human individuals, blacks were not yet seen as worthy of explicit emancipation or military participation at this early stage of the war. The First Confiscation Act simply dismissed slaves from the employment of owners deemed to have forfeited their right to slaves' labor as a result of disloyalty to the United States. Congress passed the stronger Second Confiscation Act the following year.

Be it enacted . . . That every person who shall hereafter commit the crime of treason against the United States, and shall be adjudged guilty thereof, shall suffer death, and all his slaves, if any, shall be declared and made free; or, at the discretion of the court, he shall be imprisoned for not less than five years and fined not less than ten thousand dollars, and all his slaves, if any, shall be declared and made free[.] . . .

SEC. 5. *And be it further enacted*, That, to insure the speedy termination of the present rebellion, it shall be the duty of the President of the United States to cause the seizure of all the estate and property, money, stocks, credits, and effects of the persons hereinafter named in this section, and to apply and use the same and the proceeds thereof for the support of the army of the United States[.] . . .

SEC. 9. *And be it further enacted*, That all slaves of persons who shall hereafter be engaged in rebellion against the government of the United States, or who shall in any way give aid or comfort thereto, escaping from such persons and taking refuge within the lines of the army; and all slaves captured from such persons or deserted by them and coming under the control of the government of the United States; and all slaves of such persons found *on* (or) being within any place occupied by rebel forces and afterwards occupied by the forces of the United States, shall be deemed captives of war, and shall be forever free of their servitude, and not again held as slaves.

SEC. 10. *And be it further enacted*, That no slave escaping into any State, Territory, or the District of Columbia, from any other State, shall be delivered up, or in any way impeded or hindered of his liberty, except for crime, or some offence against the laws, unless the person claiming said fugitive shall first make oath that the person to whom the labor or service of such fugitive is alleged to be due is his lawful owner, and has not borne arms against the United States in the present rebellion, nor in any way given aid and comfort thereto; and no person engaged in the military or naval service of the United States shall . . . assume to decide on the validity of the claim of any person to the service or labor of any other person, or surrender up any such person to the claimant, on pain of being dismissed from the service.

SEC. 11. *And be it further enacted*, That the President of the United States is authorized to employ as many persons of African descent as he may deem necessary and proper for the suppression of this rebellion, and for this purpose he may organize and use them in such manner as he may judge best for the public welfare. . . .

2. AN ACT TO AMEND THE ACT CALLING FORTH THE MILITIA TO EXECUTE THE LAWS OF THE UNION, SUPPRESS INSURRECTIONS, AND REPEL INVASIONS, APPROVED FEBRUARY TWENTY-EIGHT, SEVENTEEN HUNDRED AND NINETY-FIVE, AND THE ACTS AMENDATORY THEREOF, AND FOR OTHER PURPOSES, 12 STAT. 597 (JULY 17, 1862) (ACT AUTHORIZING BLACK ENLISTMENTS)

This act authorized the arming of black men, but it also provided black soldiers with pay unequal to that received by whites. The act also freed any black man who labored for or served in the U.S. armed forces, along with his mother, wife, and children, but only so long as each family member's owner "levied war or has borne arms against the United States, or adhered to their enemies by giving them aid and comfort." On the other hand, the act did not recognize even black soldiers as national citizens.

. . . SEC. 12. *And be it further enacted*, That the President be, and he is hereby, authorized to receive into the service of the United States, for the purpose of constructing intrenchments, or performing camp service, or any other labor, or any military or naval service for which they may be found competent, persons of African descent, and such persons shall be enrolled and organized under such regulations, not inconsistent with the Constitution and laws, as the President may prescribe.

SEC. 13. *And be it further enacted*, That when any man or boy of African descent, who by the laws of any State shall owe service or labor to any person who, during the present rebellion, has levied war or has borne arms against the United States, or adhered to their enemies by giving them aid and comfort, shall render any such service as is provided for in this act, he, his mother and his wife and children, shall forever thereafter be free, any law, usage, or custom whatsoever to the contrary notwithstanding: *Provided*, That the mother, wife and children of such man or boy of African descent shall not be made free by the operation of this act except where such mother, wife or children owe service or labor to some person who, during the present rebellion, has borne arms against the United States or adhered to their enemies by giving them aid and comfort. . . .

SEC. 15. *And be it further enacted*, That all persons who have been or shall be hereafter enrolled in the service of the United States under this act shall receive the pay and rations now allowed by law to soldiers, according to their respective grades: *Provided*, That persons of African descent, who under this law shall be employed, shall receive ten dollars per month and one ration, three dollars of which monthly pay may be in clothing. . . .

3. PRELIMINARY EMANCIPATION PROCLAMATION (SEPTEMBER 22, 1862)

Five days after the battle of Antietam, where the Union army repulsed General Robert E. Lee's invasion of Maryland, President Lincoln issued this preliminary

emancipation proclamation. Lincoln now declared an attack on the root of Southern society as part of prosecuting the Civil War.

I, ABRAHAM LINCOLN, President of the United States of America, and Commander-in-chief of the Army and Navy thereof, do hereby proclaim and declare that hereafter, as heretofore, the war will be prosecuted for the object of practically restoring the constitutional relation between the United States and each of the States, and the people thereof, in which States that relation is or may be suspended or disturbed.

That it is my purpose, upon the next meeting of Congress, to again recommend the adoption of a practical measure tendering pecuniary aid to the free acceptance or rejection of all Slave States, so called, the people whereof may not then be in rebellion against the United States, and which States may then have voluntarily adopted, or thereafter may voluntarily adopt, immediate or gradual abolishment of slavery within their respective limits; and that the effort to colonize persons of African descent, with their consent, upon this continent or elsewhere, with the previously obtained consent of the governments existing there, will be continued.

That on the first day of January, in the year of our Lord one thousand eight hundred and sixty-three, all persons held as slaves within any state or designated part of a State, the people whereof shall then be in rebellion against the United States, shall be then, thenceforward, and forever free; and the Executive Government of the United States, including the military and naval authority thereof, will recognize and maintain the freedom of such persons, and will do no act or acts to repress such persons, or any of them, in any efforts they may make for their actual freedom.

That the Executive will, on the first day of January aforesaid, by Proclamation, designate the States, and parts of States, if any, in which the people thereof respectively shall then be in rebellion against the United States[.] . . .

That attention is hereby called to an act of Congress, entitled "An act to make an additional Article of War," approved March 13, 1862, and which act is in the words and figure following:

"*Be it enacted* . . . That hereafter the following shall be promulgated as an additional article of war for the government of the Army of the United States, and shall be obeyed and observed as such:

"Article—. All officers or persons in the military or naval service of the United States are prohibited from employing any of the forces under their respective commands for the purpose of returning fugitives from service or labor who may have escaped from any persons to whom such service or labor is claimed to be due; and any officer who shall be found guilty by a court-martial of violating this article shall be dismissed from the service." . . .

Also to the ninth and tenth sections of an act entitled "An Act to suppress insurrection, to punish treason and rebellion, to seize and confiscate property of rebels, and for other purposes," approved July 17, 1862 [appearing on page 102 in this book]. . . .

And the Executive will in due time recommend that all citizens of the United States who shall have remained loyal thereto throughout the rebellion shall (upon the restoration of the constitutional relation between the United States and their respective States and people, if that relation shall have been suspended or disturbed) be compensated for all losses by acts of the United States, including the loss of slaves. . . .

4. OPINION OF ATTORNEY GENERAL BATES ON CITIZENSHIP, 10 OP. ATT'Y GEN. 382 (NOVEMBER 1862)

Despite the Supreme Court's exclusionary ruling in *Dred Scott v. Sandford*, Secretary of the Treasury Salmon Chase asked Attorney General Edward Bates for his official opinion as to whether the United States could recognize black men as citizens, making them thus eligible to command American ships, after a federal revenue cutter detained a schooner captained by a black man. Bates rejected Chief Justice Taney's reasoning in the *Dred Scott* case and held that blacks were U.S. citizens as a result of their native birth.

. . . Who is a citizen? What constitutes a citizen of the United States? I have often been pained by the fruitless search in our law books and the records of our courts, for a clear and satisfactory definition of the phrase *citizen of the United States*. I find no such definition, no authoritative establishment of the meaning of the phrase, neither by a course of judicial decisions in our courts, nor by the continued and consentaneous action of the different branches of our political government. For aught I see to the contrary, the subject is now as little understood in its details and elements, and the question as open to argument and to speculative criticism, as it was at the beginning of the Government. Eighty years of practical enjoyment of citizenship, under the Constitution, have not sufficed to teach us either the exact meaning of the word, or the constituent elements of the thing we prize so highly.

. . . [T]here is a very common error to the effect that the right to vote for public officers is one of the constituent elements of American citizenship, the leading faculty indeed of the citizen, the test at once of his legal right, and the sufficient proof of his membership of the body politic. No error can be greater than this, and few more injurious to the right understanding of our constitutions and the actual working of our political governments. . . . Besides those who are excluded specially on account of some personal defect, such as paupers, idiots, lunatics, and men convicted of infamous crimes, and, in some States, soldiers, all females and all minor males are also excluded. And these, in every community, make the majority; and yet, I think, no one will venture to deny that women and children, and lunatics, and even convict felons, may be citizens of the United States.

. . . [I]t is manifest that American citizenship does not necessarily depend upon nor coexist with the legal capacity to hold office and the right of suffrage, either or both of them. The Constitution of the United States, as I have said, does not define citizenship; neither does it declare who may vote, nor who may hold office, except in regard to a few of the highest national functionaries. And the several States, as far as I know, in exercising that power, act independently and without any controlling authority over them, and hence it follows that there is no limit to their power in that particular but their own prudence and discretion; and therefore we are not surprised to find that these faculties of voting and holding office are not uniform in the different States, but are made to depend upon a variety of facts, purely discretionary, such as age, sex, race, color, property, residence in a particular place, and length of residence there.

On this point, then, I conclude that no person in the United States did ever exercise the right of suffrage in virtue of the naked, unassisted fact of citizenship. . . .

In my opinion, the Constitution uses the word citizen only to express the political quality of the individual in his relations to the nation; to declare that he is a member of the body politic, and bound to it by the reciprocal obligation of allegiance on the one side and protection on the other. . . . The phrase, "a citizen of the United States," without addition or qualification, means neither more nor less than a member of the nation. And all such are, politically and legally, equal—the child in the cradle and its father in the Senate, are equally citizens of the United States. And it needs no argument to prove that every citizen of a State is, necessarily, a citizen of the United States; and to me it is equally clear that every citizen of the United States is a citizen of the particular State in which he is domiciled.

And, as to voting and holding office, as that privilege is not essential to citizenship, so the deprivation of it by law is not a deprivation of citizenship. No more so in the case of a negro than in the case of a white woman or child. . . .

It occurs to me that the discussion of this great subject of national citizenship has been much embarrassed and obscured by the fact that it is beset with artificial difficulties extrinsic to its nature, and having little or no relation to its great political and national characteristics. And these difficulties, it seems to me, flow mainly from two sources: First. The existence among us of a large class of people whose physical qualities visibly distinguish them from the mass of our people, and mark a different race, and who, for the most part, are held in bondage. This visible difference and servile connection present difficulties hard to be conquered, for they unavoidably lead to a more complicated system of government, both legislative and administrative, than would be required if all our people were of one race, and undistinguishable by outward signs. And this, without counting the effect upon the opinions, passions, and prejudices of men. Second. The common habit of many of our best and most learned men . . . of testing the political status and governmental relation of our people by standards drawn from the laws and history of ancient Greece and Rome, without . . . taking sufficient account of the organic differences between their governments and ours.

. . . [O]ur Constitution, in speaking of *natural-born citizens*, uses no affirmative language to make them such, but only recognizes and reaffirms the universal principle, common to all nations, and as old as political society, that the people born in a country do constitute the nation, and, as individuals, are *natural* members of the body politic.

If this be a true principle, and I do not doubt it, it follows that every person born in the country is, at the moment of birth, *prima facie* a citizen; and he who would deny it must take upon himself the burden of proving some great disfranchisement strong enough to override the *"natural-born"* right as recognized by the Constitution in terms the most simple and comprehensive, and without any reference to race or color, or any other accidental circumstance. . . .

In every civilized country the individual is *born* to duties and rights, the duty of allegiance and the right to protection; and these are correlative obligations, the one the price of the other, and they constitute the all-sufficient bond of union between the individual and his country; and the country he is born in *is, prima facie, his* country. . . .

I have said that, *prima facie*, every person in this country is born a citizen; and that he who denies it in individual cases assumes the burden of stating the exception to the general rule, and proving the fact which works the disfranchisement. There are but a few exceptions commonly made and urged as disqualifying facts. I lay no stress upon the small and admitted class of the *natural-born* composed of the children of foreign ministers and the like; and—

1. *Slavery*, and whether or no it is legally possible for a slave to be a citizen. On that point I make no question, because it is not within the scope of [Secretary of the Treasury Salmon Chase's] inquiry, and does not concern the person to whom your inquiry relates.

2. *Color.*—It is strenuously insisted by some that "persons of color," though born in the country, are not capable of being citizens of the United States. As far as the Constitution is concerned, this is a naked assumption; for the Constitution contains not one word upon the subject. The exclusion, if it exist, must then rest upon some fundamental fact, which, in the reason and nature of things, is so inconsistent with citizenship that the two cannot coexist in the

same person. Is mere *color* such a fact? Let those who assert it prove that it is so. It has never been so understood nor put into practice in the nation from which we derive our language, laws, and institutions, and our very morals and modes of thought; and, as far as I know, there is not a single nation in Christendom which does not regard the new-found idea with incredulity, if not disgust. What can there be in the mere *color* of a man (we are speaking now not of *race*, but of *color* only) to disqualify him for bearing true and faithful allegiance to his native country, and for demanding the protection of that country? And these two, allegiance and protection, constitute the sum of the duties and rights of a "natural-born citizen of the United States."

3. *Race.*—There are some who, abandoning the untenable objection of *color*, still contend that no person descended from *negroes of the African race* can be a citizen of the United States. Here the objection is not *color* but *race* only. The individual objected to may be of very long descent from African negroes, and may be as white as leprosy, or as the intermixture for many generations with the Caucasian race can make him; still, if he can be traced back to *negroes of the African race*, he cannot, they say, be a citizen of the United States. And why not? The Constitution certainly does not forbid it, but is silent about *race* as it is about *color*. . . .

But it is said that African negroes are a degraded race, and that all who are tainted with that degradation are forever disqualified for the functions of citizenship. I can hardly comprehend the thought of the absolute incompatibility of degradation and citizenship. I thought that they often went together. But, if it be true with regard to races, it seems to me more cogently true with regard to individuals. And, if I be right in this, there are many sorrowful examples in the legislation and practice of various States in the Union to show how low the citizen may be degraded by the combined wisdom and justice of his fellow-citizens. In the early legislation of a number of the States the most humiliating punishments were denounced against persons guilty of certain crimes and misdemeanors—the lash, the pillory, the cropping of the ears, and the branding of the face with an indelible mark of infamy. And yet a lower depth—in several of the States the common punishment of the crime of *vagrancy* was *sale into bondage at public auction*! And yet I have not read that such unfortunates thereby lost their natural-born citizenship, nor that their descendants are doomed to perpetual exclusion and degradation.

I am inclined to think that these objections, as to color and ancestral race, arise entirely from a wrong conception of the nature and qualities of citizenship, and from the loose and unguarded phraseology too often used in the discussion of the subject. . . .

In discussing this subject, it is a misleading error to fail to mark the natural and characteristic distinction between political *rights* and political *powers*. The former belong to all citizens alike, and cohere in the very name and nature of citizenship. The latter—participation in the powers of government by voting and exercising office—does not belong to all citizens alike, nor to any citizen, merely in virtue of citizenship. His *power* always depends upon extraneous facts and superadded qualifications, which facts and qualifications are common to both citizens and aliens. . . .

. . . Every citizen of the United States is a component member of the nation, with rights and duties, under the Constitution and laws of the United States, which cannot be destroyed or abridged by the laws of any particular State. The laws of the State, if they conflict with the laws of the nation, are of no force. The Constitution is plain, beyond cavil, upon this point. . . . And from this I assume that every person who is a citizen of the United States, whether by birth or naturalization, holds his great franchise by the laws of the United States, and above the control of any particular State. Citizenship of the United States is an integral thing, incapable of legal existence in fractional parts. Whoever, then, has that franchise is a whole citizen, and a citizen of the whole nation, and cannot be . . . such citizen in one State and not in another. . . .

. . . [T]he Constitution speaks of *citizens* only, without any reference to their rank, grade, or class, or to the number or magnitude of their rights, privileges, and immunities—*citizens* simply, without an adjective to qualify, enlarge, or diminish their rights and capacities. Therefore, if there be grades and classes of citizens, still the lowest individual of the lowest possible class is a citizen, and as such fills the requirement of the Constitution. . . .

[T]he celebrated case of Scott *vs.* Sandford . . . is sometimes cited as a direct authority against the capacity of free persons of color to be citizens of the United States. That is an entire mistake. The case, as it stands of record, does not determine, nor purport to determine, that question. . . .

. . . [I]t seems [Scott] desired to bring his action in the circuit court of the United States in Missouri; and, to enable him to do that, he had to allege citizenship, because Mr. Sanford, the defendant, was a citizen of New York, and unless the plaintiff were a citizen of Missouri (or some other State,) the national court had no jurisdiction of the case.[3] . . .

In this particular case the Supreme Court did first examine and consider the plea in abatement, and did adjudge that it was a good plea, sufficient to oust the jurisdiction of the circuit court. And hence it follows, as a necessary legal consequence, that whatever was done in the circuit court after the plea in abatement, and touching the merits of the case, was simply void[.] . . .

In this argument I raise no question upon the legal validity of the judgment in Scott *vs.* Sandford. I only insist that the judgment in that case is limited in law . . . to the plea in abatement; and, consequently, that whatever was said in the long course of the case, as reported, (240 pages,) respecting the legal merits of the case, and respecting any supposed legal disability resulting from the mere fact of color . . . was . . . of no authority as a judicial decision. . . .

And now, upon the whole matter, I give it as my opinion that the *free man of color*, mentioned in your letter, if born in the United States, is a citizen of the United States[.] . . .

5. EMANCIPATION PROCLAMATION (JANUARY 1, 1863)

Citing his authority as commander in chief of the armed forces during wartime, Lincoln by the Emancipation Proclamation declared free all slaves located in territory then in rebellion against the United States.

Whereas, on the twentysecond day of September, in the year of our Lord one thousand eight hundred and sixty two, a proclamation was issued by the President of the United States . . . [Lincoln quotes the third and fourth paragraphs of the September 22 proclamation on page 104 in this book.]

Now, therefore I, Abraham Lincoln, President of the United States, by virtue of the power in me vested as Commander-in-Chief, of the Army and Navy of the United States in time of actual armed rebellion against authority and government of the United States, and as a fit and necessary war measure for suppressing said rebellion, do, on this first day of January, in the year of our Lord one thousand eight hundred and sixty three, and in accordance with my purpose so to do publicly proclaimed for the full period of one hundred days, from the day first above mentioned, order and designate as the States and parts of States wherein the people thereof respectively, are this day in rebellion against the United States, the following, towit:

Arkansas, Texas, Louisiana, (except the Parishes of St. Bernard, Plaquemines, Jefferson, St. Johns, St. Charles, St. James[,] Ascension, Assumption, Terrebonne, Lafourche, St. Mary, St. Martin, and Orleans, including the City of New Orleans) Mississippi, Alabama, Florida, Georgia, South Carolina, North Carolina, and Virginia, (except the fortyeight counties designated as West Virginia, and also the counties of Berkley, Accomac, Northampton, Elizabeth City, York, Princess Ann, and Norfolk, including the cities of Norfolk & Portsmouth[)]; and which excepted parts are, for the present, left precisely as if this proclamation were not issued.

And by virtue of the power, and for the purpose aforesaid, I do order and declare that all persons held as slaves within said designated States, and parts of States, are, and henceforward shall be free; and that the Executive government of the United States, including the military and naval authorities thereof, will recognize and maintain the freedom of said persons.

And I hereby enjoin upon the people so declared to be free to abstain from all violence, unless in necessary self-defence; and I recommend to them that, in all cases when allowed, they labor faithfully for reasonable wages.

And I further declare and make known, that such persons of suitable condition, will be received into the armed service of the United States to garrison forts, positions, stations, and other places, and to man vessels of all sorts in said service.

And upon this act, sincerely believed to be an act of justice, warranted by the Constitution, upon military necessity, I invoke the considerate judgment of mankind, and the gracious favor of Almighty God. . . .

6. ABRAHAM LINCOLN TO JAMES C. CONKLING (AUGUST 26, 1863)

James C. Conkling invited Lincoln to speak at a mass meeting of Unionists in Springfield, Illinois. While declining the invitation to attend in person, Lincoln sent the following letter to be read aloud. In it, Lincoln addressed criticism about the Emancipation Proclamation.[4]

. . . You dislike the emancipation proclamation; and, perhaps, would have it retracted. You say it is unconstitutional—I think differently. I think the constitution invests its commander-in-chief, with the law of war, in time of war. The most that can be said, if so much, is, that slaves are property. Is there—has there

Fig. 5. "President Lincoln, Writing the Proclamation of Freedom." Lincoln sits in his study working on the Emancipation Proclamation, his left hand placed on a Bible, which in turn rests on a copy of the Constitution in his lap. A bust of Unionist Andrew Jackson rests on a mantelpiece to Lincoln's right, while a bust of James Buchanan, who did little to stop secessionism, hangs by a rope around its neck behind Lincoln. The scales of justice appear behind Lincoln's right shoulder, while a rail-splitter's maul lies near his feet. (David G. Blythe, 1863; Library of Congress)

Fig. 6. Caricature of Lincoln writing the Emancipation Proclamation, by Adalbert Volck. A Confederate agent, Volck emigrated from Bavaria and settled in Baltimore, where he practiced dentistry and ridiculed Lincoln and other officials and generals in his sketches. Lincoln's foot rests on the Constitution, the Devil holds his inkstand, a personification of Liberty is hooded in the background, and the paintings on the wall depict abolitionist John Brown and the slave revolt in Haiti. (1864; Library of Congress)

ever been—any question that by the law of war, property, both of enemies and friends, may be taken when needed? And is it not needed whenever taking it, helps us, or hurts the enemy? Armies, the world over, destroy enemies' property when they can not use it; and even destroy their own to keep it from the enemy. Civilized belligerents do all in their power to help themselves, or hurt the enemy, except a few things regarded as barbarous or cruel. Among the exceptions are the massacre of vanquished foes, and non-combatants, male and female.

But the proclamation, as law, either is valid, or is not valid. If it is not valid, it needs no retraction. If it is valid, it can not be retracted, any more than the dead can be brought to life. Some of you profess to think its retraction would operate favorably for the Union. Why better *after* the retraction, than *before* the issue? There was more than a year and a half of trial to suppress the rebellion before the proclamation issued, the last one hundred days of which passed under an explicit notice that it was coming, unless averted by those in revolt, returning to their allegiance. The war has certainly progressed as favorably for us, since the issue of the proclamation as before. I know as fully as one can know the opinions of others, that some of the commanders of our armies in the field who have given us our most important successes, believe the emancipation policy, and the use of colored troops, constitute the heaviest blow yet dealt to the rebellion; and that, at least one of those important successes, could not have been achieved when it was, but for the aid of black soldiers. Among the commanders holding these views are some who have never had any affinity with what is called abolitionism, or with republican party politics; but who hold them purely as military opinions. I submit these opinions as being entitled to some weight against the objections, often urged, that emancipation, and arming the blacks, are unwise as military measures, and were not adopted, as such, in good faith.

You say you will not fight to free negroes. Some of them seem willing to fight for you; but, no matter. Fight you, then, exclusively to save the Union. I issued the proclamation on purpose to aid you in saving the Union. Whenever you shall have conquered all resistance to the Union, if I shall urge you to continue fighting, it will be an apt time, then, for you to declare you will not fight to free negroes.

I thought that in your struggle for the Union, to whatever extent the negroes should cease helping the enemy, to that extent it weakened the enemy in his resistance to you. Do you think differently? I thought that whatever negroes can be got to do as soldiers, leaves just so much less for white soldiers to do, in saving the Union. Does it appear otherwise to you? But negroes, like other people, act upon motives. Why should they do any thing for us, if we will do nothing for them? If they stake their lives for us, they must be prompted by the strongest motive—even the promise of freedom. And the promise being made, must be kept.

The signs look better. The Father of Waters again goes unvexed to the sea. Thanks to the great North-West for it. Nor yet wholly to them. Three hundred miles up, they met New-England, Empire, Key-Stone, and Jersey, hewing their way right and left. The Sunny South too, in more colors than one, also lent a hand. On the spot, their part of the history was jotted down in black and white. The job was a great national one; and let none be banned who bore an honorable part in it. And while those who have cleared the great river may well be proud, even that is not all. It is hard to say that anything has been more bravely, and well done, than at Antietam, Murfreesboro, Gettysburg, and on many fields of lesser note. Nor must Uncle Sam's Web-feet be forgotten. At all the watery margins they have been present. Not only on the deep sea, the broad bay, and the rapid river, but also up the narrow muddy bayou, and wherever the ground was a little damp, they have been, and made their tracks. Thanks to all. For the great republic—for the principle it lives by, and keeps alive—for man's vast future,—thanks to all. . . .

Fig. 7. "Breaking that 'Backbone.'" Confederate president Jefferson Davis holds the dog-like monster of Rebellion beneath a sign that says it has a backbone that cannot be broken. Union generals Henry W. Halleck and George B. McClellan swing in unison hammers marked "Skill" and "Strategy," while Secretary of War Edwin Stanton waits holding a hammer labeled "Draft." Behind them, a dejected man holds a tiny hammer labeled "Compromise." On the far right, President Abraham Lincoln converses with Stanton while holding an axe labeled "Emancipation Proclamation." Stanton: "Halleck may use his skill and Mac his strategy, but this draft will do the business." Lincoln: "You can try him with that, but I'm afraid this axe of mine is the only thing that will fetch him." (Currier & Ives, 1862 or 1863; Library of Congress)

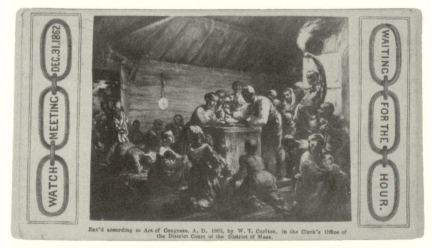

Fig. 8. Carte de visite of the William Tolman Carleton painting *Waiting for the Hour*, depicting African American men, women, and children eagerly gathered on December 31, 1862, around a man with a watch, waiting for the Emancipation Proclamation to take effect. (Library of Congress)

7. Speech of Frederick Douglass from *Addresses of the Hon. W. D. Kelley, Miss Anna E. Dickenson, and Mr. Frederick Douglass, at a Mass Meeting, Held at National Hall, Philadelphia, July 6, 1863, for the Promotion of Colored Enlistments* (July 6, 1863)

Blacks in the North immediately volunteered to serve as soldiers when the Civil War broke out, but white Northerners rejected their offer. It therefore remained to be seen whether blacks would enlist enthusiastically in the armed forces once Congress passed legislation authorizing them to serve. They did. In this rousing recruitment speech, Frederick Douglass asked blacks to forget about past strictures and take heart at changes already taking place. Douglass also called on black men to affirm their American citizenship by grasping the Union musket.

. . . There are those among us who say they are in favor of taking a hand in this tremendous war, but they add they wish to do so on terms of equality with white men. They say if they enter the service, endure all the hardships, perils and suffering—if they make bare their breasts, and with strong arms and courageous hearts confront rebel cannons, and wring victory from the jaws of death, they should have the same pay, the same rations, the same bounty and the same favorable conditions every way afforded to other men.

I shall not oppose this view. There is something deep down in the soul of every man present which assents to the justice of the claim thus made, and honors the manhood and self-respect which insists upon it. (Applause.)[5] I say at once, in peace and in war, I am content with nothing for the black man short of equal and exact justice. The only question I have, and the point at which I differ from those who refuse to enlist, is whether the colored man is more likely to obtain justice and equality while refusing to assist in putting down this tremendous rebellion than he would be if he should promptly, generously and earnestly give his hand and heart to the salvation of the country in this its day of calamity and peril. Nothing can be more plain, nothing more certain than that the speediest and best possible way open to us to manhood, equal rights and elevation, is that we enter this service. For my own part, I hold that if the Government of the United States offered nothing more, as an inducement to colored men to enlist, than bare subsistence and arms, considering the moral effect of compliance upon ourselves, it would be the wisest and best thing for us to enlist. (Applause.) There is something ennobling in the possession of arms, and we of all other people in the world stand in need of their ennobling influence.

. . . There are two governments struggling now for possession of and endeavoring to bear rule over the United States[.] . . . These two governments are to-day face to face, confronting each other with vast armies, and grappling each other upon many a bloody field, north and south, on the banks of the Mississippi, and under the shadows of the Alleghenies. Now, the question for every colored man is, or ought to be, what attitude is assumed by these respective governments and armies towards the rights and liberties of the colored race in this country; which is for us, and which is against us! (Cries of That's the question.)

Now, I think there can be no doubt as to the attitude of the Richmond or confederate government. . . . [Its] purpose is nothing more nor less than to make the slavery of the African race universal and perpetual on this continent. . . . [I]f the Abolitionists are the cause of the war, they are the cause of it only because they have sought the abolition of slavery. View it in any way you please, therefore, the rebels are fighting for the existence of slavery—they are fighting for the privilege, the horrid privilege, of sundering the dearest ties of human nature—of trafficking in slaves and the souls of men—for the ghastly privilege of scourging women and selling innocent children. (Cries of That's true.)

. . . [The Confederate government] is based upon the idea that colored men are an inferior race, who may be enslaved and plundered forever and to the heart's content of any men of different complexion, while the Federal Government recognizes the natural and fundamental equality of all men. (Applause.)

I say, again, we all know that this Jefferson Davis government holds out to us nothing but fetters, chains, auction blocks, bludgeons, branding-irons, and eternal slavery and degradation. If it triumphs in this contest, woe, woe, ten thousand woes, to the black man! Such of us as are free, in all the likelihoods of the case, would be given over to the most excruciating tortures, while the last hope of the long-crushed bondman would be extinguished forever. (Sensation.)

Now, what is the attitude of the Washington government toward the colored race? What reasons have we to desire its triumph in the present contest? Mind, I do not ask what was its attitude towards us before this bloody rebellion broke out. I do not ask what was its disposition when it was controlled by the very men who are now fighting to destroy it when they could no longer control it. . . .

I do not ask what was the attitude of this government when many of the officers and men who had undertaken to defend it, openly threatened to throw down their arms and leave the service if men of color should step forward to defend it, and be invested with the dignity of soldiers. Moreover, I do not ask what was the position of this government when our loyal camps were made slave hunting grounds, and United States officers performed the disgusting duty of slave dogs to hunt down slaves for rebel masters. These were all dark and terrible days for the republic. I do not ask you about the dead past. I bring you to the living present. Events more mighty than men, eternal Providence, all-wise and all-controlling, have placed us in new relations to the government and the government to us. What that government is to us to-day, and what it will be to-morrow, is made evident by a very few facts. Look at them, colored men. Slavery in the District of Columbia is abolished forever; slavery in all the territories of the United States is abolished forever; the foreign slave trade, with its ten thousand revolting abominations, is rendered impossible; slavery in ten States of the Union is abolished forever; slavery in the five remaining States is as certain to follow the same fate as the night is to follow the day. The independence of Hayti is recognized; her Minister sits beside our Prime Minister, Mr. Seward, and dines at his table in Washington, while colored men are excluded from the cars in Philadelphia; showing that a black man's complexion in Washington, in the presence of the Federal Government, is less offensive than in the city of brotherly love. Citizenship is no longer denied us under this government.

Under the interpretation of our rights by Attorney General Bates, we are American citizens. We can import goods, own and sail ships, and travel in foreign countries with American passports in our pockets; and now . . . the President at Washington, the Cabinet and the Congress, the generals commanding and the whole army of the nation unite in giving us one thunderous welcome to share with them in the honor and glory of suppressing treason and upholding the star-spangled banner. The revolution is tremendous, and it becomes us as wise men to recognize the change, and to shape our action accordingly. (Cheers and cries of We will.)

I hold that the Federal government was never, in its essence, anything but an anti-slavery government. Abolish slavery to-morrow, and not a sentence or syllable of the Constitution need be altered. It was purposely so framed as to give no claim, no sanction to the claim of property in man. If in its origin slavery had any relation to the government, it was only as the scaffolding to the magnificent structure, to be removed as soon as the building was completed. There is in the Constitution no East, no West, no North, no South, no black, no white, no slave, no slaveholder, but all are citizens who are of American birth.

Such is the government, fellow citizens, you are now called upon to uphold with your arms. Such is the government you are called upon to co-operate with in burying rebellion and slavery in a common grave. (Applause.) Never since the world began was a better chance offered to a long enslaved and oppressed people. The opportunity is given us to be men. With one courageous resolution we may blot out the hand-writing of ages against us. Once let the black man get upon his person the brass letters U. S.; let him get an eagle on his button, and a musket on his shoulder, and bullets in his pocket, and there is no power on the earth or under the earth which can deny that he has earned the right of citizenship in the United States. . . .

Do not flatter yourselves, my friends, that you are more important to the government than the government is to you. You stand but as the plank to the ship. This rebellion can be put down without your help. Slavery can be abolished by white men; but liberty so won for the black man, while it may leave him an object of pity, can never make him an object of respect.

. . . [T]his is no time for hesitation. Do you say you want the same pay that white men get? I believe that the justice and magnanimity of your country will speedily grant it. But will you be over nice about this manner? Do you get as good wages now as white men get by staying out of the service? Don't you work for less every day than white men get? You know you do. Do I hear you say you want black officers? Very well, and I have not the slightest doubt that in the progress of this war we shall see black officers, black colonels, and generals even. But is it not ridiculous in us in all at once refusing to be commanded by white men in time of war, when we are everywhere commanded by white men in time of peace? . . .

Do I hear you say you offered your services to Pennsylvania and were refused? I know it. But what of that? The State is not more than the nation. The greater includes the lesser. Because the State refuses, you should all the more readily turn to the United States. (Applause.) When the children fall out, they should refer their quarrel to the parent. "You came unto your own, and your own received you not." But the broad gates of the United States stand open night and day. Citizenship in the United States will, in the end, secure your citizenship in the State.

Figs. 9 and 10. Hubbard Pryor as a slave and as a private in the 44th U.S. Colored Infantry, showing the transformative moment that took place for many blacks when they joined the Union army. (1864, National Archives)

Young men of Philadelphia, you are without excuse. The hour has arrived, and your place is in the Union army. Remember that the musket—the United States musket with its bayonet of steel—is better than all mere parchment guarantees of liberty. In your hands that musket means liberty; and should your constitutional right at the close of this war be denied, which, in the nature of things, it cannot be, your brethren are safe while you have a Constitution which proclaims your right to keep and bear arms. (Immense cheering.)

Fig. 11. Black artist David Bustill Bowser designed the six-foot-square silk colors that black civilians donated and presented to the 6th U.S. Colored Infantry in Philadelphia in the late summer of 1863. A female personification of Liberty holds aloft a flag and exhorts a black soldier, armed and sharply uniformed, while a black child applauds in the background. (Library of Congress)

8. Letter of Black Soldier James Henry Gooding to Abraham Lincoln Protesting Unequal Pay (September 28, 1863) (National Archives)

Discrimination in pay seriously lowered morale among African American troops and served as a badge of inferiority, yet blacks in the field seized upon this issue to articulate their vision of a different constitutional regime that respected their equality. The War Department originally intended to pay black soldiers the same as whites, $13 a month with a $3.50 clothing allowance, and with higher salaries for noncommissioned officers. Despite his Republican credentials, however, Solicitor William Whiting reviewed the Act of July 17, 1862, which authorized the enlistment of blacks, and held that black soldiers stood entitled to receive only the pay contemplated by the act for black laborers (the provision read, "That all persons who have been or shall be hereafter enrolled in the service of the United States under this act shall receive the pay and rations now allowed by law to soldiers, according to their respective grades: *Provided*, That persons of African descent, who under this law shall be employed, shall receive ten dollars per month and one ration, three dollars of which monthly pay may be in clothing"). On June 4, 1863, the federal government changed its policy so that black troops would receive ten dollars a month in pay, regardless of rank, with an additional three dollars deducted as a clothing allowance. Shortly after the men of the 54th Massachusetts Volunteer Infantry charged Fort Wagner and heard of the atrocities committed against African Americans during the New York City Draft Riot, they learned of reduction in their pay.

As the ideal of equality generated by putting on the blue uniform clashed with the contradiction of unequal pay, many black soldiers refused to accept less money than was their due, even where this created tremendous hardship for families at home. Some black soldiers felt emboldened to write directly to high-ranking officials to assert an impatient demand for change. Other black soldiers mutinied. While many white officers understood the legitimate basis of these mutineers' protests and tried to avoid imposing capital punishment on them (technically, the refusal to accept pay itself fell within the rubric of mutiny as defined by the Articles of War), some black soldiers faced execution for their impatient demand for equality. These soldiers revealed the paradox of the black military experience: rejecting the unequal treatment they experienced in not being paid the same as their white comrades, they were nonetheless tried pursuant to the same code of military discipline and standards of due process afforded white soldiers.

Camp of 54th Mass Colored Regt
Morris Island. Dept of the South. Sept 28th, 1863.
Your Excelency, Abraham Lincoln:

Your Excelency will pardon the presumtion of an humble individual like myself, in addressig you, but the earnest Solicitation of my Comrades in Arms, besides the genuine interest felt by myself in the matter is my excuse, for placing before the Executive head of the Nation our Common Grievance: On the 6th of the last Month, the Paymaster of the department informed us, that if we would decide to recieve the sum of $10 (ten dollars) per month, he would come and pay us that sum, but, that, on the sitting of Congress, the Regt would, in his opinion, be *allowed* the other 3 (three.) . . . Now the main question is, Are we *Soldiers*, or are we *Labourers*[?] We are fully armed, and equipped, have done all the various Duties pertaining to a Soldier[']s life, have conducted ourselves to the complete satisfaction of General Officers, who were if any[thing], prejudiced *against* us, but who now accord us all the encouragement, and honour due us; have shared the perils, and Labour, of Reducing the first stronghold that flaunted a Traitor Flag; and more, Mr. President. Today the Anglo Saxon Mother, Wife, or Sister are not alone, in tears for departed Sons, Husbands and Brothers. The patient, Trusting Descendants of Afric's Clime, have dyed the ground with blood, in defense of the Union, and Democracy. Men too your Excellency, who know in a measure the cruelties of the Iron heel of oppression, which in years gone by, the very Power, their blood is now being spilled to maintain, ever ground them to the dust. But When the war trumpet sounded o'er the land, when men knew not the Friend from the Traitor, the Black man laid his life at the Altar of the Nation,—and he was refused. When the arms of the Union were beaten, in the first year of the War, And the Executive called [for] more food for its ravaging maw, again the black man begged the privilege of Aiding his Country in her need, to be again refused. And now, he is in the War; and how has he conducted himself? Let their dusky forms rise up, out [of] the mires of James Island, and give the answer. Let the rich mould around Wagner[']s parapets be upturned, and there will be found an Eloquent answer. Obedient and patient, and Solid as a wall are they. All we lack, is a paler hue, and a better acquaintance with the Alphabet. Now your Excellency, We have done a Soldier[']s Duty. Why cant we have a Soldier[']s pay? You caution the Rebel Chieftain, that the United States knows no distinction, in her Soldiers; She insists on having all her Soldiers, of whatever creed or Color, to be treated according to the usages of War. Now if the United States exacts uniformity of treatment of her Soldiers from the Insurgents, would it not be well, and consistent, to set the example herself by paying all her *Soldiers* alike? We of this Regt were not enlisted under any "contraband" act. But we do not wish to be understood as rating our Service of more Value to the Government than the service of the exslave. Their Service *is* undoubtedly worth much to the Nation, but Congress made express provision touching their case, as slaves freed by military necessity, and assuming the Government to be their temporary Gaurdian;—Not so with us. Freemen by birth, and consequently, having the advantage of *thinking* and acting for ourselves, so far as the Laws would allow us. We do not consider ourselves fit subject for the Contraband act. We appeal to you, Sir, as the Executive of the Nation, to have us justly Dealt

with. The Regt. do pray that they be assured their service will be fairly appreci-
ated by paying them as American *Soldiers*, not as menial hierlings. Black men
you may well know, are poor; three dollars per month, for a year, will suply
their needy Wives, and little ones, with fuel. If you, as Chief Magistrate of the
Nation, will assure us, of our whole pay. We are content our Patriotism, our
enthusiasm will have a new impetus, to exert our energy more and more to aid
Our Country. Not that our hearts ever flagged in Devotion, spite the evident
apathy displayed in our behalf, but We feel as though our Country spurned us,
now we are sworn to serve her.

Please give this a moment's attention[.]

> Corporal James Henry Gooding
> Co. C, 54th Mass. Regt
> Morris Island S.C.

THE GALLANT CHARGE OF THE FIFTY FOURTH MASSACHUSETTS (COLORED) REGIMENT.
On the Rebel works at Fort Wagner, Morris Island near Charleston. July 18. 1863, and death of Colonel Rob.ʳ G. Shaw.

Fig. 12. "The Gallant Charge of the Fifty Fourth Massachusetts (Colored) Regiment." This
romanticized depiction of combat shows black soldiers valiantly charging the ramparts of
Fort Wagner and fighting against Confederate troops as men and as equals. Shortly after
the men of the 54th Massachusetts charged Fort Wagner and heard of the atrocities committed against African Americans during the New York City Draft Riot, both of which
occurred in mid-July 1863, they learned of the reduction in their pay. (Currier & Ives, c.
1863; Library of Congress)

9. Petition of Seventy-four Members of the Black 55th Massachusetts to Lincoln Threatening Mutiny in Protest of Unequal Pay (July 16, 1864) (National Archives)

Camp 55th Massachusetts Volunteer Infantry
Folly island South Carolina
July 16th 1864

To The President of the United States

Sir We The Members of Co D of the 55th Massachusetts vols Call the attention of your Excellency to our case

1st First We wase enlisted under the act of Congress of July 18.61 Placing the officers non Commissioned officers & Privates of the volunteer forces in all Respects as to Pay on the footing of Similar Corps of the Regular Army[.] 2nd We Have Been in the Field now thirteen months & a Great many yet longer We Have Recieved no Pay & Have Been offered only Seven Dollars Pr month Which the Paymaster Has said was all He Had ever Been authorized to Pay Colored Troops this was not acording to our enlistment—Consequently—We Refused the Money the Commonwealht of Massechusetts then Passed an act to make up all Deficienceys which the general Government Refused To Pay But this We Could not Recieve as The Troops in the general Service are not Paid Partly By Government & Partly By State 3rd that to us money is no object—we came to fight For Liberty justice & Equality. These are gifts we Prise more Highly than Gold For these We Left our Homes our Familys Friends & Relatives most Dear to take as it ware our Lives in our Hands To Do Battle for God & Liberty

4th after the elaps of over thirteen months spent cheerfully & willingly Doing our Duty most faithfuly in the Trenches Fatiegue Duty in camp and Conspicious valor & endurence in Battle as our Past History will Show

P 5th therefore we Deem these sufficient Reasons for Demanding our Pay from the Date of our enlisment & our imediate Discharge Having Been enlisted under False Prentence as the Past History of the Company will Prove

6th Be it further Resolved that if imediate Steps are not takened to Relieve us we will Resort to more stringent mesures

We Have the Honor to Remin your Obedint Servants The Members of Co D
[seventy-four signatures]

10. Congressional Debate Regarding Equalization of African American Soldiers' Pay (*Congressional Globe*, 38th Congress, 1st Session, 1864)

In the light of black protest, as well as petitions from sympathetic whites, Congress in February 1864 turned to the issue of equalizing pay for black troops.

February 5, 1864:

Mr. FESSENDEN. As these soldiers enlisted to serve for a given sum, I wish simply to inquire what propriety there is in our going back and paying them this increase for services already rendered. So far as putting these men on the same footing with other soldiers is concerned, I have always been in favor of it, and shall favor it now; but I think we ought to be a little careful in our expenditures. We must not consider that the Treasury can meet everything. If there is any particular reason for going back and paying them this increase for the time they have been in the service I should like to hear it.

Mr. WILSON. I think as an act of justice that this bill should be retrospective; in fact I have no doubt about it. Many of these men were assured when they entered the service they would receive the same compensation as other soldiers. The first colored regiment in the country was raised in South Carolina under an express order that they should have the same pay as other troops, and the first pay they received was the same pay; but since that time it has been changed.

Now, sir, the gross injustice that has been done by the country toward these men I think ought to be corrected. I have letters on this subject from several colonels in the field, Colonel Hallowell, of the Massachusetts fifty-fourth; Colonel Hartwell, of the Massachusetts fifty-fifth; and Colonel Tilghman, of one of the United States colored regiments. Colonel Tilghman says that some of the men in his regiment enlisted with the expectation and understanding that they were to have the same compensation as other troops. The raising of the Massachusetts fifty-fourth was commenced on the 10th day of last February, and it went into the service on the 28th day of May. They have never received a dollar, and will not receive a dollar, because they were promised the same compensation as other troops, and they demand it as a right. The Legislature of the State has authorized them to be paid by the State, and they have declined to take pay from the State. They say they were promised to be put on the same footing with other troops; that they were enlisted under the act of 1861, and they do not choose to take it from the State.

Mr. POMEROY. . . . I think the Treasury of the United States can stand justice, and I do not think that we do well in legislating any injustice anywhere. . . .

I can see very well why the confederates would not recognize our colored soldiers: because we did not recognize them. I can see why they would not exchange them: because we have never put them on a level with our other soldiers. We ourselves are measurably responsible for that.

February 10, 1864:

Mr. LANE, of Indiana. . . . We promised them ten dollars a month. We have paid them ten dollars a month.

But gentlemen say they were deceived by the representations of their recruiting officers. The recruiting officers were the agents of the General Government. If they transcended their power and made representations that the law did not authorize, they, as agents, are legally liable, but the principal, never.

But I cannot see any injustice or any possible breach of good faith if we pay these soldiers all that we promised to pay them; and I think we have paid them an abundant compensation. They do not deserve to be paid as much as white soldiers. Many of our white soldiers left a profitable business at home, by which they were able to make money. These colored soldiers are refugees from the house of bondage, who have never heretofore got one cent of pay, and ten dollars is more compensation to them than thirteen dollars to a white soldier. They are fighting for a higher boon than money. They are fighting for their freedom. They were receiving not one cent at the time we agreed to pay them ten dollars a month; and I cannot conceive of any possible injustice or hardship in the Government holding them to their bargain.

April 22, 1864:

Mr. WILSON. I have another amendment which I wish to add to the bill as an additional section: [Wilson introduced language from a bill passed by the Senate providing, among other things, that all blacks in the military service "shall receive the same uniform, clothing, arms, equipments, camp equipage, rations, medical and hospital attendance, pay, and emoluments other than bounty, as other soldiers of the regular or volunteer forces of like arm of the service, from and after the 1st day if January, 1864; and that every person of color who shall hereafter be mustered into the service shall receive such sums in bounty as the President shall order in the different States and parts of the United States, not exceeding $100," and that all blacks in the military service "shall be entitled to receive the pay and clothing allowed by law to other volunteers in the service from the date of their muster into the service: *Provided*, That the same shall have been pledged or promised to them by any officer or person who, in making such pledge or promise acted by authority of the War Department." Because the House had not yet acted on the measure, Wilson incorporated the bill into a pending appropriations measure.]

... The ... amendment [comprises] the identical provisions of the bill which passed the Senate by a nearly unanimous vote seven weeks ago, to equalize the pay of troops in the military service of the United States. That bill, however, has not been acted upon by the House of Representatives, and the interests of the country are suffering on account of the non-action of the House. Major Foster, to whom is committed the organization of colored troops, informed me to-day that the enlistment of colored troops in the northern States has nearly ceased. The pressing needs of the country demand the enlistment of all the men we can obtain, black or white. Surely the country cannot expect that colored men will enlist in a service so hazardous to their liberty and their lives for *seven* dollars per month, when they can earn three or four times that amount in the peaceful and safe avocations of life. Intelligence comes to us from various sections of the country that some colored regiments in the field are in a state of discontent bordering on insubordination and mutiny on account of the treatment they have received on the part of the Government concerning their pay. Some of these regiments were enlisted under the solemn pledges of officers of the Government that they should receive the same compensation as white troops. Other regiments have been organized during the past six months with assurances of men in whom they had a right to confide that the Congress of the United States would promptly place them on an equality with other soldiers. Thousands of colored men have entered the service of the country under the plighted faith of officers of the Government, or on the assurances of gentlemen, of influence and character, that the Government would equalize the pay, and put them on an equality with other defenders of the Republic. This long delay of Congress to do justice to men who are bravely periling liberty and life for a Government that cannot or does not protect them against rebel barbarities cannot but depress their spirits and imbitter their feelings, and thereby impair the discipline and diminish the power of colored regiments. I was told yesterday by Mr. Webster, of Philadelphia, who has just returned from General Butler's department, that he found some of the colored regiments in a state of discontent tending to insubordination and mutiny. . . .

Some of the regiments first raised in South Carolina were promised and received thirteen dollars per month, but that promise has not been kept, and they are now paid only seven dollars per month. The discontent in these regiments has become so great that a mutiny broke out in the third South Carolina volunteers, and the leader of it, who was a sergeant, has been shot for mutiny, and others are under arrest and they too may be tried and shot for violation of discipline, impelled by a burning sense of our injustice. I am informed by a gentleman from Ohio of intelligence and character, who has just returned from General Butler's department, that the tenth United States colored infantry was paid on the day the intelligence was received of the bloody massacre at Fort Pillow. Such was the intense excitement growing out of the intelligence of that brutal butchery, combined with the fact that they received seven dollars per month from the hand of the same paymaster that had paid thirteen dollars per month to white soldiers, that two companies were only restrained by the influence of their officers from breaking out into open mutiny.

Sir, we have raised about eighty thousand colored troops. They are obedient, faithful, brave. At Port Hudson, Milliken's Bend, Wagner, Olustee, Paducah, Fort Pillow, everywhere wherever they have been called to meet the enemies of our country, they have proved their courage, constancy, and devotion. . . . These heroic men have toiled for the country, fought for the country, bled for the country, suffered for the country, and died for the country that has broken its plighted faith to them.

Sir, can we, dare we hope for the blessing of Heaven upon our cause while we perpetrate these wrongs or suffer them to remain unredressed? Can we demand that the rebels shall give to our colored soldiers the rights of civilized warfare while we refuse to them equality of rights? Can we redress the brutal and bloody butchery at Fort Pillow while we continue this injustice? Sir, the whole country is horrified at the barbarities perpetrated by the rebels upon our colored soldiers. The civilized world will be shocked as it reads of the bloody butchery at Fort Pillow. But, sir, I feel that the nation is doing a wrong to the colored soldiers hardly less wicked than the wrongs perpetrated upon them by slaveholding traitors. Let us right their wrongs. Let the Senate adopt this amendment. The issue will then be distinctly presented to the House of Representatives, and the Representatives of the people will, I am confident, promptly concur in righting the grievous wrongs of our country's heroic defenders.

In the end, an 1864 appropriations bill held that all blacks mustered into the armed forces were entitled to the same equipment and pay dating to January 1, 1864; all persons enlisted under the October 17, 1863, call for volunteers stood entitled to the same bounty without regard to color; and all blacks free as of April 19, 1861, who enlisted in the armed services stood entitled to the same pay, bounty, and clothing from the time of their enlistment. Thus, even in the moment of their success, a final wrinkle caused black soldiers to balk: in order to receive equal pay, the law required some blacks to swear that they were free on April 19, 1861, the day the Union first called on states to provide volunteer troops. Colonel Edward N. Hallowell of the 54th Massachusetts devised a "Quaker Oath" whereby each soldier could swear that "no man had the right to demand unrequited labor" of them so that either slave or free could answer in the affirmative. In prevailing on the issue of pay, blacks validated their new status and rejected notions of caste in citizenship, an especially impressive accomplishment considering the minimal political influence blacks held at the time.

11. Transcripts of Three Civil War Courts-Martial of African American Soldiers (Sampson Goliah, Wallace Baker, and Samuel Green)

Courts-martial records allow insight into the lives and voices of black soldiers on both a public and personal level and also reveal how courts-martial became an important forum for debate at a moment when blacks and whites struggled with the fluid contours of the changing status of African Americans. Both in revolting and in defending themselves against subsequent charges, black soldiers refuted their past

as slaves to claim rights as freedmen, soldiers, and citizens. Some cases show the extent to which blacks protested perceived inequities committed at the hands of the government, particularly unequal pay and arbitrary treatment by superior officers. These cases reflect black anger aimed at white discrimination but also demonstrate how the empowerment some African Americans felt upon donning the Union blue uniform led them to rebel against further injustice. These black soldiers demanded, sometimes at the cost of their lives, equal treatment and rights, and in so doing, many of those executed for mutiny made an argument that blacks had an equal place in the polity and in the army that protected it. In this way, African American mutineers embraced an alternative legal order, seeking to change laws distinguishing between whites and blacks and to bring official law and practices into conformity with their vision. These soldiers situated themselves as U.S. citizens by opposing discrimination, defying legal precedents that failed to acknowledge their equality, and actively supporting their interpretation of legal meanings and practices, even if the law did not yet recognize them as American citizens. African Americans thus turned the court into an important junction on the road to freedom and citizenship, even when it punished those who violated military law.

Moreover, while black soldiers likely suffered more frequent instances of arbitrary abuse at the hands of white regimental officers than white soldiers endured, and endemic racism in the Union army tainted the disciplinary process on other levels, the records reveal that officers on general court-martial panels wrestled with providing fair judicial process to black defendants while maintaining necessary discipline so that African American soldiers received equal treatment and justice in cases involving capital-level crimes. While most mutineers' protests were well grounded in legitimate grievances—and for that reason, some may argue with merit that by definition they were unfairly punished—that did not change the gravity of their crime in the eyes of military law. Nonetheless, in many cases, authorities consciously tried to avoid imposition of the death penalty, even where the Articles of War called for it.

Most of the general courts-martial transcripts are marked by the businesslike conduct of officers determined to do their duty as members of the court.[6] Black or white, no prisoner could be sentenced to death by court-martial except by concurrence of two-thirds of its members. While a few procedural irregularities exist in some cases, these deviations likely reflect the fact that soldiers, not attorneys, conducted these trials. Across the board in the extant files, defendants had the opportunity to object to members of the court and, whether they took advantage of it or not, were advised that they had the right to representation. African American defendants who declined counsel still had the right to question white witnesses, while black testimony, even that offered by slaves, frequently played a prominent role in their trials. While judge advocates and defense counsels sometimes made race an issue, or witnesses used it as an identifying factor, the records do not indicate altered procedure or standards because of a defendant's race. Where crimes occurred at night, panels sought to establish if sufficient light existed for witnesses to establish identification accurately.

In June 1864, before Lincoln signed legislation on July 4, 1864, opening federal courts to black witnesses, the judge advocate's office affirmed that blacks could testify before military courts regardless of any disqualifying laws in the state in which the court sat. Some proceedings relied exclusively on African American testimony, affirming blacks' right to testify and familiarizing these soldier-witnesses with the legal process. Astonishingly, both free blacks and emancipated slaves experienced something formerly unavailable to almost all of them: the privilege of testifying against white defendants. Thus, black soldiers and civilians offered testimony against white officers and enlisted men who engaged in improper recruitment practices or committed financial crimes against soldiers. Black soldiers enjoyed rights and opportunities previously denied them in civilian life because as soldiers they were entitled to uniform application of the Articles of War and other statutes concerning military discipline and trial. Rather than devise a separate scheme to address military discipline within the United States Colored Troops, in this regard the federal government treated blacks on par with white soldiers from the beginning of African American army service during the Civil War.

Sampson Goliah Court-Martial, 55th Massachusetts Infantry (National Archives)

On April 19, 1864, a mutiny erupted aboard a steamer transporting the 55th Massachusetts Infantry between Hilton Head and Folly Island, South Carolina, as Sampson Goliah defied white officers, freed himself from being tied to the ship's rigging while other soldiers revolted, fought with a lieutenant, and took the officer's pistol. At Goliah's court-martial, two white officers cited the pay issue as the salient cause of tension within the unit, and in a successful plea to spare Goliah from execution, the prosecutor did the same. As other white officers came to realize, black soldiers mutinied not out of nervous energy generated by camp malaise or the privations of combat service but as political action undertaken by men who felt newly entitled to equality by their wearing of the uniform.

In Camp South End Folly Island S.C.
May 7th 1864,
10, oclock A.M.

. . . The Court then proceeded to the trial of private *Sampson Goliah* Company "A" 55th Regiment Mass. Vols., who was called into Court; and having heard the order read convening the Court, was asked if he had any objection to any member named in the order; to this he replied in the negative. The Court and Judge Advocate were then duly sworn in the presence of the prisoner and the prisoner . . . was arraigned on the following Charge and specifications

Charge Mutiny

Specification 1st In this that he private Sampson Goliah Co. "A" 55 Mass. Vols. when ordered by his Superior Officer 2d Lt. J. A. Bean, 55th Regt Mass. Vols, to keep quiet did refuse to obey the same, this on board U.S. Steam Transport "Sentinel" between Hilton Head S.C. and Folly Island S.C. on or about the evening of the 19th day of April 1864,

Specification 2d In this that he private Sampson Goliah . . . when ordered by his Superior Offic[e]r, Captain William Nutt, 55th Regt. Mass. Vols., to keep quiet did refuse to obey saying, "I wont keep quiet for Captain Nutt, or any other God damn white man" or words to that effect, this on board U.S. Steam Transport "Sentinel" . . . the 19th Day of April 1864,

Specification 3rd In this, that he private Sampson Goliah . . . when brought before his commanding Officer Col. A. S. Hartwell, Commanding 55th Mass. Vols., and by him ordered to give his name, did refuse to obey the same, this on board U.S. Steam Transport "Sentinel" . . . the 19th day of April 1864,

Specification 4th In this that he private Sampson Goliah . . . after having been tied to the rigging for his mutinous conduct and having been taken therefrom by several mutinous comrades, did seize from the person of 2nd Lt Bean, while in the discharge of his duty as Officer of the Guard, a pistol and did cock the same. This on board the U.S. Steam Transport "Sentinel" . . . the 19th day of April 1864,

Specification 5th In this that he private Sampson Goliah . . . did violently and by force resist his superior Officers Capt William Nutt and 2d Lt. Bean, 55th Regt. Mass. Vols. This on board the United States Steam Transport "Sentinel" . . . the 19th day of April 1864,

Specification 6th In this that he private Sampson Goliah . . . did raise both his hands and attempt to strike his superior Officer Capt William Nutt 55th Regt Mass Vols. This on board U.S. Steam Transport "Sentinel" . . . the 19th day of April 1864,

Specification 7th In this that he private Sampson Goliah . . . did call upon his comrades "shoot the damned scoundrel He has struck me" or words to that effect. This on board U.S. Steam Transport "Sentinel" . . . the 19th day of April 1864,

To which charge and Specifications the prisoner pleaded as follows:

[Goliah pleaded not guilty to all specifications and the charge in general.]

2nd Lt J. A. Bean a witness for the prosecution being duly sworn testified as follows.

By Judge Advocate State your name, rank, and Regiment.

Answer Jacob A. Bean, 2nd Lt 55 Mass. Vols. Co "D[.]"

By Judge Advocate How long have you known the prisoner?

Answer [A]bout 3 weeks. I have known him by sight.

By Judge Advocate Where were you April 19th 1864?

Answer On board Steamer "Sentinel," between Hilton Head and Folly Island.

By Judge Advocate Were you on any special duty on board the Sentinel?

Answer I was Officer of the Guard.

By Judge Advocate State what you saw occur on board the Steamer Sentinel on or about the evening of 19th of April.

Answer This prisoner was between decks. I heard loud talk, between decks. I went down there and ordered them to keep quiet, it was after taps. I went the 2nd time. I went the 3rd time. I saw the prisoner lying down and he rose up on his left elbow, and was talking loud and Holloing and using some profane language. I heard the remark made of "Hard bread and salt horse" by some one in the crowd[.] I stepped along to him and ordered him on deck, he did not get up. I asked him if he was going and he said "No, he would not go there for any damned White Officer" [and] "If I laid my hands on to him he would smash me." I called to the Guard, they did not come. I saw Captain Nutt, and called him, and when he came I immediately went for the guard. A Corporal and a file came and took him on deck. I got a pair of Irons, I mean Handcuffs, + they were put on to him. I don't know who put them on but I saw them on him.

The Guard was ordered to keep him on deck. A short time after, Col. Hartwell, came where I was on deck, near the Guard where the prisoner was, + wanted to know the circumstances of the prisoner being hand-cuffed. I told him the nature of the case + he ordered the Captain of the boat to tie him to the rigging, the Captain then tied him + the Col. ordered me to keep him there nearly two hours unless he was willing to tell what his name was. When the prisoner was between decks he refused to tell Captain Nutt, what his name was and also he refused on deck to tell the Col. his name. When he had been tied about an hour and a half, every thing had been quiet + I was on the opposite side of the boat from the prisoner. I saw some 12 to 15 men appear on deck all at one time, walking towards the prisoner. I immediately walked towards them and inquired of them what they were there for. [T]hey said "they came there to cut the prisoner down[,]" "he had been tied there long enough[,]" "they would not allow one of their men tied by a citizen." I ordered them to go away about their business, to go and lie down. They turned around and started away, there were two men among them who raised the cry "let's cut him down" and the body of the men returned towards the prisoner. I ordered them this time away and told the guard to fix bayonetts + keep them back. [T]hey turned back a second time they still kept the cry, "let[']s cut him down" there were more of them. They wanted to know what good one man could do to prevent their coming forward "there are five Companies of us and they will all be on deck in a few moments[.]"

I was between the prisoner and the crowd at this time. The prisoner stepped up on to the Guard of the boat or railing, and commenced untieing the rope that he was tied with, with his teeth. I took him by the leg and pulled him off. [H]e had got the knot so far untied by this time that it slipped and untied.

Just at this time a man came from the crowd with a knife in his right hand and attempted to cut the rope. [D]uring this time the prisoner had got loose himself, *they did not cut the rope.* [T]he crowd closed up [illegible words]. I drew a pistol and as I drew it the prisoner caught it with both hands and two other men or more besides the prisoner had hold of me, the prisoner wrenched the pistol from my hand and immediately cocked it. [I]t was too dark to see. I saw him raise his hands up + heard the clicking of the cock. I immediately caught hold of him, and the prisoner + I together were carried together by the crowd to the hatchway and the prisoner and one or two more went down stairs, kind of slid down. I remained on deck to keep the remainder where they were, for some little time I saw nothing. The Col. notified me if I could find out where the prisoner was to report to him. I ascertained where he was + reported to him. [H]e ordered 3 of the sergeants who were on deck to go below and bring him on deck. [T]hey went below and brought the prisoner on deck. I did not see him when he first came up. [T]he Surgeon was called and declared him not injured to any extent. [T]he Hand-cuffs which had been put on him were broken[.] When he came on deck + another pair were put on him and he was put under guard + I was relieved between the hours of 11, + 12, oclock.

Question by Judge Advocate Why was the Captain of the vessel told to tie the prisoner?

Answer I heard the Col. ask him the question, if he knew how to do it. [H]e said he did, and I suppose that to be the reason.

By Judge Advocate Do you know anything of the Character of the prisoner previous?

Answer I do not.

Question by prisoner How do you know it was me making the fuss [page cut off][?]

Answer I do not know that it was you every time.

By prisoner Did you hear me use the words "Salt Horse and Hard Tack"?

Answer I could not say for certain, that you used that expression. The prisoner was talking loud.

By prisoner What did I say to you when you told me to come on deck?

Answer When I first told him to come on deck he wanted to know what it was for[.] I asked him if he was going he said "no."

Question by Court Was the Captain of the boat a Commissioned Officer of the United States?

Answer I don[']t know. I supposed him to be. [H]e was *not* in uniform.

Capt. William Nutt, a witness for the prosecution being duly sworn testifies as follows

Question by Judge Advocate State your name, Rank, + Regiment.

Answer Wm Nutt Captain 55 Mass Vols Company "D."

By Judge Advocate How long have you known the prisoner?

Answer I only recollect him since the night that this alleged mutiny occurred[.]

By Judge Advocate Where were you on the 19th day of April 1864?

Answer On board the steamer Sentinel in the Harbor at Hilton Head.

Judge Advocate State to the Court what you saw occur on board on or about the evening of the 19th of April.

Answer Just after taps that evening, I was in the Mess-room + I heard considerable noise between decks where a part of the companies were quartered. I saw Lt. Bean, + heard him ordering the men to keep quiet and they would not do it. [H]e told the prisoner especially to keep quiet, the prisoner said "he wouldn't for him and no other man." I ordered them to keep still he the pris. swore there "he would not keep still, for me and for no Other God damned white man" "we've bene humbuged long enough", "you Massachusetts men have bene humbugging us long enough," "we are going to do as we please after this." I told Lt. Bean he'd better send for the guard. As he used the word *we* I did not know how serious the affair might be. [T]here was much sympathy with him after the Lt. had gone after the Guard, he talked so abusive of every body that I did not know but that the man was crazy. I asked him what his name was, he told me "it was none of my God damned business[.]" I asked him if he knew who I was, he said "Yes by God" "I do" you are Captain Nutt. I then told him again to keep quiet. [H]e then said he would keep quiet when he got ready. [T]he guard came pretty soon then and I directed the guard to take him on deck. I told them if he refused to run him through with their bayonetts. [H]e went up on deck then and I put a pair of hand-cuffs on him. I told him again to keep still or I would gag him. He then stopped his noise. I then went back to the messroom and turned in. Perhaps an hour after that, I heard quite a noise on deck. [I]mmediately several of the men came down the stairs with a rush. I got up and took the first sword I could get hold of and followed by Capt. Crane went to the men's quarters. I saw Col Hartwell there and he was directing the crowd to keep Still. I heard him give the command "Stop their noise[.]" I passed by him and saw the prisoner. [T]he prisoner was making considerable noise, and also some of the men in Company "D." I ordered my men to go to their quarters, + told the prisoner to keep quiet and he swore he would not. I repeated the command and he brought up both hands as though he was intending to strike me. [A]s he lifted his hands I struck him with my sword. [H]e then called out "Shoot the damned cuss" "he has struck me." [H]e called on them several times to shoot and said "Where are my friends, have they all deserted me." He then dropped his head down on a level with my breast and made towards me as though he were going to butt me up against the side of the vessel[.]

I had my sword in my hand. [H]e jumped towards me and up against the point of my sword. [T]he point of the sword touched him about his breast. [H]e then fell down beside me[.] I supposed he was seriously hurt, but it was proved afterwards that he was not. I turned my attention to others in the crowd, and when I again looked around after him, the prisoner, he was gone.

The crowd soon dispersed. I then told Col. Hartwell what I had done and I supposed the prisoner was bleeding. I had nothing more to do with the prisoner that night[.] I saw the sergeants bring him on deck. . . .

By Judge Advocate Was there any General dissatisfaction in your Regt. about this time, for other reasons?

Answer There was.

By Judge Advocate On what account was it?

Answer Because they they [*sic*] had not been paid according to the *terms* of their Enlistment.

By Judge Advocate Had the Col. of the Regiment tried to get their full pay?

Answer I so understood it sir.

Judge Advocate Do you know that the prisoner ever was nearly insane or inclined that way?

Answer No sir.

By Judge Advocate At the time of his acting thus towards you, did he seem to know what he was about?

Answer First he did not. Afterward he did.

Question by prisoner Did I . . . strike you first or not?

Answer He did.

By prisoner Was it not the lick you gave me, that made me stagger first away from you and then back towards you?

Answer It could not be possible. [H]e was midships. I was the nearest the side of the vessel. [T]here was an interval between the striking and the lunge.

Question by the Court Has there been any mutinous conduct manifested on the part of the men about their pay prior to the 19th April 1864,?

Answer Not that I know of. [T]here had bene grumbling +co.

Colonel Hartwell, a witness for the prosecution being duly sworn, testifies as follows.

Question by Judge Advocate State your Name, Rank, Regiment.

Answer Alfred S. Hartwell, Col. 55th Mass. Vols.,

By Judge Advocate How long have you known the prisoner by sight?

Answer Since the evening of the alleged mutiny.

By Judge Advocate Where were you on the evening of the 19th day of April?

Answer I was at Hilton Head until eight oclock in the evening. I went on board the Steamer "Sentinel" at that hour.

By Judge Advocate State what you saw occur on board the "Sentinel" about this time.

Answer I saw the Officer of the Guard, Lt. Bean, who told me about the voice down below, I ordered the man he had arrested—the prisoner—brought to me. I asked the prisoner his name. [H]e would not give it and I repeated the question. [H]e muttered some answer, what I could not understand. And I ordered the Captain of the boat to tie him to the rigging. Captain of the boat did so. I left orders that the prisoner should be kept 2 hours tied up[.] . . . I went to sleep and was aroused by the Captain of the boat. I went out and saw the prisoner near the hatchway struggling with Lt. Bean, the Officer of the Guard and several other officers. I next saw him at the foot of the ladder, saw the prisoner raise both hands in a menacing manner against Captain Nutt, as if he intended to strike him.

By Judge Advocate What happened after he raised both hands?

Answer Capt Nutt's sword was drawn and the prisoner disappeared in the darkness and I supposed the prisoner was struck down by Capt. Nutt. The prisoner was not found for perhaps ½ an hour, when he was brought up on deck and another pair of Hand-cuffs were put on in place of those which had been broken while he was below. I then kept him on deck under guard.

By Judge Advocate Did you see the prisoner take a pistol from Lt. Bean?

Answer I did not.

By Judge Advocate Did you hear any oaths or insulting words used by the prisoner towards any officer?

Answer I only remember a few words, and those were insulting.

By Judge Advocate Was there or was there not any general dissatisfaction in your Regiment?

Answer There was.

Judge Advocate On what account?

Answer Because the Regiment had not been paid at all, nor offered pay according to terms of Enlistment.

I should like to state that this was the first violent or mutinous expression of their feelings and that I have reason to think that very few men sympathize with these proceedings.

Question by the prisoner Did you not order me first to keep quiet?

Answer Not to my knowledge.

Question by prisoner Do you think that I raised my hands up on self defence or to strike Captain Nutt?

Answer Evidently to strike Capt. Nutt.

Question by Judge Advocate Was it dark at this time?

Answer It was after nine oclock in the evening.

By the prisoner Did you not hear me tell Capt. Nutt, not to strike me, that I was hand-cuff[ed] and could do nothing?

Answer I did not.

By Judge Advocate Why did you tell the Captain of the boat to tie the prisoner?

Answer Because he had experience in tieing men up to the rigging. I could not do it properly.

By Judge Advocate Was he a Commissioned Officer of the United States[?]

Answer I do not know.

The prosecution was here closed. The Court here Adjourned to to [*sic*] meet again on Monday the 9th instant, at 11, o'clock A.M.

> In Camp South End Folly Island S.C.
>
> May 9th 1864,
>
> 11, A.M.

The Court met pursuant to Adjournment.

Present all the members and the Judge Advocate.

The prisoner was then brought into Court.

The proceedings of Yesterday having been read by the Judge Advocate, the Court proceeded with the trial of *private Sampson Goliah Company "A" 55 Mass. Vols.*

Charles C. Porter, a witness for the defence being duly sworn, testifies as follows:

Question by Judge Advocate State your Name, Rank and Regiment.

Answer Charles C. Porter, private, Co. "A" 55 Regt. Mass. Vols.

By Judge Advocate How long have you known the prisoner?

Answer Ever since he has been in the Regiment.

By Judge Advocate Were you on board the Steamer "Sentinel" at the time this occurrence took place?

Answer Yes sir.

By Judge Advocate State what you saw occur on or about the evening of the 19th day of April.

Answer On the passage up, we had been singing and talking between decks, the same as we had been doing the evening before. The first that I noticed of anything was when the officer of the Day came down. I saw him reach out his hand and whether he took hold of the prisoner or not I cannot say[.] [S]aid he "you go long with me" the prisoner then said "I don't allow any white man to collar me" said he, "I can go" or "go with the Guard" or something to that effect. I believe then that Captain Nutt, was called for and he came. I believe he then went on deck.

By Judge Advocate Did you hear the prisoner use any oath towards Captain Nutt?

Answer I don[']t know but there were some words used in an exciting manner that were spoken. [H]e seemed to be willing to go on deck if not compelled but the compelling seemed to excite.

By Judge Advocate Did you see the prisoner on the upper deck?

Answer [N]o sir.

By Judge Advocate Did you hear the officer of the day or Capt Nutt tell the prisoner to keep quiet?

Answer I don[']t don[']t [*sic*] recollect.

Question by the Prisoner Did you see or hear anything that occured after I came down stairs Hand-Cuffed?

Answer I saw nothing. I never heard the prisoner use any bad language generally in camp. [H]e generally performed his duties faithfully as a soldier.

Question by the Court What do you mean by some words used against Captain Nutt, were they oaths or not?

Answer I could not distinguish there was so much general noise.

David Wilkins, a witness for the defence, being duly sworn, testified as follows:

By Judge Advocate State your Name, Rank and Regiment.

Answer David Wilkins Co. "A" 55 Reg. Mass. Vols.

By Judge Advocate How long have you known the prisoner?

Answer Since he came into the Regiment in about June 1863, we have tented together at different times.

By Judge Advocate Were you on board the Steamer "Sentinel" on her passage from Hilton SC to Folly Island S.C. April 19th /64?

Answer Yes sir.

By Judge Advocate What did you see occur on or about the evening of the 19th April?

Answer On that evening Sampson was lying down between decks. I was not far from him. [H]e was laughing like the rest. [T]here was an officer came down, he wanted the prisoner to come up on deck. Sampson got up on his feet and said "you can't take me" and the officer laid his hands on him. [T]he prisoner told him that he did not [missing word in transcript] any white man to put his hands on him. [T]he officer again told him to go on deck and as soon as he said that he called the corporal of the guard. Captain Nutt came in then, and I could not say what Captain Nutt said. I was sitting down and the crowd was standing between. [T]here was considerable noise made. I know that he went very promptly soon after the guard came.

By Judge Advocate Did you hear Goliah refuse to be quiet?

Answer I did not hear, I was near enough to hear any orders given by the officers + I don[']t think he told him to be quiet. Goliah said "you can[']t take me" after the officer told him to go up stairs.

Question by Court At what time did this disturbance occur?

Answer I do not know sir. It was after taps[.] I could distinguish Sampson 12 feet off.

Elijah Richardson a witness for the defence, being duly sworn, testifies as follows:

By Judge Advocate State your Name, Rank, Regiment.

Answer Elijah Richardson private Co. "A" 55th Regt Mass. Vols.

By Judge Advocate How long have you known the prisoner?

Answer Ever since he came into the Regiment; about a year ago.

Judge Advocate Were you on board the U.S. Steamer "Sentinel" coming from Hilton Head to Folly Island S.C.?

Answer Yes sir.

By Judge Advocate What did you see occur on or about the evening the 19th of April 1864 in[stant]?

Answer All I saw was an Officer came down stairs. [H]e told Goliah to come go on deck with him. The Officer then took hold of him and the prisoner . . . said to "take his hands off he allowed no man to collar him" neither white nor black, the guard had come then and he went up stairs.

By Judge Advocate Did Goliah seem willing to go if he was unmolested?

Answer Yes sir.

By Judge Advocate Did you hear Goliah refuse to obey any officer?

Answer No sir.

By Judge Advocate Did you see anything that occurred on deck?

Answer No sir. I was not there.

By Judge Advocate Did it seem to you that Goliah wanted to create trouble?

Answer No sir.

By Judge Advocate Did the other men make most of the noise and disturbance or not?

Answer I don[']t think it was Goliah.

The prisoner having no further testimony to offer then made the following statement in his defence:

Prisoner[']s Statement

In the first place Lt. Bean, came down stairs. I got up when he told me to go up stairs, and when I reached down to get my Coat he grabbed me by the collar. I then said to him "let me go". I then asked him "what he took hold of me for", he said he wanted me to go up stairs[.] I said "I will go without being dragged or pulled". [A]t that time Captain Nutt came and said "he could drive me or put his hands on me either one". I told him to "go away I can go away with the officer of the Guard as well as I could with him". I told Lt. Bean, to take the man who was making the fuss, not to take me[.] I thought it was hard to suffer for what other men did. [T]his is the first time there had been any trouble with me in the Regiment. When Captain Nutt came up stairs he put the Handcuffs on me. I had no thought of striking Capt. Nutt at all. Captain Nutt drew his sword and offered to strike me[.] I raised my two hand which were in Irons to defend the blow. I knew I did not want to strike a man with a revolver and drawn sword and me hand cuffed.

The Judge Advocate then made the following reply:

Remarks of the Judge Advocate

Article 7th of the "Articles of War" reads as follows—

"Any officer or soldier, who shall begin, excite, cause or join in any mutiny or sedition in any troop or company in the service of the United States, or in any party, post, detachment or guard, shall suffer death, or such other punishment, as by a court-martial shall be inflicted."

Article 9th reads "Any officer or soldier who shall strike his superior officer, or draw or lift up any weapon, or offer any violence against him, being in the execution of his office, on any pretence whatsoever, or shall disobey any lawful command of his superior officer, shall suffer death or such other punishment as shall, according to the nature of his offence, be inflicted upon him by the sentence of a court-martial."

It is for the court to determine whether the evidence adduced is sufficient to bring the alleged offence under the cognizance of either of the above articles.

[Stephen] Benét, a high authority, declares "By *mutiny* is understood resistance to lawful military authority; this resistance may be either active or passive. . . . It is not necessarily an aggregate offence committed by many individuals, or by more than one. It may originate and conclude with a single person."

The same authority says "The crime of mutiny must be proved by acts, or words, in connection with acts." . . .

The testimony is concurrent that the prisoner did "disobey the lawful commands of his superior officer", and did "offer violence against him".

It is clearly established that there was on the part of the prisoner "resistance to lawful military authority."

But it is a grave responsibility upon the court to determine whether these acts are stamped with that awful criminality contemplated by the 7th and 9th Articles.

Your oath to "well and truly try and determine the matter now before you" calls upon you to declare whether these acts of the prisoner are of that aggravated nature called *mutiny*. The court should fully satisfy itself whether the element of conspiracy entered into the offence. That those acts were committed there can be no doubt, but do they mean mutiny in the highest degree[?] A grave offence has unquestionably been committed, and one to which heavy penalties should be offered, but whether that offence is so gross that the extreme rigor of the law should be applied, is a question to be determined by the court.

The court must distinguish between the acts of the prisoner and the acts of other men. The question should be asked "would a man who intended mutiny wait till he was hand-cuffed, before the overt act of mutiny was committed"? It is the duty of the Judge Advocate, further, to call the attention of the court to other and extraordinary circumstances, which by no means excuse, yet mitigate the offence.

Col. Hartwell testifies there had been previously a prevalent discontent in the regiment "because the men had never even been offered pay according to the terms of their enlistment." It is for the court to see that the dignity of the law is maintained as well as the rights of the prisoner secured.

The Case was then submitted to the Court.

The Court then took a recess of 15 minutes.

Upon the assembling of the Court it was closed; and having maturely deliberated upon the testimony adduced, is of the Opinion that *private Sampson Goliah of Company "A" 55th Massachusetts Volunteers, is* [guilty of all specifications and the charge in general.]

And does, therefore, sentence him, private Sampson Goliah Co. "A" Mass. Vols., "to be confined at hard labor for the remainder of his term of Enlistment, at such place as the Commanding Officer may deem fit; to forfeit all pay and allowances which are now or may become due him until the expiration of that period. And then to be dishonorably discharged the service of the United States."

Bankson T. Morgan
Lieut. Colonel 54th N.Y.V.
President Court Martial

James M. Walton
Captain 54th Reg. Mass. Vols.
Judge Advocate

[The proceedings and sentence were reviewed and approved by district commander Brigadier General Schimmelfennig and department commander Major General J. G. Foster.]

Wallace Baker Court-Martial, 55th Massachusetts Infantry (National Archives)

Likely concerned with growing insubordination within the 55th Massachusetts Infantry, substantially the same court-martial panel tried Wallace Baker as tried Sampson Goliah, but it imposed a far harsher sentence: death.

In Camp South End Folly Is. S.C.
May 17th 1864
2 o'clock P.M.

Present are the members and the Judge Advocate.

The Court then proceeded to the trial of Private Wallace Baker, Company "I," 55th Mass Vols Infty. who was called into Court and having heard the order convening the Court read, was asked if he had any objection to any member named in the order, to this he replied in the negative.

The Court and Judge Advocate were then duly sworn in the presence of the prisoner, and the prisoner, private Wallace Baker, Company "I," 55th Mass. Vols. Infty was then arraigned on the following charges and specifications.

Charge I. "Mutiny."

Specification. In this, that he Private Wallace Baker . . . being ordered by his superior Officer 2d Lieut. T. F. Ellsworth 55th Mass. Vols to go into his quarters, did refuse to do so, at the same time striking Lt. Ellsworth two violent blows in the face, and that he private Wallace Baker, did then endeavor to take from 2d Lt Ellsworth his sword, and did at the same time repeat the blows several times.

All this at Camp of 55th Mass Vols Infty, Folly Island, S.C. on or about the 1st day of May 1864,

Charge II Disobedience of Orders

Specification. In this that he Wallace Baker . . . being ordered by 2d Lt. T. F. Ellsworth, 55th Mass. Vols. Infantry, to go into his quarters did refuse to obey saying, "I shan't do it, I'll be damned if [I]'ll go, I'll go to the guard-house first" or words to that effect.

This at Camp of 55th Mass Vols Folly Island S.C., on or about the 1st day of May 1864.

Charge III Contempt and disrespect to his superior Officer.

Specification. In this that he Wallace Baker . . . did say to 2d Lt. T. F. Ellsworth . . . "You damned White Officer do you think that you can strike me, and I not strike you back again, I will do it. I'm damned if I don't," or words to that effect.

This at Camp of 55th Mass. Vols, Folly Island S.C. on or about the 1st day of May 1864,

Charge IIII Conduct prejudicial to good order and Military Discipline

Specification. In this that he Wallace Baker . . . did refuse to obey the orders of his superior Officer 2d Lt. T. F. Ellsworth . . . and did strike his Superior Officer 2d Lt Ellsworth, and did use very abusive language against him, in the presence of his Company "I" of the 55th Regt Mass. Vols.

All this at the Camp of 55th Mass. Vols. Folly Island S.C. on or about the 1st day of May, 1864.

To which Charges and specifications the prisoner pleaded as follows:

[Baker pleaded not guilty to all charges and specifications.]

Lt. Ellsworth a witness for the prosecution being duly sworn testifies as follows:—

By Judge Advocate—State your name, rank, + Regiment.

Answer—Thomas F. Ellsworth, 2d Lieut. Co. "I," 55th Regiment Massachusetts Volunteers.

By J Advocate—Was there any disturbance in your Company Street on or about May 1st with which the prisoner Baker was connected?

Answer—Yes sir.

By J. Ad. State what then occurred.

Answer—During Inspection on May 1st private Baker fell into line nearly the last man, without his round-about on, his gun in front of him, and his round-about in his left hand.[7] I told him to bring his gun to a shoulder. [H]e told me that he had not got his Equipments on yet. I asked him "why he hadn't them on," he said "he had not had time." I told him "that he had had all the afternoon to get ready" and he remarked "I'm not going to hurry" or words to that effect. I said to him, "what is that you say Baker?" and he repeated the above sentence. I told him "to keep his mouth shut and come to attention as I have ordered him before." [H]e still continued to talk and I went to him, I asked him "if he meant to obey me", he replied he "was not going to hurry" I told him "to shoulder his gun and go to his quarters, pack his knapsack and report to me after parade or inspection." Before I had dismissed the company, he went to his tent, took off his equipments, and came out on the left of his company three or four paces in advance. On his appearance without his equipments and taking no notice of my order to pack his knapsack, the company began to laugh. [T]he inspection was then over, I then went to Baker, and ordered him to his tent to do as I had told him. He then said, "I won[']t go" or words to that effect, and "you are going to make me stand at attention[,]" "I won't do it[,]" "I'll be damned if I will[.]" I then ordered him again to "go immediately[.]" [H]e said "Lt, I won[']t stand to attention for you or any other damned white officer" or words to that effect[.] I seized him by the collar and shoved him towards his tent, he then doubled up his fist—his right hand—and knocked my left hand loose, which had hold of his collar by the throat. [H]e then struck me two violent blows in the right cheek. I then drew my sword (he was in front) and attempted to cut him down, he raised his right hand and caught the blow of the sword on his left arm and on his left shoulder. [H]e then seized my sword and then struck me 3 or 4 very severe blows with his fist on my forehead, he then took hold of the sword with both hands, and I attempted to get it away from him. In the wrestle, he got the sword over my head on the back of my neck, my head was leaning on his breast. One of my hands had hold of the sword by the hilt, and the other near where the sword rested on my neck. I called for the orderly sergeant, he did not come and I called for the other sergeants, neither of them came and I sent for the captain. The captain came and ordered him to let loose the sword; he Baker then let go with one hand. I opened it through the other hand, and in taking it through the other hand he struck me. It must have cut him, for he jumped and struck me 4 or 5 very severe blows on my face and the back of my head. I sheathed my sword and seized him by the throat and back of the neck, and ordered a guard to take him to the Guard-House. The men did not seem too inclined to take him there, so I took him there with the assistance of the Captain. I ordered the sergeant of the guard to have him bucked and [missing word in transcript] until further orders. [D]uring the affair I attempted to strike him several times, but struck him about three.

By Judge Advocate—When you were wrestling with the prisoner, are you sure that he struck you blows—and that it was not the jarring of his Elbows or other part of his body?

Answer—He drew deliberately back in front of me, and struck me several blows in the face.

By Judge Advocate—Did the prisoner show any willingness to go to the guard-house, if you did not employ harsh means?

Answer—He did not sir. I ordered him to his quarters a second time before I took hold of him, and he said "I[']ll be damned if [I]'ll go[,]" "I will go to the guard-house first.["]

By Judge Advocate—Did the prisoner know that the line was being formed for inspection or parade?

Answer[—]Yes sir, by the Bugle call and it was given out by the orderly previously.

Question by Prisoner—Was I in my shirt sleeves when I fell into line or had I my coat on and my Equipments?

Answer—He had (I think) a blouse on and had his cartridge box over his shoulder. [H]e had his waist belt in his left hand.

By Prisoner—Was I buckling on my Equipments and getting ready when I fell into line, or doing nothing?

Answer—He was coming along trying to put his Equipments on and when he got into the ranks placed his gun in front of him in order to buckle his belt I suppose.

By Prisoner[—]Was I doing anything at the time you ordered me to attention to prevent me from obeying you?

Answer—No. When I first ordered him I did not know what he was doing. I believe he was putting on his Equipment.

By Pris.—How long have you known the prisoner?

Answer[—]Since the 20th April[.]

By Judge Advocate for Pris.[—]Has he ever before acted in any way as a man with an unbalanced mind?

Answer—Not to my knowledge[.]

By Judge Advocate for Pris.[—]Was he thought always a man of sound mind?

Answer—I don't know. One of the men who I spoke to with regard to this matter said he was not bright, or words to that effect "he was half witted" or something like that.

By Judge Advocate for Pris[,] Was the prisoner a man who you did, and would employ in any intelligent and responsible duty?

Answer—He was. [H]e has been on picket on the outposts of this Island.

Question by a Member [of the Court.][—]Did the Captain stand by all this time, (that is after you sent for him) and see this affair, and did he not interfere?

Question objected to by Judge Advocate on the ground of its being entirely irrelevant to the question at issue.

The Court was cleared for deliberation and on the opening of the court the objection was sustained.

*Question by the Court[.][—]*Did the prisoner attack you any other way than by striking you?

Answer—Yes sir, he attempted to seize hold of me so as to get me down, and he bit my thumb severely.

Question by Court—How long a time did the affair last from the time that you took the prisoner by the coat till he was marched to the gaurd-house?

Answer—About 15 minutes, about half that time between the arrival of the Captain and his being taken to the guard-house.

Captain Gordon a witness for the prosecution being duly sworn, testifies as follows:—

By Judge Advocate—State your name, rank, and Regiment.

*Answer[—]*John Gordon, Captain Co "I," 55th Mass Vols.

By Judge Advocate—Did you see the affair between Lt. Ellsworth and private *Baker* on or about the 1st of May[?]

Answer—I saw a part of it sir.

By Judge Advocate—State briefly what you saw of it.

Answer—I heard Lt. Ellsworth call "Captain"[.] I stepped out of my tent into the company street, and saw Lt. Ellsworth having hold of Baker's collar in front with his left hand I saw several blows exchanged between the two. I saw Baker strike Lt. Ellsworth several times as if to make him let go of him. I immediately stepped up to *Baker* and placed my hand upon his shoulder and commanded him to "stop instantly," no other blows were struck after that. [B]ut it was perhaps a moment before I succeeded in making *Baker* let go his hold, he would not until Lieut. released his hold. I told Lieut. Ellsworth to take him to the gaurd-house, and after dispersing the crowd, went to my tent.

By Judge Advocate—Did Baker obey your orders promptly at the time?

Answer—No sir.

By Judge Advocate—Did he use any disrespectful language or action to you at the time?

Answer—When I placed my hand upon his shoulder he said "hands off".

By Judge Advocate—How long have you known the prisoner?

Answer—Since he enlisted in my company from June 1st 1863.

By Judge Advocate—Have you always considered him a reliable man before, and a man of sound mind?

Answer—I have considered him a man of sound mind.

By Judge Advocate—Was there nothing else occurred but the blows you speak of, after you came out?

Answer—I heard a great many insulting words used by *Baker* to Lt. Ellsworth.

By Judge Ad.—How long did the disturbance last?

Answer—I am unable to say. The part I saw of it was from 3 to 5 minutes.

Question by a member—What is the general character of the prisoner?

Question objected to by Court and withdrawn[.]

Private Way a witness for the *prosecution* being duly sworn testifies as follows:—

By Judge Advocate—State your name, rank, and Regiment.

Answer—Henry Way, private Co "I" 55th Mass. Vols.

By Judge Advocate—Did you see the disturbance in your company st. between the prisoner *Baker* and Lieut Ellsworth, on May 1st[?]

Answer—I saw part of it, the latter part.

By Judge Advocate—State what you saw.

Answer—When we fell out into line for inspection *Baker* happened to be a little late, and was fixing something about his pants, and Lieutenant told him "to bring his piece to a shoulder[.]" [A]fter that I could not understand what Baker said. But the Lieut. told him "to be still". I don't know any more about it, except that Lieut. told him to go to his quarters. After inspection I saw the Lieut. and Baker having hold of each other, they were scuffling around, I saw them both make efforts to strike each other. I was about twenty five paces from them[.] Lieut. had his head bent down by the grasp around his neck of *Baker*. I heard no swearing or bad language by Lieut. I did not see Baker bite Lieutenant by the thumb.

The Court then adjourned to meet to-morrow the 18th instant at 10 oclock A.M.

In camp

South End Folly Island S.C.

May 18th, 1864

10, oclock A.M.

The Court met pursuant to adjournment. . . .

The prisoner was brought into Court and the proceedings of yesterday having been read by the Judge Advocate the court proceeded with the trial of private Wallace Baker Co. "I" 55 Reg. Mass. Captain Gordon, a witness for the prosecution was recalled by the Court.

Captain Gordon, a witness for the prosecution being duly sworn, testifies as follows:—

By Judge Advocate—Have the Articles of War ever been read to the prisoner?

Answer—They have sir. I have read them myself to the to the [*sic*] Company. I have read them always at inspections every sabbath mornings. Sometimes during the week.

The prosecution was here closed.

Private Frank Gardner a witness for the defence being duly sworn, testifies as follows:—

By prisoner—State your name, rank, and Regiment.

Answer—Frank Gardner, private Co "I" 55th Regt. Mass. Vols.

By prisoner[—][D]o you know the prisoner?

Answer—Yes sir—his name is Wallace Baker. I have known him ever since May or June 1863.

By Defence—[D]id you see the affair in the street of Company "I" between Lt. Ellsworth and the prisoner *Baker*?

Answer—Yes sir.

By J.A. for pris[.][—]Did you hear Baker refuse to do duty?

Answer—I heard him say he would rather go to the guard-house than pack his knap-sack.

By J.A. for Pris.[—]Did he go afterwards and pack his knap-sack?

Answer—No sir.

By Judge Advocate—Did you see Lt. Ellsworth take hold of Baker?

Answer—Yes sir.

By J.A. for Pris.[—]Did not Baker only defend himself from being hurt, or did he strike Lt. Ellsworth?

Answer—Lieut caught Baker by his collar, and struck him with his fist, he took out his sword and struck him once with his sword, and the strap on the hilt got caught over the Lieut's hand. [T]hen Baker caught hold of the sword to keep him from hitting him with it. Lt. told *Baker* to let loose the sword. *Baker* told him if he did not trouble him any more he would let loose the sword. At this time the Lt. called for a sergeant, and a man by the name of White and neither came, at that time he hit Baker again with his fist. Baker then struck him back again, and several blows were given on both sides[.]

By Judge Advocate[—]Have you known Baker before he came into the regiment?

Answer—No sir.

By J.A. for Prisoner—Was he generally a quiet man?

Answer—No sir, has a way of his own kind of carrying on, but raised no fuss in the company.

By J. Advocate—Did you ever see *Baker* act as thou[gh] he were out of his mind?

Answer—He has very simple ways at times, he is very hard to understand anything[.]

By Judge Advocate—Was he called simple or anything like that in the company?

Answer—Amongst the company they call him a kind of foolish fellow, because he is so hard to understand anything.

By Judge Advocate—Do you recollect anything he ever did that was simple or as though he were out of his mind?

Answer—No sir, it was just in talking[.]

By Judge Advocate—Have you ever been on picket with Baker? Did he understand his duties well?

Answer—I never knew him to fire off his piece just for the fun of it, he generally was punctual in falling into line with a few exceptions.

Private Henry Call a witness for the defence being duly sworn testifies as follows:—

By Judge Advocate for Prisoner—State your name, rank, and Regiment.

Answer[—]Henry Call, private Co. "I" 55th Mass. Vols.

By J.A. for Pris.—Do you know the prisoner?

Answer—Yes sir, his name is Wallace Baker, I have known him since he has been in the Regiment in June 1863.

By Judge Advocate—Was it your opinion that he was of sound mind?

Answer—I always thought that when a man addressed him a sensible word he did not appear to have good knowledge, he was though simple in the company. He has been in our company always, the orderly has spoken to him several times and *Baker* would jaw back because he thought he ought not to be ruled by another man. My opinion is that he is *not* a sensible man and, does *not* know what he says. Baker seemed queer in his actions generally in the company, when the rest of the men wanted to play he would misunderstand them and want to fight.

[P]rivate Morris Darnell a witness for the defence being duly sworn, testifies as follows:—

By Judge Advocate—State your name, rank, and Regiment.

Answer[—]Morris Darnell, private Co "I" 55th Mass. Vols.

By Judge Advocate—Do you know the prisoner?

Answer—Yes sir, his name is Wallace Baker, I have known him since he came to the Regiment in June 1863.

By Judge Advocate—Have you or have you not thought Baker a simple man?

Answer—I have never thought him very rational, he talks very singular at times, and his manner of addressing anybody is kind of strange. It was the way he talks generally and acts made me think him simple and the way he argues. . . .

The defence was here closed.

The prisoner having no defence to offer, and the Judge Advocate no reply to make. The Court was then closed, and, having maturely deliberated upon the testimony adduced is of the opinion that private Wallace Baker Co "I" 55 Mass. Vols. Infty, is—

Guilty of Specification to first Charge, Except the words, —"and that he private Wallace Baker, did then endeavor to take from Lt. Ellsworth, his sword."

Guilty of the 1st Charge

Guilty of Specification to 2nd Charge

Guilty of 2nd Charge

Not Guilty of Specification to 3rd Charge

Not Guilty of the 3rd Charge

Guilty of Specification to 4th Charge

Guilty of the 4th Charge

And does, therefore, sentence him, private Wallace Baker, Co "I" 55th Regiment Massachusetts Volunteers,—

"To be shot to death with musketry at such time and place as the commanding officer may deem fit."

Two thirds of the members concurring therein.

H. Northey Hooper

Lt. Col. 54th Mass. Vols.

President

James M. Walton

Capt 54th Reg. Mass. Vols

Judge Advocate

After the district and department commanders reviewed and approved the proceedings and sentence, Wallace Baker died by firing squad.

Fig. 13. The 26th U.S. Colored Infantry in training at Camp William Penn before heading into action in South Carolina. For African Americans, military discipline proved especially critical in transforming former slaves into soldiers and, despite some excesses by white officers, served as a force for unit cohesiveness. Military regulations also provided blacks with a paradoxical relationship between freedom and equality. Most black soldiers understood the difference between the army's rule of law and the capricious wielding of individual authority under slavery, though a few soldiers nonetheless resisted white officers as the replacement of one master by another. (National Archives)

Samuel Green Court-Martial, 109th U.S. Colored Infantry (National Archives)

Due process afforded Sergeant Samuel Green, who defended himself without counsel, the opportunity to win acquittal based on his cross-examination of a white officer and the testimony he elicited by his questioning of two black defense witnesses. In this case, note also how black noncommissioned officers played integral roles in mediating discipline. Their place in the chain of command made them responsible for carrying out officers' orders, and many of them understood the need for discipline to ensure unit cohesion and effectiveness during military service and to lay the foundation for more general black improvement. On the other hand, the position held by African American noncommissioned officers sometimes proved uncomfortable. Black soldiers at times resented their enforcement of orders issued by whites, while they also faced additional charges, as a result of their rank, if they participated in a mutiny or failed to try to stop one.

October 19th 1865 9 o'clock A.M.

Proceedings of a General Court Martial which convened at Indianola Texas

. . .

The Court then proceeded to the trial of 1st Sergeant Samuel Green Co. "D" 109th U.S.C. Inf. who was called before the Court and the order appointing it read in his presence.

The accused was asked if he had any objections to any member of the Court named in the order, to which he replied in the negative.

The Court was then, in his presence, duly sworn by the Judge Advocate and the Judge Advocate was sworn by the President of the Court, also in the presence of the accused.

The accused, 1st Sergt. Samuel Green Co "D" 109th U.S.C. Infantry was then arraigned on the following charge and specification

Charge

"Violation of the 7th Article of War["]

Specification In this that 1st Sergeant Samuel Green Co "D" 109th U.S.C. Infantry did in a noisy manner go to his commanding officer Capt. A. H. Keene commanding Co "D" 109th U.S.C. Infantry and did say "That man must be released" (meaning Private Allen Johnson Co D 109th U.S.C. Infantry) who was at that time confined in irons on the deck of the U.S. Steamer Thomas A. Scott as a prisoner. "We came away from home to get rid of such treatment as this[,]" "It is not alone in our Company but on the whole boat," "if he is not released it will raise the devil," or words to that effect, and did incite others to act also in a mutinous manner.

This on board the Steamer Thomas A. Scott off Pensacola Harbor on or about the Sixth day of June 1865.

To which Charge and Specification the accused pleaded as follows.

To the Specification "Not Guilty"

To the Charge "Not Guilty"

Captain A. H. Keene, 109th U.S.C. Inf. a witness for the prosecution being duly sworn says:

Question by J.A. State to the Court your name and rank?[8]

Answer. A. H. Keene, Captain, 109th U.S.C. Infantry.

Question by J.A. Are you acquainted with the prisoner?

Answer. I am!

Question by J.A. Were you present on board the Steamer Thomas A. Scott, on or about the 6th day of June 1865?

Answer[.] I was!

Question by J.A. Was there a disturbance or mutiny among the soldiers on board the Steamer Thomas A. Scott on or about the 6th day of June 1865[?]

Answer. There was!

Question by J.A. State to the Court all you [missing word in transcript] in regard to that mutiny and the part taken in it by the prisoner?

Answer. The disturbance was occasioned by one of my Company being tied up for neglect of duty[.] During the first of the evening that day there was a party visited me composed of men from Companies on the boat. The prisoner was at the head of the party and came to the cabin door when the officers were sitting in the cabin and called for me. I stepped out of the cabin near the aft hatchway and the prisoner said "Captain those men must be released. [I]f they are not released it will raise the devil" or words to that effect, and he further said that "We came from home to get rid of such treatment as this,["] referring to the prisoners who were confined on deck. I don[']t remember of his saying anything else or taking any part in the release of the prisoners. He made some remarks which I can[']t remember showing sympathy with the prisoners!

Question by J.A. What was the bearing of the prisoner when he visited you and made use of the remarks specified?

Answer[.] I considered it at the time to be disrespectful and I considered the words in the form of a demand instead of a request and accompanied with a threat that if the prisoners were not released it would raise the devil!

Question by J.A. Did you consider the remark that "if the men were not released it would raise the devil" a threat that the men would do so if the prisoners were not released?

Answer. I did!

Question by J.A. Did he incite others to act in a mutinous manner?

Answer. By his example I think he did. I do not know that he encouraged it by words or advice to others!

Question by J.A. Did the prisoner appear to be the leader of the party who visited you?

Answer. He was at the head of the party, but I don[']t know whether he was in command of them. [H]e was at their head when he came to the cabin!

"Cross Examined"

Question by the Accused. What remarks did you make to the accused at the time it is alleged he visited you?

Answer. If I remember I order[ed] the prisoner among the rest to go forward and cease such demonstrations and that I would see to the men who were being punished!

Question by accused. Did you not ask the accused the names of those who were engaged in the demand for the release of the prisoners?

Answer[.] I think I did!

Question by accused[.] Did you not tell the accused to go back and quiet the men and that you would use your influence with the Lieut. Colonel Commanding to get the prisoners loose?

Answer[.] The first part of the question I would answer in the affirmative. The other part I did not. If I remember the exact words I told him to go and quiet the men and that I would see the Lieut. Col. but I did not intimate that I would use my influence to secure there [*sic*] release!

Question by accused. Did you order the men forward or did the Lieut. Col. after you had reported to him?

Answer[.] I ordered them forward before reporting to him and afterward the Lieut. Col. himself then [ordered them] forward!

Question by accused. Did you tell the accused that you would see the Lieut. Col. about the release of the prisoners who were tied?

Answer[.] I did not!

"By the Court"

Question by the Court. When you ordered the prisoner and his party forward was your order obeyed?

Answer. As I gave the order the men started back toward the bow. I turned to see the Lieut. Col. in the cabin. [A]t the same time, some of the men stopped. It was not obeyed by all of the party!

Question by the Court. Was the prisoner among those who obeyed your order?

Answer. I can[']t remember whether he remained or went!

Question by the Court. Did you see the prisoner at any time during the mutiny after your conversation with him?

Answer. I did. [I]t was on the forward part of the boat near the wheel house!

Question by the Court. At what time was this?

Answer[.] It was about one half hour after the men were cut down. I saw him a number of times!

Question by the Court. What was the prisoner doing at the time you saw him?

Answer. At this time there was considerable excitement among the men, he was walking among the rest. I got the impression at the time that he was sympathizing with the men who were being punished, I can[']t recollect the words used. He was doing nothing but talking!

Question by the Court. What reasons have you for thinking that he was sympathizing with the prisoners?

Answer[.] From language that he used at the time!

Question by the Court. State as nearly as you can what his language was?

Answer. I remember hearing him speak what he said at the cabin door, that we came away from home to get rid of such treatment as that, referring to the prisoners who were being punished. The general tone of his conversation seemed to be in sympathy with the prisoners!

Question by the Court. At what time of day did the prisoner make the demand for the release of the prisoners?

Answer. Between 8 and 9 in the evening!

Sergeant Henry Tyler Co "D" 109th U.S.C. Infantry, a witness for the prosecution being duly sworn says:

Question by J.A. State to the Court your name and rank?

Answer[.] Henry Tyler, Sergt. Co "D" 109th U.S.C. Infantry!

Question by J.A. Are you acquainted with the prisoner?

Answer[.] I am!

Question by J.A. Were you present on board the Steamer Thomas A. Scott on or about the 6th day of June 1865?

Answer. Yes sir!

Question by J.A. Was there a mutiny among the soldiers of the 109th U.S.C. Infantry on board the Steamer Thomas A. Scott on or about the 6th day of June 1865?

Answer. Yes sir!

Question by J.A. State to the Court all you know in regard to that mutiny and the part taken in it by the prisoner?

Answer[.] Sergeant Green said if the boys were to loose the men who were tied up they would turn around and cuss them for it. [A]nd the boys said to Sergt. Green that they had been putting irons on the boys, and Sergt. Green said that he would go down and see the Captain about it. He went down and called the Captain out and was talking to him. I couldn[']t get near enough to hear what he was saying to him. [T]he last words the Captain told the [missing word in transcript] were for him to go back and try and quiet the men and he would go and see the Lieut. Colonel about it!

Question by J.A. Did you hear the Captain when he made these remarks to the prisoner?

Answer[.] Yes sir! I heard that!

Question by J.A. Did the prisoner try to excite the men to create disturbance?

Answer[.] No sir! Not while I was present!

Question by J.A. Was the prisoner in command of the party who visited the Captain?

Answer[.] He went down himself and a good many followed after him. I don[']t know whether he was in command of these or not!

Question by J.A. Did you hear the prisoner make use of any language tending to create disturbance or excite mutiny among the men?

Answer. No sir.

Cross Examined

Question by the accused. Did you not hear the accused advise the men not to create any disturbance and tell them that all armies had to have regulations and if they were not obeyed the men would be punished?

Answer. Yes sir! he used those words! . . .

"The Prosecution here Closed"

1st Sergeant James Dahomey, Co "D" 109th U.S.C. Inf. a witness for the defence being duly sworn says:

Question by the Judge Advocate. State to the Court your name and rank?

Answer. James Dahomey 1st Sergeant Co "D" 109th U.S.C. Inf.!

Question by Judge Advocate[.] Are you acquainted with the prisoner?

Answer. I am!

Question by the Accused[.] Was the accused in Command of the party who visited Capt. Keene and demanded the release of the prisoners who were being punished?

Answer. No sir he was not!

Question by accused. State all you know in regard to the circumstance of the party visiting Capt. Keene?

Answer. When the men rose in the first place I talked with them and they got very calm. Sergt. Tyler Co "D" came around and raised them again. I quieted him down the second time and he came and raised them again[.] I quieted them down the third time and he came for them. Sergt. Tyler said that "Sergt Dahomey is a damned coward and that he would get twelve (12) men without calling on Company [']D['] and cut the men loose who were tied.["] [H]e raised the men then and I could do nothing with them and then the orderly of the Company Sam. Green says that he would go down to the Captain and see if he couldn[']t do something with them and he went down to the Captain but I could not hear what he said. I followed on after him myself with Corpl[.] Milam. Sgt Green called the Captain out of his room. [W]hen he called him out of the room Sergeant Tyler and his gang were there and I could not get up near them!

Question by accused. Did not accused use every means in his power to quiet the men?

Answer[.] Yes sir! he came up and talked to them and tried to get them down he said "boys you don[']t know what you are a doing. You go and cut one of them down and he will try and kill you a few moments afterwards.["] [T]hen he said, "I advise you every one to leave those boys alone." . . .

Question by accused[.] Did not accused visit Capt. Keene for the purpose of preventing a disturbance on the boat?

Answer. That is what he told me he was agoing to do. All I heard him say was that he would go and see the Captain and see what could be done about it!

Cross Examined

Question by Judge Advocate. How many men had Serg. Tyler with him when he went to the Capt.?

Answer. I can[']t tell exactly. I think he was standing in front of them. [T]he boat was full of men. I think there was about 20 or 30 with him.

Corporal James Milam, Co "D" 109th U.S.C. Infantry a witness for the defence being duly sworn says

Question by Judge Advocate. State to the Court your name and rank?

Answer. James Milam, Corporal Co "D" 109th U.S.C. Infantry.

Question by Judge Advocate. Are you acquainted with the prisoner?

Answer. Yes sir!

Question by the Accused[.] Was the accused in command of the party who visited Capt. Keene and demanded the release of the prisoners who were being punished?

Answer. No sir. Orderly Green said he would report to the Captain if the boys didn[']t stop their noise!

Question by accused. State all you know in regard to the circumstances connected with the visit of the men to Capt. Keene?

Answer. Orderly Green went down and I was behind the orderly and Sergt. Dahomey was next to me, and Sergt. Tyler was behind Sergt. Dahomey. [T]he men followed along after Sergt. Tyler. [A]fter they got down to the Captain I turned and went back!

Question by accused. Did the accused make use of any language tending to excite the men to create disturbance?

Answer. He did not while I was in his presence!

Question by accused. Did not the accused use every means in his power to quiet the men?

Answer. When the fuss came up he spoke to the boys and said they ought not to do that if they went down and let loose [the] Arrested he would be ready to kill them in five minutes after. I don[']t remember anything else!

Question by accused. Did not the accused tell the men that they came out to put down the rebellion and if they rebelled it would make it worse?

Answer. Yes sir, that is what he said, he said that they didn[']t understand the rule of the army!

Cross Examined

Question by Judge Advocate. How long after the disturbance commenced were you with the prisoner?

Answer. I wasn[']t with him very long after. I seen him a number of times after I left him!

The accused having no further testimony to offer made the following remarks in his defence

"The boys asked me if I was going into the fuss and I asked them what, and they said cutting the boys loose, and I asked them were they tied up and they told me they were and I replied to them that they would have to do like I did when I got into difficulty and they asked me how I done and I told them I got out the best way I could. Then they went on and I told them that all armies had to have regulations and all men were sworn in to obey orders. [I]t was no use for them to cut up about the boys for if they cut the boys loose they would want to fight them[.] I told them that just such men as they were cutting up about started the rebellion in the commencement and I didn[']t see the use of 10 men rebelling against a regiment or a regiment against the United States Army. I told them that it had not been but a few weeks since the Colonel had talked to us about such things and now it was awful to think about let alone to do it. Then some wild fellow said that some men who upheld the officers were no better than they were and that they could destroy them as well as the officers. I replied that I didn[']t tie the men and didn[']t have it done and that I wasn[']t going to have anything to do with them[.] I remarked to Sergt Dahomey and Corporal Milam that I would go and report to the Captain about the thing. I went down and the Captain asked if it was our Company who was making the disturbance and I said it wasn[']t ours any more than it was the balance of the men, and he said you go and try and delay the men and I will go and see the Lieut Colonel. [A]s we parted, I said 'Yes Captain I think it would be better than have any fuss here on the ship out on the water.' The Lieutenant Colonel came out and said 'Sergt. you take the men to their quarters' and I went to them and said 'Come on away from there' and I went up to the bow of the boat[.]

["]The Captain came and requested me to get the men to their quarters and he would see the Lieut Colonel and do all he could to get the prisoners released, and he said nothing more to me. I have been hard at work ever since I was arrested!"

The Judge Advocate submitted the case without remark.

The Court was then closed for deliberation and having maturely considered the evidence adduced find the accused 1st Sergeant Samuel Green Co "D" 109th U.S.C. Infantry as follows

Of the Specification "Not Guilty"

Of the Charge "Not Guilty"

And do therefore acquit him. . . .

M. Bailey
Maj. 7th U.S.C.I.
President
Geo. H. Cook.
Capt. 8th U.S.C. Arty. "Heavy"
Judge Advocate

Major General D. S. Stanley reviewed and approved the proceedings and ordered Green released from arrest and returned to duty. Green mustered out as a private, worked in a tannery, and joined a Grand Army of the Republic post after the war. After his first wife died in May 1874, leaving him with five children, Green married an ex-slave named Mary and had eight children with her (one was stillborn, six were under the age of sixteen when Samuel died, and one was born after his death). Green also raised as his own, until her death, a child that Mary had in April 1873 with another man not her husband and with whom she never lived. Green died in Kentucky in 1892.

Fig. 14. Company E, 4th U.S. Colored Infantry, at Fort Lincoln, D.C. (Library of Congress)

12. AN ACT TO AMEND AN ACT ENTITLED "AN ACT FOR ENROLLING
AND CALLING OUT THE NATIONAL FORCES, AND FOR OTHER
PURPOSES," APPROVED MARCH THIRD, EIGHTEEN HUNDRED AND
SIXTY-THREE, 13 STAT. 6 (FEBRUARY 24, 1864) (ACT FREEING ALL
BLACK SOLDIERS DRAFTED INTO THE ARMY, REGARDLESS OF
WHETHER THEIR MASTERS WERE LOYAL TO THE UNION)

**In February 1864, the freedom granted by the July 1862 legislation and the Emancipa-
tion Proclamation expanded to include black conscripts or volunteers (though not
their families) owned by Southern Unionists. Congress also provided that in loyal
slave states that remained in the Union, the one hundred dollar bounty payable to
each black conscript would go to his owner, as well as compensation in an amount
not more than three hundred dollars, as determined by state-level commissions.**

SEC. 24. *And be it further enacted*, That all able-bodied male colored persons, between the ages of twenty and forty-five years, resident in the United
States, shall be enrolled according to the provisions of this act, and of the act
to which this is an amendment, and form part of the national forces; and when
a slave of a loyal master shall be drafted and mustered into the service of the
United States, his master shall have a certificate thereof, and there thereupon
such slave shall be free; and the bounty of one hundred dollars, now payable

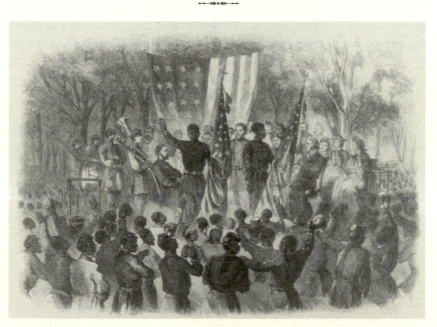

Fig. 15. Black politicization increased dramatically as a result of military service. This illustration shows black soldiers conducting an Emancipation Day commemoration at Port
Royal, South Carolina (*Frank Leslie's Illustrated Newspaper*, January 24, 1863)

by law for each drafted man, shall be paid to the person to whom such drafted person was owing service or labor at the time of his muster into the service of the United States. The Secretary of War shall appoint a commission in each of the slave States represented in Congress, charged to award each loyal person to whom a colored volunteer may owe service a just compensation, not exceeding three hundred dollars, for each such colored volunteer, payable out of the fund derived from commutations, and every such colored volunteer on being mustered into the service shall be free. And in all cases where men of color have been heretofore enlisted or have volunteered in the military service of the United States, all the provisions of this act, so far as the payment of bounty and compensation are provided, shall be equally applicable as to those who may be hereafter recruited. But men of color, drafted or enlisted, or who may volunteer into the military service, while they shall be credited on the quotas of the several states, or subdivisions of states, wherein they are respectively drafted, enlisted, or shall volunteer, shall not be assigned as state troops, but shall be mustered into regiments or companies as United States colored troops. . . .

13. A RESOLUTION TO ENCOURAGE ENLISTMENTS AND TO PROMOTE THE EFFICIENCY OF THE MILITARY FORCES OF THE UNITED STATES, 13 RES. 571 (MARCH 3, 1865) (RESOLUTION FREEING THE WIVES AND CHILDREN OF ALL BLACKS IN THE ARMED FORCES OF THE UNION)

Not until March 1865 did Congress hold "forever free" the wife and children of any person mustered into the service and, acknowledging the difficulties slavery posed for validating marriage, required only evidence that the soldier and his wife lived together or "associated as husband and wife" at the time of enlistment, regardless of any form or ceremony, and whether recognized by law or not.

Resolved by the Senate and House of Representatives . . . That . . . it is hereby enacted that the wife and children, if any he have, of any person that has been, or may be, mustered into the military or naval service of the United States, shall, from and after the passage of this act, be forever free, any law, usage, or custom whatsoever to the contrary notwithstanding; and in determining who is or was the wife and who are the children of the enlisted person herein mentioned, evidence that he and the woman claimed to be his wife cohabited together, or associated as husband and wife, and so continued to cohabit or associate at the time of the enlistment, or evidence that a form or ceremony of marriage, whether such marriage was or was not authorized or recognized by law, has been entered into or celebrated by them, and that the parties thereto thereafter lived together, or associated or cohabited as husband and wife, and so continued to live, cohabit, or associate at the time of the enlistment, shall be deemed sufficient proof of marriage for the purposes of this act, and the children born of any such marriage shall be deemed and taken to be the children embraced within the provisions of this act, whether such marriage shall or shall not have been dissolved at the time of such enlistment.

14. *CEREMONIES AT THE RECEPTION OF WELCOME TO THE COLORED SOLDIERS OF PENNSYLVANIA, IN THE CITY OF HARRISBURG, NOV. 14, 1865, BY THE GARNET LEAGUE* (HARRISBURG: TELEGRAPH STEAM BOOK AND JOB OFFICE, 1865)

Celebrations organized by African Americans to welcome home black veterans provided an immediate forum for blacks to articulate publicly their vision of a new postwar legal scheme. On November 14, 1865, a crowd of both whites and blacks enthusiastically thronged Harrisburg's flag-adorned streets in a ceremony hosted by the city's chapter of the Pennsylvania State Equal Rights League.

HARRISBURG, NOV. 14, 1865.

A PROPITIOUS DAY

The reception of the returned colored troops of Pennsylvania, to-day, was a well arranged, orderly and an enthusiastic turn-out of colored citizens. No day could

Fig. 16. One of the most compelling moments experienced by many black soldiers was the reception they received by new freedpeople as the Union army advanced toward ultimate victory. Here, jubilant ex-slaves greet the 55th Massachusetts as the regiment enters Charleston, South Carolina (*Harper's Weekly*, March 18, 1865)

Fig. 17. A black regiment musters out at Little Rock, Arkansas. Muster out ceremonies helped many black soldiers transition into a civilian life formerly unknown to most of them, that of freedmen, and juxtaposed the sadness of parting with the joy of reunion with families and a new confidence for future political action. One black correspondent wrote about a U.S. Colored Infantry regiment's disbandment: "[W]hen discharged, see them turn away with a sad, lingering gaze upon that old flag which they have borne so proudly upon the many battlefields. . . . Then, as the order is given to break ranks, see how eagerly they grasp the hand of their comrades in earnest friendship for the last time. A tear courses down their bronzed cheeks, as they hastily say the parting word in final adieu to that comrade who has with them passed through all dangers" ("Hannibal," Western Theological Seminary, October 27, 1865 [*Christian Recorder,* November 5, 1865]). The correspondent also wrote of his expectation that these veterans would take the lead in continuing to prosecute black expectations for equality. (Alfred R. Waud, 1866; Library of Congress)

have been chosen more propitious for the occasion. It has been one of the finest of this most pleasant Indian summer. Besides the soldiers on parade, there were over six thousand colored strangers in town. The demonstration, which was gotten up mainly at the expense of the colored men of the State Capital, was worthy of the occasion, and is truly a compliment to the Committee of Arrangements.

THE TEMPER OF THE PEOPLE

Thus far there has been no disturbance of any description whatever; all is passing off smoothly and in order, with a considerable show of good nature and a great display of enthusiasm, which speak well for both colors. In the streets, through which the parade passed, crowds of white citizens, ladies and gentlemen, blocked up the sidewalks to view the procession. The regular marching of the soldiers in line was admired by all.

The colored people of Harrisburg, of both sexes, were out in force. . . . The music was good, and the different civic associations were gaily decorated.

MOTTOES, &C.

One of these organizations, the Equal Rights League, of Reading, carried a large portrait of Abraham Lincoln, the Savior of his country. They all, by some token or other, manifested their love of country.

Over the principal streets, in that portion of the city which is most thickly populated by the colored people, they sprung arches of evergreen with wreathed banners, bearing inscriptions of welcome to the colored soldiers. On one arch was inscribed:

HE WHO DEFENDS FREEDOM IS
WORTHY OF ALL ITS FRANCHISES.

The citizens, generally, all over the city displayed the Stars and Stripes from their doors and windows.

[The procession, led by black correspondent Thomas Morris Chester as chief marshal, included black veterans on foot and disabled soldiers riding in carriages, William Howard Day and other black leaders, several Equal Rights League chapters, a band, women members of the Garnet League, members of a Masonic Lodge, and large numbers of black citizens on foot. The column marched to the capitol grounds, and after an opening prayer, a band played "My Country, 'tis of Thee." There, with veterans of the 3rd, 6th, 8th, 22nd, 24th, 32nd, 41st, 43rd, 45th, and 127th U.S. Colored Infantry, 11th U.S. Colored Heavy Artillery, and 54th and 55th Massachusetts Infantry Regiments in attendance, a series of resolutions was read on the grounds of the most important public space in Pennsylvania:]

The colored citizens of Pennsylvania . . . in order to give a heartfelt welcome to their gallant brothers who at their country's call braved all the perils and privations of war, deem this assembling a proper opportunity to reiterate their unswerving adherence to the truths held to be self-evident in the Declaration of our Independence, and to urge upon their white fellow-citizens, that in all faith to God and the world, the Federal Government and the respective State Governments of the several States in the American Union should be the practical embodiments and commentaries of the political creed expressed in that document: We, therefore, as colored native born citizens, claim for ourselves all the rights, privileges and franchises enjoyed by our fellow-citizens of another race.

Is our manhood challenged? We point for its successful vindication to the two hundred thousand black soldiers of our recent conflict; to those heroes among them whom God has kindly spared to return to their homes; to the silent and unmarked mounds where their dead comrades, the willing sacrifices for an imperiled Union sleep; to the proud record of the achievements of the dead and living at Vicksburg and Port Hudson, at Fort Wagner and Olustee, at Milliken's Bend and beleaguered Petersburg; on many a battle-field from the Mississippi's banks to the Atlantic's border, and from the mountain chains of Virginia to the Floridian everglades; at each and every point where Rebellion was to be met, faced, and threatened.

Admitting, then, our manhood, for in the light of all this evidence, it must needs be admitted, is there any pretence that we, through traitorous practices, have forfeited our right to liberty and the pursuit of happiness? Is our loyalty, our patriotism questioned? Go to the White House, and scan the crowds of repentant Rebels, seeking for pardon. How many black faces can be counted among them? How many ought in all reason to be there? Not one. In the annals of our civil war it will be recorded, to the honor of black Americans, that they proved invariably true to the mother land that has been false to them, and that denied to them at first an opportunity of taking part in a white man's war.

They afterwards nobly responded to the call for aid made upon them, for less pay than their fellow soldiers were receiving, and with no hopes of promotion to urge them on to deeds of daring, and now, having borne their part in the salvation of their beloved country and the vindication of her Government, can these unselfish heroes contemplate that Government with the consciousness that it derives its power from their consent? Is he who handled the bullet in war permitted to handle the ballot in peace? Massachusetts, indeed, welcomes her colored soldiers back to the enjoyment of all her franchises, but how is it with other States? How is it with Pennsylvania?

To the shame of the Keystone State be it spoken that she remands back those dark hued warriors, who risked life in her defence, to a degrading tutelage, and that she grudgingly accords to them the inalienable rights of men, while she withholds from them those governmental instrumentalities whereby alone these rights can be perfectly secured. In view then, of our claims as men and as American citizens, in view of the deprivations to which we are subjected in the State of Pennsylvania, notwithstanding all the proofs of our manhood and loyalty, and in view of the glorious conduct whereby our immortal brothers have so triumphantly vindicated that manhood and loyalty, be it by us here assembled,

Resolved, First, in all gratitude, That our thanks in such measure as no language can express, are due to our brothers, the colored soldiers of the American Union; that we recognize in them the instrumentalities, under Divine Providence, for the vindication of our aspersed humanity; that we sincerely mourn for those who have nobly fallen, and that all tender our most cordial welcome-home to the gallant brave who survive.

Resolved, That we confidently expect those heroes to add to their soldierly deportment which characterized them in the service all the worthy traits which adorn civilians, so that they and we, by an exhibition of correct morals and refined enlightenment, may compel all unprejudiced observers to acknowledge our just claims to all the rights of citizenship.

Resolved, That we earnestly appeal to our white fellow citizens to show their gratitude to their colored defenders by undoing the mighty wrong done to the colored freemen of Pennsylvania in that amendment of the State Constitution which deprived them of the elective franchise.

Resolved, That while the United States are bound by the Federal Constitution to guarantee to every State in this Union a republican form of government: such a form of government truly interpreted by the lights afforded by the Declaration of Independence is utterly incompatible with distinctions based on race or color; that an incompatibility of this nature is not one of the light and transient causes on account of which a Government long established should not be changed; and that an enforcement of Article 4, Section 4, of the Federal Constitution, is, therefore, importuned.

Resolved, That our grateful acknowledgements are due and are hereby tendered to those members of the Federal and State Legislatures who have advocated the rights of the colored men, and to all persons who give their sympathies and efforts to the work of securing the equality of all men before the law.

Resolved, That this, the land of our birth, is, if possible, more endeared to us and rendered ours more rightfully by the services of colored soldiers, in its defense, and that we cannot but regard any attempt at our expatriation, as a class, as an additional injustice offered to us. . . .

CHAPTER 4

RIGHTS DURING THE CIVIL WAR AND RECONSTRUCTION: POTENTIAL, CHANGE, AND OPPOSITION

The fluidity of the Civil War and its aftermath marked a moment of potential. Ex-slaves suddenly transformed from chattel property to persons and, in light of African American military service, could never go back to bondage again. In an opinion on citizenship, Attorney General Edward Bates helped set the groundwork for future civil rights legislation by explicitly rejecting the *Dred Scott* ruling and articulating that blacks could be American citizens. Northern and Southern blacks validated their manhood by joining the armed forces and bolstered their declarations of equality by successfully protesting unequal pay.

Military service also reinvigorated the antebellum African American convention movement, where blacks articulated their vision as to the contours of their new citizenship status with more coherence and potency than before the war, and forced whites to confront their expectations. The shared experiences of military service—including victory regarding the pay issue, increased political and national awareness, greater organization and unity, and growing appreciation for education and the value of African American labor—strengthened unity within the black community at the same time it afforded a powerful argument in support of expectations that those who defended the Union deserved full and equal membership in its society. Beginning with the National Convention in Syracuse, New York, in October 1864, blacks began to meet once again in national and statewide conventions, including in Virginia, Tennessee, North Carolina, Arkansas, Georgia, Alabama, and even South Carolina almost immediately upon the close of the war.

Speeches by whites also indicate the moment of potential during the 1860s. An oration by Massachusetts Republican George S. Boutwell defined Union victory as a triumph against treason and a restoration of the ideals of the Declaration of Independence. Benjamin Runkle, a Union officer and superintendent of Freedmen's Affairs in Kentucky, urged blacks to embrace the Republican free labor ethos and pursue self-reliance, self-improvement, education, and property; to cultivate moral character; and to avoid alcohol.

In this context, Congress passed, and courts enforced, a series of legislative measures that began to define and modernize the rights and practices associated with national citizenship and enforce civil rights for blacks for the first time. The most obvious and profound manifestation of legal change during the Civil War came in the form of Civil War Amendments that emancipated the slaves (the Thirteenth), defined American citizens in nationalistic terms as those persons born or naturalized in the United States and thus entitled to "equal protection of the laws" and not to be deprived of "life, liberty, or property, without due process of law" (the Fourteenth), and granted black men the right to vote (the Fifteenth). These amendments and accompanying legislation, such as the Civil Rights Act of 1866, represented a major revision of American constitutionalism and federalism: they not only engraved the Union's battlefield victory onto the law but also strengthened the American nation-state by establishing the primacy of national citizenship over that of the states, defining the body of national citizens, and marking out some of the rights associated with that status. Moreover, the amendments and legislation recognized millions of freedpeople as national citizens, and freedmen as voters, within years of the exclusionary *Dred Scott* case. In so doing, these amendments and other legislation helped restore to practice the egalitarian ideals articulated in the Declaration of Independence. The Civil Rights Act of 1866 defined for the first time some of the rights attendant to national citizenship, mandating in harmony with the Republican Party's free labor ideology that "all persons born in the United States and not subject to any foreign power, excluding Indians not taxed, are . . . citizens of the United States" and that "citizens, of every race and color . . . shall have the same right, in every State and Territory in the United States, to make and enforce contracts, to sue, be parties, and give evidence, to inherit, purchase, lease, sell, hold, and convey real and personal property, and to full and equal benefit of all laws and proceedings for the security of person and property, as is enjoyed by white citizens, and shall be subject to like punishment, pains, and penalties, and to none other, any law, statute, ordinance, regulation, or custom, to the contrary notwithstanding." The admittedly short-lived Civil Rights Act of 1875 went even further, desegregating public accommodations and removing racial discrimination in inns, public conveyances, and theaters before its nullification by the Supreme Court in 1883.

On the other hand, the need for legislation such as the Civil Rights Act of 1866, and the Enforcement Acts between 1870 and 1872, illuminates the enduring nature of Southern white racism and the existence of forces that sought to destroy blacks' newfound freedom and equality in the law. Despite their uplifting transformation, blacks continued to confront paradox and duality as practical realities unceasingly challenged egalitarian ideals. Southern Black Codes gave African Americans rights but heavily restricted and regulated them at the same time. State-level vagrancy legislation and blacks' continuing economic dependence and inability to pursue land ownership on a meaningful scale made it excruciatingly difficult for them to improve their lot. Even more troubling was the rise of a vicious racist counterrevolution organized across the South, with apologists in the North, which sought to tamp out blacks' new enjoyment of rights and intimidate white Republican governments.

In opposition to legislation and constitutional amendments that enshrined the Union victory and blacks' rights in law, the Ku Klux Klan operated outside of the law across the South by 1868 to preserve white dominance and the political and economic subordination of blacks. Through the murder and beatings of African American students and those involved in politics, attacks on whites seeking to assist these freedpeople, and the burning of black churches, schools, and homes, the Klan spread a wave of intimidation and terror through the South by the time black troops had demobilized.

Ten percent of black delegates to state constitutional conventions in the South in 1867–68 became victims of Klan violence, and seven were murdered. In 1871–72, the Klan burned thirty Mississippi black schools and churches, and in the period between January and March 1871 assassinated sixty-three Mississippi blacks. In December 1874 in Vicksburg, Mississippi, the site of one of the Union's greatest military triumphs during the Civil War, an armed White Line force ousted black veteran Peter Crosby from his elected position as sheriff. The paramilitary force did more than that, moreover, murdering in cold blood fleeing blacks who had no intention of resisting. At least twenty-nine, if not more, blacks lay dead at the end of this violent spree, many of their bodies rotting in the open because their families feared to claim and bury them. Similar brutality erupted at Clinton, Mississippi, in early September 1875 as White Liners attended a Republican barbecue with concealed weapons. After creating a verbal confrontation, one shot into the head of a black man at point-blank range, and full-scale mayhem ensued. Some armed blacks fired back before scattering in fear for their lives, but white militia organized in posses ranged through the area for days, pursuing and butchering black leaders and white carpetbaggers, leaving their bodies exposed to animals and the elements. Between thirty and fifty men died.

The delegates to an October 1871 Southern States Convention of Colored Men realized that there were rights granted by the law but curtailed in actual practice as they met in the House chamber in Columbia, South Carolina. Delegates from Alabama, Arkansas, Florida, Georgia, Louisiana, Maryland, Mississippi, North Carolina, South Carolina, Tennessee, Texas, and the District of Columbia demanded an end to Southern white attempts to circumvent the Union's military victory and the Civil War Amendments through the use of vicious extralegal secret organizations such as the Ku Klux Klan. J. H. Burch of Baton Rouge perceptively called for convergence of legal doctrine and real-life practices: "If we look all over the Southern States, we will find the highways and the byways marked by the bleaching bones of white and colored men, who have fought, bled and died that colored men might assume, even in South Carolina, the rights and privileges of manhood. We stand here in the hall of the House of Representatives of South Carolina, a body of colored men discussing American politics, civil rights, education and labor. Let me ask those gentlemen who now look me in the face, how long is it since they dared walk the streets without a pass after the clock struck nine at night?"[1]

By 1875, 2,141 blacks had been killed and another 2,115 wounded by white supremacists in Louisiana alone since the end of the war. Some of these deaths occurred singly, others in massacres such as one in the small hamlet of Colfax, Louisiana, where whites butchered and mutilated dozens of blacks on Easter Sunday 1873 after they sought to assert their political rights. In September 1874, a full-blown White League militia army numbering 5,000 men defeated 3,500 Republicans in battle on Canal Street in the heart of New Orleans's business district, forcing the temporary flight of Governor William P. Kellogg until federal troops arrived. This was not the first time New Orleans witnessed large-scale violence aimed at curbing black and Republican power: on July 30, 1866, as Republicans sought to reconvene a state constitutional convention and enfranchise black Louisianans, a white mob stormed the convention and attacked blacks parading in support outside the Mechanics' Institute where the delegates met. Police joined whites in shooting and beating blacks, and by the end of the riot, at least thirty-four blacks (and likely more) and three white Unionists lay dead, with over a hundred injured.

Congress responded to this resurgence of open warfare in parts of the South with a series of five Enforcement Acts between 1870 and 1872. The newly created Department of Justice proved successful in punishing civil rights violations in the South in the early 1870s, pursuant to these Enforcement Acts and other civil rights legislation, as hundreds of members of white supremacist groups faced prosecution, conviction, and imprisonment. While this again vindicated black rights and equal enjoyment of citizenship before the law, it also illuminated in no uncertain terms that powerful forces of resistance would challenge the developments of the Civil War era and that these changes would not go untested. If contingency and choice of action led to the advancements of the Civil War era, they also allowed for their erosion with regard to African Americans.

The activities of the Klan contrasted with the newfound ability and courageous determination of ex-slaves in the South to hold conventions, vote, move about, speak, and do other things formerly prohibited to them when in bondage. Many Americans hailed the Fifteenth Amendment's ratification in the spring of 1870 as the end of the "black question." Blacks celebrated across the land, and Frederick Douglass jubilantly announced, "Never was revolution more complete," creating "a new world" where "[t]he black man is free, the black man is a citizen, the black man is enfranchised . . . no more a despised and hated creature, but a man, and, what is more a man among men." According to Douglass, blacks now stood "upon an equal footing with all other men, and that the glory or shame of our future is to be wholly our own" in a new country where "[c]haracter, not color, is to be the criterion" and blacks had the opportunity to rise or fall, succeed or fail, as their own actions and choices dictated.[2] On the other hand, states remained free to define voting qualifications so long as they avoided exclusion based on race, color, or previous condition of slavery. Thus, poll taxes and literacy tests, coupled with extralegal intimidation and brutish violence, prevented many blacks from exercising the franchise as a practical matter. This violence severely impeded Republican voting, efforts of the Freedmen's Bureau, and the ability of blacks to live as citizens in practical terms: for example, the Republican vote in Claiborne County, Mississippi, went from 1,844 in 1873 to 496 in 1875. In Yazoo County, with over 12,000 blacks, only seven Republican ballots were cast in 1875, and that number dropped to two on Election Day in 1876.

The materials excerpted in this chapter convey the tangled nature of legal evolution in post–Civil War America. Arranged chronologically, they show the simultaneous competing voices and strategies people used to advance or inhibit legal change.

1. *Proceedings of the National Convention of Colored Men, Held in the City of Syracuse, N.Y. October 4, 5, 6, and 7, 1864; with the Bill of Wrongs and Rights and the Address to the American People* (Boston: Geo. C. Rand & Avery, 1864)

Beginning with the National Convention in Syracuse, New York, in October 1864, blacks began to meet once again in national and statewide conventions, including in former Confederate states almost immediately upon the close of the war. Black conventions fostered legal change by lobbying legislators, showing that blacks could engage rationally with constitutional questions, calling on Republicans to be consistent to their party's ideals, and challenging white and black Americans to live up to the principles of the Declaration of Independence.

Black delegates to these conventions reiterated time and again that African American military service rewrote the rules excluding blacks from citizenship. Black conventioneers repeatedly cast themselves as the keepers of the "true" American Founding and further bolstered their claim to citizenship and inclusion in the process. Additionally, many conventions adopted the martial spirit and sense of nationalism learned by black soldiers, rousing the African American community as a whole with references to duty, sacrifice, and continued struggle. The experience that nearly all black soldiers served in federal, not state, regiments, helped bolster African American identification of the federal jurisdiction as superior to that of the states. African American conventioneers now deployed on a different type of battlefield, one on which Americans wrestled with how they would interpret the Constitution after the Civil War and upon which blacks insistently declared that their military service and birth within the United States gave them every right to participate. Transcending freedom in name only, blacks centered their discussions on whether a simple test of loyalty could determine who was and who was not a citizen and articulated their expectations of real freedom, complete with equality and guaranteed rights.

Importantly, black conventions and the organizations they created demonstrated a high level of competent self-governance, something that flaunted common white prejudice. Many conventions kept precise minutes that reveal a meticulous devotion to the rules of parliamentary procedure, as delegates formed committees, debated motions, and drafted reports. Blacks also formed a National Equal Rights League, with state and local chapters governed by well-considered constitutions that allowed for trial and censure, suspension, or banishment of members who violated bylaws or committed offenses contrary to the league's interests. Local chapters proved active: the 220 members of Philadelphia's Garnet League, for example, established schools, sponsored essay contests, and hired lawyers for wronged black soldiers. The Pennsylvania League organized public rallies, circulated petitions, and sent letters to newspapers. By funding court cases and lobbying politicians, the state league brought the issue of streetcar segregation to the foreground until state legislators enacted a bill in 1867 prohibiting segregation or exclusion of blacks by railways.

Blacks shrewdly connected their loyalty to ongoing debates about suffrage and the success of the Republican agenda at a time when determinations on these issues had not yet been made. In the immediate aftermath of war, Republicans such as George S. Boutwell took up the point articulated by African Americans, blending idealism and pragmatism in arguing for black suffrage because of black service as well as "because his power at the ballot-box is now essential to us, just exactly as his power in the field with the bayonet was essential to us during the war." Dramatically, the immediate aftermath of war generated a round of statewide conventions across the South, including states where blacks had formerly been unable to gather, much less weigh in on constitutional issues. Though mirroring many of the same themes as the national conventions and those held in Northern states, the Southern state conventions more directly dealt with the impact of slavery, emancipation, and Southern white racism, because their participants experienced these firsthand. These conventions even more vividly contrasted black loyalty against the treason of white Confederates, stridently arguing that choice of allegiance trumped race. Southern blacks, unsatisfied with a legal freedom that rang hollow, demanded concrete rights that gave a broader definition to their freedom.

Congress took note of the Civil War era conventions, as Massachusetts senator Charles Sumner and others routinely presented petitions and memorials for consideration by both houses of Congress. On December 21, 1865, Sumner presented a memorial from an August 1865 Tennessee convention "representing two hundred and eighty thousand citizens of the United States, colored citizens of the State of Tennessee," before Republican senator Jacob Howard presented the petition of 3,740 blacks from South Carolina calling for protection of their civil rights in light of "their unquestioned loyalty, exhibited by them alike as bond or free, as soldier or laborer, in the Union lines under the protection of the Government, or within the rebel lines under the domination of the rebellion[.]"[3] Similarly, on January 5, 1866, Sumner highlighted the explosive situation in the Deep South by presenting a petition from a convention of Alabama blacks who assembled in Mobile, "representing four hundred and thirty-six thousand nine hundred and thirty citizens of the United States" and calling for federal protection for blacks in the face of church burnings

and violence against them, along with a similar petition from Mississippi blacks who could not even meet in convention due to the fear of violence against them.[4]

The National Convention of Colored Men assembled . . . in Syracuse, N.Y., October 4, 1864, at 7 o'clock, P.M. . . .

Moved by Professor E. D. Bassett, of Pennsylvania, that the delegation from each State now proceed to select one from its number; the persons so selected to constitute a Committee to nominate permanent officers for the Convention.

Dr. Randolph, of New York, moved as an amendment, that the nomination and election of permanent officers be in open Convention.

The amendment was sustained by Stephen Myers, and Wm. H. Johnson, of New York, and opposed by E. Weaver, of Pennsylvania.

Robert Hamilton, of New York, moved to amend the amendment, so as to elect by ballot.

Mr. Downing, of Rhode Island, opposed Mr. Hamilton's amendment. He thought that the appointment of a Nominating Committee would relieve the matter of all difficulty.

The Convention then negatived both amendments, and adopted the original motion made by Professor Bassett. . . .

The Nominating Committee, through their Chairman . . . unanimously reported . . . [Frederick Douglass for president, sixteen vice presidents, and five secretaries].

The report of the Committee was received, the name of Frederick Douglass being greeted with great applause.

The report of the Committee was then adopted as a whole. . . .

The Convention, on motion, adjourned to meet in Wieting Hall, Wednesday morning, Oct. 5, at 9 o'clock.

[Wednesday, October 5]

. . . On motion, H. H. Garnet and Enoch Moore were appointed a Committee to borrow the battle-flag of the First Louisiana Colored Troops, to suspend across the platform. . . .

The beautiful flag was then presented by Rev. Mr. Garnet. He alluded to Capt. Ingraham, who led the attack at Port Hudson when the brave Cailloux fell. Capt. Ingraham then gave a feeling narrative of the events connected with the flag. His remarks were greeted with great applause. The whole audience rose, and united in giving three hearty cheers for Capt. Ingraham, the brave men who were with him, and the battle-flag which they bore. . . .

[Thursday, October 6]

. . . John S. Rock, Esq., of Boston . . . said, "I come from Massachusetts, where we are jealous of every right. I received information a few days ago that a sergeant in the Fifty-fourth Massachusetts Regiment, who is a splendid penman, had been detailed by his captain as a clerk in his department; and that, when the officer in command learned this, he immediately ordered the sergeant back to his regiment, saying in his order, that 'no negro will be allowed to hold any position in this department except that of a cook or a laborer.' A copy of this order was forwarded to me; and I immediately presented the case to our most excellent Governor, who was going to Washington that evening. The result is, the sergeant is restored back to his position as clerk, and the officer who made the order has suddenly left for the North. . . .

"All we ask is equal opportunities and equal rights. This is what our brave men are fighting for. They have not gone to the battle-field for the sake of killing and being killed; but they are fighting for liberty and equality. (Applause.)[5] We ask the same for the black man that is asked for the white man; nothing more, and nothing less. When our men fight bravely, as they always do, they don't like to be cheated out of the glory and the positions they so dearly earn. Many of our grandfathers fought in the Revolution, and they thought they were fighting for liberty; but they made a sad mistake, and we are now obliged to fight those battles over again, and I hope, this time, to a better purpose. We are all loyal. Why are we not treated as friends? This nation spurned our offers to rally around it, for two long years, and then, without any guaranties, called upon us at a time when the loyal white men of the North hesitated. We buried the terrible outrages of the past, and came magnanimously and gallantly forward. In the heroism displayed at Milliken's Bend, Port Hudson, Fort Wagner, Olustee, in the battles now going on before Richmond, and everywhere where our men have faced the foe, they have covered themselves all over with glory. (Applause.) They have nobly written with their blood the declaration of their right to have their names recorded on the pages of history among the true patriots of this American Revolution for Liberty. (Applause.) Witness, if you please, the moral heroism of the Massachusetts soldiers, spurning the offers of seven dollars a month, which the Government insultingly tempted them with for eighteen months, when it was known that they were without means, and that many of them had wives at home and children crying to them for bread when there was none to give them. But they bore it manfully, and have lived to see the right triumph. (Applause.) My friends, we owe much to the colored soldiers; not only to the Massachusetts men, but to every brave man who has taken up the musket in defence of liberty. (Applause.) They have done wonders for the race. Let us stand by them and their families, and be ready at any and at all times to assist them, and to give them a word of cheer.

"Though we are unfortunately situated, I am not discouraged. Our cause is flying onward with the swiftness of Mercury. Every day seems almost to be an era in the history of our country. . . .

[The Convention founded the National Equal Rights League, in keeping with a belief that "the interests of colored men generally will be best subserved and advanced by a union of all our energies and the use of all our means in a given direction," specifically, "to encourage sound morality, education, temperance, frugality, industry, and promote every thing that pertains to a well-ordered and dignified life; to obtain by appeals to the minds and conscience of the American people, or by legal process when possible, a recognition of the rights of the colored people of the nation as American citizens." The constitution of the National Equal Rights League provided for election of officers at annual meetings and the establishment of local chapters of the league, "provided that no distinction on account of color or sex shall be permitted in such auxiliary or subordinate association(.)" The constitution also established an executive committee to "call the people of those States together in convention or otherwise, and urge them to take the steps necessary to secure the rights and improvements for the attainment, of which this League is formed. They shall encourage the publication of such documents as may be of advantage to our cause; and may, at their discretion, publish brief appeals, arguments or statements of fact, which may have a tendency to promote the ends of the Association. . . ."]

DECLARATION OF WRONGS AND RIGHTS, MADE BY THE COLORED MEN OF THE UNITED STATES OF AMERICA IN CONVENTION ASSEMBLED, IN SYRACUSE, N.Y. OCT. 4, 1864.

1st. As a branch of the human family, we have for long ages been deeply and cruelly wronged by people whose might constituted their right; we have been subdued, not by the power of ideas, but by brute force, and have been unjustly deprived not only of many of our natural rights, but debarred the privileges and advantages freely accorded to other men.

2d. We have been made to suffer well-nigh every cruelty and indignity possible to be heaped upon human beings; and for no fault of our own.

3d. We have been taunted with our inferiority by people whose statute-books contained laws inflicting the severest penalties on whomsoever dared teach us the art of reading God's word; we have been denounced as incurably ignorant, and, at the same time, have been, by stern enactments, debarred from taking even the first step toward self-enlightenment and personal and national elevation; we have been declared incapable of self-government by those who refused us the right of experiment in that direction, and we have been denounced as cowards by men who refused at first to trust us with a musket on the battle-field.

4th. As a people, we have been denied the ownership of our bodies, our wives, homes, children, and the products of our own labor; we have been compelled, under pain of death, to submit to wrongs deeper and darker than the earth ever witnessed in the case of any other people; we have been forced to silence and inaction in full presence of the infernal spectacle of our sons groaning under the lash, our daughters ravished, our wives violated, and our firesides desolated, while we ourselves have been led to the shambles and sold like beasts of the field.

5th. When the nation in her trial hour called her sable sons to arms, we gladly went to fight her battles: but were denied the pay accorded to others, until public opinion demanded it; and then it was tardily granted. We have fought and conquered, but have been denied the laurels of victory. We have fought where victory gave us no glory, and where captivity meant cool murder on the field, by fire, sword, and halter; and yet no black man ever flinched.

6th. We are taxed, but denied the right of representation. We are practically debarred the right of trial by jury; and institutions of learning which we help to support are closed against us.

We submit to the American people and world the following Declaration of our Rights, asking a calm consideration thereof:

1st. We declare that all men are born free and equal; that no man or government has a right to annul, repeal, abrogate, contravene, or render inoperative, this fundamental principle, except it be for crime; therefore we demand the immediate and unconditional abolition of slavery.

2d. That, as natives of American soil, we claim the right to remain upon it: and that any attempt to deport, remove, expatriate, or colonize us to any other land, or to mass us here against our will, is unjust; for here were we born, for this country our fathers and our brothers have fought, and here we hope to remain in the full enjoyment of enfranchised manhood, and its dignities.

3d. That, as citizens of the Republic, we claim the rights of other citizens. We claim that we are, by right, entitled to respect; that due attention should be given to our needs; that proper rewards should be given for our services, and that the immunities and privileges of all other citizens and defenders of the nation's honor should be conceded to us. We claim the right to be heard in the halls of Congress; and we claim our fair share of the public domain, whether acquired by purchase, treaty, confiscation, or military conquest.

4th. That, emerging as we are from the long night of gloom and sorrow, we are entitled to, and claim, the sympathy and aid of the entire Christian world; and we invoke the considerate aid of mankind in this crisis of our history, and in this hour of sacrifice, suffering, and trial.

These are our wrongs; these a portion of what we deem to be our rights as men, as patriots, as citizens, and as children of the common Father. To realize and attain these rights, and their practical recognition, is our purpose. We confide our cause to the just God, whose benign aid we solemnly invoke. To him we appeal.

ADDRESS OF THE COLORED NATIONAL CONVENTION TO THE PEOPLE OF THE UNITED STATES.

Fellow-Citizens,—

The members of the Colored National Convention . . . warmly embrace the occasion to congratulate you upon the success of your arms, and upon the prospect of the speedy suppression of the slaveholders' rebellion. Baptized in the best blood of your noblest sons, torn and rent by a strife full of horrors,—a strife undertaken and prosecuted for aims and objects the guiltiest that can enter the wicked hearts of men long in the practice of crime,—we ardently hope with you that our country will come out of this tremendous conflict, purer, stronger, nobler, and happier than ever before. Having shared with you, in some measure, the hardships, perils, and sacrifices of this war for the maintenance of the Union and Government, we rejoice with you also in every sign which gives promise of its approaching termination, and of the return of our common country again to those peaceful, progressive, and humanizing activities of true national life, from which she has been so wantonly diverted by the insurrection of slaveholders. . . .

. . . The warm blood of your brave and patriotic sons is still fresh upon the green fields of the Shenandoah. Mourning mingles everywhere with the national shout of victory; and though the smoke and noise of battle are rolling away behind the southern horizon, our brave armies are still confronted in Georgia and Virginia by a stern foe, whose haughtiness and cruelty have sprung naturally from his long and undisputed mastery over men. The point attained in the progress of this war is one from which you can if you will view to advantage the calamities which inevitably follow upon long and persistent violation of manifest duty; and on the other hand, the signs of final triumph enable you to anticipate the happy results which must always flow from just and honorable conduct. The fear of continued war, and the hope of speedy peace, alike mark this as the time for America to choose her destiny. Another such opportunity as is now furnished in the state of the country, and in the state of the national heart, may not come again in a century. Come, then, and let us reason together.

We shall speak, it is true, for our race,—a race long oppressed, enslaved, ignored, despised, slandered, and degraded; but we speak not the less for our country, whose welfare and permanent peace can only result from the adoption of wise and just measures towards our whole race, North and South.

. . . [W]hile joyfully recognizing the vast advances made by our people in popular consideration, and the apparent tendency of events in our favor, we cannot conceal from ourselves, and would not conceal from you, the fact that there are many and powerful influences, constantly operating, intended and calculated to defeat our just hopes, prolong the existence of the source of all our ills,—the system of slavery,—strengthen the slave power, darken the conscience of the North, intensify popular prejudice against color, multiply unequal and discriminating laws, augment the burdens long borne by our race, consign to oblivion the deeds of heroism which have distinguished the colored soldier, deny and despise his claims to the gratitude of his country, scout his pretensions to American citizenship, establish the selfish idea that this is exclusively the white man's country, pass unheeded all the lessons taught by these four years of fire and sword, undo all that has been done towards our freedom and elevation, take the musket from the shoulders of our brave black soldiers, deny them the constitutional right to keep and bear arms, exclude them from the ballot-box where they now possess that right, prohibit the extension of it to those who do not possess it, overawe free speech in and out of Congress, obstruct the right of peaceably assembling, re-enact the Fugitive-slave Bill, revive the internal slave-trade, break up all diplomatic relations with Hayti and Liberia, reopen our broad territories to the introduction of slavery, reverse the entire order and tendency of the events of the last three years, and postpone indefinitely that glorious deliverance from bondage[.] . . .

. . . [Y]ou will not blame us if we manifest anxiety in regard to the position of our recognized friends, as well as that of our open and declared enemies; for our cause may suffer even more from the injudicious concessions and weakness of our friends, than from the machinations and power of our enemies. The weakness of our friends is strength to our foes. When the "Anti-slavery Standard," representing the American Anti-slavery Society, denies that that society asks for the enfranchisement of colored men, and the "Liberator" apologizes for excluding the colored men of Louisiana from the ballot-box, they injure us more vitally than all the ribald jests of the whole proslavery press. . . .

. . . The weakness and hesitation of our friends, where promptness and vigor were required, have invited the contempt and rigor of our enemies. . . . It is, therefore, not the malignity of enemies alone we have to fear, but the deflection from the straight line of principle by those who are known throughout the world as our special friends. We may survive the arrows of the known negro-haters of our country; but woe to the colored race when their champions fail to demand, from any reason, equal liberty in every respect!

We have spoken of the existence of powerful re-actionary forces arrayed against us, and of the objects to which they tend. . . . The first and most powerful is slavery; and the second, which may be said to be the shadow of slavery, is prejudice against men on account of their color. The one controls the South, and the other controls the North. Both are original sources of power, and generate peculiar sentiments, ideas, and laws concerning us. The agents of those two evil influences are various: but the chief are, first, the Democratic party; and, second, the Republican party. The Democratic party belongs to slavery; and the Republican party is largely under the power of prejudice against color. While gratefully recognizing a vast difference in our favor in the character and composition of the Republican party, and regarding the accession to power of the Democratic party as the heaviest calamity that could befall us in the present juncture of affairs, it cannot be disguised, that, while that party is our bitterest enemy, and is positively and actively re-actionary, the Republican party is negatively and passively so in its tendency. What we have to fear from these two parties,—looking to the future . . . is, alas! only too obvious. The intentions, principles, and policy of both organizations, through their platforms, and the antecedents and the recorded utterances of the men who stand upon their respective platforms, teach us what to expect at their hands, and what kind of a future they are carving out for us, and for the country which they propose to govern. . . . Under the apparently harmless verbiage, "*private rights*," "*basis of the Federal Union*," and under the language employed in denouncing the Federal Administration for "*disregarding the Constitution in every part*," "*pretence of military necessity*," we see the purpose of the Democratic party to restore slavery to all its ancient power, and to make this Government just what it was before the rebellion,—simply an instrument of the slave-power. . . . From this party we must look only for fierce, malignant, and unmitigated hostility. Our continued oppression and degradation is the law of its life, and its sure passport to power. . . . We therefore pray, that whatever wrath, curse, or calamity, the future may have in store for us, the accession of the Democratic party to the reins of power may not be one of them; for this to us would comprise the sum of all social woes.

How stands the case with the great Republican party in question? We have already alluded to it as being largely under the influence of the prevailing contempt for the character and rights of the colored race. This is seen by the slowness of our Government to employ the strong arm of the black man in the work of putting down the rebellion: and in its unwillingness, after thus employing him, to invest him with the same incitements to deeds of daring, as white soldiers; neither giving him the same pay, rations, and protection, nor any hope of rising in the service by meritorious conduct. It is also seen in the fact, that in neither of the plans emanating from this party for reconstructing the institutions of the Southern States, are colored men, not even those who had *fought* for the country, recognized as having any political existence or rights whatever.

Even in the matter of the abolition of slavery,—to which, by its platform, the Republican party is strongly committed, as well by President Lincoln's celebrated Proclamation of the first of January, 1863 . . . there is still room for painful doubt and apprehension. It is very evident, that the Republican party, though a party composed of the best men of the country, is not prepared to make the abolition of slavery, in all the Rebel States, a consideration precedent to the re-establishment of the Union. However antislavery in sentiment the President may be, and however disposed he may be to continue the war till slavery is abolished, it is plain that in this he would not be sustained by his party. A single reverse to our arms, in such a war, would raise the hands of the party in opposition to their chief. The hope of the speedy and complete abolition of slavery, hangs, therefore, not upon the disposition of the Republican party, not upon the disposition of President Lincoln; but upon the slender thread of

Rebel power, pride, and persistence. In returning to the Union, slavery has a fair chance to live; out of the Union, it has a still better chance to live: but, fighting against the Union, it has no chance for any thing but destruction. Thus the freedom of our race and the welfare of our country tremble together in the balance of events.

. . . [O]ur Republican Administration is not only ready to make peace with the Rebels, but to make peace with slavery also; that all executive and legislative action launched against the slave-system, whether of proclamation or confiscation, will cease the instant the Rebels shall disband their armies, and lay down their arms. The hope that the war will put an end to slavery, has, according to this exposition, only one foundation; and that is, that the courts and Congress will so decree. But what ground have we here? Congress has already spoken, and has refused to alter the Constitution so as to abolish Slavery. The Supreme Court has yet to speak; but what it will say, if this question shall come before it, is very easily divined. We will not assert positively what it will say; but indications of its judgment are clearly against us. What then have we? Only this, as our surest and best ground of hope; namely, that the Rebels, in their madness, will continue to make war upon the Government, until they shall not only become destitute of men, money, and the munitions of war, but utterly divested of their slaves also.

. . . We come before you altogether in new relations. Hitherto we have addressed you in the generic character of a common humanity; only as men: but to-day, owing to the events of the last three years, we bring with us an additional claim to consideration. By the qualities displayed, by the hardships endured, and by the services rendered the country, during these years of war and peril, we can now speak with the confidence of men who have deserved well of their country. While conscious of your power and of our comparative weakness, we may still claim for our race those rights which are not less ours by our services to the country than by the laws of human nature. All, therefore, that justice can demand, and honor grant, we can now ask, without presumption and without arrogance, of the American people.

Do you, then, ask us to state, in plain terms, just what we want of you, and just what we think we ought to receive at your hands? We answer. First of all, the complete abolition of the slavery of our race in the United States. We shall not stop to argue. We feel the terrible sting of this stupendous wrong, and that we cannot be free while our brothers are slaves. The enslavement of a vast majority of our people extends its baleful influence over every member of our race; and makes freedom, even to the free, a mockery and a delusion: we therefore, in our own name, and in the name of the whipped and branded millions, whose silent suffering has pleaded to the humane sentiment of mankind, but in vain, during more than two hundred years for deliverance, we implore you to abolish slavery. In the name of your country, torn, distracted, bleeding, and while you are weeping over the bloody graves of more than two hundred thousand of your noblest sons, many of whom have been cut down, in the midst of youthful vigor and beauty, we implore you to abolish slavery. In the name of peace, which experience has shown cannot be other than false and delusive while the rebellious spirit of Slavery has an existence in the land, we implore you to abolish slavery. In the name of universal justice, to whose laws great States not less than individuals are bound to conform, and the terrible consequences of whose violation are as fixed and certain as the universe itself, we implore you to abolish slavery; and thus place your peace and national welfare upon immutable and everlasting foundations.

Why would you let slavery continue? What good thing has it done, what evil thing has it left undone, that you should allow it to survive this dreadful war, the natural fruit of its existence? Can you want a second war from the same cause? Are you so rich in men, money, and material, that you must provide for future depletion? . . . Can you expect any better results from compromises in the future, than from compromises with slavery in the past? . . .

Do you answer, that you have no longer any thing to fear? that slavery has already received its death-blow? that it can only have a transient existence, even if permitted to live after the termination of the war? We answer, So thought your Revolutionary fathers when they framed the Federal Constitution; and to-day, the bloody fruits of their mistake are all around us. . . . [A]bolition is essential to your national peace and unity. . . . You have repeatedly during this wanton slaveholding and wicked Rebellion, in the darkest hours of the struggle, appealed to the Supreme Ruler of the universe to smile upon your armies, and give them victory: surely you will not now stain your souls with the crime of ingratitude by making a wicked compact and a deceitful peace with your enemies. . . . Your antislavery professions have drawn to you the sympathy of liberal and generous minded men throughout the world[.] . . . Will you now proclaim your own baseness and hypocrisy by making a peace which shall give the lie to all such professions? You have over and over again, and very justly, branded slavery as the inciting cause of this Rebellion[.] . . . Will you now, when the evil in question has placed itself within your constitutional grasp, and invited its own destruction by its persistent attempts to destroy the Government, relax your grasp, release your hold, and to the disappointment of the slaves deceived by your proclamations, to the sacrifice of the Union white men of the South who have sided with you in this contest with slavery, and to the dishonor of yourselves and the amazement of mankind, give new and stronger lease of life to slavery? We will not and cannot believe it.

There is still one other subject, fellow-citizens,—one other want,—looking to the peace and welfare of our common country, as well as to the interests of our race; and that is, political equality. We want the elective franchise in all the States now in the Union, and the same in all such States as may come into the

Union hereafter. We believe that the highest welfare of this great country will be found in erasing from its statute-books all enactments discriminating in favor or against any class of its people, and by establishing one law for the white and colored people alike. Whatever prejudice and taste may be innocently allowed to do or to dictate in social and domestic relations, it is plain, that in the matter of government, the object of which is the protection and security of human rights, prejudice should be allowed no voice whatever. In this department of human relations, no notice should be taken of the color of men; but justice, wisdom, and humanity should weigh alone, and be all-controlling.

Formerly our petitions for the elective franchise were met and denied upon the ground, that, while colored men were protected in person and property, they were not required to perform military duty. . . .

But now even this frivolous though somewhat decent apology for excluding us from the ballot-box is entirely swept away. Two hundred thousand colored men . . . are now in the service, upon field and flood, in the army and the navy of the United States; and every day adds to their number. They are there as volunteers, coming forward with other patriotic men at the call of their imperilled country; they are there also as substitutes filling up the quotas which would otherwise have to be filled up by white men who now remain at home; they are also there as drafted men, by a certain law of Congress, which, for once, makes no difference on account of color: and whether they are there as volunteers, as substitutes, or as drafted men, neither ourselves, our cause, nor our country, need be ashamed of their appearance or their action upon the battle-field. Friends and enemies, rebels and loyal men,—each, after their kind,—have borne conscious and unconscious testimony to the gallantry and other noble qualities of the colored troops.

Your fathers laid down the principle, long ago, that universal suffrage is the best foundation of Government. We believe as your fathers believed, and as they practised; for, in eleven States out of the original thirteen, colored men exercised the right to vote at the time of the adoption of the Federal Constitution. . . .

. . . We say, therefore, that having required, demanded, and in some instances compelled, us to serve with our time, our property, and our lives, coupling us in all the obligations and duties imposed upon the more highly favored of our fellow-citizens in this war to protect and defend your country from threatened destruction, and having fully established the precedent by which, in all similar and dissimilar cases of need, we may be compelled to respond to a like requisition,—we claim to have fully earned the elective franchise; and that you, the American people, have virtually contracted an obligation to grant it, which has all the sanctions of justice, honor, and magnanimity, in favor of its prompt fulfilment. Are we good enough to use bullets, and not good enough to use ballots? May we defend rights in time of war, and yet be denied the exercise of those rights in time of peace? Are we citizens when the nation is in peril, and aliens when the nation is in safety? May we shed our blood under the star-spangled banner on the battle-field, and yet be debarred from marching under it to the ballot-box? Will the brave white soldiers, bronzed by the hardships and exposures of repeated campaigns, men who have fought by the side of black men, be ashamed to cast their ballots by the side of their companions-in-arms? May we give our lives, but not our votes, for the good of the republic? Shall we toil with you to win the prize of free government, while you alone shall monopolize all its valued privileges? Against such a conclusion, every sentiment of honor and manly fraternity utters an indignant protest. . . .

. . . We are asked, even by some Abolitionists, why we cannot be satisfied, for the present at least, with personal freedom; the right to testify in courts of law; the right to own, buy, and sell real estate; the right to sue and be sued. We answer, Because in a republican country, where general suffrage is the rule, personal liberty, the right to testify in courts of law, the right to hold, buy, and sell property, and all other rights, become mere privileges, held at the option of others, where we are excepted from the general political liberty. What gives to the newly arrived emigrants, fresh from lands governed by kingcraft and priestcraft, special consequence in the eyes of the American people? It is not their virtue, for they are often depraved; it is not their knowledge, for they are often ignorant; it is not their wealth, for they are often very poor: why, then, are they courted by the leaders of all parties? The answer is, that our institutions clothe them with the elective franchise, and they have a voice in making the laws of the country. Give the colored men of this country the elective franchise, and you will see no violent mobs driving the black laborer from the wharves of large cities, and from the toil elsewhere by which he honestly gains his bread. . . . The possession of that right is the keystone to the arch of human liberty: and, without that, the whole may at any moment fall to the ground; while, with it, that liberty may stand forever,—a blessing to us, and no possible injury to you. If you still ask why we want to vote, we answer, Because we don't want to be mobbed from our work, or insulted with impunity at every corner. We are men, and want to be as free in our native country as other men.

. . . You are strong, we are weak; you are many, we are few; you are protected, we are exposed. Clothe us with this safeguard of our liberty, and give us an interest in the country to which, in common with you, we have given our lives and poured out our best blood. You cannot need special protection. Our degradation is not essential to your elevation, nor our peril essential to your safety. You are not likely to be outstripped in the race of improvement by persons of African descent; and hence you have no need of superior advantages, nor to burden them with disabilities of any kind. Let your Government be what all governments should be,—a copy of the eternal laws of the universe; before which all men stand equal as to rewards and punishments, life and death, without regard to country, kindred, tongue, or people.

But what we have now said, in appeal for the elective franchise, applies to our people generally. A special reason may be urged in favor of granting colored men the right in all the rebellious States.

... [W]hoever lives to see this rebellion suppressed at the South, as we believe we all shall, will also see the South characterized by a sullen hatred towards the National Government. It will be transmitted from father to son, and will be held by them "as sacred animosity." The treason, mowed down by the armies of Grant and Sherman, will be followed by a strong undergrowth of treason which will go far to disturb the peaceful operation of the hated Government.

Every United-States mail-carrier, every custom-house officer, every Northern man, and every representative of the United-States Government, in the Southern States, will be held in abhorrence; and for a long time that country is to be governed with difficulty. We may conquer Southern armies by the sword; but it is another thing to conquer Southern hate. Now what is the natural counterpoise against this Southern malign hostility? This it is: give the elective franchise to every colored man of the South who is of sane mind, and has arrived at the age of twenty-one years, and you have at once four millions of friends who will guard with their vigilance, and, if need be, defend with their arms, the ark of Federal Liberty from the treason and pollution of her enemies. You are sure of the enmity of the masters,—make sure of the friendship of the slaves; for, depend upon it, your Government cannot afford to encounter the enmity of both.

... To break with your friends, and make peace with your enemies; to weaken your friends, and strengthen your enemies; to abase your friends, and exalt your enemies; to disarm your friends, and arm your enemies; to disfranchise your loyal friends, and enfranchise your disloyal enemies,—is not the policy of honor, but of infamy.

But we will not weary you. Our cause is in some measure before you. The power to redress our wrongs, and to grant us our just rights, is in your hands. You can determine our destiny,—blast us by continued degradation, or bless us with the means of gradual elevation. We are among you, and must remain among you; and it is for you to say, whether our presence shall conduce to the general peace and welfare of the country, or be a constant cause of discussion and of irritation,—troubles in the State, troubles in the Church, troubles everywhere.

To avert these troubles, and to place your great country in safety from them, only one word from you, the American people, is needed, and that is JUSTICE: let that magic word once be sounded, and become all-controlling in all your courts of law, subordinate and supreme; let the halls of legislation, state and national, spurn all statesmanship as mischievous and ruinous that has not justice for its foundation; let justice without compromise, without curtailment, and without partiality, be observed with respect to all men, no class of men claiming for themselves any right which they will not grant to another,—then strife and discord will cease; peace will be placed upon enduring foundations;

Fig. 18. "And Not This Man?" Columbia, as a female personification of the United States, poignantly challenges whites over how a black war veteran, who lost a leg in service to the Union, still could not vote. (Thomas Nast, *Harper's Weekly*, August 5, 1865)

and the American people, now divided and hostile, will dwell together in power and unity.

2. An Act to establish a Bureau for the Relief of Freedmen and Refugees, 13 Stat. 507 (March 3, 1865)

In 1863, the War Department created the American Freedmen's Inquiry Commission, composed of Samuel Gridley Howe, James McKaye, and Robert Dale Owen. The commission visited Union-occupied portions of the South and recommended the creation of a Bureau of Emancipation to assist the freed slaves in their transition to self-reliance. After much debate, in March 1865, Congress established the Freedmen's Bureau to distribute necessities to the freedpeople and oversee "all subjects relating to refugees and freedmen from rebel states." Congress sought to ensure that the bureau would exist only as a temporary measure: it limited its existence to one year and did not appropriate funds for its support, leaving it to draw funds from the War Department.

Be it enacted . . . That there is hereby established in the War Department, to continue during the present war of rebellion, and for one year thereafter, a bureau of refugees, freedmen, and abandoned lands, to which shall be committed, as hereinafter provided, the supervision and management of all abandoned lands, and the control of all subjects relating to refugees and freedmen from rebel states, or from any district of country within the territory embraced in the operations of the army, under such rules and regulations as may be prescribed by the head of the bureau and approved by the President. The said bureau shall be under the management and control of a commissioner to be appointed by the President, by and with the advice and consent of the Senate[.] . . .

SEC. 2. *And be it further enacted*, That the Secretary of War may direct such issues of provisions, clothing, and fuel, as he may deem needful for the immediate and temporary shelter and supply of destitute and suffering refugees and freedmen and their wives and children, under such rules and regulations as he may direct.

SEC. 3. *And be it further enacted*, That the President may, by and with the advice and consent of the Senate, appoint an assistant commissioner for each of the states declared to be in insurrection, not exceeding ten in number, who shall, under the direction of the commissioner, aid in the execution of the provisions of this act. . . . And any military officer may be detailed and assigned to duty under this act without increase of pay or allowances. . . .

SEC. 4. *And be it further enacted*, That the commissioner, under the direction of the President, shall have authority to set apart, for the use of loyal refugees and freedmen, such tracts of land within the insurrectionary states as shall have been abandoned, or to which the United States shall have acquired title by confiscation or sale, or otherwise, and to every male citizen, whether refugee or freedman, as aforesaid, there shall be assigned not more than forty acres of such land, and the person to whom it was so assigned shall be protected in the use and enjoyment of the land for the term of three years at an annual rent not exceeding six per centum upon the value of such land, as it was appraised by the state authorities in the year eighteen hundred and sixty, for the purpose of taxation, and in case no such appraisal can be found, then the rental shall be based upon the estimated value of the land in said year, to be ascertained in such manner as the commissioner may by regulation prescribe. At the end of said term, or at any time during said term, the occupants of any parcels so assigned may purchase the land and receive such title thereto as the United States can convey, upon paying therefor the value of the land, as ascertained and fixed for the purpose of determining the annual rent aforesaid. . . .

3. An Act to incorporate the Freedman's Savings and Trust Company, 13 Stat. 510 (March 3, 1865)

At the same time it founded the Freedmen's Bureau, Congress established the Freedman's Savings and Trust Company, also known as the Freedman's Savings Bank, to encourage former slaves to save money. Thousands of blacks made small deposits with the initially successful bank, as did some churches and societies. Sadly, economic downturn, risky speculation, and mismanagement led to the bank's failure, and in 1874, all branches closed their doors. Some depositors received partial compensation for their lost money, while others lost the entirety of their accounts. The collapse of the Freedman's Savings Bank chilled black trust in banks for years.

. . . SEC. 5. *And be it further enacted*, That the general business and object of the corporation hereby created shall be to receive on deposit such sums of money as may be from time to time offered therefor, by, or on behalf of, persons heretofore held in slavery in the United States, or their descendants, and investing the same in the stocks, bonds, treasury notes, or other securities of the United States.

SEC. 6. *And be it further enacted*, That it shall be the duty of the trustees of the corporation to invest, as soon as practicable, in the securities named in the next preceding section, all sums received by them beyond an available fund, not exceeding one third of the total amount of deposits with the corporation, at the discretion of the trustees, which available funds may be kept by the trustees to meet current payments of the corporation, and may by them be left on deposit at interest or otherwise, or in such available form as the trustees may direct. . . .

SEC. 8. *And be it further enacted*, That all sums received on deposit shall be repaid to such depositor when required, at such time, with such interest, not exceeding seven per centum per annum, and under such regulations as the board of trustees shall, from time to time, prescribe, which regulations shall be posted up in some conspicuous place in the room where the business of the corporation shall be transacted, but shall not be altered so as to affect any deposit previously made. . . .

SEC. 12. . . . *And provided, also,* Whenever it shall appear that, after the payment of the usual interest to depositors, there is in the possession of the corporation an excess of profits over the liabilities amounting to ten per centum upon the deposits, such excess shall be invested for the security of the depositors in the corporation; and thereafter, at each annual examination of the affairs of the corporation, any surplus over and above such ten per centum shall, in addition to the usual interest, be divided rateably among the depositors, in such manner as the board of trustees shall direct. . . .

4. GEORGE S. BOUTWELL, *RECONSTRUCTION: ITS TRUE BASIS.*
SPEECH OF HON. GEORGE S. BOUTWELL, AT WEYMOUTH,
MASS., JULY 4, 1865 (BOSTON: WRIGHT & POTTER, 1865)

A former state representative and governor of Massachusetts, Boutwell served as member of an 1861 peace convention that sought to avert Civil War. Boutwell represented Massachusetts in Congress as a Republican from 1863 to 1869, served as President Ulysses S. Grant's secretary of the treasury from 1869 to 1873, and represented Massachusetts in the Senate from 1873 to 1877. Note in the below speech how Boutwell offers both idealistic and pragmatic reasons to support granting blacks suffrage.

. . . We are able . . . for the first time to rejoice in the complete, or, at least, in the near fulfilment of the great truths contained in the second paragraph of the Declaration of Independence. Our ancestors said: "We hold these truths to be self-evident; that all men are created equal, and that they are endowed by their Creator with certain natural, essential and unalienable [*sic*] rights, among which are life, liberty, and the pursuit of happiness." . . . We have passed through a great struggle, which was a necessary incident of our national life, due to the fact, which now we can comprehend, and which it is neither disgrace to our fathers, nor dishonor to us, to confess, that our national system contained a fundamental error; namely, that it was possible to set up and maintain permanently a government based in part upon the principle that "all men are created equal," and in part upon the principle that a certain portion of mankind have the right to hold a certain other portion in bondage. . . .

. . . Justice, *justice,* is the only foundation for statesmanship, the only security for national life, and our fathers, in departing from the principle of justice, in the original construction of this government, left to their posterity the woes through which we have passed. . . . I feel assured, however, that whatever may be the prejudices of some, whatever may be the influence of tradition upon others, whatever may be the distinctions of race or color that exist among us, the people of this country are finally to re-establish the government upon the distinct enunciation of the doctrine that "all men are created equal." Building upon that foundation, the nation will withstand the storms and the floods of time; but if you build upon injustice, upon wrong, upon distinctions of race, of color, or upon caste, you build upon the sand, and when the storms come, and the winds blow, and the rains fall, then will the structure that you have reared be brought down in ruin upon your heads.

Nor is the triumph of the day limited to restoration of the Union as a result, and the overthrow of slavery as an incident of the war. We have placed the United States, as a nation, in the front rank of the nations of the earth. . . . [I]n the subjugation of the rebels of the South, we have conquered both England and France, as well as the enemies of Republican institutions the world over. . . .

The war for freedom and the Union has been carried on by the whites and negroes born on this continent, by the Irish and the Germans, and indeed by representatives of every European race. With this fresh experience we ought to make it a part of the organic government that no State shall make any distinction in the enjoyment of the elective franchise on account of race or color. . . .

. . . Upon the constitutional basis, political power will be apportioned, in 1870, in this wise: To the four and a half million negroes in the South, thirty Representatives; to the nine million white people in the South, sixty Representatives—ninety Representatives from the South. To the twenty-two million of people in the North, one hundred and forty-four Representatives in Congress. Now, what is the inevitable result of the doctrine that these eleven rebellious States are States in the Union, and have a right to be represented as States? It is this: that the nine million of white people in the South are to do all the voting in the fifteen old slave States[.] . . . These white voters of the South are to elect ninety Representatives to Congress. And who are these white men of the South? They are the men who have been in arms against the Republic and against the soldiers of the Republic. They are of a race which through two centuries has been contaminated by the vilest crime, the crime of slavery, until the whole public sentiment of the South has become debauched, until it has given birth to conspiracies, for the perpetration of the crimes of arson, of murder, of treason, of assassination, in all their hideous and unnamable forms; such crimes as could not have been committed, or even contemplated, in any other country or by any other people. . . . [W]ill the people of this country, if they have a prejudice against the negro race . . . exclude the negroes from the ballot-box, and allow it to be controlled by these nine million, or the representatives of these nine million, of white people in the South? . . . On the other hand, the black man, despised, down-trodden, with no reason to cheer or bless the flag of the Republic, which to him, from the foundation of the government until the signal shot upon Fort Sumter, had been only the ensign of oppression, with no reminiscences or traditions in its behalf, has proved true to the country, has led and guided and cheered the soldier, has enlisted in the armies of the Republic, has fought for the integrity of the nation and the safety of freedom; and can it be—*can it be* in the heart of any man of the twenty million of inhabitants in the North, with an ingratitude unexampled save in the instance of Judas Iscariot, now to consign these people, their race, and their posterity to the tender mercies of the men who instituted Libby Prison and Andersonville, who sent to the islands of the ocean for the pestilence with which they hoped to blast the cities of the North, who instituted arson as a plan, and finally closed their career of systematic and organized crime by the assassination of the President of the Republic? Do you propose to allow these people to send ninety representatives into the Congress of the United States, when according to numbers they would be entitled to but sixty? . . .

. . . We do not, to-day, ask suffrage for the negroes because they are competent to judge of questions of public policy, but we ask for suffrage for them because they are in favor of this government, and the white people of the South are against it. . . . I am in favor of allowing him to vote, without going into any inquiry whether he can read and write, because his power at the ballot-box is now essential to us, just exactly as his power in the field with the bayonet was essential to us during the war. . . . We have taken the bayonet, in time of war, out of the hands of our rebel enemies. What are we invited to do? To put the ballot, which is the instrument of power in time of peace, into the hands of our enemies, and deprive our friends of the privilege of exercising that power. . . . Are the people of this country more disposed to put power into the hands of rebels because they are white, than into the hands of patriots who happen to be black? . . .

By the Emancipation Proclamation, we have taken the initiatory steps towards the freedom of the negro; but how are liberties secured? . . . Their security is in the ballot. We say that men possess certain "natural, essential and unalienable rights." How are those rights to be defended? Either by the bayonet or by the ballot. If the negroes are to protect themselves in their rights, it is for the country to give them the means by giving them the ballot. . . .

. . . I am compelled to declare to you . . . heinous as are the crimes of these Southern men . . . that if the people of the North . . . now that they have secured the restoration of the Union by the services and sacrifices of the negro, in common with their own services and their own sacrifices, should surrender him, bound hand and foot, as he will be, if he does not enjoy the right of suffrage, into the custody of his enemies, made doubly ferocious by the events of this war, and into the custody of your enemies . . . your position upon the page of history . . . will be only less infamous than theirs. I know of no excuse that we can offer to ourselves, I know of no excuse that we can offer to this generation in other countries, I know of no excuse that we can offer to mankind in the coming ages, if, after having accepted the services and the blood of these men in defence of the flag, of liberty and of the Union, we turn and conspire with these their ancient oppressors and trample our faithful allies in the dust. . . .

5. Charles B. Brockway, *A Soldier's Sentiments: Speech of Capt. Charles B. Brockway, At the Great Knob Mountain Meeting, Columbia County, Pa., on Wednesday, August 30, 1865* ([Pennsylvania?]: n.p., [1865?])

On the other hand, this Democratic veteran opposed the Republican agenda and displayed the persistent racism that affected many people, even in the North.

. . . Among the first acts of the administration violating our contract, was the publication of the emancipation proclamation. At the time I was confined in Libby Prison . . . but the sufferings of imprisonment were nothing compared to the mental torture on finding the high and noble cause for which I enlisted debased by being made a struggle for giving freedom to a few degraded negroes. Leading Republicans, it is true, urged the measure as a *military necessity*, as if twenty millions of white men could not subdue eight millions South without the aid of a few cowardly negroes. . . . The natural result of this ill-timed proclamation was to stop recruiting in the North, and from that time large bounties and heavy drafts had to be resorted to fill our armies, while so long as the war was for the Union more volunteers were offered than the administration would accept. Another effect was to consolidate the South. . . .

. . . You and I have lost beloved comrades, nay, suffered ourselves; yet we must be insulted with assurances that these friends died, or we suffered, not for the Union, not in defence of the Constitution, but to make the negro our equal. . . .

The war being over, the question occurs, how shall we secure the objects for which we fought? In the first place, we should return to trial by jury. The time for courts-martial and military commissions, I apprehend, is over, or at least *should be*. . . .

We would also demand the restoration of the writ of *habeas corpus*, so that men can be no longer sent to bastiles without due process of law. . . .

We would also support President Johnson in his endeavors to bring back the Southern States to their loyalty. We want Virginia, South Carolina, and the rest in the Union, not as territories, but as free, sovereign, and independent States, as they were when Washington gave them to us. . . .

But, fellow-citizens, I must enter a special protest against the doctrines of negro equality. On this question the soldier feels the most sensitive, and is the most earnest in repudiating it. . . . [W]e resent the insult, and boldly declare that a more cowardly crew were never drawn up in line of battle. . . . [D]uring that terrible fight at Spottsylvania, when our gallant men were falling by thousands . . . these government pets were kept well to the rear, ready to run at the first signal. . . .

Now, fellow-citizens, let us try no rash experiments with the people of the South. Let us not exasperate but conciliate. Let us not adopt such a course as will justify rebellion in their eyes, or that of their descendants. Furthermore, let us insist that no preference hereafter be shown to the negro. If he is as good as the white man let him take the same chances. How is it now? A Freedman's Bureau is erected especially for the care of negroes, and homes, farms, schools and the like furnished them at our expense. Nay, New England in her love for them sends school teachers, money &c., while she sells the poor crippled soldier who happens to become a township charge to the lowest bidder. Why do these men adopt these negroes as their brethren? *They want their votes.* Horace Greeley says emancipation will add 800,000 votes to the Republican party, and H. Winter Davis, of Maryland, another high authority, says "It is votes, numbers, not intelligence, we want." . . .

6. The Thirteenth Amendment (Declared Ratified December 18, 1865)

Section 1. Neither slavery nor involuntary servitude, except as a punishment for crime whereof the party shall have been duly convicted, shall exist within the United States, or any place subject to their jurisdiction.

Section 2. Congress shall have power to enforce this article by appropriate legislation.

7. Various State Black Code Laws, Reprinted in 39th Congress, 2nd Session, Senate Executive Document No. 6, *Laws in Relation to Freedmen* (1867)

In the face of the Thirteenth Amendment, states across the South passed Black Codes that afforded blacks some rights but heavily restricted and regulated them at the same time. Many of the Black Codes included labor provisions that governed contracts and wages, licensing at exorbitant fees for blacks for certain crafts or occupations, and the arrest of blacks who without "good cause" quit their employment. In many former slave states, legislation applicable to loosely defined vagrants (for instance, Alabama included in its definition of vagrant a "stubborn or refractory servant" and a "laborer or servant who loiters away his time") subjected unemployed blacks to heavy fines and sometimes authorized their being hired out or forced to labor as part of a chain gang.

Alabama

AN ACT to protect freedmen in their rights of person and property in this State.

SECTION 1. *Be it enacted . . .* That all freedmen, free negroes, and mulattoes shall have the right to sue and be sued, plead and be impleaded, in all the different and various courts of this State, to the same extent that white persons now have by law. And they shall be competent to testify only in open court, and only in cases in which freedmen, free negroes, and mulattoes are parties, either plaintiff or defendant; and in civil and criminal cases, for injuries in the persons and property of freedmen, free negroes, and mulattoes, and in all cases civil or criminal in which a freedman, free negro, or mulatto is a witness against a white person, or a white person against a freedman, free negro, or mulatto, the parties shall be competent witnesses, and neither interest in the question or suit, nor marriage, shall disqualify any witness from testifying in open court.

Approved December 9, 1865.

AN ACT concerning vagrants and vagrancy.

SECTION 1. *Be it enacted . . .* That the commissioner's court of any county in this State . . . may cause to be hired out such as are vagrants, to work in chain-gangs, or otherwise, for the length of time for which they are sentenced, and the proceeds of such hiring must be paid into the county treasury for the benefit of the helpless in said poor-house, or house of correction.

SEC. 2. *Be it further enacted,* That the following persons are vagrants, in addition to those already declared to be vagrants by law. . . : A stubborn or refractory servant; a laborer or servant who loiters away his time, or refuses to comply with any contract for any term of service without just cause; and any such person may be sent to the house of correction in the county in which such offence is committed; and for want of such house of correction the common jail of the county may be used for that purpose.

SEC. 3. *Be it further enacted,* That when a vagrant is found any justice of the peace must . . . issue his warrant . . . to bring such person before him; and if, upon examination and hearing of testimony, it appears to the justice that such person is a vagrant, he shall assess a fine of fifty dollars and costs against such vagrant, and in default of payment he must commit such vagrant to the house of correction, or, if no such house, to the common jail of the county, for a term not exceeding six months, or until such costs, fine, and charges are paid, or such party is otherwise discharged by law: *Provided,* That when committed to jail under this section, the commissioner's court may cause him to be hired out in like manner as in section one of this act.

SEC. 4. *Be it further enacted,* That when any person shall be convicted of vagrancy as provided for in this act, the justice of the peace before whom such conviction is had may, at his discretion, either commit such person to jail, to the house of correction, or hire such person to any person who will hire the same for a period not longer than six months for cash, giving three days' notice of the time and place of hiring; and the proceeds of such hiring, after paying all costs and charges, shall be paid into the county treasury for the benefit of the helpless in the poor-house. . . .

Approved December 15, 1865.

AN ACT to define the relative duties of master and apprentice.

SECTION 1. *Be it enacted* . . . That it shall be the duty of the sheriffs, justices of the peace, and other civil officers . . . in this State to report to the probate courts of their respective counties, at any time, all minors under the age of eighteen years, within their respective counties, beats or districts, who are orphans, without visible means of support, or whose parent or parents have not the means, or who refuse to provide for and support said minors, and thereupon it shall be the duty of said probate court to apprentice said minor to some suitable and competent person, on such terms as the court may direct, having a particular care to the interest of said minor: *Provided*, If said minor be a child of a freedman, the former owner of said minor shall have the preference, when proof shall be made that he or she shall be a suitable person for that purpose[.] . . .

SEC. 2. *Be it further enacted*, That when proof shall be fully made before such court that the person or persons to whom said minor shall be apprenticed shall be a suitable person to have the charge and care of said minor, and fully to protect the interest of said minor, the said court shall require the said master or mistress to execute bond, with security, to the State of Alabama, conditioned that he or she shall furnish said minor with sufficient food or clothing, to treat said minor humanely, furnish medical attention in case of sickness, teach, or cause to be taught, him or her to read and write, if under fifteen years old, and will conform to any law that may be hereafter passed for the regulation of the duties and relation of the master and apprentice.

SEC. 3. *Be it further enacted*, That in the management and control of said apprentices, said master or mistress shall have power to inflict such moderate corporal chastisement as a father or guardian is allowed to inflict on his or her child or ward at common law: *Provided*, That in no case shall cruel or inhuman punishment be inflicted.

SEC. 4. *Be it further enacted*, That if any apprentice shall leave the employment of his or her master or mistress without his or her consent, said master or mistress may pursue and capture said apprentice . . . and in the event of a refusal on the part of said apprentice so to return, then said justice [of the peace] shall commit said apprentice to the jail of said county, on failure to give bond, until the next term of the probate court; and it shall be the duty of said court at the next term thereafter to investigate said case, and if the court shall be of opinion that said apprentice left the employment of his or her master or mistress without good cause, to order him or her to receive such punishment as may be provided by the vagrant laws which may then be in force in this State, until he or she shall agree to return to his or her master or mistress: *Provided*, That if the court shall believe that said apprentice had good cause to quit the employment of his or her master or mistress, the court shall discharge such apprentice from said indenture, and may also enter a judgment against the master or mistress for not more than one hundred dollars, for the use and benefit of said apprentice, to be collected on execution, as in other cases. . . .

Approved February 23, 1866.

Florida

AN ACT prescribing additional penalties for the commission of offences against the State, and for other purposes.

. . . SEC. 12. *Be it further enacted*, That it shall not be lawful for any negro, mulatto, or other person of color to own, use, or keep in his possession . . . any bowie-knife, dirk, sword, fire-arms, or ammunition of any kind, unless he first obtain a license to do so from the judge of probate of the county in which he may be a resident for the time being; and the said judge of probate is hereby authorized to issue such license upon the recommendation of two respectable citizens of the county, certifying to the peaceful and orderly character of the applicant; and any negro, mulatto, or other person of color so offending, shall be deemed to be guilty of a misdemeanor, and upon conviction shall forfeit to the use of the informer all such fire-arms and ammunition, and . . . shall be sentenced to stand in the pillory for one hour, or be whipped, not exceeding thirty-nine stripes, or both, at the discretion of the jury. . . .

SEC. 14. *Be it further enacted*, That if any negro, mulatto, or other person of color shall intrude himself into any religious or other public assembly of white persons, or into any railroad car or other public vehicle set apart for the exclusive accommodation of white people, he shall be deemed to be guilty of a misdemeanor, and upon conviction shall be sentenced to stand in the pillory for one hour, or be whipped, not exceeding thirty-nine stripes, or both, at the discretion of the jury; nor shall it be lawful for any white person to intrude himself into any religious or other public assembly of colored persons, or into any railroad car or other public vehicle set apart for the exclusive accommodation of persons of color, under the same penalties.

Approved January 15, 1866.

AN ACT in relation to contracts of persons of color.

SECTION 1. *Be it enacted* . . . That all contracts with persons of color shall be made in writing, and fully explained to them, before two credible witnesses, which contract shall be in duplicate, one copy to be retained by the employer, and the other filed with some judicial officer of the State and county in which the parties may be residing at the date of the contract, with the affidavit of one or both witnesses, setting forth that the terms and effect of such contract were fully explained to the colored person, and that he, she or they had voluntarily entered into and signed the contract, and no contract shall be valid unless so executed and filed: *Provided*, That contracts for service or labor for less time than thirty days may be made by parol.

SEC. 2. And whereas it is essential to the welfare and prosperity of the entire population of the State that the agricultural interest be sustained and placed upon a permanent basis, it is therefore enacted, That when any person of color shall enter into a contract as aforesaid, to serve as a laborer for a year or any other specified term on any farm or plantation in this State, if he shall refuse or neglect to perform the stipulations of his contract by wilful disobedience of orders, wanton impudence, or disrespect to his employer or his authorized agent . . . he or she shall be liable . . . to be arrested and tried before the criminal court of the county, and upon conviction shall be subject to the pains and penalties prescribed for the punishment of vagrancy: *Provided*, That it shall be optional with the employer to require that such laborer be remanded to his service instead of being subjected to the punishment aforesaid: *Provided further*, That if it shall on such trial appear that the complaint is not well founded, the court shall dismiss such complaint and give judgment in favor of such laborer against the employer for such sum as may appear to be due under the contract, and for such damages as may be assessed by the jury. . . .

SEC. 4. *Be it further enacted*, That if any person employing the service or labor of another, under contract . . . shall violate his contract by refusing or neglecting to pay the stipulated wages or compensation agreed upon, or any part thereof, or by turning of the employé before the expiration of the term, unless for sufficient cause, or unless such right is reserved by the contract, the party so employed may make complaint thereof before the judge of the criminal court, who shall at an early day, on reasonable notice to the other party, cause the same to be tried by a jury to be summoned for the purpose, who, in addition to the amount that may be proved to be due under the contract, may give such damages as they in their discretion may deem to be right and proper, and the judgment thereon shall be a first lien on the crops of all kinds in the cultivation of which such laborer may have been employed: *Provided*, That either party shall be entitled to an appeal to the circuit court, as in cases of appeal from justices of the peace. . . .

Approved January 12, 1866.

Mississippi

AN ACT to amend the vagrant laws of the State.

SECTION 1. *Be it enacted* . . . That all rogues and vagabonds, idle and dissipated persons, beggars, jugglers, or persons practicing unlawful games or plays, runaways, common drunkards, common night-walkers, pilferers, lewd, wanton, or lascivious persons, in speech or behavior, common railers and brawlers, persons who neglect their calling or employment, misspend what they earn, or do not provide for the support of themselves or their families, or dependants, and all other idle and disorderly persons, including all who neglect all lawful business, habitually misspend their time by frequenting houses of ill-fame, gaming-houses, or tippling shops, shall be deemed and considered vagrants, under the provisions of this act, and on conviction thereof shall be fined not exceeding one hundred dollars, with all accruing costs, and be imprisoned, at the discretion of the court, not exceeding ten days.

SEC. 2. *Be it further enacted*, That all freedmen, free negroes and mulattoes in this State, over the age of eighteen years, found on the second Monday in January, 1866, or thereafter, without lawful employment or business, or found unlawfully assembling themselves together, either in the day or night time, and all white persons so assembling themselves with freedmen, free negroes or mulattoes, or usually associating with freedmen, free negroes or mulattoes, on terms of equality, or living in adultery or fornication with a freed woman, free negro or mulatto, shall be deemed vagrants, and on conviction thereof shall be fined in a sum not exceeding, in the case of a freedman, free negro, or mulatto, fifty dollars, and a white man two hundred dollars, and imprisoned, at the discretion of the court, the free negro not exceeding ten days, and the white man not exceeding six months. . . .

SEC. 5. *Be it further enacted*, That all fines and forfeitures collected under the provisions of this act shall be paid into the county treasury for general county purposes, and in case any freedman, free negro or mulatto shall fail for five days after the imposition of any fine or forfeiture upon him or her for violation of any of the provisions of this act to pay the same, that it shall be, and is hereby, made the duty of the sheriff of the proper county to hire out said freedman, free negro or mulatto, to any person who will, for the shortest period of service, pay said fine or forfeiture and all costs[.] . . .

SEC. 6. *Be it further enacted*, That the same duties and liabilities existing among white persons of this State shall attach to freedmen, free negroes and mulattoes, to support their indigent families and all colored paupers; and that in order to secure a support for such indigent freedmen, free negroes, and mulattoes, it shall be lawful, and it is hereby made the duty of the boards of county police of each county in this State, to levy a poll or capitation tax on each and every freedman, free negro, or mulatto, between the ages of eighteen and sixty years, not to exceed the sum of one dollar annually to each person so taxed, which tax . . . shall . . . constitute a fund to be called the Freedmen's Pauper Fund, which shall be applied by the commissioners of the poor for the maintenance of the poor of the freedmen, free negroes, and mulattoes of this State, under such regulations as may be established by the boards of county police in the respective counties of this State.

SEC. 7. *Be it further enacted*, That if any freedman, free negro, or mulatto shall fail or refuse to pay any tax levied according to the provisions of the sixth section of this act, it shall be *prima facie* evidence of vagrancy, and it shall be the duty of the sheriff to arrest such freedman, free negro, or mulatto, or such person refusing or neglecting to pay such tax, and proceed at once to hire for the shortest time such delinquent tax-payer to any one who will pay the said tax[.] . . .

Approved November 24, 1865.

South Carolina

AN ACT to amend the criminal law.

. . . 14. It shall not be lawful for a person of color to be owner, in whole or in part, of any distillery where spirituous liquors of any kind are made, or of any establishment where spirituous liquors of any kind are sold by retail; nor for a person of color to be engaged in distilling spirituous liquors, or in retailing the same, in a shop or elsewhere. A person of color who shall do anything contrary to the provisions herein contained shall be guilty of a misdemeanor, and upon conviction may be punished by fine or corporal punishment and hard labor, as to the district judge or magistrate before whom he may be tried shall seem meet. . . .

22. No person of color shall migrate into and reside in this State unless, within twenty days after his arrival within the same, he shall enter into a bond, with two freeholders as sureties, to be approved by the judge of the district court or a magistrate, in a penalty of one thousand dollars, conditioned for his good behavior and for his support, if he should become unable to support himself. And in case any such person shall fail to execute the bond as aforesaid, the district judge or any magistrate is hereby authorized and required, upon complaint and due proof thereof, to issue his warrant, commanding such person of color to leave the State within ten days thereafter. . . .

Approved December 19, 1865.

AN ACT to establish and regulate the domestic relations of persons of color, and to amend the law in relation to paupers and vagrancy.

. . . 61. The servant may depart from the master's service for an insufficient supply of wholesome food; for an unauthorized battery upon his own person, or one of his family, not committed in defence of the person, family, guests or agents of the master, nor to prevent a crime or aggravated misdemeanor; invasion by the master of the conjugal rights of the servant; or his failure to pay wages when due; and may recover wages due for services rendered to the time of his departure. . . .

72. No person of color shall pursue or practice the art, trade, or business of an artisan, mechanic, or shop-keeper, or any other trade, employment, or business (besides that of husbandry or that of a servant under a contract for service or labor) on his own account and for his own benefit, or in partnership

with a white person, or as agent or servant of any person, until he shall have obtained a licence therefor from the judge of the district court, which licence shall be good for one year only. This licence the judge may grant upon petition of the applicant, and upon being satisfied of his skill and fitness, and of his good moral character, and upon payment by the applicant to the clerk of the district court of one hundred dollars, if a shop-keeper or peddler, to be paid annually, and ten dollars if a mechanic, artisan, or to engage in any other trade, also to be paid annually: *Provided, however,* That upon complaint being made, and proved to the district judge, of an abuse of such license, he shall revoke the same: *And provided also,* That no person of color shall practice any mechanical art or trade unless he shows that he has served an apprenticeship in such art or trade, or is now practicing such art or trade. . . .

Approved December 21, 1865.

8. *Mass Meeting of the Citizens of New-York, Held at the Cooper Institute, February 22d, 1866, To Approve the Principles Announced in the Messages of Andrew Johnson, President of the United States* (New York: George F. Nesbitt & Co., 1866)

. . . Hon. DAVID DUDLEY FIELD then presented the following address and resolutions:

. . . The element of disturbance, and, as we think, the only one, is the political condition of the freedmen; the late slaves whom we have emancipated by the great Constitutional Amendment. There is no substantial disagreement among loyal men respecting their civil rights. We all agree that they must have all the civil rights of any other class of citizens; the rights of person and of property, the right to sue and to testify; in short, they must have *equality before the law.* But whether they should also have the suffrage is the dividing question. Those who insist that they should have it, do so chiefly on these grounds: some of them say that the elective franchise is a natural right; that every person has a just title to participate in the enactment of the laws by which he is governed; others say, that the blacks aided us in the suppression of the rebellion, and therefore should be endowed with the privilege of participating in the government of the country which they helped to save, others still maintain that the suffrage is the only safeguard of the colored race for the preservation of their freedom and civil rights.

On the other hand these propositions are denied, and two other considerations are put forward: first, that in respect to the States, whether those lately in rebellion or those which have ever been loyal, the Federal Government has no right to interfere with the question of the elective franchise; and second, that in respect to the District of Columbia and the territories which are subject to the legislation of Congress, the question is one of expediency, depending upon the circumstances of each particular case, the elective franchise being not a right but a trust; and that wherever great numbers of the blacks are in an ignorant and debased condition it would be unwise and dangerous to admit them to the suffrage. These are the opposing claims, and it cannot be denied that the judgment which men will form upon them depends much upon their theory of government. They who believe in the democratic republican theory inherited from the Fathers will guard with scrupulous fidelity the rights of the States as they were reserved by the Constitution. . . .

There can be no question whatever that the power of determining who shall, and who shall not, enjoy the elective franchise belongs exclusively to the respective States. New-York has no more right to say who shall or who shall not vote in Virginia, than Virginia has to say who shall or shall not vote in New-York. . . .

Because the blacks have fought for the country, that does not necessarily give them a right to govern it, or to participate in its government. If it were otherwise, every brave boy, from sixteen to twenty-one, who fought in the Union ranks . . . should have a vote, instead of waiting for years to participate in the government to which he is subjected.

The blacks fought for a country, and they have it; they fought for their freedom and they have obtained it. For, thanks to God, the sun of this glorious morning has not seen a single slave through all the unbroken land from sea to sea. We would welcome our emancipated brother to the rights of manhood; we would take him by the hand and bid him stand up and be of good cheer, for, henceforth, no man can call himself his master. But when we are asked to give all the men of his race, at the moment of their emancipation, the right to participate in the Government, we must answer in the words of one of their own number, more intelligent than many others, white or black, "the able bodied only bear arms, the able-minded only should vote."

To insist that the blacks will not be protected in their freedom and all their rights, if they have not the elective franchise, is to forget that by the second clause of the Great Amendment it is provided that "Congress shall have power to enforce this article by appropriate legislation." It is also to forget that the men and women of the South are of like sentiments and instincts with ourselves, and something, certainly, may be expected from their regard to their interests and from their sense of justice.

It is a curious feature of the Freedmen's Bill, which the President has just vetoed, that it took the blacks under the protection of the Federal Government, as if they were not able to take care of themselves, while the same persons who urged through the measure are the most clamorous to give this same dependent population a large share in the Government of the country. . . .

9. AN ACT TO PROTECT ALL PERSONS IN THE UNITED STATES IN THEIR CIVIL RIGHTS, AND FURNISH THE MEANS OF THEIR VINDICATION, 14. STAT. 27 (APRIL 9, 1866)

The racial inequities of the Black Codes helped bring about passage of the Civil Rights Act of 1866, which comported with the Republican Party's free labor ideology, provided a definition of national citizenship rights for the first time, and sought to enforce the Thirteenth Amendment by prohibiting the reconstitution of slavery in fact, if not in law. The Black Codes, and persistent racist activity in the South, made clear what would happen if the federal government refrained from acting.

On January 5, 1866, Senator Lyman Trumbull of Illinois, chair of the Senate Judiciary Committee, introduced what would become the Civil Rights Bill of 1866. Referencing Black Codes that discriminated against African Americans, Trumbull emphasized that "[t]here is very little importance in the general declaration of abstract truths and principles"—the freedom of the slaves and the principles of the Declaration of Independence—"unless they can be carried into effect."[6] Some opponents believed the bill subverted federalism: it applied nationwide, went beyond protection for freedpeople alone, and truncated the traditional view that state law created citizenship rights. "Can any man believe that the founders of this Republic . . . would have ever entered into the Union," asked Delaware senator Eli Saulsbury, "if they had supposed that in the short term of eighty years their children would be subjected to the absolute control and the omnipotent will of the Federal Congress?"[7] Kentucky senator Garrett Davis bluntly summed up his main objection: "[T]his is a white man's Government," and "the negro is not a citizen here" unless made so by force.[8]

On the other hand, Michigan senator Jacob Howard asserted that the bill did not invade the "legitimate rights of the States" but "simply gives to persons who are of different races or colors the same civil rights." Moreover, Howard trusted that, having employed "nearly two hundred thousand" blacks "in the prosecution of our just and righteous war," the nation could not "now be found so recreant to duty, so wanting in simple justice, as to turn our backs upon the race and say to them, 'We set you free, but beyond this we give you no protection; we allow you again to be reduced to slavery by your old masters, because it is the right of the State which has enslaved you for two hundred years thus to do.'"[9] In response to Senator Davis's admonition that "the power to change the Constitution is a power simply to amend; it is not a power to revolutionize . . . it is not a power to change our form of Government," Maine senator Lot Morrill asked, "Are we not in the midst of a civil and political revolution which has changed the fundamental principles of our Government in some respects? Sir, is it no revolution that you have changed the entire system of servitude in this country?" According to Morrill, the end of slavery created a "revolution grander and sublimer in its consequences than the world has witnessed hitherto."[10]

Toward the end of the debates in the Senate, Massachusetts Republican Henry Wilson provided an eloquent summation on February 2, 1866. After reminding his colleagues that at least six of the former Confederate states passed laws "as iniquitous as the old slave codes," Wilson declared that by the Thirteenth Amendment and "[b]y the will of the nation freedom and free institutions for all, chains and fetters for none, are forever incorporated in the fundamental law of regenerated and united America. Slave codes and auction blocks, chains and fetters and bloodhounds are things of the past, and the chattel stands forth a man with the rights and the powers of the freemen. For the better security of these new-born civil rights we are now about to pass the greatest and the grandest act in this series of acts that have emancipated a race and disenthralled a nation."[11] Later that day, the Senate approved the bill by a vote of 33 to 12, with 5 absences; the House of Representatives followed suit by a vote of 111 to 38, with 34 not voting, on March 13, 1866.

President Andrew Johnson vetoed the bill on March 27, 1866, on the grounds that, in his opinion, the freedpeople were not fit for citizenship and because he felt the legislation inappropriately revised the relationship between the federal and state governments by now allowing the federal government to interfere with a state's ability to discriminate between the races as its government saw fit. On April 9, 1866, exactly a year after General Robert E. Lee's surrender at Appomattox, the House of Representatives joined the Senate's vote of a few days earlier to overturn Johnson's veto, and the Civil Rights Act became law.

Be it enacted . . . That all persons born in the United States and not subject to any foreign power, excluding Indians not taxed, are hereby declared to be citizens of the United States; and such citizens, of every race and color, without regard to any previous condition of slavery or involuntary servitude, except as a punishment for crime whereof the party shall have been duly convicted, shall have the same right, in every State and Territory in the United States, to make and enforce contracts, to sue, be parties, and give evidence, to inherit, purchase, lease, sell, hold, and convey real and personal property, and to full and equal benefit of all laws and proceedings for the security of person and property, as is enjoyed by white citizens, and shall be subject to like punishment, pains, and penalties, and to none other, any law, statute, ordinance, regulation, or custom, to the contrary notwithstanding.

SEC. 2. *And be it further enacted*, That any person who, under color of any law, statute, ordinance, regulation, or custom, shall subject, or cause to be subjected, any inhabitant of any State or Territory to the deprivation of any right secured or protected by this act, or to different punishment, pains, or penalties on account of such person having at any time been held in a condition of slavery or involuntary servitude, except as a punishment for crime whereof the party shall have been duly convicted, or by reason of his color or race, than is prescribed for the punishment of white persons, shall be deemed guilty of a misdemeanor, and, on conviction, shall be punished by fine not exceeding one thousand dollars, or imprisonment not exceeding one year, or both, in the discretion of the court.

SEC. 3. *And be it further enacted*, That the district courts of the United States . . . shall have, exclusively of the courts of the several States, cognizance of all crimes and offences committed against the provisions of this act, and also . . . of all causes, civil and criminal, affecting persons who are denied or cannot enforce in the courts or judicial tribunals of the State or locality where they may be any of the rights secured to them by the first section of this act; and if any suit or prosecution, civil or criminal, has been or shall be commenced in any State court, against any such person, for any cause whatsoever, or against any officer, civil or military, or other person, for any arrest or imprisonment, trespasses, or wrongs done or committed by virtue or under color of authority derived from this act or the act establishing a Bureau for the relief of Freedmen and Refugees, and all acts amendatory thereof, or for refusing to do any act upon the ground that it would be inconsistent with this act, such defendant shall have the right to remove such cause for trial to the proper district or circuit court[.] . . .

SEC. 4. *And be it further enacted*, That the district attorneys, marshals, and deputy marshals of the United States, the commissioners appointed by the circuit and territorial courts of the United States, . . . the officers and agents of the Freedmen's Bureau, and every other officer who may be specially empowered by the President of the United States, shall be, and they are hereby, specially authorized and required, at the expense of the United States, to institute proceedings against all and every person who shall violate the provisions of this act[.] . . .

SEC. 9. *And be it further enacted*, That it shall be lawful for the President of the United States, or such person as he may empower for that purpose, to employ such part of the land or naval forces of the United States, or of the militia, as shall be necessary to prevent the violation and enforce the due execution of this act. . . .

10. AN ACT FOR THE DISPOSAL OF THE PUBLIC LANDS FOR HOMESTEAD ACTUAL SETTLEMENT IN THE STATES OF ALABAMA, MISSISSIPPI, LOUISIANA, ARKANSAS, AND FLORIDA, 14 STAT. 66 (JUNE 21, 1866) (SOUTHERN HOMESTEAD ACT)

The Southern Homestead Act opened public land in the South to development and gave blacks and loyal whites first choice of plots until 1867. While broad in potential, the act made little impact. Few blacks possessed sufficient capital to take advantage of the act, while much of the available public land was located in remote areas or was unsuitable for farming anyway. Whites acting as agents for lumber companies claimed most of the land disposed of under this law.

Be it enacted . . . That from and after the passage of this act all the public lands in the States of Alabama, Mississippi, Louisiana, Arkansas, and Florida shall be disposed of according to the stipulations of the homestead law of twentieth May, eighteen hundred and sixty-two, . . . and the act supplemental thereto, approved twenty-first of March, eighteen hundred and sixty-four, but with this restriction, that until the expiration of two years from and after the passage of this act, no entry shall be made for more than a half-quarter section, or eighty acres; and in lieu of the sum of ten dollars required to be paid by the second section of said act, there shall be paid the sum of five dollars at the time of the issue of said patent; . . . *Provided,* That no distinction or discrimination shall be made in the construction or execution of this act on account of race or color[.]

SEC. 2. *And be it further enacted . . .* That until the first day of January, eighteen hundred and sixty-seven, any person applying for the benefit of this act shall, in addition to the oath, hereinbefore required, also make oath that he has not borne arms against the United States, or given aid and comfort to its enemies. . . .

11. *UNITED STATES V. RHODES*, 27 F. CAS. 785
(CIRCUIT COURT, D. KENTUCKY 1866)

A jury found guilty several whites who burglarized a black woman in Kentucky on a May 1866 night. The U.S. attorney tried the case in the U.S. district court because Kentucky state law prohibited blacks from testifying. Defense counsel challenged the verdict on the basis that the Civil Rights Act of 1866 gave no grounds for trying the case in federal court, and that the act went beyond the Thirteenth Amendment's scope. Supreme Court justice Noah Swayne, writing in his capacity as circuit court judge of the Circuit Court of Kentucky, upheld the constitutionality of the Civil Rights Act of 1866. Swayne relied on the Thirteenth Amendment's authorization that Congress could enforce it by appropriate legislation and prohibit a reconstitution of slavery except in name. Swayne added that the amendment "throws its protection over every one, of every race, color, and condition within that jurisdiction, and guards them against the recurrence of the evil," slavery, so that "[t]he constitution, thus amended, consecrates the entire territory of the republic to freedom, as well as to free institutions" for all future time.

[Noah] SWAYNE, Circuit Justice. This is a prosecution under the [1866 Civil Rights Act]. The defendants having been found guilty by a jury, the case is now before us upon a motion in arrest of judgment.

Three grounds are relied upon in support of the motion. It is insisted: I. That the indictment is fatally defective. II. That the case which it makes, or was intended to make, is not within the act of congress upon which it is founded. III. That the act itself is unconstitutional and void.

I. As to the indictment, if either count be sufficient, it will support the judgment of the court upon the verdict. Our attention will be confined to the second count. That count alleges that the defendants, being white persons, "on the 1st of May, 1866, at the county of Nelson, in the state and district of Kentucky, at the hour of eleven of the clock in the night of the same day, feloniously and burglariously did break and enter the dwelling house there situate of Nancy Talbot, a citizen of the United States of the African race . . . who was then and there, and is now, denied the right to testify against the said defendants, in the courts of the state of Kentucky, . . . with intent the goods and chattels, moneys and property of the said Nancy Talbot, in the said dwelling house then and there being, feloniously and burglariously to steal, take, and carry away, contrary to the statute in such case made and provided, and against the peace and dignity of the United States."

The objection urged against this count is, that it does not aver that "white citizens" enjoy the right which it is alleged is denied to Nancy Talbot. This fact is vital in the case. Without it our jurisdiction cannot be maintained. It is averred that she is a citizen of the United States, of the African race, and that she is denied the right to testify against the defendants, they being white persons. Section 669 of the Code of Civil Practice of Kentucky gives this right to white persons under the same circumstances. This is a public statute, and we are bound to take judicial cognizance of it. It is never necessary to set forth matters of law in a criminal pleading. The indictment is, in legal effect, as if it averred the existence and provisions of the statute. The enjoyment of the right in question by white citizens is a conclusion of law from the facts stated. . . . The objection to this count cannot be sustained.

II. Is the offense charged, within the statute? [Here Judge Swayne recites portions of the Civil Rights Act of 1866.]

. . . When the act was passed there was no state where ample provision did not exist for the trial and punishment of persons of color for all offenses; and no locality where there was any difficulty in enforcing the law against them. There was no complaint upon the subject. The aid of congress was not invoked in that direction. It is not denied that the first and second sections were designed solely for their benefit. The third section, giving the jurisdiction to which this question relates, provides expressly that if sued or prosecuted in a state court under the circumstances mentioned, they may at once have the cause certified into a proper federal court. [The fourth through ninth sections describe the mechanism wherein district attorneys, marshals, commissioners, freedmen's bureau agents, and other officers had a duty to institute proceedings at the expense of the United States against people who violated the statutes; the sections also made it unlawful for persons to obstruct their efforts or aid a person in evading arrest after a warrant has issued.]

. . . It is incredible that all this machinery, including the agency of the freedmen's bureau, would have been provided, if the intention were to limit the criminal jurisdiction conferred by the third section to colored persons, and exclude all white persons from its operation. . . .

The difficulty was that where a white man was sued by a colored man, or was prosecuted for a crime against a colored man, colored witnesses were excluded. This in many cases involved a denial of justice. Crimes of the deepest dye were committed by white men with impunity. Courts and juries were frequently hostile to the colored man, and administered justice, both civil and criminal, in a corresponding spirit. Congress met these evils by giving to the colored man everywhere the same right to testify "as is enjoyed by white citizens," abolishing the distinction between white and colored witnesses, and by giving to the courts of the United States jurisdiction of all causes, civil and criminal, which concern him, wherever the right to testify as if he were white is denied to him or cannot be enforced in the local tribunals of the state.

The context and the rules of interpretation to be applied permit of no other construction. Such was clearly the intention of congress, and that intention constitutes the law. . . .

III. Is the act warranted by the constitution? . . . The thirteenth amendment is the last one made. It trenches directly upon the power of the states and of the people of the states. It is the first and only instance of a change of this character in the organic law. It destroyed the most important relation between capital and labor in all the states where slavery existed. It affected deeply the fortunes of a large portion of their people. It struck out of existence millions of property. The measure was the consequence of a strife of opinions, and a conflict of interests, real or imaginary, as old as the constitution itself. These elements of discord grew in intensity. Their violence was increased by the throes and convulsions of a civil war. The impetuous vortex finally swallowed up the evil, and with it forever the power to restore it. Those who insisted upon the adoption of this amendment were animated by no spirit of vengeance. They sought security against the recurrence of a sectional conflict. They felt that much was due to the African race for the part it had borne during the war. They were also impelled by a sense of right and by a strong sense of justice to an unoffending and long-suffering people. These considerations must not be lost sight of when we come to examine the amendment in order to ascertain its proper construction.

The act of congress confers citizenship. Who are citizens, and what are their rights? The constitution uses the words "citizen" and "natural born citizens;" but neither that instrument nor any act of congress has attempted to define their meaning. . . .

The fact that one is a subject or citizen determines nothing as to his rights as such. They vary in different localities and according to circumstances. Citizenship has no necessary connection with the franchise of voting, eligibility to office, or indeed with any other rights, civil or political. Women, minors, and persons non compos are citizens, and not the less so on account of their disabilities. . . . Here, until the thirteenth amendment was adopted, the power belonged entirely to the states, and they exercised it without question from any quarter, as absolutely as if they were not members of the Union. . . .

"The powers not delegated to the United States by this constitution, nor prohibited by it to the states, are reserved to the states respectively or to the people." Const. Amend. What the several states under the original constitution only could have done, the nation has done by the thirteenth amendment. . . .

This brings us to the examination of the thirteenth amendment. . . .

Before the adoption of this amendment, the constitution, at the close of the enumeration of the powers of congress, authorized that body "to make all laws which shall be necessary and proper for carrying into execution the foregoing powers, and all other powers vested by this constitution in the government of the United States, or any department or officer thereof." . . .

. . . Before proceeding further, it would be well to pause and direct our attention to what has been deemed appropriate in the execution of some of the other powers confided to congress in like general terms.

(1) "The power to lay and collect taxes, duties, and imposts." This includes authority to build custom houses; to employ revenue cutters; to appoint the necessary collectors and other officers; to take bonds for the performance of their duties; to establish the needful bureaus; to prescribe when, how, and in what the taxes and duties shall be paid; to rent or build warehouses for temporary storing purposes; to define all crimes relating to the subject in its various ramifications, with their punishment; and to provide for their prosecution.

(2) "To regulate commerce with foreign nations, among the several states, and with the Indian tribes." This carries with it the power to build and maintain lighthouses, piers, and breakwaters; to employ revenue cutters; to cause surveys to be made of coasts, rivers, and harbors; to appoint all necessary officers, at home and abroad; to prescribe their duties, fix their terms of office and compensation; and to define and punish all crimes relating to commerce within the sphere of the constitution. . . .

These are but a small part of the powers which are incidental and appropriate to the main powers expressly granted. It is Utopian to believe that without such constructive powers, the powers expressed can be so executed as to meet the intentions of the framers of the constitution, and to accomplish the objects for which governments are instituted. The constitution provides expressly for the exercise of such powers to the full extent that may be "necessary and proper." No other limitation is imposed. . . .

The present effect of the amendment was to abolish slavery wherever it existed within the jurisdiction of the United States. In the future it throws its protection over every one, of every race, color, and condition within that jurisdiction, and guards them against the recurrence of the evil. The constitution, thus amended, consecrates the entire territory of the republic to freedom, as well as to free institutions. The amendment will continue to perform its function throughout the expanding domain of the nation, without limit of time or space. Present possessions and future acquisitions will be alike within the sphere of its operation.

Without any other provision than the first section of the amendment, congress would have had authority to give full effect to the abolition of slavery thereby decreed. . . . The second section of the amendment was added out of abundant caution. It authorizes congress to select, from time to time, the means that might be deemed appropriate to the end. . . . It is only when the authority given has been clearly exceeded, that the judicial power can be invoked. . . .

When the late Civil War broke out, slavery of the African race subsisted in fifteen states of the Union. The legal code relating to persons in that condition was everywhere harsh and severe. . . .

Slaves were imperfectly, if at all, protected from the grossest outrages by the whites. Justice was not for them. The charities and rights of the domestic relations had no legal existence among them. The shadow of the evil fell upon the free blacks. They had but few civil and no political rights in the slave states. Many of the badges of the bondman's degradation were fastened upon them. Their condition, like his, though not so bad, was helpless and hopeless. . . .

On January 1, 1863, President Lincoln issued his proclamation of emancipation. Missouri and Maryland abolished slavery by their own voluntary action. Throughout the war the African race had evinced entire sympathy with the Union cause. At the close of the Rebellion two hundred thousand had become soldiers in the Union armies. The race had strong claims upon the justice and generosity of the nation. Weighty considerations of policy, humanity, and right were superadded. Slavery, in fact, still subsisted in thirteen states. Its simple abolition, leaving these laws and this exclusive power of the states over the emancipated in force, would have been a phantom of delusion. The hostility of the dominant class would have been animated with new ardor. Legislative oppression would have been increased in severity. Under the guise of police and other regulations slavery would have been in effect restored, perhaps in a worse form, and the gift of freedom would have been a curse instead of a blessing to those intended to be benefited. They would have had no longer the protection which the instinct of property leads its possessor to give in whatever form the property may exist. It was to guard against such evils that the second section of the amendment was framed. It was intended to give expressly to congress the requisite authority, and to leave no room for doubt or cavil upon the subject. The results have shown the wisdom of this forecast. Almost simultaneously with the adoption of the amendment this course of legislative oppression was begun. Hence, doubtless, the passage of the act under consideration. In the presence of these facts, who will say it is not an "appropriate" means of carrying out the object of the first section of the amendment, and a necessary and proper execution of the power conferred by the second? Blot out this act and deny the constitutional power to pass it, and the worst effects of slavery might speedily follow. It would be a virtual abrogation of the amendment.

It would be a remarkable anomaly if the national government, without this amendment, could confer citizenship on aliens of every race or color, and citizenship, with civil and political rights, on the "inhabitants" of Louisiana and Florida, without reference to race or color, and cannot, with the help of the amendment, confer on those of the African race, who have been born and always lived within the United States, all that this law seeks to give them. . . .

The amendment reversed and annulled the original policy of the constitution, which left it to each state to decide exclusively for itself whether slavery should or should not exist as a local institution, and what disabilities should attach to those of the servile race within its limits. The whites needed no relief or protection, and they are practically unaffected by the amendment. The emancipation which it wrought was an act of great national grace, and was doubtless intended to reach further in its effects as to every one within its scope, than the consequences of a manumission by a private individual.

We entertain no doubt of the constitutionality of the act in all its provisions. . . . We are happy to know that if we have erred the supreme court of the United States can revise our judgment and correct our error. The motion is overruled, and judgment will be entered upon the verdict.

12. *IN RE TURNER*, 24 F. CAS. 337 (CIRCUIT COURT, D. MARYLAND 1867)

Shortly after the Civil War, some states passed apprenticeship laws that authorized removal of black children from their parents. In this case, the chief justice of the Supreme Court, sitting as a circuit justice, held such apprenticeships to be involuntary servitude prohibited by the Thirteenth Amendment and the Civil Rights Act of 1866.

[Salmon P.] CHASE, Circuit Justice.

. . . The petitioner, Elizabeth Turner, a young person of color, and her mother, were, prior to the adoption of the Maryland constitution of 1864, slaves of the respondent. That constitution went into operation on November 1, 1864, and prohibited slavery. Almost immediately thereafter many of the freed people of Talbot county [Maryland] were collected together under some local authority, the nature of which does not clearly appear, and the younger persons were bound as apprentices, usually, if not always, to their late masters. Among others, Elizabeth, the petitioner, was indentured to Hambleton by an indenture dated November 3, two days after the new constitution went into operation.

Upon comparing the terms of this indenture (which is claimed to have been executed under the laws of Maryland relating to negro apprentices) with those required by the law of Maryland in the indentures for the apprenticeship of white persons, the variance is manifest. The petitioner, under this indenture, is not entitled to any education; a white apprentice must be taught reading, writing, and arithmetic. The petitioner is liable to be assigned and transferred at the will of the master to any person in the same county; the white apprentice is not so liable. The authority of the master over the petitioner is described in the law as a "property and interest;" no such description is applied to authority over a white apprentice. It is unnecessary to mention other particulars.

... The following propositions ... decide the case:

1. The first clause of the thirteenth amendment to the constitution of the United States interdicts slavery and involuntary servitude, except as a punishment for crime, and establishes freedom as the constitutional right of all persons in the United States.

2. The alleged apprenticeship in the present case is involuntary servitude, within the meaning of these words in the amendment.

3. If this were otherwise, the indenture set forth in the return does not contain important provisions for the security and benefit of the apprentice which are required by the laws of Maryland in indenture of white apprentices, and is, therefore, in contravention of that clause of the first section of the civil rights law enacted by congress on April 9, 1866, which assures to all citizens without regard to race or color, "full and equal benefit of all laws and proceedings for the security of persons and property as is enjoyed by white citizens."

4. This law having been enacted under the second clause of the thirteenth amendment, in enforcement of the first clause of the same amendment, is constitutional, and applies to all conditions prohibited by it, whether originating in transactions before or since its enactment.

5. Colored persons equally with white persons are citizens of the United States. The petitioner, therefore, must be discharged from restraint by the respondent.

The chief justice passed the following order: Ordered by the court, this 16th day of October, A.D. 1867, that Elizabeth Turner be discharged from the custody of Philemon T. Hambleton, upon the ground that the detention and restraint complained of is in violation of the constitution and laws of the United States; and it is further ordered that the costs of this proceeding be paid by the petitioner.

13. THREE RECONSTRUCTION ACTS (1867)

In 1866, President Johnson undertook the "swing around the circle," in which he sought to influence upcoming elections by delivering speeches across the country. Johnson succeeded in influencing the election, but not in the way he had hoped: the president's harangues embarrassed even some of his supporters, and the Republicans gained a veto-proof majority in Congress. Radical Republicans seized the initiative by passing three Reconstruction Acts that placed the former Confederate states under military control and required them to draft constitutions framed by delegates elected by male citizens over the age of twenty-one regardless of race (but excepting those disfranchised for participation in the rebellion) and to adopt the Fourteenth Amendment before they could be readmitted to representation in Congress and have military governance withdrawn.

An Act to provide for the more efficient Government of the Rebel States, 14 Stat. 428 (March 2, 1867)

WHEREAS no legal State governments or adequate protection for life or property now exists in the rebel States of Virginia, North Carolina, South Carolina, Georgia, Mississippi, Alabama, Louisiana, Florida, Texas, and Arkansas; and whereas it is necessary that peace and good order should be enforced in said States until loyal and republican State governments can be legally established: Therefore,

Be it enacted . . . That said rebel States shall be divided into military districts and made subject to the military authority of the United States as hereinafter prescribed[.] . . .

SEC. 2 *And be it further enacted*, That it shall be the duty of the President to assign to the command of each of the said districts an officer of the army, not below the rank of brigadier-general, and to detail a sufficient military force to enable such officer to perform his duties and enforce his authority within the district to which he is assigned.

SEC. 3 *And be it further enacted*, That it shall be the duty of each officer assigned as aforesaid, to protect all persons in their rights of person and property, to suppress insurrection, disorder, and violence, and to punish, or cause to be punished, all disturbers of the public peace and criminals; and to this end he may allow local civil tribunals to take jurisdiction of and to try offenders, or, when in his judgment it may be necessary for the trial of offenders, he shall have power to organize military commissions or tribunals for that purpose, and all interference under color of State authority with the exercise of military authority under this act, shall be null and void.

SEC. 4 *And be it further enacted*, That all persons put under military arrest by virtue of this act shall be tried without unnecessary delay, and no cruel or unusual punishment shall be inflicted, and no sentence of any military commission or tribunal hereby authorized, affecting the life or liberty of any person, shall be executed until it is approved by the officer in command of the district, and the laws and regulations for the government of the army shall not be affected by this act, except in so far as they conflict with its provisions: *Provided*, That no sentence of death under the provisions of this act shall be carried into effect without the approval of the President.

SEC. 5 *And be it further enacted*, That when the people of any one of said rebel States shall have formed a constitution of government in conformity with the Constitution of the United States in all respects, framed by a convention of delegates elected by the male citizens of said State, twenty-one years old and upward, of whatever race, color, or previous condition, who have been resident in said State for one year previous to the day of such election, except such as may be disfranchised for participation in the rebellion or for felony at common law, and when such constitution shall provide that the elective franchise shall be enjoyed by all such persons as have the qualifications herein stated for electors of delegates, and when such constitution shall be ratified by a majority of the persons voting on the question of ratification who are qualified as electors for delegates, and when such constitution shall have been submitted to Congress for examination and approval, and Congress shall have approved the same, and when said State, by a vote of its legislature elected under said constitution, shall have adopted the [Fourteenth] amendment to the Constitution of the United States . . . and when said article shall have become a part of the Constitution of the United States, said State shall be declared entitled to representation in Congress . . . and then and thereafter the preceding sections of this act shall be inoperative in said State: *Provided*, That no person excluded from the privilege of holding office by said proposed amendment to the Constitution of the United States, shall be eligible to election as a member of the convention to frame a constitution for any of said rebel States, nor shall any such person vote for members of such convention.

SEC. 6 *And be it further enacted*, That, until the people of said rebel States shall be by law admitted to representation in the Congress of the United States, any civil governments which may exist therein shall be deemed provisional only, and in all respects subject to the paramount authority of the United States at any time to abolish, modify, control, or supersede the same; and in all elections to any office under such provisional governments all persons shall be entitled to vote, and none others, who are entitled to vote under the provisions of the fifth section of this act; and no person shall be eligible to any office under any provisional governments who would be disqualified from holding office under the provisions of the third *article* of said constitutional amendment.

*An Act supplementary to an Act entitled "An Act to provide
for the more efficient Government of the Rebel States," passed
March second, eighteen hundred and sixty-seven, and to
facilitate Restoration, 15 Stat. 2 (March 23, 1867)*

Be it enacted . . . That before the first day of September, eighteen hundred and sixty-seven, the commanding general in each district defined by an act entitled "An act to provide for the more efficient government of the rebel States," passed March second, eighteen hundred and sixty-seven, shall cause a registration to be made of the male citizens of the United States, twenty-one years of age and upwards, resident in each county or parish in the State or States included in his district, which registration shall include only those persons who are qualified to vote for delegates by the act aforesaid, and who shall have taken and subscribed the following oath or affirmation: "I, _____, do solemnly swear (or affirm), in the presence of Almighty God, that I am a citizen of the State of _____; that I have resided in said State for _____ months next preceding this day, and now reside in the county of _____, or the parish of _____, in said State (as the case may be); that I am twenty-one years old; that I have not been disfranchised for participation in any rebellion or civil war against the United States, nor for felony committed against the laws of any State or of the United States; that I have never been a member of any State legislature, nor held any executive or judicial office in any State and afterwards engaged in insurrection or rebellion against the United States, or given aid or comfort to the enemies thereof; that I have never taken an oath as a member of Congress of the United States, or as an officer of the United States, or as a member of any State legislature, or as an executive or judicial officer of any State, to support the Constitution of the United States, and afterwards engaged in insurrection or rebellion against the United States, or given aid or comfort to the enemies thereof; that I will faithfully support the Constitution and obey the laws of the United States, and will to the best of my ability, encourage others so to do, so help me God"; which oath or affirmation may be administered by any registering officer.

Sec. 2. *And be it further enacted*, That after the completion of the registration hereby provided for in any State, at such time and places therein as the commanding general shall appoint and direct, of which at least thirty days' public notice shall be given, an election shall be held of delegates to a convention for the purpose of establishing a constitution and civil government for such State loyal to the Union, said convention in each State, except Virginia, to consist of the same number of members as the most numerous branch of the State legislature of such State in the year eighteen hundred and sixty, to be apportioned among the several districts, counties, or parishes of such State by the commanding general, giving to each representation in the ratio of voters registered as aforesaid as nearly as may be. The convention in Virginia shall consist of the same number of members as represented the territory now constituting Virginia in the most numerous branch of the legislature of said State in the year eighteen hundred and sixty, to be apportioned as aforesaid.

Sec. 3. *And be it further enacted*, That at said election the registered voters of each State shall vote for or against a convention to form a constitution therefor under this act. . . . If a majority of the votes given on that question shall be for a convention, then such convention shall be held as hereinafter provided; but if a majority of said votes shall be against a convention, then no such convention shall be held under this act: *Provided*, That such convention shall not be held unless a majority of all such registered voters shall have voted on the question of holding such convention.

Sec. 4. *And be it further enacted,* That . . . if a majority of the votes given on that question shall be for a convention, the commanding general, within sixty days from the date of election, shall notify the delegates to assemble in convention, at a time and place to be mentioned in the notification, and said convention, when organized, shall proceed to frame a constitution and civil government according to the provisions of this act, and the act to which it is supplementary; and when the same shall have been so framed, said constitution shall be submitted by the convention for ratification to the persons registered under the provisions of this act at an election to be conducted by the officers or persons appointed or to be appointed by the commanding general, as hereinbefore provided, and to be held after the expiration of thirty days from the date of notice thereof, to be given by said convention; and the returns thereof shall be made to the commanding general of the district.

Sec. 5. *And be it further enacted,* That if, according to said returns, the constitution shall be ratified by a majority of the votes of the registered electors qualified as herein specified, cast at said election, at least one half of all the registered voters voting upon the question of such ratification, the president of the convention shall transmit a copy of the same, duly certified, to the President of the United States, who shall forthwith transmit the same to Congress, if then in session, and if not in session, then immediately upon its next assembling; and if it shall moreover appear to Congress that the election was one at which all the registered and qualified electors in the State had an opportunity to vote freely and without restraint, fear, or the influence of fraud, and if the Congress shall be satisfied that such constitution meets the approval of a majority of all the qualified electors in the State, and if the said constitution shall be declared by Congress to be in conformity with the provisions of the act to which this is supplementary, and the other provisions of said act shall have been complied with, and the said constitution shall be approved by Congress, the State shall be declared entitled to representation, and senators and representatives shall be admitted therefrom as therein provided. . . .

An Act supplementary to an Act entitled "An Act to
provide for the more efficient Government of the Rebel
States," passed on the second day of March, eighteen hundred
and sixty-seven, and the Act supplementary thereto, passed on
the twenty-third day of March, eighteen hundred
and sixty-seven, 15 Stat. 14 (July 19, 1867)

Be it enacted . . . That it is hereby declared to have been the true intent and meaning of the [prior two Reconstruction Acts] that the governments then existing in the rebel States of Virginia, North Carolina, South Carolina, Georgia, Mississippi, Alabama, Louisiana, Florida, Texas, and Arkansas were not legal State governments; and that thereafter said governments, if continued, were to be continued subject in all respects to the military commanders of the respective districts, and to the paramount authority of Congress.

Sec. 2. *And be it further enacted,* That the commander of any district named in said act shall have power, subject to the disapproval of the General of the army of the United States, and to have effect till disapproved, whenever in the opinion of such commander the proper administration of said act shall require it, to suspend or remove from office, or from the performance of official duties and the exercise of official powers, any officer or person holding or exercising, or professing to hold or exercise, any civil or military office or duty in such district under any power, election, appointment or authority derived from, or granted by, or claimed

Fig. 19. "The First Vote," depicting a craftsman, city dweller, and black veteran casting their votes under the 1867 Reconstruction Acts. (Alfred R. Waud, *Harper's Weekly,* November 16, 1867)

under, any so-called State or the government thereof, or any municipal or other division thereof, and upon such suspension or removal such commander, subject to the disapproval of the General as aforesaid, shall have power to provide from time to time for the performance of the said duties of such officer or person so suspended or removed, by the detail of some competent officer or soldier of the army, or by the appointment of some other person, to perform the same, and to fill vacancies occasioned by death, resignation, or otherwise. . . .

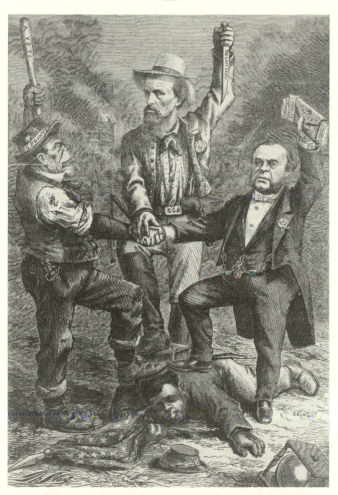

Fig. 20. "This Is a White Man's Government," depicting an Irish American, Nathan Bedford Forrest, and August Belmont as chair of the Democratic Party trampling a black Union veteran, while the Colored Orphan Asylum burns in the background (a reference to the New York City Draft Riot). The caption below reads, "'We regard the Reconstruction Acts (so called) of Congress as usurpations, and unconstitutional, revolutionary, and void.'—*Democratic Platform*." (Thomas Nast, *Harper's Weekly*, September 5, 1868)

14. ARTICLES OF IMPEACHMENT AGAINST PRESIDENT
ANDREW JOHNSON (PRESENTED TO THE SENATE ON
MARCH 4, 1868) (*SUPPLEMENT TO THE CONGRESSIONAL
GLOBE*, 40TH CONGRESS, 2ND SESSION, 1868)

In 1864, the Republican Party, calling itself the National Union Party, attempted to broaden its appeal by nominating Andrew Johnson, a Southerner and a War Democrat, to the vice presidency. After Lincoln's death, President Johnson antagonized Radical Republicans in Congress with his lenient attitude toward the South and his hostility toward legislation to protect the newly freed slaves, especially as the nation confronted race riots in Memphis and New Orleans in May and July 1866, respectively. Congress passed both the Freedmen's Bureau Bill and the Civil Rights Act of 1866 over Johnson's veto and, in an effort to keep Republican Edwin Stanton at his post as secretary of war, passed in March 1867 the Tenure of Office Act, which prohibited Johnson from dismissing any officer confirmed by the Senate without Senate approval. Radical Republicans imposed their own plan for Reconstruction and placed the states of the former Confederacy under military rule with the Reconstruction Acts of March 2, March 23, and July 19, 1867. In August 1867, Johnson dismissed Stanton from office, but the Senate overruled him pursuant to the Tenure of Office Act. In January 1868, Johnson again dismissed Stanton as secretary of war, and on February 24, 1868, the House of Representatives resolved to impeach Johnson. On March 4, the House presented the following articles to the Senate, and after trial, the Senate acquitted Johnson by a single vote. The Tenure of Office Act, meanwhile, remained law until its repeal in 1887.

Articles exhibited by the House of Representatives of the United States, in the name of themselves and all the people of the United States, against Andrew Johnson, President of the United States, in maintenance and support of their impeachment against him for high crimes and misdemeanors.

ARTICLE I.

That said Andrew Johnson, President of the United States, on the 21st day of February, in the year of our Lord 1868, at Washington, in the District of Columbia, unmindful of the high duties of his office, of his oath of office, and of the requirement of the Constitution that he should take care that the laws be faithfully executed, did unlawfully and in violation of the Constitution and laws of the United States issue an order in writing for the removal of Edwin M. Stanton from the office of Secretary for the Department of War, said Edwin M. Stanton having been theretofore duly appointed and commissioned, by and with the advice and consent of the Senate of the United States, as such Secretary, and said Andrew Johnson, President of the United States, on the 12th day of August, in the year of our Lord 1867, and during the recess of said Senate, having suspended by his order Edwin M. Stanton from said office, and within twenty days after the first day of the next meeting of said Senate, that is to say, on the 12th day of December, in the year last aforesaid, having reported to said Senate such suspension, with the evidence and reasons for his action in the case and the name of the person designated to perform the duties of such office temporarily until the next meeting of the Senate, and said Senate thereafterward, on the 13th day of January, in the year of our Lord 1868, having duly considered the evidence and reasons reported by said Andrew Johnson for said suspension, and having refused to concur in said suspension, whereby and by force of the provisions of an act entitled "An act regulating the tenure of certain civil offices," passed March 2, 1867, said Edwin M. Stanton did forthwith resume the functions of his office, whereof the said Andrew Johnson had then and there due notice, and said Edwin M. Stanton, by reason of the premises, on said 21st day of February, being lawfully entitled to hold said office of Secretary for the Department of War, which said order for the removal of said Edwin M. Stanton is in substance as follows, that is to say:

EXECUTIVE MANSION,
WASHINGTON, D.C., *February* 21, 1868.

SIR: By virtue of the power and authority vested in me as President by the Constitution and laws of the United States, you are hereby removed from office as Secretary for the Department of War, and your functions as such will terminate upon receipt of this communication.

You will transfer to Brevet Major General Lorenzo Thomas, Adjutant General of the Army, who has this day been authorized and empowered to act as Secretary of War *ad interim*, all records, books, paper and other public property now in your custody and charge.

Respectfully yours, ANDREW JOHNSON.

Hon. EDWIN M. STANTON, *Washington, D.C.*

Which order was unlawfully issued, with intent then and there to violate the act entitled "An act regulating the tenure of certain civil offices," passed March 2, 1867; and, with the further intent contrary to the provisions of said act, in violation thereof, and contrary to the provisions of the Constitution of the United States, and without the advice and consent of the Senate of the United States, the said Senate then and there being in session, to remove said Edwin M. Stanton from the office of Secretary for the Department of War, the said Edwin M. Stanton being then and there Secretary of War, and being then and there in the due and lawful execution of the duties of said office, whereby said Andrew Johnson, President of the United States, did then and there commit, and was guilty of a high misdemeanor in office.

[Articles II–IX consist of additional charges related to Johnson's violations of the Tenure of Office Act.]

ARTICLE X.

That said Andrew Johnson, President of the United States, unmindful of the high duties of his office and the dignity and proprieties thereof, and of the harmony and courtesies which ought to exist and be maintained between the executive and legislative branches of the Government of the United States, designing and intending to set aside the rightful authorities and powers of Congress, did attempt to bring into disgrace, ridicule, hatred, contempt and reproach the Congress of the United States and the several branches thereof, to impair and destroy the regard and respect of all the good people of the United States for the Congress and legislative power thereof, (which all officers of the government ought inviolably to preserve and maintain,) and to excite the odium and resentment of all good people of the United States against Congress and the laws by it duly and constitutionally enacted; and in pursuance of said design and intent, openly and publicly, and before divers assemblages of the citizens of the United States convened in divers parts thereof to meet and receive said Andrew Johnson as the Chief Magistrate of the United States, did, on the 18th day of August, in the year of our Lord 1866, and on divers other days and times, as well before as afterward, make and deliver, with a loud voice certain intemperate, inflammatory, and scandalous harangues, and did therein utter loud threats and bitter menaces as well against Congress as the laws of the United States duly enacted thereby, amid the cries, jeers, and laughter of the multitudes then assembled and within hearing, which are set forth in the several specifications hereinafter written, in substance and effect, that is to say:

Specification First.—In this, that at Washington, in the District of Columbia, in the Executive Mansion, to a committee of citizens who called upon the President of the United States, speaking of and concerning the Congress of the United States, heretofore, to wit, on the 18th day of August, in the year of our Lord 1866, did, in a loud voice, declare in substance and effect, among other things, that is to say:

"So far as the executive department of the Government is concerned, the effort has been made to restore the Union, to heal the breach, to pour oil into the wounds which were consequent upon the struggle, and (to speak in common phrase) to prepare, as the learned and wise physician would, a plaster healing in character and coextensive with the wound. We thought, and we think, that we had partially succeeded; but as the work progresses, as reconstruction seemed to be taking place, and the country was becoming reunited, we found a disturbing and marring element opposing us. In alluding to that element, I shall go no further than your convention and the distinguished gentleman who has delivered to me the report of the proceedings, I shall make no reference to it that I do not believe the time and the occasion justify.

"We have witnessed in one department of the government every endeavor to prevent the restoration of peace, harmony and union. We have seen hanging upon the verge of the government, as it were, a body called or which assumes to be the Congress of the United States, while in fact it is a Congress of only part of the States. We have seen this Congress pretend to be for the Union, when its every step and act tended to perpetuate disunion and make a disruption of States inevitable." ****

"We have seen Congress gradually encroach step by step upon constitutional rights, and violate, day after day and month after month, fundamental principles of the Government. We have seen a Congress that seemed to forget that there was a limit to the sphere and scope of legislation. We have seen a Congress in a minority assume to exercise power which, allowed to be consummated, would result in despotism or monarchy itself."

Specification Second.—In this, that at Cleveland, in the State of Ohio, heretofore, to wit, on the 3d day of September, in the year of our Lord 1866, before a public assemblage of citizens and others, said Andrew Johnson, President of the United States, speaking of and concerning the Congress of the United States, did, in a loud voice, declare in substance and effect, among other things, that is to say:

"I will tell you what I did do. I called upon your Congress that is trying to break up the Government."

* * *

"In conclusion, beside that, Congress had taken much pains to poison the constituents against him. But what had Congress done? Have they done anything to restore the union of these States? No: on the contrary, they had done everything to prevent it; and because he stood now where he did when the rebellion commenced he had been denounced as a traitor. Who had run greater risks or made greater sacrifices than himself? But Congress, factious and domineering, had undertaken to poison the minds of the American people."

Specification Third.—In this, that at St. Louis, in the State of Missouri, heretofore, to wit, on the 8th day of September, in the year of our Lord 1866, before a public assemblage of citizens and others, said Andrew Johnson, President of the United States, speaking of and concerning the Congress of the United States, did, in a loud voice, declare in substance and effect, among other things, that is to say:

"Go on. Perhaps if you had a word or two on the subject of New Orleans you might understand more about it than you do. And if you will go back—if you will go back and ascertain the cause of the riot at New Orleans, perhaps you will not be so prompt in calling out 'New Orleans.' If you will take up the riot at New Orleans and trace it back to its source or its immediate cause, you will find out who was responsible for the blood that was shed there. If you will take up the riot at New Orleans and trace it back to the Radical Congress you will find that the riot at New Orleans was substantially planned. If you will take up the proceedings in their caucuses you will understand that they there knew that a convention was to be called which was extinct by its power having expired; that it was said that the intention was that a new government was to be organized, and on the organization of that government the intention was to enfranchise one portion of the population, called the colored population, who had just been emancipated, and at the same time disfranchise white men. When you design to talk about New Orleans you ought to understand what you are talking about. When you read the speeches that were made, and take up the facts on the Friday and Saturday before that convention sat, you will there find that speeches were made incendiary in their character, exciting that portion of the population, the black population, to arm themselves and prepare for the shedding of blood. You will also find that that convention did assemble in violation of law, and the intention of that convention was to supersede the reorganized authorities in the State government of Louisiana, which had been recognized by the Government of the United States; and every man engaged in that rebellion in that convention, with the intention of superseding and up-turning the civil government which had been recognized by the Government of the United States, I say that he was a traitor to the Constitution of the United States, and hence you find that another rebellion was commenced having its origin in the Radical Congress."

* * *

"So much for the New Orleans riot. And there was the cause and the origin of the blood that was shed; and every drop of blood that was shed is upon their skirts, and they are responsible for it. I could test this thing a little closer, but will not do it here to-night. But when you talk about the causes and conse-quences that resulted from proceedings of that kind, perhaps, as I have been introduced here, and you have provoked questions of this kind, though it does not provoke me. I will tell you a few wholesome things that have been done by this Radical Congress in connection with New Orleans and the extension of the elective franchise.

"I know that I have been traduced and abused. I know it has come in advance of me here, as elsewhere, that I have attempted to exercise an arbitrary power in resisting laws that were intended to be forced upon the Government; that I had exercised that power; that I had abandoned the party that elected me, and that I was a traitor, because I exercised the veto power in attempting and did arrest for a time a bill that was called a "Freedmen's Bureau" bill, yes, that I was a traitor. And I have been traduced, I have been slandered, I have been maligned, I have been called Judas Iscariot, and all that. Now, my countrymen here to-night, it is very easy to indulge in epithets; it is easy to call a man a Judas and cry out traitor; but when he is called upon to give arguments and facts he is very often found wanting. Judas Iscariot—Judas. There was a Judas and he was one of the twelve apostles. Oh! yes, the twelve apostles had a Christ, and he never could have had a Judas unless he had had twelve apostles. If I have played the Judas, who has been my Christ that I have played the Judas with? Was it Thad. Stevens? Was it Wendell Phillips? Was it Charles Sumner? These are the men that stop and compare themselves with the Saviour, and everybody that differs with them in opinion, and to try and to stay and arrest the diabolical and nefarious policy, is to be denounced as a Judas."

* * *

"Well, let me say to you, if you will stand by me in this action; if you will stand by me in trying to give the people a fair chance, soldiers and citizens, to participate in these offices, God being willing, I will kick them out. I will kick them out just as fast as I can.

"Let me say to you, in concluding, that what I have said is what I intended to say. I was not provoked into this, and I care not for their menaces, the taunts, and the jeers. I care not for threats, I do not intend to be bullied by enemies nor overawed by my friends. But, God willing, with your help I will veto their measures whenever any of them come to me."

Which said utterances, declarations, threats, and harangues, highly censurable in any, are peculiarly indecent and unbecoming in the Chief Magistrate of the United States, by means whereof said Andrew Johnson has brought the high office of the President of the United States into contempt, ridicule, and disgrace, to the great scandal of all good citizens, whereby said Andrew Johnson, President of the United States, did commit, and was then and there guilty of, a high misdemeanor in office.

ARTICLE XI.

That said Andrew Johnson, President of the United States, unmindful of the high duties of his office and of his oath of office, and in disregard of the Constitution and laws of the United States, did heretofore, to wit: on the 18th day of August, 1866, at the city of Washington, in the District of Columbia, by public speech, declare and affirm in substance that the Thirty-Ninth Congress of the United States was not a Congress of the United States authorized by the Constitution to exercise legislative power under the same; but, on the contrary, was a Congress of only part of the States, thereby denying and intending to deny, that the legislation of said Congress was valid or obligatory upon him, the said Andrew Johnson, except in so far as he saw fit to approve the same, and also thereby denying and intending to deny the power of the said Thirty-Ninth Congress to propose amendments to the Constitution of the United States; and, in pursuance of said declaration, the said Andrew Johnson, President of the United States, afterward, to wit: on the 21st day of February, 1868, at the city of Washington, in the District of Columbia, did unlawfully and in disregard of the requirements of the Constitution, that he should take care that the laws be faithfully executed, attempt to prevent the execution of an act entitled "An act regulating the tenure of certain civil offices," passed March 2, 1867, by unlawfully devising and contriving, and attempting to devise and contrive, means by which he should prevent Edwin M. Stanton from forthwith resuming the functions of the office of Secretary for the Department of War, notwithstanding the refusal of the Senate to concur in the suspension therefore made by said Andrew Johnson of said Edwin M. Stanton from said office of Secretary for the Department of War, and also by further unlawfully devising and contriving, and attempting to devise and contrive, means then and there to prevent the execution of an act entitled "An act making appropriations for the support of the Army for the fiscal year ending June 30, 1868, and for other purposes," approved March 2, 1867, and also to prevent the execution of an act entitled "An act to provide for the more efficient government of the rebel States," passed March 2, 1867; whereby the said Andrew Johnson, President of the United States, did then, to wit: on the 21st day of February, 1868, at the city of Washington, commit and was guilty of a high misdemeanor in office.

15. AMERICAN CITIZENSHIP REDEFINED: THE FOURTEENTH AMENDMENT (DECLARED RATIFIED JULY 28, 1868) AND THE ACT OF JULY 27, 1868

The Civil Rights Act of 1866 defined in the law for the first time some of the rights associated with national citizenship. Concerned that a future Congress could repeal the act, Republicans sought a more permanent safeguard for the definition of national citizenship. On June 13, 1866, Congress passed and sent to the states for ratification the Fourteenth Amendment. Around this same time, Congress considered the issue of expatriation rights, the doctrine that individuals could divest themselves of their birth citizenship and change their allegiance, without permission from their native government, by emigrating to and naturalizing in the country of their choice. Americans had generally embraced expatriation rights since the Founding, but confusion reigned over the actual protection enjoyed by naturalized American citizens who returned to visit their homeland. The Constitution remained silent on the standing of naturalized Americans, Congress refrained from legislating on it, and conflicting rulings from the judiciary and State Department further muddled the matter. Meanwhile, most of Europe, including Britain, adhered to the principle of perpetual allegiance, that a subject could not disclaim birth allegiance even by swearing loyalty to another country. Shortly after the Civil War, Irish nationalists in the United States called Fenians attacked Canada and agitated for Ireland's release from British rule. When Britain began arresting Irish-born naturalized American citizens who returned to Ireland after the Civil War and charged them not as American citizens but as British subjects, the opposing viewpoints held by Britain and the United States regarding expatriation rights came to a head.

The Fourteenth Amendment, declared ratified by the nation on January 28, 1868, overturned Chief Justice Roger Taney's ruling in *Dred Scott*. The amendment defined in the Constitution that all persons born or naturalized in the United States,

regardless of color or former slave status, were American citizens. Furthermore, the amendment sanctified the idea that the same rights and protections enjoyed by native-born Americans applied to naturalized citizens in the United States, except for exclusion for the foreign-born from eligibility to serve as president or vice president. The Act of July 27, 1868, extended the concept of equal rights and protections for naturalized American citizens when those citizens traveled abroad. In conjunction with the Fourteenth Amendment, the Act of July 27, 1868, still in force today, explicitly linked expatriation rights to those listed in the Declaration of Independence and affirmed that naturalization placed foreign-born citizens on the same footing as those born on United States soil. By upholding the right of individuals to opt out of their birthright citizenship and choose a new allegiance without the consent of their native country, the Act of July 27, 1868, affirmed the voluntary and consensual nature of citizenship. As nation-building measures, both the Fourteenth Amendment and the Act of July 27, 1868, affirmed the power of the government of the United States to define its citizenry as well as protect it. As for Britain, American diplomatic pressure forced it to abandon the doctrine of perpetual allegiance pursuant to an 1870 treaty.

15(a). The Fourteenth Amendment (Declared Ratified July 28, 1868)

Section 1. All persons born or naturalized in the United States, and subject to the jurisdiction thereof, are citizens of the United States and of the State wherein they reside. No State shall make or enforce any law which shall abridge the privileges or immunities of citizens of the United States; nor shall any State deprive any person of life, liberty, or property, without due process of law, nor deny to any person within its jurisdiction the equal protection of the laws.

Section 2. Representatives shall be apportioned among the several States according to their respective numbers, counting the whole number of persons in each State, excluding Indians not taxed. But when the right to vote at any election for the choice of electors for President and Vice-President of the United States, Representatives in Congress, the executive and judicial officers of a State, or the members of the legislature thereof, is denied to any of the male inhabitants of such State, being twenty-one years of age, and citizens of the United States, or in any way abridged, except for participation in rebellion or other crime, the basis of representation therein shall be reduced in the proportion which the number of such male citizens shall bear to the whole number of male citizens twenty-one years of age in such State.

Section 3. No Person shall be a Senator or Representative in Congress, or elector of President and Vice-President, or hold any office, civil or military, under the United States, or under any State, who having previously taken an oath, as a member of Congress, or as an officer of the United States, or as a member of any State legislature, or as an executive or judicial officer of any State, to support the Constitution of the United States, shall have engaged in insurrection or rebellion against the same, or given aid or comfort to the enemies thereof. But Congress may by a vote of two thirds of each house remove such disability.

Section 4. The validity of the public debt of the United States, authorized by law, including debts incurred for payment of pensions and bounties for services in suppressing insurrection or rebellion, shall not be questioned. But neither the United States nor any State shall assume or pay any debt or obligation incurred in aid of insurrection or rebellion against the United States, or any claim for the loss or emancipation of any slave; but all such debts, obligations and claims shall be held illegal and void.

Section 5. The Congress shall have power to enforce, by appropriate legislation, the provisions of this article.

15(b). An Act concerning the Rights of American Citizens in foreign States, 15 Stat. 223 (July 27, 1868)

WHEREAS the right of expatriation is a natural and inherent right of all people, indispensable to the enjoyment of the rights of life, liberty, and the pursuit of happiness; and whereas in the recognition of this principle this government has freely received emigrants from all nations, and invested them with the rights of citizenship; and whereas it is claimed that such American citizens, with their descendents, are subjects of foreign states, owing allegiance to the governments thereof; and whereas it is necessary to the maintenance of public peace that this claim of foreign allegiance should be promptly and finally disavowed; Therefore,

Be it enacted... That any declaration, instruction, opinion, order, or decision of any officers of this government which denies, restricts, impairs, or questions the right of expatriation, is hereby declared inconsistent with the fundamental principles of this government.

Sec. 2. *And be it further enacted*, That all naturalized citizens of the United States, while in foreign states, shall be entitled to, and shall receive from this government, the same protection of persons and property that is accorded to native-born citizens in like situations and circumstances.

Sec. 3. *And be it further enacted*, That whenever it shall be made known to the President that any citizen of the United States has been unjustly deprived of his liberty by or under the authority of any foreign government, it shall be the duty of the President forthwith to demand of that government the reasons for such imprisonment, and if it appears to be wrongful and in violation of the rights of American citizenship, the President shall forthwith demand the release of such citizen, and if the release so demanded is unreasonably delayed or refused, it shall be the duty of the President to use such means, not amounting to acts of war, as he may think necessary and proper to obtain or effectuate such release, and all the facts and proceedings relative thereto shall as soon as practicable be communicated by the President to Congress.

16. Benjamin P. Runkle, *Address Delivered by Bvt. Col. Ben. P. Runkle, U.S.A. Chief Supt. Freedmen's Affairs, State of Kentucky, to the Freedmen of Louisville, October, 1868* (Louisville: Calvert, Tippett & Co., 1868)

In this speech to blacks in Louisville, Kentucky's superintendent of Freedmen's Affairs inspired his audience by recounting how blacks helped to save the Union and in the process began to become fitted for citizenship. Runkle declared that those who defended the nation should have a say in its governance, and he urged blacks to embrace the Republican free labor ethos by pursuing education and property, cultivating moral character, and avoiding alcohol.

. . . We will consider for a moment, the mighty work of the last seven years. The year 1861 found you four million of bondsmen—from the Bluegrass hills of Kentucky to the rice swamps of the Savannah, and the everglades of Florida—from the beautiful mountains of Virginia to the broad plains of Texas, four million people toiled in the damps of morning, in the hot noon day, and until the going down of the sun, waiting, yet scarce expecting the coming of a better day. . . .

. . . At last when the government, casting aside the last lingering remnants of prejudice, determined to use all the power it could command to crush the rebellion it offered the musket to the black man—the musket without the promise of bounty and without the sword—How they responded let the names of 125,000 black men on the rolls of the National Army answer! how they used their arms, let Fort Wagner and Port Hudson respond!

Then amid the ringing of steel, the roar of cannon, and the crash of musketry, was a people born, from darkness to light, from bondage to freedom; and stood, their shackles broken, forever free, waiting in the dim uncertain morning of this new day, waiting counsel and advice, standing on the borders of the promised land, waiting to be taught the responsibilities and duties of their new destiny as American citizens. And the hand that had burst the shackles, did not stop with the work of four years war. The Bureau followed in the track of the army; and with it came books, school houses, and teachers. A people were to be brought forth from the depths of ignorance, taught and made fit to receive and enjoy the rights and privileges of American Citizens, and a great and beneficient government, aided by the benevolent people of the north, came promptly to do the work. . . .

History does not record a greater work. No! none half so great—the fetters stricken from the limbs of four million people and that people protected, educated and guided in the way to become fitted for citizens of a free nation, and that in the space of seven short years. . . .

. . . [H]ow are you to gain the rights and privileges which you desire? What are these rights and privileges? You want the legal rights of American citizens.

You want equality before the law. You do not want social equality. I shall not stop to discuss this. I know that you do not want, ask for, or expect it. You have had too much of it already. It would be the ruin and destruction of both races. If an Allmighty God had intended the races to be one, He, in his infinite wisdom, would have made them one. Man cannot set aside the decrees of the Allmighty. We know this, you know it. Your enemies know it, they have no more fear of Negro equality than of Indian equality. It is the cry of unscrupulous demagogues, appealing to the prejudices of the people. It is ridiculous—it is impossible, let it pass! But equality before the law! It is a *different a very different thing*.

Life, liberty, the possession of property and the pursuit of happiness, should be guaranteed to every man who treads American soil, no matter what his color, cast or condition. . . .

[Runkle then discusses that blacks want the right to possess property, to labor for fair wages, and to till the soil without fear of attack, "the right to buy land, to pay for it, to build your little homes, to provide for your wives and children by your own fire-sides, to rest after your daily labor beneath your own roof without the fear of having your houses broken into, your families insulted, and yourselves dragged forth to be beaten or murdered on any pretence, whether it be that you served in the Union Army, or that the regulators are determined that you shall not live separate from your late masters, or that you have committed some offence against the laws of the land," the right to walk the streets and go to "places of amusement, Theatres or Circuses, subject to the rules governing such places, and all you ask is that the law of the land may protect you from the jeers, insults, assaults of evil-minded men," and the right to build schools and churches. He then points out that to protect these rights, blacks need the right to testify in court, sit on juries, and vote.]

. . . When this nation struggled for its life against the hosts of the Rebellion, when it was necessary, *absolutely necessary*, to strain every nerve, and bend every energy to save the Republic, did it stop to enquire whether the man who answered to the call and grasped the rifle was white or black? No! and when the ranks of the insurgents bore hard upon our bleeding and broken lines, when men fell thick and fast, when we saw "Old Glory" surrounded by the glittering bayonets coming to the rescue, did it matter to us whether the faces in that column were white or black? No, so they came under that same banner and went in with a loyal cheer it was all right. Why should we who stood side by side in the same armies, who stood or fell as fortune willed, who were likely to fall before the foe on the same field and go side by side with the black man to the bar of the same just God, why should we object to vote with them side by side at the same ballot box to support the same eternal principles? I do not believe we would be called upon to answer whether we fought in a white or black regiment; but on *what side we fought*, on the side of *God, liberty and humanity*, or on the side of *darkness, the Devil and Slavery*. Again, I repeat, every man who is liable to bear arms in defence of his country should have the right to vote, and as certain as the sun shines by day, so certain will that right be conceded. . . .

You must not expect the Congress of the United States to reconstruct this State and give you these rights and privileges, this cannot be done.

But from the people of Kentucky as a free gift worthily bestowed you must receive them. Prove to these people that you are worthy and well qualified, educate public sentiment by your daily walk and conversation, prove your fitness by your acts, and the powerful voice of Justice will plead and win your cause. Your destiny is in your own hands.

And now, in view of all this what is your duty? To educate your children and yourselves, strain every nerve, leave nothing undone which shall tend to fit you for the duties and responsibilities of the undeveloped future. Cultivate and raise the standard of morals among your people, and acquire property, get and keep the allmighty dollar[.] . . .

In the end, your leaders will be ranked among the cultivated men of the nation, and you will be known as a happy and prosperous people.

But first there are other things to be done, you must elevate the *standard of morals among your people*. Encourage morals and religion. Teach your people to occupy their minds with thoughts of good deeds—to turn from the evil and pursue the good, remember that there is a Providence over-ruling all—let your hearts be penetrated with a piety, and an honesty so strong that good faith and fidelity shall reign among you, more than fear of laws and punishments. That you shall do right for the sake of right; true religion will soften your manners and elevate your minds—good morals will nourish and strengthen the better impulses of your natures, the nobler promptings of your hearts. More than this, they will make you respected in the land, and strengthen you where you are now weak. . . . When I saw the black man free, working for his bread and the bread of his family, I rejoiced, but when I saw him entering the dram shop and wasting his wages for drink, which ruins both soul and body, I thought that with the good comes the evil, and with the blessing a curse—My friends shun the dram shop as you would the gates of hell, and the whisky cup as you would the cup of death. Again I trust the practice of "taking up" will disap pear from among you. To be sure there are many other people who behave very badly, yet they throw around their conduct a "mantle of concealment, and of outward decorum," this will profit them nothing in the next world, though it evidently does in this. . . .

. . . And lastly, save your money, acquire property and preserve it. It will give you importance, standing and consideration. Let every man strive to be a land owner, to have a home, however lowly, however small, *a home of his own*. Let him gather around his hearth-stone his wife and little ones, and with no fear of oppressive landlords, thank God that his lot is cast in this free land, and be happy. . . .

The future is yours, and if you but do your duty, "the wings of old time shall come laden with flowers." If you but do your duty the issue cannot be doubtful. This nation has, by the aid of the God of battles, solved the problem of American Slavery with the sword, and by the help of the same Omnipotent Arm we will solve the question of the education and elevation of this people, with school houses and books, with the pen, the printing press and the diffusion of knowledge among the masses of the people. And before these agencies prejudice, hatred, malice and uncharitableness shall go down in the dust, even as the armed columns of the rebellion went down before the bayonets of the loyal legions of this land. I repeat, the march of Christianity and civilization cannot be stopped by the evil deeds and words of men.

17. The Fifteenth Amendment (Declared Ratified March 30, 1870)

Section 1. The right of citizens of the United States to vote shall not be denied or abridged by the United States or by any State on account of race, color, or previous condition of servitude.

Section 2. The Congress shall have power to enforce this article by appropriate legislation.

Fig. 21. "Uncle Sam's Thanksgiving Dinner." A celebration of egalitarianism, Uncle Sam carves a turkey at a large table surrounded by men, women, and children of different races and nationalities. Uncle Sam's female counterpart, Columbia, sits at the far left of the table between a black man and a Chinese family. In the background, a banner celebrates the as-yet not ratified Fifteenth Amendment, and the table's centerpiece is labeled "self-government/universal suffrage." Behind Uncle Sam is a painting depicting Castle Garden, a major entry point for immigrants at the time before Ellis Island replaced it. (Thomas Nast, *Harper's Weekly*, November 20, 1869; Library of Congress)

THE RESULT OF THE FIFTEENTH AMENDMENT.
And the Rise and Progress of the African Race in America and its final Accomplishment, and Celebration on May 19ᵗʰ A.D.1870.

Fig. 22. "The Result of the Fifteenth Amendment, And the Rise and Progress of the African Race in America and its final Accomplishment, and Celebration on May 19th A.D. 1870." Many Americans hailed the Fifteenth Amendment's ratification in the spring of 1870 as the end of the "black question." Blacks celebrated across the land, Wendell Phillips's American Anti-Slavery Society disbanded ten days after ratification of the Fifteenth Amendment, and Frederick Douglass jubilantly announced, "Never was revolution more complete," creating "a new world" where "[t]he black man is free, the black man is a citizen, the black man is enfranchised . . . no more a despised and hated creature, but a man, and, what is more a man among men." According to Douglass, blacks now stood "upon an equal footing with all other men, and . . . the glory or shame of our future is to be wholly our own" in a new country where "[c]haracter, not color, is to be the criterion" ("At Last, at Last, the Black Man Has a Future: An Address Delivered in Albany, New York, on 22 April, 1870," in *The Frederick Douglass Papers, Series One*, ed. John W. Blassingame and John R. McKivigan [New Haven: Yale University Press, 1991], 4:265–72, 266–67, 270–71). (c. 1870; Library of Congress)

---

18. *Ku Klux Klan Hearings*, 42nd Congress, 2nd Session, Multiple Reports (1872)

In contrast to legal rights granted by the Civil War Amendments, these excerpts describe the violent opposition of Southern white racists.

[On July 6, 1871, white farmer William M. Champion, living near Spartanburgh, South Carolina, testified:]

... *Question.* Go on and state if, at any time, you have been visited by any men in disguise; and, if so, what they did and said to you, and all that occurred.

Answer. Yes—but I hate to tell it. Sunday night before the last State election, which I think was on the 19th day of October, I was visited by a crowd of disguised men. There were some who were not disguised; they were in my house, when I awoke, ripping, and tearing, and cursing, and hallooing "You d——d radical son of a b——h." ... They then blindfolded me, and told me I had but a few minutes to live . . . and if I had any praying to do, to pray. . . . They took me then and led me off, and took down my shirt and breeches, and whipped me, I could not tell you how much, as much as I was able to bear. I think I was about to faint and they ceased whipping me. There were some negroes they had there, but I had never seen them. I saw when they led me to the place that there was a number of them there before they blindfolded me. Well, they made me kiss the negro man's posterior, and held it open and made me kiss it, and as well as I remember a negro woman's, too, and also her private parts, and they told me to have sexual connection with her. I told them they knew, of course, I could not do that. They struck me, and some of them begged for me. They asked how I liked that for nigger equality. I told them it was pretty tough. They told me if I voted the radical ticket they would kill me. They led me on with them, and double-quicked me back a piece. They made me whip the negro some after they took off the blindfold. I could see and knew who I was whipping. They made me whip him some—that is, one of the negroes; they had three negroes there. . . .

Question. Was your back bruised?

Answer. Of course it was bruised; my shirt, when I took it off, was stiff with blood; but they said they couldn't see any broken skin.

Question. Where did the blood come from, then?

Answer. From the beating and bruising; it just oozed through. It was black, and so sore that I could scarcely go anywhere for days. I could scarcely swallow. They choked me so that my throat was sore, and they beat me everywhere.

Question. Had you anything to do with the election?

Answer. They appointed me one of the managers of the election in the township of Limestone. . . . Now, the neighborhood I live in was democratic, and I joined the Union League. . . .

Question. Had you been in the rebel service?

Answer. No sir; I had a sore leg, and never was mustered. I was a Union man in principle when the war came, and remained so. . . .

Question. Are you afraid to stay in your house?

Answer. Yes, sir.

Question. Why?

Answer. I am afraid of being visited again.

Question. To what extent does that feeling prevail in your part of the country? Are there other people who sleep out at night?

Answer. Yes, sir. I guess the whole republican party do. I suppose there are hardly any but what have laid out.

Question. Do you mean by that white and colored?

Answer. Yes, sir[.] . . .

Question. Do they lie out of their houses in the woods at night?

Answer. Yes sir; and they take the weather as it comes. We do not go anywhere else; we are afraid to go to a republican's house for fear it will be visited, and we can't go to the democrats' houses.

Question. Do you believe that this is a well-grounded fear—of these people visiting you and inflicting violence upon you—that drives you out?

Answer. I do; you can look at that letter, and see whether you think I am wrong in my feelings, (producing a letter.) . . .

"HEADQUARTERS KU-KLUX CLAN, *Algood, S.C.*

"Mr. BUSTER CHAMPION: We have been told that our visit to you was not a sufficient hint. We now notify you to leave the country within thirty days from the reception of this notice, or abide the consequences.

"K.K.K.

"NOVEMBER 8, 1870."

[On July 8, 1871, black farmer Jackson Surratt, living near Spartanburgh, South Carolina, testified:]

. . . *Question.* Have you been visited at any time by the Ku-Klux?

Answer. Yes, sir.

Question. When?

Answer. About two months ago, on a Sunday night, and the Saturday following.

Question. Go on and tell us all about it. . . .

Answer. I waked up in my bed, and I heard somebody running against the door. There was two. I hallooed, "Wait, and I will open it." They stopped. When I got up they had bursted a piece off, but it was not open. I opened it wide, and one said, "Have you ever went radical?" I told them I had. The other hallooed, "Blindfold him;" and he jerked me out of the door and blindfolded me; and they said, "Take a walk with me," and they took me off about fifty yards. . . . They told me to get down on my knees. I got down. He said, "Did you vote radical?" I said, "Yes, sir." He said, "What made you do it?" I said, "Because I was with the white people when I voted that way." They said, "Did you think the white people was right?" I told them I had no other source to cling to. I did not go by myself. I thought it was as right as anybody. He says, "Did the radical party promise to kill all us democrats?" I said, "They never told me that." He said, "If you tell me a lie we will murder you right here." I said, "I will tell you the truth." They said, "Didn't they say they would kill us?" "No," says I. Says he, "Are you lying? You are damn good now; but didn't you get up and go and vote before breakfast?" I says, "I did, in order to not lose much time. It was near my home, and I was busy cutting grass, and I didn't want to lose time." Says he, "You slipped off and went." "No, I didn't," says I, "I went along slow." "What made you vote radical?" Says I, "I did not know any better." Says he, "Do you think you will do any better?" I said, "I will do the best I know how." They said, "Damn you, that is not the best. You have been talked to, to go democrat, and, damn you, you didn't do it, and we will show you to-night." Then they said for me to pray for them. I prayed. They said then, "Just hit him a lick apiece;" and they hit me a lick apiece, and all the time they had me blindfolded, and they made me run to the house, and I had just time to look where the house was before I ran. . . . [T]hey gave me fourteen licks[.] . . .

Question. Did they come again?

Answer. Yes, sir. On the next Saturday night they come. . . . When they came again I had a clock and it struck one, and I laid there, and the first thing I heard the yard was full of horses, and they were rearing and cursing, "Open the door or we will kill the last one of you." I was scared, and opened it; and they cried, "Gentlemen, blindfold him." They started off with me, and they run in the house and cursed and tore and jerked my daughter out, and jerked my wife and my wife's son out of bed, and the first thing I knew they were bringing them all out. . . . They took us about seventy yards and made me let down the fence, and made me and my wife jump two logs together. They made us lie down about three steps apart, and they began to cut switches. They made us all lie down—my wife and all. They had us nearly naked. It was getting warm weather. . . . They cut switches, and they hit my wife's son a lick, and asked him what he was doing. He told them he did not know what he was doing. . . . I said to myself, "I believe if I lie here they will put me and all my folks through, so that I can't do any good," . . . and I rose on all fours and jumped and ran about fifty yards and stumped my foot, but I raised up and ran on and took right through the woods, and ran until I run over a log, and I found they were not after me[.] . . .

[Jackson's wife, Jane Surratt, then testified:]

. . . Answer. They came to my house and took me out and whipped me. They asked, did I work; I told them I did; they said I didn't; I said I did, as far as I was able; I was not able to do hard work; and they just whipped me on.

Question. How many of them came to your house?

Answer. I was so frightened I don't know; I don't recollect how many, but I think there was six or seven, if I am not mistaken; but I was so frightened that I don't remember.

Question. Did they take out anybody else but you?

Answer. Yes, sir; my husband and daughter and my son, and whipped them all at the same time. They didn't whip him then; they had whipped him before; he got away; but they whipped the balance of us.

Question. How much did they whip you?

Answer. I don't know, but I think that they gave me near forty lashes, or quite forty.

Question. On what part of your person?

Answer. They whipped me from my ankles clear up to about here, above my waist. They made us all lay down.

Question. Were you whipped hard?

Answer. Yes, sir; they whipped us with things bigger than my thumb.

Question. With what?

Answer. Switches and sticks, I call them.

Question. Did it hurt you?

Answer. Yes, sir. Sunday and Monday I couldn't hold my child on my lap to suckle it; I had to lay it on the bed and stand by it. I had no way to rest except on the flat of my belly. I couldn't rest.

Question. What did they do to your son and daughter?

Answer. They whipped them. They whipped my son miserably bad; they whipped my daughter very bad; she has not been able to do much since; I don't believe she will ever get over it.

Question. Did they say why they whipped you, except that you did not work?

Answer. That was all. They told her she didn't make a good hand last spring. He was hired out, and they told him he didn't make a good hand[.] . . .

Fig. 23. "Visit of the Ku-Klux." This illustration disturbingly depicts white racist terrorism against black freedpeople in the South. (Frank Bellow, *Harper's Weekly*, February 24, 1872; Library of Congress)

[On July 12, 1871, Mervin Givens, a black man living near Spartanburgh, South Carolina, testified:]

... *Answer.* They broke in on me and frightened me right smart, being asleep. ... They pulled the pillow-slip over my head and told me if I took it off they would shoot me. They carried me out and whipped me powerful.

Question. With what?

Answer. With sticks and hickories. They whipped me powerful.

Question. How many lashes?

Answer. I can't tell. I had no knowledge at all about it. May be a hundred or two. Two men whipped me and both at once.

Question. Did they say anything to you?

Answer. They cursed me and told me I had voted the radical ticket, and they intended to beat me so I would not vote it again. . . .

Question. Were they disguised?

Answer. Yes, sir.

Question. How[?]

Answer. They had on some sort of gray-looking clothes, and much the same sort of thing over their face. One of them had a sort of high hat with tassel and sort of horns. . . .

19. AN ACT TO ENFORCE THE RIGHT OF CITIZENS OF THE UNITED STATES TO VOTE IN THE SEVERAL STATES OF THIS UNION, AND FOR OTHER PURPOSES, 16 STAT. 140 (MAY 31, 1870)

Congress responded to racist violence in parts of the South with a series of five Enforcement Acts between 1870 and 1872. The first Enforcement Act, approved just two months after the Fifteenth Amendment was declared ratified, reiterated that American citizens could vote without regard to race, color, or previous slavery; provided enforcement provisions to secure this Fifteenth Amendment right; and mandated that the civil rights secured by prior legislation such as the Civil Rights Act of 1866 applied to everyone, including aliens. Subsequent Enforcement Acts emphasized the link between civil and political rights and required an increasingly nationalized system of elections, complete with federal supervision. The Enforcement Acts imposed criminal penalties against those who tried to interfere with black voting rights and sought to suppress organizations such as the Ku Klux Klan, including by presidential suspension of the writ of habeas corpus and use of federal troops.

Be it enacted . . . That all citizens of the United States who are or shall be otherwise qualified by law to vote at any election by the people in any State, Territory, district, county, city, parish, township, school district, municipality, or other territorial subdivision, shall be entitled and allowed to vote at all such elections, without distinction of race, color, or previous condition of servitude;

any constitution, law, custom, usage, or regulation of any State or Territory, or by or under its authority, to the contrary notwithstanding.

SEC. 2. *And be it further enacted*, That if by or under the authority of the constitution or laws of any State, or the laws of any Territory, any act is or shall be required to be done as a prerequisite or qualification for voting, and by such constitution or laws persons or officers are or shall be charged with the performance of duties in furnishing to citizens an opportunity to perform such prerequisite, or to become qualified to vote, it shall be the duty of every such person and officer to give to all citizens of the United States the same and equal opportunity to perform such prerequisite, and to become qualified to vote without distinction of race, color, or previous condition of servitude; and if any such person or officer shall refuse or knowingly omit to give full effect to this section, he shall, for every such offence, forfeit and pay the sum of five hundred dollars to the person aggrieved thereby, to be recovered by an action on the case, with full costs, and such allowance for counsel fees as the court shall deem just, and shall also, for every such offence, be deemed guilty of a misdemeanor, and shall, on conviction thereof, be fined not less than five hundred dollars, or be imprisoned not less than one month and not more than one year, or both, at the discretion of the court.

SEC. 3. *And be it further enacted*, That whenever, by or under the authority of the constitution or laws of any State, or the laws of any Territory, any act is or shall be required to [be] done by any citizen as a prerequisite to qualify or entitle him to vote, the offer of any such citizen to perform the act required to be done as aforesaid shall, if it fail to be carried into execution by reason of the wrongful act or omission aforesaid of the person or officer charged with the duty of receiving or permitting such performance or offer to perform, or acting thereon, be deemed and held as a performance in law of such act; and the person so offering and failing as aforesaid, and being otherwise qualified, shall be entitled to vote in the same manner and to the same extent as if he had in fact performed such act; and any judge, inspector, or other officer of election whose duty it is or shall be to receive, count, certify, register, report, or give effect to the vote of any such citizen who shall wrongfully refuse or omit to receive, count, certify, register, report, or give effect to the vote of such citizen upon the presentation by him of his affidavit stating such offer and the time and place thereof, and the name of the officer or person whose duty it was to act thereon, and that he was wrongfully prevented by such person or officer from performing such act, shall for every such offence [face the same punishment articulated in Section 2].

SEC. 4. *And be it further enacted*, That if any person, by force, bribery, threats, intimidation, or other unlawful means, shall hinder, delay, prevent, or obstruct, or shall combine and confederate with others to hinder, delay, prevent, or obstruct, any citizen from doing any act required to be done to qualify him to vote or from voting at any election as aforesaid, such person shall for every such offence [face the same punishment articulated in Section 2]. . . .

20. An Act to enforce the Provisions of the Fourteenth Amendment to the Constitution of the United States, and for other Purposes, 17 Stat. 13 (April 20, 1871)

Be it enacted . . . That any person who, under color of any law, statute, ordinance, regulation, custom, or usage of any State, shall subject, or cause to be subjected, any person within the jurisdiction of the United States to the deprivation of any rights, privileges, or immunities secured by the Constitution of the United States, shall, any such law, statute, ordinance, regulation, custom or usage of the State to the contrary notwithstanding, be liable to the party injured in any action at law, suit in equity, or other proper proceeding for redress; such proceeding to be prosecuted in the several district or circuit courts of the United States, with and subject to the same rights of appeal, review upon error, and other remedies provided in like cases in such courts, under the provisions of the [Civil Rights Act of 1866]; and the other remedial laws of the United States which are in their nature applicable in such cases.

SEC. 2. That if two or more persons within any State or Territory of the United States shall conspire together to overthrow, or to put down, or to destroy by force the government of the United States, or to levy war against the United States, or to oppose by force the authority of the government of the United States, or by force, intimidation, or threat to prevent, hinder, or delay the execution of any law of the United States, or by force to seize, take, or possess any property of the United States contrary to the authority thereof, or by force, intimidation, or threat to prevent any person from accepting or holding any office or trust or place of confidence under the United States, or from discharging the duties thereof, or by force, intimidation, or threat to induce any officer of the United States to leave any State, district, or place where his duties as such officer might lawfully be performed, or to injure him in his person or property on account of his lawful discharge of the duties of his office, or to injure his person while engaged in the lawful discharge of the duties of his office, or to injure his property so as to molest, interrupt, hinder, or impede him in the discharge of his official duty, or by force, intimidation, or threat to deter any party or witness in any court of the United States from attending such court, or from testifying in any matter pending in such court fully, freely, and truthfully, or to injure any such party or witness in his person or property on account of his having so attended or testified, or by force, intimidation, or threat to influence the verdict, presentment, or indictment, of any juror or grand juror in any court of the United States, or to injure such juror in his person or property on account of any verdict, presentment, or indictment lawfully assented to by him, or on account of his being or having been such juror, or shall conspire together, or go in disguise upon the public highway or upon the premises of another for the purpose, either directly or indirectly, of depriving any person or any class of persons of the equal protection of the laws, or of equal privileges or immunities under the laws, or for the purpose of preventing or hindering the constituted authorities of any State from giving or securing to all persons within such State the equal protection of the laws, or shall conspire together for the purpose of in any manner impeding, hindering, obstructing or defeating the due course of justice in any State or Territory, with intent to deny to any citizen of the United States the due and equal protection of the laws, or to injure any person in his person or his property for lawfully enforcing the right of any person or class of persons to the equal protection of the laws, or by force, intimidation, or threat to prevent any citizen of the United States lawfully entitled to vote from giving his support or advocacy in a lawful manner towards or in favor of the election of any lawfully qualified person as an elector of President or Vice-President of the United States, or as a member of the Congress of the United States, or to injure any such citizen in his person or property on account of such support or advocacy, each and every person so offending shall be deemed guilty of a high crime, and, upon conviction thereof in any district or circuit court of the United States or district or supreme court of any Territory of the United States having jurisdiction of similar offences, shall be punished by a fine not less than five hundred nor more than five thousand dollars, or by imprisonment, with or without hard labor, as the court may determine, for a period of not less than six months nor more than six years, as the court may determine, or by both such fine and imprisonment as the court shall determine. . . .

SEC. 3. That in all cases where insurrection, domestic violence, unlawful combinations, or conspiracies in any State shall so obstruct or hinder the execution of the laws thereof, and of the United States, as to deprive any portion or class of the people of such State of any of the rights, privileges, or immunities, or protection, named in the Constitution and secured by this act, and the constituted authorities of such State shall either be unable to protect, or shall, from any cause, fail in or refuse protection of the people in such rights . . . it shall be lawful for the President, and it shall be his duty to take such measures, by the employment of the militia or the land and naval forces of the United States, or of either, or by other means, as he may deem necessary for the suppression of such insurrection, domestic violence, or combinations[.] . . .

SEC. 4. That whenever in any State or part of a State the unlawful combinations named in the preceding section of this act shall be organized and armed, and so numerous and powerful as to be able, by violence, to either overthrow or set at defiance the constituted authorities of such State, and of the United States within such State, or when the constituted authorities are in complicity with, or shall connive at the unlawful purposes of, such powerful and armed combinations . . . in every such case such combinations shall be deemed a rebellion against the government of the United States, and during the continuance of such rebellion, and within the limits of the district which shall be so under the sway thereof, such limits to be prescribed by proclamation, it shall be lawful for the President of the United States, when in his judgment the public safety shall require it, to suspend the privileges of the writ of habeas corpus, to the end that such rebellion may be overthrown: *Provided*, That all the provisions of the second section of [the Habeas Corpus Act of March 3, 1863] . . . shall be in full force so far as the same are applicable to the provisions of this section[.] . . .

SEC. 5. That no person shall be a grand or petit juror in any court of the United States upon any inquiry, hearing, or trial of any suit, proceeding, or prosecution based upon or arising under the provisions of this act who shall, in the judgment of the court, be in complicity with any such combination or conspiracy; and every such juror shall, before entering upon any such inquiry, hearing, or trial, take and subscribe an oath in open court that he has never, directly or indirectly, counseled, advised, or voluntarily aided any such combination or conspiracy[.] . . .

SEC. 6. That any person or persons, having knowledge that any of the wrongs conspired to be done and mentioned in the second section of this act are about to be committed, and having power to prevent or aid in preventing the same, shall neglect or refuse to do so . . . such person or persons shall be liable to the person injured . . . for all damages caused by any such wrongful act which such first-named person or persons by reasonable diligence could have prevented[.] . . .

21. *Coger v. The North Western Union Packet Co.*,
37 Iowa 145 (Supreme Court of Iowa, 1873)

In this case, the Supreme Court of Iowa relied on the Civil Rights Act of 1866 to affirm a judgment against a steam liner that segregated a black woman who tried to dine with white passengers.

[Joseph M.] BECK, Ch. J.—I. The plaintiff, being in the city of Keokuk, went upon the steamer S. S. Merrill, one of defendant's line of packets navigating the Mississippi river . . . to be transported to her home at the city of Quincy, in the State of Illinois. She is a quadroon, being partly of African descent, and was employed as the teacher of a school for colored children in the city where she resided. She applied at the office of the vessel for a ticket and was given one entitling her to transportation, but not to a state-room nor to meals, such as those which, under the custom and regulations of defendant's steamers, are given to colored persons. This, after its terms were explained to her, she returned to the clerk of the boat and its price was returned to her. She claimed the right to be transported as other first-class passengers, and offered to pay accordingly. This being refused she, at the time, declined to accept a ticket on any other conditions and left the boat. She afterward returned and purchased a ticket, containing the conditions of the one she had refused to accept, printed in red ink thereon in these words: "The holder of this ticket is entitled to meals at an assigned table and first-class cot only—besides transportation." The following words were written across the face of the ticket: "This does not include meals." Before the hour of dinner she sent the chamber-maid to purchase a ticket for that meal and one was brought her with the words, "colored girl," written thereon. Plaintiff applied to the clerk at his office to be informed of the meaning of the writing and was told that it was a ticket of the character sold to persons of her color and entitled her to dinner at a table on the guards of the boat and that, under the conditions of her ticket for transportation, she could be seated for meals in whatever place the clerk saw proper to assign her. She returned the ticket to the clerk, refusing to accept it with the conditions as explained, and the price was repaid to her. After this she requested a gentleman to buy her a ticket for dinner, who bought her one without any indorsements or conditions. It does not appear that the officers of the boat knew, when this ticket was purchased, for whom it was intended. When dinner was announced she seated herself at the ladies' table in the cabin at a place designated for certain ladies traveling on the boat; this, it does not appear, she knew before seating herself. She was then informed by one of the officers of the boat that she must leave the table, that the seat she occupied was reserved and that her dinner would be, in a short time, ready for her at the place designated by the clerk. . . . She refused, and thereupon the captain of the boat was sent for, who repeated the request, and, being denied compliance, he proceeded by force to remove her from the table and the cabin of the boat. She resisted so that considerable violence was necessary to drag her out of the cabin, and, in the struggle, the covering of the table was torn off and dishes broken, and the officer received a slight injury. The defendant's witnesses testify that she used abusive, threatening and coarse language during and after the struggle, but this she denies. Certain it is, however, that by her spirited resistance and her defiant words, as well as by her pertinacity in demanding the recognition of her rights and in vindicating them, she has exhibited evidence of the Anglo-Saxon blood that flows in her veins. While we may consider that the evidence, as to her words and conduct, does not tend to establish that female delicacy and timidity so much praised, yet it does show an energy and firmness in defense of her rights not altogether unworthy of admiration. But neither womanly delicacy nor unwomanly courage has any thing to do with her legal rights and the remedies for their deprivation. These are to be settled without regard to such personal traits of character. . . .

II. . . . As we regard the case, the sole question presented for our determination is this: Had the defendant, as a common carrier of passengers, the authority to establish and enforce regulations depriving an individual of color of the privileges and rights accorded to white persons traveling upon its steamers, and to enforce rules whereby the former were required to submit to treatment and accept accommodations different from those of the latter; or, more briefly and in a word, are the rights and privileges of persons transported by public carriers affected by race or color? . . .

IV. In our opinion the plaintiff was entitled to the same rights and privileges while upon defendant's boat, notwithstanding the negro blood, be it more or less, admitted to flow in her veins, which were possessed and exercised by white passengers.

These rights and privileges rest upon the equality of all before the law, the very foundation principle of our government. If the negro must submit to different treatment, to accommodations inferior to those given to the white man, when transported by public carriers, he is deprived of the benefits of this very principle of equality. His contract with a carrier would not secure him the same privileges and the same rights that a like contract, made with the same party by his white fellow citizen, would bestow upon the latter. If he buys merchandise of the tradesman, or corn of the farmer, no principle of equality or justice will permit him to be supplied with an inferior article, or short weight or measure, because of his dark complexion. Why can it be claimed that his ticket for transportation upon a steamboat may assign him to a cot for sleep, or a place upon the guards for his dinner? It may be claimed that as he does not get accommodations equal to the white man he is not charged as great a price. But this does not modify the injustice and tyranny of the rule contended for. It amounts to a denial of equality. It says to the negro, you may have inferior accommodations at a reduced price, but no others. Who could defend the rule when carried to its legitimate end? . . . The absurdity and gross injustice of the rule—nay, its positive wickedness, as all other principles intended to inflict oppression and wrong, are readily exposed by tracing it to its natural consequences.

The doctrines of natural law and of Christianity forbid that rights be denied on the ground of race or color; and this principle has become incorporated into the paramount law of the Union. It has been recognized by this court in a decision wherein it is held that the directors of a public school could not forbid a colored child to attend a school of white children simply on the ground of negro parentage, although the directors provided competent instruction for her at a school composed exclusively of colored children. *Clark v. The Board of Directors, etc.*, 24 Iowa, 267.

The decision is planted on the broad and just ground of the equality of all men before the law, which is not limited by color, nationality, religion or condition in life. This principle of equality is announced and secured by the very first words of our State constitution which relate to the rights of the people, in language most comprehensive, and incapable of misconstruction, namely: "All men are, by nature, free and equal." Art. 1, § 1. Upon it we rest our conclusion in this case.

V. But the doctrine of equality and its application to the rights of the plaintiff, as presented in the record before us, depend, for support, not alone upon the constitution of this State and adjudications of this court. They are recognized and secured by the recent constitutional amendments and legislation of the United States. . . .

The persons contemplated by the [Fourteenth] amendment are: 1. All persons born or naturalized in the United States, and subject to the jurisdiction thereof. These are secured the right of citizenship of the United States, and protected against abridgment of their privileges and immunities. 2. All persons within the jurisdiction of the States. These are protected in life, liberty and property, and secured the equal protection of the laws.

Plaintiff belongs to both classes of persons, to whom rights are secured and protection extended, by the amendment under consideration. . . .

Under [the 1866 Civil Rights Act], equality in rights is secured to the negro. The language is comprehensive and includes the right to property and all rights growing out of contracts. It includes within its broad terms every right arising in the affairs of life. The right of the passenger under the contract of transportation with the carrier is included therein. The colored man is guaranteed equality and equal protection of the laws with his white neighbor. These are the rights secured to him as a citizen of the United States, without regard to his color, and constitute his privileges, which are secured by the constitutional amendment above considered. The peculiar privilege of the colored man intended to be guarantied by these constitutional and statutory provisions, is equality with the white man in all affairs of life, over which there may be legislation, or of which the courts may take cognizance. He is secured in life, liberty and property, and the remedies provided by law to enforce the rights pertaining thereto. As to all these, there cannot be laws imposing disabilities upon him, or depriving him of equal benefits, equal advantages and equal protection, with other citizens. . . .

VI. It is insisted that the rights claimed by plaintiff, for the deprivation of which she prosecutes this suit, are social, and are not, therefore, secured by the constitution and statutes, either of the State or of the United States. Without doubting that social rights and privileges are not within the protection of the laws and constitutional provisions in question, we are satisfied that the rights and privileges which were denied plaintiff are not within that class. She was refused accommodations equal to those enjoyed by white passengers. She offered to pay the fare required of those who had the best accommodations the boat afforded. She was unobjectionable in deportment and character. The advantages of the contract made with other passengers was denied her. Her money would not purchase for her that which the same sum would entitle a white passenger to receive. In these matters her rights of property were invaded, and her right to demand services to which she was lawfully entitled was denied. She complains not because she was deprived of the society of white persons. Certainly no one will claim that the passengers in the cabin of a steamboat are there in the character of members of what is called society. Their companionship as travelers is not esteemed by any class of our people to create social relations. Neither are these created by the seat at a common table. Those of high pretensions in society—the good and virtuous, may mingle as passengers in the cabin, and sit at the same table with the lowly and vicious without a thought that the social barriers erected by the haughty assumptions of pride and wealth, or the just requirements of moral and good manners are broken down, and the high and low, good and bad, are thus brought to a common level of conventional society. . . . It cannot be doubted that she was excluded from the table and cabin, not because others would have been degraded and she elevated in society, but because of prejudice entertained against her race, growing out of its former condition of servitude—a prejudice, be it proclaimed to the honor of our people, that is fast giving way to nobler sentiments, and, it is hoped, will soon be entombed with its parent, slavery. The object of the amendments of the federal constitution and of the statutes above referred to, is to relieve citizens of the black race from the effects of this prejudice, to protect them in person and property from its spirit. . . .

VIII. It is urged that the plaintiff was rightfully removed from the table because she occupied a seat reserved for other passengers. The instructions given to the jury fairly announce the right of the officers of the boat to enforce reasonable rules. For disobedience thereto, and those reserving seats for ladies traveling without escort, or for other proper reasons, may be included in the number, it may be admitted she could have been properly removed from such reserved seats. But . . . she could not have been lawfully removed from the seat she occupied on account of her color. The cause of her removal was thus properly left to the jury, and there is no reason to doubt the correctness of the conclusion they reached upon this question of fact.

IX. It is also insisted that the treatment she received was justified by her bad language and improper behavior. . . . Whether her treatment resulted from the enforcement of such rules, or of others aimed at her exclusion on account of color, were questions for the jury, and were left to them by the instructions. There is no just ground of complaint with their findings thereon.

X. Certain instructions were asked by defendant and refused, to the effect that the dinner ticket having been procured by the plaintiff through deception, and without the knowledge of the officers of the boat, entitled her to no rights other than those given by the transportation ticket. It does not appear that the rules and custom of the boat required tickets to be purchased in person by the individuals using them, or that a ticket not thus obtained conferred no rights upon the party acquiring it. Having obtained the ticket in a manner not forbidden by the regulations of the boat or by law, she was entitled thereby to all the rights which it would have conferred upon a white person if obtained in the same way.

The foregoing discussion disposes of all the objections made by defendant's counsel to the rulings of the district court. In our opinion they are correct. The judgment is therefore Affirmed.

22. *VICKSBURGH TROUBLES*, 43RD CONGRESS, 2ND SESSION, HOUSE REPORT NO. 265 (1875)

In response to a massacre of blacks in Vicksburg, Mississippi, Congress formed an investigative committee comprised of Republicans Omar D. Conger of Michigan, Stephen A. Hurlbut of Illinois, and Charles G. Williams of Wisconsin and Democrats R. Milton Speer of Pennsylvania and William J. O'Brien of Maryland. Note the two very different perspectives articulated by the Republican majority report and the Democratic minority report.

COLORED WITNESSES AFRAID TO TESTIFY.

There was great reluctance on the part of the colored people to testify at all; and it was not until after the widows of some of the murdered men, with a courage born of despair, had told their painful story, that bravery enough to tell the truth came to the men, and some even then refused to testify from fear of consequences.

Personally and under their own notice your committee saw enough to indicate the cloud of apprehension that rested on the minds of the people.

From the evidence before us it was clear that for days and weeks a large portion of the colored population of the county had been hiding in the cane or in the woods for fear of death and injury. . . .

STATEMENT OF FACTS.

At the November election of 1873 Peter Crosby was elected sheriff of Warren County by a very large majority of unquestioned votes. Under the law of Mississippi the sheriff is *ex-officio* tax-collector, and is required to give bond in each capacity. Crosby gave bond as sheriff and as tax-collector, which bonds were approved by the court charged with that duty—the board of supervisors of Warren County. Having thus qualified in pursuance of law, he entered upon the duties of his office. Shortly after his election, there was formed in Vicksburgh an association called the "tax-payers' league." The causes which led to the formation of this league, as set forth by its members, were the heavy burdens of taxation both in the city and county, and the alleged misapplication of funds and extravagance in appropriations of the officials, both of the city and county.

It does not appear that there was anything secret in the organization nor specially partisan in the requisites for membership, and at first its proclaimed objects and mode of operation seem to have been proper. It does also appear that a very large addition to the taxes was made for educational purposes, and that the colored people are, to a great extent, availing themselves of the advantages of education.

But early in the year 1874 another organization begins to make its appearance, narrower in its proportions, illegal in its views, and basing itself upon the embodiment of force and the readiness to use violence for the purpose of controlling and overthrowing the will of the majority, lawfully expressed in the form of elections.

THE "WHITE LINE."

This interior organization has not yet assumed definitely, in the State of Mississippi, such precise form and so distinct an existence as in the State of Louisiana, but is unquestionably an extension into Mississippi of the "White League" organization, whose headquarters are in New Orleans. In Warren County it is sometimes called the "white line," and by that name is familiarly spoken of by the leading papers of Vicksburgh, as well as by some of the prominent witnesses before this committee. It is also known as "people's clubs," but in all instances, the formation of the clubs or civil organization is accompanied by establishing within the clubs themselves a military organization, officered, equipped, and armed.

Thus the clubs and the tax-payers' league are open associations apparently directed toward objects in which all citizens might lawfully unite, but controlled from within by the military and partisan organizations whose purposes are special and unlawful.

The purposes of these clubs or white line companies are these, as they are openly avowed or secretly cherished:

1. They are *first* to make a census and enrollment of all the white men in the State.

2. To incorporate into the interior military organizations all the whites who will join with them.

3. To set aside, by whatever means may be necessary, the election of colored men to office, and to nullify in practice the enabling and enforcement acts of Congress, granting and enforcing the right of all citizens, without distinction of color, to hold offices, if properly elected to them.

4. To allow none but white men to be elected to office or to hold office.

It is proper here to state that the colored vote of Warren County exceeds the white vote by about thirty-five hundred majority.

PERSECUTION OF CROSBY.

It happened that within a short time after Crosby filed his first bonds one of the sureties thereon died, and Crosby was required to make a new bond. Nearly all the heavy property-holders of Warren County were politically opposed to Crosby, and it became necessary for him to look for sureties elsewhere, as the league and the white line controlled public sentiment to such an extent that few men of property or position dared to go upon his bond.

The laws of Mississippi appear to permit sureties upon such bonds from any portion of the State, and availing himself of this permission, Crosby prepared and filed a second bond, which was accepted by the only tribunal which, under the laws of the State, had authority in the first instance to accept or reject.

Under these circumstances the white line determined to make their first effort toward the political purposes of their organization in the city of Vicksburgh and to control both the registration and the election of city officers. This election was in August, 1874. The city was known and admitted to have been republican by a majority of between 300 and 400, and undoubtedly had a clear majority of lawful votes of colored people. . . .

Six or seven military organizations were formed, varying from sixty to one hundred men each, all of which were armed and all fully officered, and all undoubtedly reporting to and commanded by some central authority in the executive committee. . . .

INTIMIDATION IN VICKSBURGH.

For four weeks or more this self-constituted and unlawful organization held the city of Vicksburgh under show of force. They patrolled the streets by day and especially by night; they placed sentinels and relieved guards; they had their passwords and their countersigns; they admitted whom they pleased and kept out whom they pleased; they watched the steamboat-landings, the ferries, and the roads; they attended in armed bodies at the registration of voters, in clear violation of law; and impressed upon the whole city that fear which comes naturally from an organized and irresponsible mob, prepared for violence, and the more to be dreaded by peaceful people, because of the mystery which surrounded their numbers, their leaders, their purposes, and their threats.

By this means they secured the registration of many white men not entitled to vote, and drove or frightened from the registration many citizens qualified to vote.

Sustained by this armed body, if not incited by them, evil-disposed people interfered with and threatened the registrar in the discharge of his official duty, and he was compelled on one occasion to make his escape from a window in the rear of the place of registration, and was also compelled by the same armed force to violate law by re-opening his registration after the time fixed by law.

The day of election for city officers came, and it is said it was very quiet and peaceable, for the work of intimidation was already done, and one or more of these illegal companies were on hand to parade the streets, and keep up the show of illegal force. There was no pretense of legal authority for these demonstrations.

It is true that there had been organized in Vicksburgh three companies of State militia, fully armed, equipped, and officered, but two of these companies of white men had become merged in the people's club, and the State arms distributed among these illegal organizations, and it would have been dangerous in the then state of feeling to have called on the colored company to resist such unlawful combination. . . .

The opposition candidates were elected by about two hundred majority, and the city government, created by the aid of the mob, passed fully under its control.

This point of advantage, being thus secured, became the base of larger operations in the same direction. The organization became more insolent and more dictatorial. The city papers, which were but the echo of the violent elements, were constantly full of the most gross, calumnious, and abusive articles, and proclaimed with too bold a frankness the declared purpose to revolutionize the county and the State in the same way. The white line was rapidly extended.

But the sheriff by the law of the State is not only tax-collector, he is one of three officers to whom is given the power to select the registrars of the county. This was an additional political reason for getting rid of Crosby. The agitation as to the sufficiency of his bond was kept up. It was known to all the leaders that there were two methods given by due process of law of inquiring into the sufficiency of his bond, and removing him if insufficient, and that the courts were open and the judges men of unimpeached character, just and fearless in the administration of their high office; but they did not choose to pursue either of these lawful methods. They preferred to follow the course which they had begun, and to drive the officer of the law from his position by force and threats.

DISPLACING THE SHERIFF.

Accordingly the tax-payers' league called a meeting on the 2d of December, not of the league itself, but of all citizens, and, after rejecting by an overwhelming vote a very proper resolution which declared that legal remedies were not exhausted, they passed another demanding the resignation of all the county officials, and appointed a committee of ten to wait on them, inform them of the resolution, demand their resignation, and report the results to the meeting.

This committee called upon the sheriff and chancery clerk, Crosby and Davenport, demanded their resignation, and reported their refusal back to the meeting.

Thereupon the entire body of not less than five hundred men adjourned to the court-house to enforce their demand. Davenport fled from the mob. Crosby, having abundant reason to fear for his life, signed a resignation prepared for him, and the sheriff's office, court-house, jail, and county property, by this same irresponsible mob, were put into the custody and control of one of their number.

Thus the regularly-elected officers of the county were by duress ousted from office, the entire records, papers, offices, court-house, and all county property unlawfully and riotously seized upon by an unlawful combination of men, not only without warrant of law, but in direct and palpable violation and deliberate transgression of all principles and forms of law known to any civilized people. . . .

CROSBY'S CARD.

. . . The rumor spread through the city that the entire available strength of the black people of the county would move upon Vicksburgh . . . and the rumor was exaggerated, perhaps purposely, into alarming proportions. The old horror of servile insurrection, which has darkened every hearth in the South in the olden time, was again appealed to, and horrible phantoms of death, robbery, rape, and arson were called up again to excite the popular mind. . . . It is proper here to state that Crosby and his friends had been engaged on Saturday with fair prospects of success in endeavoring to procure the execution of a bond which should be wholly satisfactory as to solvency.

THE MASSACRE.

About 3 o'clock in the morning of Monday, the 7th, the alarm was struck by the watchman on the court-house cupola, but it proved to be a false alarm. Between 7 and 8 the same watchman, E. D. Richardson, struck the alarm again, reporting that a considerable body of men were approaching on the Cherry-street road, information of whose approach was given by Dr. Hunt. In a very short time the court-house square was filled by a large number of excited men, armed with all sorts of weapons.

Dr. O'Leary, the mayor of the city, put the city under martial law, and delegated supreme command over the armed citizens to Horace H. Miller, an officer of some experience on the confederate side in the late war. Why he did not give this command to some of the many State militia officers on the ground . . . it is impossible to say, further than that it is a just inference that it was given to Colonel Miller from his known and declared position in the white line.

On assuming command, Colonel Miller first seized upon Crosby as the probable chief of the movement, and placed him under guard at the court-house. He then detailed parties of mounted men to patrol Vicksburgh and drive all colored people off the streets—orders which were executed with extreme brutality, as will appear. Having thus secured his rear, this skillful officer moved out with a force of about eighty to one hundred well-armed men on Cherry street, and soon confronted a body of colored men under Andrew Owens. Miller rode up where they had halted in a deep cut, on the brow of a hill, within the city limits, having first disposed his own force on the slope of the opposite hill, with a ravine and bridge between the two, and having advanced in due form a line of skirmishers to cover the bridge.

Owens, the leader of the blacks, informed Colonel Miller that they were coming in in obedience to an order from Crosby as sheriff. Miller stated that Crosby was captured and the party could do no good, but might receive much harm. Owens then demanded to see Crosby and take orders from him, and stated that he was willing to withdraw if Crosby said so. This request was granted by Miller, and Owens was escorted under guard to the court-house, where he saw Crosby and was told by him to go home.

On returning to his people, he informed Colonel Miller that he should take his men home, and they immediately proceeded to return by the way they came.

THE FLEEING NEGROES FIRED UPON.

It is clearly in testimony that they did so, and that no shot was fired by them. They retired, not in any military order, but in a confused and noisy group, about half a mile, when suddenly, and without any orders from any officer, fire was opened upon them by the whites. This fire appears to have commenced from some mounted men, who during the time of the parley had gained the flank of the colored people, but immediately became general, and was followed by a rush of all the whites who had proper arms, upon these unresisting and retreating men, who in good faith were carrying out the agreement.

There could not have been, at the outside, more than one hundred and twenty-five colored men in Owens's party, and of these, certainly not one-half armed with any weapon but a pistol, and many wholly unarmed, and none of them armed with weapons of effectiveness. It was no battle; it was a simple massacre, unutterably disgraceful to all engaged in it. The attack began without orders; your committee do not believe that Colonel Miller ever would have given such an order, but when it began, his undisciplined mob ran on entirely beyond his control.

. . . To lead eighty or one hundred men under heavy fire down an exposed hill, to cross a bridge and storm the opposing height in the presence of a foe superior in numbers, is an exploit worthy of the heroic days of the republic, but the truth of history compels your committee to say that there was no enemy in sight or reach during the wonderful evolution, and, further, that no white man was killed or wounded, or in any danger except from the careless shooting of his own comrades. The black people on being fired upon scattered in all directions, singly or in groups of two or three, and occasionally returned an ineffectual fire.

The killing of these men, thus retiring in good faith, was murder, willful, cowardly, and in violation of all laws of peace or of war.

Eight or nine colored men were killed here, and about twenty rescued by Colonel Miller, and sent as prisoners, under escort, to the court-house. . . .

ASSASSINATIONS OF COLORED MEN.

But scenes far worse, far more painful, remain. Some excuse may be made for crime committed in hot blood, while the actual struggle is going on. The better sort at Vicksburgh, the thoughtful and the humane—for there are such—who had lent themselves to the substitution of mobs for law, or who were swept away by a storm which they could raise but not control, were now helpless. The baser sort always come to the front when the restraints of law are removed, and are masters of those who, under the reign of law, control them.

It is in evidence that the aids deputed by Colonel Miller ordered every colored man they met off the street, and that in so doing they shot three unresisting and unarmed men. And yet these men, who murdered these American citizens in cold blood on the streets of Vicksburgh, are men who by birth, education, and family relations stand high in society as now constituted in that city. Exaggerated statements of the peril of the city are telegraphed to all parts of the country; the Associated Press receives and distributes these false dispatches; and the whole country is ablaze with excitement over the "insurrection at Vicksburgh." Offers of aid to the people of the beleaguered city come back from all quarters, and on the same night of the seventh of December, one hundred and sixty armed men from Louisiana pour in to the rescue. . . .

No longer law; no longer order. The city filled with men drunken with excitement, or worse; full of violence; full of unrestrained passion; that night of December 7 is a perfect carnival of released rascality. Decent people shut their doors and bar their windows, while the bad and dangerous element which exists in all cities, but especially in river towns, is thoroughly master of the situation.

Unauthorized searches by self-constituted authority into private houses; searches for arms converted, as is usual, into robbery and thieving; insolent abuse of quiet people—all these wrongs are to be justly apprehended where neither the form nor the substance of law remains.

One poor old man, half crazed, but harmless, sitting quietly in a neighbor's house, is brutally shot to death in the presence of terrified women and shrieking children. He gained his wretched living by hunting and fishing, and had a shotgun. No one pretended that Tom Bidderman had anything to do with the fight, but he was black, and had a gun in his house, and so they murdered him for amusement as they were going from the city to restore order in the country.

Patrols of mounted men, members of the people's clubs, traversed the settlements and executed their own hellish ideas of justice.

On that same Monday, after the sham fight was over, about noon, a party of five mounted men rode down to the house of Robert Banks, about two miles from Vicksburgh and off from the road. They dismounted and bade the old man hold their horses and went into the house. There were Mrs. Banks and five or six other frightened women, and young Robert Banks, a boy of eighteen. They asked the boy if he had any weapons, and he gave them a pistol which was in the house. Then they struck him, and, as he fled, pursued him through the house, and shot him to death. Returning, they came where the father still stood, holding their horses, ordered him to walk out to the front, and, in the presence of his family, deaf to the entreaties of the wife and mother, these cold-blooded assassins of the son, murdered the father also.

A poor old man, Mingo Green, very old and so decrepit that he was compelled to support his steps with a cane, a local exhorter of some note, chanced to meet a party of these patrols, and was put to death, and left lying in the road with the top of his head cut smooth off, or, as the witness expressed it, "the whole inside of his head showed white like a china bowl."

A man named Buck Worrell, peaceable and unoffending, living some eight miles from Vicksburgh, not accused, even, of any complicity in the difficulty, was on the Tuesday after chased by these patrols from his own house up to the house of Mr. Edwards, a white man for whom he worked, where he prayed protection of the ladies there present. Miss Martha Edwards, to whom he appealed, merely said that she did not want him killed in her yard. They respected the young lady's wishes, and took him into the road and shot him dead in the presence of his wife. This was done by Hebron's company, one of the people's clubs.

Handy Hilliard, in no way connected with the troubles, living quietly at home with his wife and children, near Vicksburgh, was murdered in cold blood. . . .

THE BODIES OF MURDERED NEGROES NEGLECTED, ETC.

. . . [I]n the whole affair two white men—Brown and Vaughn—appear to have been killed, and twenty-nine blacks, more than half of whom were deliberately put to death in cold blood. How many more are missing and unaccounted for, lying in the cane, it is impossible to ascertain. One of the witnesses stated that we (the committee) never could find out; "but we watch where the buzzards hover, and there we find the dead men."

. . . On the 8th of December Crosby, being still under guard, signed another resignation of his office. . . . Crosby swears that the resignation was not voluntary but under fear. . . . [U]pon the resignation being presented to the board of supervisors, Crosby was released from confinement and sent under escort to Jackson.

On the 9th of December, the board of supervisors made an order reciting that a vacancy existed in the office of sheriff by the resignation of Peter Crosby, and calling a special election to fill the vacancy, to be held on the 31st of December. . . . [A. J. Flanigan, who captained one of the "illegal companies," won.]

RELATION OF THE RACES.

By the events of the war and the legislation of the nation the whole fabric of society in the South has been subverted; the traditions, prejudices, habits, and inherited beliefs of a whole people have been overthrown by force from without, superior and irresistible.

Master and slave, each trained for generations to their several positions—one strengthened in absolute and unapproachable dominion by law, by habit, by religious teaching, by pride of birth and of race, by every feeling and prejudice by which the life of man can be molded; the other weakened by long years of inferiority, by habitual recognition of infinite distance, by enforced labor, by subjection to blows or other punishment at the simple whim or caprice of his owner—these elements of society, for two hundred years so far apart, are brought at once and without preparation face to face on the absolute and inexorable level of legal and political equality.

Wide as were the changes effected by the war, it did not bring nor could it bring any change in human nature. War is force in its fullest development; and force, though it may compel obedience, cannot make such obedience voluntary and from the heart. No man who was not a visionary, no man who recognized the great fact that men are always governed largely by their passions and their prejudices, had any right to expect that the discrowned monarchs of the slave States would ever love the law that drove them from their dominion and impoverished them by setting free their most valued possessions. It was not in human nature to do so.

As a logical consequence, it was equally impossible for them to love the nation that had broken down their armed resistance, defeated their armies, and, by what they deemed violent and unconstitutional legislation, had enfranchised their slaves, destroyed one of their great sources of wealth, and inflicted a perpetual cause of chronic irritation by delivering their cities, counties, and States into the political control of a race whom they despise whenever they assert such legal and political rights.

Nothing but absolute necessity ever induced them even to pretend any cordiality in their acceptance either of the constitutional amendments, the reconstruction laws, or the Government that had forced these things upon them.

Your committee do not say that there exists throughout the South a hatred to the negro as such, merely because he is a negro, but the hatred to negro officers of municipalities, of States, of legislatures, is intense.

They do not like to be tried for life or for civil rights before negro juries; they do not like to be ordered on road duty by colored overseers of highways; they do not like to have laws made for them by colored legislators.

COERCING THE NEGRO VOTE.

They are as yet willing that colored men shall vote, but always under the proviso that they vote for and with white men.

In those States where the colored vote is in the majority, there are many white men, and those of high character and position, who openly avow that that colored majority must be and shall be controlled and overridden. This declaration means force and intimidation, and means nothing else, for no persuasion, no inducement, no eloquence, no fair promises have been wanting in the past to induce or bribe the colored people to abandon their attachment to the political party which liberated them and gave them these rights. All have failed, for it is unquestionably the settled belief of the black men of the South that outside of the republican party they have no protection from lapsing into slavery.

The labor and vagrant laws passed or threatened wherever the white native element prevailed are their proof.

Nothing is left but force and intimidation to bring about this result desired at the South; and that result is so precious to them that any means seem lawful and expedient.

The admitted quality of the colored race, whether it be native, or acquired and hereditary from the days of bondage, is that as a people they are incapable of combination, unfit for conspiracy, gentle in temper, and enduring to a fault. Scattered in cabins on isolated farms, unarmed and unused to deadly weapons, they are easily cowed for a while by exhibitions of violence; and the whites of the South are singularly prone to such exhibitions. The whites control the land; they control commerce; they have the press; they have the telegraph; they own or buy the correspondents; they give the color to all news; they magnify every offense by a colored man, and keep out of sight all the wrongs done by whites.

They readily unite for common purposes; they hesitate at nothing which they deem necessary for the attainment of their ends; they are essentially inclined to strike straight out by the strong hand rather than to work by rules of law.

Let the least sign of a conflict come up, and the old spirit of masterdom revives. It is insolence, intolerable insolence, then, for a black man to hesitate, to delay, when ordered by the white, and the hand to punish is swift, sure, and deadly.

If any principle is dear to the American people, it is that the voice of the majority fairly expressed shall control, and that there shall be no distinction of any form or kind in the rights which attach to every citizen, and that these rights shall be recognized in absolute equality to all; if any principle is fixed in the southern mind, it is that a white minority ought to override and break down such majority if it be composed of colored men.

To this end all these unauthorized military organizations, now spreading with fearful rapidity, point. This is their aim and purpose. "No more negroes to be elected to office," is their watchword. Careful men say boldly that the reconstruction laws are a failure. Rash men carry out in practice what the careful men say, and dragoon whole neighborhoods by the persuasion of the pistol.

DUTY OF THE NATION.

One of two things this nation must do: it must either restrain by force these violent demonstrations by the bold, fierce spirits of the whites; it must, by the exercise of all its power, if needed, secure to every man, black and white, the free exercise of the elective franchise, and punish, sternly and promptly, all who violently invade those rights; or it must say to the enfranchised voters of the South—creatures of its own word, staunch, true, and faithful to its Government—we have given you these rights—we have made you men and citizens—we have given you the right to bear arms and to vote; now work out your own salvation as others have done; fight your way up to full manhood, and prove yourselves worthy of the endowments you have received at our hands. It is for the country to decide which is the best. But the country must decide quickly.

Your committee are of the opinion that neither honor nor the true interests of the nation permit us yet to abandon this struggling population. We are largely responsible for the very weaknesses and failings that as yet unfit them to work out their destiny alone. These are the vestiges of American slavery; they are the curses that remain to us, the feebleness that springs from the old taint. . . .

. . . Law is with us the only sovereign thing, and its subversion by force is the highest treason. Tested by that rule, the occurrences at Vicksburgh deserve condemnation from every law-abiding man—every citizen who hopes for the future of his country. . . .

O. D. CONGER.

S. A. HURLBUT.

Mr. O'BRIEN, from the same committee, submitted the following as the

VIEWS OF THE MINORITY:

. . . The colored men were advancing upon the city by all roads in columns, each several hundred strong, in all, as the testimony shows, about 1,400 men. They avowed their purpose to be to reinstate Crosby in office and to get even with the white people. One of their principal leaders, Owens, threatened to wade knee-deep in the blood of white men. Some of the columns marched with military precision, and were largely composed of men used to the manual of arms. Others came forward in scattering bodies, some on horseback, but mostly on foot. They were armed with every kind of weapon—needle-guns, army muskets, shot-guns, revolvers, &c. The policemen sent out on different roads were unable to reach the colored men, for on approaching with a white handkerchief, displayed, as a flag of truce, they were fired upon and compelled to retire. . . .

The testimony shows that it was the universal opinion that if the colored men advanced into the city many lives would be sacrificed, and the city given over to plunder and the flames, and the women become the prey of the infuriated passions of the invading negroes. Notwithstanding this belief, there was no disposition evinced on the part of the whites, in resisting the invasion, to shed blood, or to take the lives of the armed men who menaced the city. The detachments that went out on the different roads were under capable officers, men of the highest respectability, and old citizens. In most cases they attempted to parley with the invaders, but found that they were disposed to fight.

The firing in every case commenced from the colored side. . . .

We cannot conceive of a more unhappy condition of society than exists as a result of the reconstruction laws and the rule of the corrupt men who were invested with authority by the policy of the national Government and the republican party. All offices in the State of any importance, from the governor down, are held by men who encourage the maintenance of the color-line, and who regard the white element of the State as disloyal and rebellious. In this category they class many men who have always supported the republican party in national politics, and many who were officers and soldiers in the Federal Army during the late war.

The white people have exhausted every means of conciliation. So long as the most depraved white men in the State can maintain their control of the majority of colored voters, and pursue the systematized robbery that characterizes their government throughout the counties, the honest and intelligent white men must be arrayed against them. The preservation of their homes and property will, without regard to political considerations, cause them to remain united as one man so long as the hope of a return to honest rule remains.

There is not the least foundation in the testimony for the charge that the white people oppose or vote against candidates for office on account of their color, nor for the pretense that any of the proceedings of the citizens of Vicksburgh, in December last, were prompted by the color of the corrupt officials. Nor can it be asserted from anything in the testimony that the whites have ever interfered with the exercise of the right of franchise by the colored men. But as to both white men and colored, when candidates for office, they do insist upon their integrity and capability.

Further, the testimony conclusively shows that there do not exist any organizations for political purposes different in character and object from those which usually prevail in all political parties in the Northern States. Political differences are tolerated with as much freedom as they obtain in any locality north of the Ohio. Intimidation of any kind for political purposes is only known in the ranks of the colored men. . . . By means of the influence exercised through their religious as well as political meetings, the great mass of the colored race are constrained to keep within the line of the republican party.

The want of confidence in the whites by the colored men in politics does not extend to matters of business, where the interest of the two races is in common. The political leaders of the colored people exert but little influence in that regard, as all branches of trade and commerce are controlled by the whites. Very few colored men are engaged in trade except as employés, and with rare exceptions they accumulate but little property. In the line of production throughout the counties, their efforts are confined to the raising of a few bales of cotton, which, with vegetables raised for home consumption, afford them a living suitable to their desires.

The relations of the two races, outside of the domain of politics, are eminently friendly. Kindness on the part of the white people toward the colored is universal, and we have little doubt would be reciprocated by them were they free from the wicked influences which control them.

The foundation of their antipathy to the whites is the devotion with which they follow their political leaders and their preachers, for the two are generally united in the same person. They seem blind to the infamous character of the men who control them for the worst purposes.

The condition of the colored people has not improved under the operation of existing- laws. From all the evidences of their state that were brought to our attention, their moral tone is of a very low degree, and would not be considered an advance from their condition before enfranchisement. The manner in which they exercise the franchise is a mockery.

Even education, so far as diffused among them, seems not to have aided them in reaching a higher plane of citizenship. Its advantages seem to be accepted only as a qualification for the role of the baser sort of politician, to the extent that every man among them who has acquired a show of learning strives to become a leader in the arena of politics. A little learning is a dangerous thing in its application to them. The educated among them are the most dangerous class in the community, as they exercise a malign and blighting influence over the future prospects of their race. They fill the offices, and with few exceptions fall an easy prey to the temptations to dishonesty and corrupt practices. Their aim seems to be to intensify the hostility already invoked against the white race, and their purposes are ably seconded by the white adventurers who find in the emoluments of political office among them a fitting reward for their unworthy and ignoble position.

The tax imposed in all the counties of the State for school purposes is very heavy and is cheerfully paid. It is fairly distributed among the two races, and there is reason to indulge the hope of a great improvement in the rising generation over the men that now so sadly misrule the State.

The general condition of the State has greatly declined. Lands to the extent of one fifth of the whole State have been forfeited for the non-payment of taxes. At the same rate of retrogression as the misgovernment of the last few years discloses it will not be many years before the State will be "the monarch of all it surveys."

To remedy these consequences of the crime of thus impoverishing and degrading the people of a sovereign state is within our duty or power.

From a review of the whole testimony we will therefore but briefly state the following conclusions:

1st. That, in the city of Vicksburgh and county of Warren, the white citizens pay about 99 per cent of the taxes, which have grown enormously oppressive, and that the negroes chiefly assess, collect, and disburse them.

2d. That the debt of the city, which in 1869 was $13,000, is now $1,400,000, as far as can be ascertained. That it has accumulated to this amount by reckless and improvident legislation and expenditure by republican officials, and is a grievous burden imposed on a population of 11,000 people, less than half of whom are white people.

3d. That a corrupt and infamous ring, composed mainly of negro officials, has existed in said city and county for several years, who, by forgeries, peculation, and systematized frauds on the revenues, have impaired the public credit, impoverished the people, and augmented the taxes to rates resulting in practical confiscation.

4th. That Peter Crosby, the sheriff and tax-collector, was the political and personal friend of these corrupt officials, and by his power in summoning juries, their conviction was rendered practically impossible. That the sheriff admitted to bail his political friends, when charged with the gravest offenses, on bonds notoriously worthless, and was the chief impediment to the administration of justice in the courts. . . .

6th. That the tax-payers' league was organized irrespective of politics or color, and that its sole object, as stated in its constitution, was to secure capable officials and honest government.

7th. That the bonds of Crosby as sheriff and tax-collector were utterly insufficient, if not absolutely worthless.

8th. That the board of supervisors was advised of the utter insufficiency of Crosby's bonds, but corruptly declined to compel him, as the law required, to give good and sufficient bonds.

9th. That the time having arrived for the collection of taxes, the taxpayers having no adequate remedy, were justified in their demand for Crosby's resignation, and that his resignation was voluntary, and not the result of violence or threats.

10th. That the conflict of December 7, resulting in the killing of two whites and twenty-four colored people, was solely and wholly caused by the armed attempt of the negroes of Warren County to invade Vicksburgh; that this invasion was incited and instigated by Peter Crosby, and that Crosby was advised and encouraged to take this course, and was promised aid in it by Governor Ames.

11th. That the defense of the city was made under the direction of the mayor, and all the preparations and conduct of the citizens were justified by nature's highest law, self-preservation. They acted in defense of their families and their homes. Any other course would have been cruelty to the families of both races, for, as General Packer testified, "it was a mercy to the women and children, white and black, that the negroes were prevented from entering the city."

12th. That the purpose of the invaders was only limited by the will of their leaders, and that if they had succeeded in entering the city they would have been assisted by a large number of well-armed and thoroughly-organized negroes in the city, who were in readiness to co-operate with them.

13th. That there is not and has not been any organized resistance at Vicksburgh on the part of the whites to lawful authority; but, on the contrary, the white people, owning nearly all the property and paying nearly all the taxes, are sincerely desirous of preserving peace and good order. Their interests, social and business, give strength to this desire, and the patience they have exhibited under accumulated wrongs and outrages, such as Citizens of a northern city would not tolerate for a day, is the marvel of our civilization.

14th. That there is no White League or political organization in Mississippi whose object it is to deny to colored men, *because of their color*, or for any

Fig. 24. "The Union as It Was. The Lost Cause, Worse Than Slavery." A chilling contrast with his idealistic "Uncle Sam's Thanksgiving Dinner," Thomas Nast in this illustration critiques the realities of Southern white racist violence. A member of the "White League" shakes hands with a Ku Klux Klan member over a shield that shows an African American couple holding a (probably) dead child, while a man hangs lynched from a tree and a school burns in the background. (Thomas Nast, *Harper's Weekly*, October 24, 1874; Library of Congress)

255

reason, any rights or privileges guaranteed by law; nor is there any political organization of white men which has any other object than to secure the election of honest and capable officials.

15th. That the call of the governor upon the President for military aid was based on partisan statements utterly devoid of truth. At the time the call was made, Vicksburgh was as quiet and peaceable as any city of the same population in the United States, and it has so remained to the present hour.

16th. After Crosby's resignation, Flanagan was elected sheriff and took peaceable possession of the office. Whether he or Crosby was the legal sheriff was a question for the courts alone to determine; and yet, in shameless disregard of civil law and of the rights of citizens, Flanagan has been marched out of the court-house by United States soldiers at the point of the bayonet.

That the condition of Mississippi is deplorable. With a governor who has declared that, if not in office, he would not reside in the State if given the whole of it; with corruption prevailing to an alarming extent in counties where negroes and political adventurers have entire control; with property depreciating and taxes increasing, utter ruin can be averted only by restoring to the people the right to govern themselves and to manage their own affairs without interference from the Federal Government.

WILLIAM J. O'BRIEN.

R. M. SPEER.

23. President Ulysses S. Grant to the United States Senate (January 13, 1875) (*Journal of the Senate of the United States*, 43rd Congress, 2nd Session)

In the face of violence against blacks and Republicans in Louisiana, President Grant dispatched General Philip H. Sheridan to use army soldiers to maintain order. Five seats of Louisiana's legislature remained contested as a result of intimidation during the 1874 election, and the five Democrats tried to take their seats without certification in January 1875. Federal troops ejected them, and Sheridan went further by declaring white supremacist terrorists as "banditti" who should be tried by military court and executed. In the face of the Southern crisis, Grant here asked Congress to take further action.

. . . To say that lawlessness, turbulence, and bloodshed have characterized the political affairs of that State since its re-organization under the reconstruction acts, is only to repeat what has become well known as a part of its unhappy history; but it may be proper here to refer to the election of 1868, by which the republican vote of the State, through fraud and violence, was reduced to a few thousands, and the bloody riots of 1866 and 1868, to show that the disorders there are not due to any recent causes or to any late action of the Federal authorities.

Preparatory to the election of 1872, a shameful and undisguised conspiracy was formed to carry that election against the republicans without regard to law or right, and to that end the most glaring frauds and forgeries were committed in the returns after many colored citizens had been denied registration, and others deterred by fear from casting their ballots. . . .

To hold the people of Louisiana generally responsible for these atrocities would not be just; but it is a lamentable fact that insuperable obstructions were thrown in the way of punishing these murderers, and the so-called conservative papers of the State not only justified the massacre, but denounced as Federal tyranny and despotism the attempt of the United States officers to bring them to justice. Fierce denunciations ring through the country about office-holding and election matters in Louisiana, while every one of the Colfax miscreants goes unwhipped of justice, and no way can be found in this boasted land of civilization and Christianity to punish the perpetrators of this bloody and monstrous crime.

Not unlike this was the massacre in August last. Several northern young men of capital and enterprise had started the little and flourishing town of Coushatta. Some of them were republicans and officeholders under [Republican governor William P.] Kellogg. They were therefore doomed to death. Six of them were seized and carried away from their homes and murdered in cold blood. No one has been punished; and the conservative press of the State denounced all efforts to that end, and boldly justified the crime. . . .

To say that the murder of a negro or a white republican is not considered a crime in Louisiana would probably be unjust to a great part of the people; but it is true that a great number of such murders have been committed, and no one has been punished therefor, and manifestly, as to them, the spirit of hatred and violence is stronger than law.

Representations were made to me that the presence of troops in Louisiana was unnecessary and irritating to the people, and that there was no danger of public disturbance if they were taken away. Consequently, early in last summer, the troops were all withdrawn from the State, with the exception of a small garrison at New Orleans Barracks. It was claimed that a comparative state of quiet had supervened. Political excitement as to Louisiana affairs seemed to be dying out. But the November election was approaching, and it was necessary for party purposes that the flame should be rekindled. . . .

I have deplored the necessity which seemed to make it my duty under the Constitution and laws to direct such interference. I have always refused except where it seemed to be my imperative duty to act in such a manner under the Constitution and laws of the United States. I have repeatedly and earnestly entreated the people of the South to live together in peace, and obey the laws; and nothing would give me greater pleasure than to see reconciliation and tranquillity everywhere prevail, and thereby remove all necessity for the presence of troops among them. I regret, however, to say that this state of things does not exist, nor does its existence seem to be desired in some localities; and as to those it may be proper for me to say that, to the extent that Congress has conferred power upon me to prevent it, neither Ku-Klux-Klans, White Leagues, nor any other association using arms and violence to execute their unlawful purposes, can be permitted in that way to govern any part of this country; nor can I see with indifference Union men or republicans ostracised, persecuted, and murdered on account of their opinions, as they now are in some localities.

24. An act to protect all citizens in their civil and legal rights, 18 Stat. Part 3, 335 (March 1, 1875) (Civil Rights Act)

The expansive Civil Rights Act of 1875 desegregated public accommodations and outlawed racial discrimination in inns, public conveyances, and theaters, but not schools, before the Supreme Court declared it unconstitutional in 1883.

Whereas, it is essential to just government we recognize the equality of all men before the law, and hold that it is the duty of government in its dealings with the people to mete out equal and exact justice to all, of whatever nativity, race, color, or persuasion, religious or political; and it being the appropriate object of legislation to enact great fundamental principles into law: Therefore,

Be it enacted . . . That all persons within the jurisdiction of the United States shall be entitled to the full and equal enjoyment of the accommodations, advantages, facilities, and privileges of inns, public conveyances on land or water, theaters, and other places of public amusement; subject only to the conditions and limitations established by law, and applicable alike to citizens of every race and color, regardless of any previous condition of servitude.

SEC. 2. That any person who shall violate the foregoing section . . . except for reasons by law applicable to citizens of every race and color, and regardless of any previous condition of servitude . . . or by aiding or inciting such denial, shall, for every offence, forfeit and pay the sum of five hundred dollars to the person aggrieved thereby, to be recovered in an action of debt, with full costs; and shall also, for every such offense, be deemed guilty of a misdemeanor, and, upon conviction thereof, shall be fined not less than five hundred nor more than one thousand dollars, or shall be imprisoned not less than thirty days nor more than one year[.] . . .

SEC. 3. That the district and circuit courts of the United States shall have, exclusively of the courts of the several States, cognizance of all crimes and offenses against, and violations of, the provisions of this act . . . and the district attorneys, marshals, and deputy marshals of the United States, and commissioners appointed by the circuit and territorial courts of the United States . . . are hereby specially authorized and required to institute proceedings against every person who shall violate the provisions of this act . . . except in respect of the right of action accruing to the person aggrieved; and such district attorneys shall cause such proceedings to be prosecuted to their termination as in other cases: *Provided*, That . . . any district attorney who shall willfully fail to institute and prosecute the proceedings herein required, shall, for every such offense, forfeit and pay the sum of five hundred dollars to the person aggrieved thereby . . . and shall, on conviction thereof, be deemed guilty of a misdemeanor, and be fined not less than one thousand nor more than five thousand dollars[.] . . .

SEC. 4. That no citizen possessing all other qualifications which are or may be prescribed by law shall be disqualified for service as grand or petit juror in any court of the United States, or of any State, on account of race, color, or previous condition of servitude; and any officer or other person charged with any duty in the selection or summoning of jurors who shall exclude or fail to summon any citizen for the cause aforesaid shall, on conviction thereof, be deemed guilty of a misdemeanor, and be fined not more than five thousand dollars. . . .

CHAPTER 5

JUDICIAL INTERPRETATION AND LIMITATION OF THE CIVIL WAR AMENDMENTS AND CIVIL RIGHTS LEGISLATION

Beginning with its ruling in the *Slaughter-House Cases* (1873), which truncated an expansive interpretation of the Fourteenth Amendment, the Supreme Court slowly whittled away the practical impact of the Civil War Amendments and legislation. Holdings in *United States v. Cruikshank* (1876) and *United States v. Harris* (1883) undermined anti-Klan legislation, while the ruling in *United States v. Reese et al.* (1876) allowed states to impose poll taxes and other measures by a holding that the Fifteenth Amendment simply prohibited race-based exclusion from voting. The *Civil Rights Cases* (1883) involved defendants from New York, Missouri, Tennessee, Kansas, and California who denied blacks access to public facilities in violation of the Civil Rights Act of 1875, which desegregated public accommodations. In ruling that the Thirteenth Amendment purged badges of slavery but did not remove racial discrimination as to inns, public conveyances, or theaters and that the Fourteenth Amendment only addressed state action and not private discrimination, the Supreme Court nullified much of the Civil Rights Act of 1875. The Court followed a winding path toward Jim Crow, however: in *Strauder v. West Virginia* (1880), it ruled that the Fourteenth Amendment prohibited states from excluding citizens from juries on account of race, and in *Ex parte Yarbrough* (1884), it upheld Congress's authority to prohibit individuals from interfering with the right of citizens to vote in federal elections.

At the same time the Supreme Court strongly promoted states' rights at the expense of vigorous interpretations of the Civil War Amendments and other congressional legislation, some Republicans recoiled at the growth of the federal government. Especially as the desire for reconciliation with the South flourished, federal protection for black rights diminished in substantial ways. In later decades, with the ascendance of Jim Crow and social Darwinism, the Supreme Court affirmed the doctrine of separate but equal in *Plessy v. Ferguson* (1896). Blacks were left to hold onto the memory of uplifting moments of equality. For them, such moments, as well as the legal changes during the Civil War era, made up the potential for the future. As black soldiers, editors, leaders, ministers, and common folk kept alive the memory of the Civil War era's achievements, they stoked the fire of hope and articulated arguments that would be brought to fruition in future civil rights movements carried on by their sons and daughters, culminating in another corrective moment a century later.

1. SLAUGHTER-HOUSE CASES, 83 U.S. 36 (1873)

In 1869, Louisiana's legislature incorporated the Crescent City Live-Stock Landing and Slaughter-House Company and granted it a monopoly by confining all slaughtering in New Orleans to its facility. While the state claimed that this was a legitimate health regulation under its police powers, designed to promote sanitation within New Orleans, independent butchers compelled to rent space from the company at a fixed rate challenged the law on the grounds, among others, that the monopoly violated the privileges or immunities clause of the Fourteenth Amendment to the Constitution. The Supreme Court restricted the application of the Fourteenth Amendment by holding that the privileges and immunities protected by that amendment were limited to those delineated in the Constitution and thus did not include many rights given by the states. In other words, the Court ruled that it was constitutional for a state to grant a business monopoly to some citizens but not to others.

The case also revisited the issue of whether the Fourteenth Amendment applied the Bill of Rights to the states. Although many Republicans believed that the Bill of Rights applied to the states even before ratification of the Fourteenth Amendment, the Supreme Court had ruled in *Barron v. Baltimore* (1833) that it did not. Now, counsel for the butchers cited legislative history to the Court showing that the drafters of the Fourteenth Amendment intended it to apply the Bill of Rights to the states. Justice Samuel Freeman Miller's opinion effectively rejected this application and left protection of the fundamental rights of American citizens to the states.

Four justices dissented based on a more robust and expansive interpretation of the Fourteenth Amendment's scope.

Mr[.] Justice [Samuel] MILLER now, April 14th, 1873, delivered the opinion of the Court.

These cases are brought here by writs of error to the Supreme Court of the State of Louisiana. They arise out of the efforts of the butchers of New Orleans to resist the Crescent City Live-Stock Landing and Slaughter-House Company in the exercise of certain powers conferred by the charter which created it, and which was granted by the legislature of that State. . . .

The records show that the plaintiffs in error relied upon, and asserted throughout the entire course of the litigation in the State courts, that the grant of privileges in the charter of defendant, which they were contesting, was a violation of the most important provisions of the thirteenth and fourteenth articles of amendment of the Constitution of the United States. . . .

The statute thus assailed as unconstitutional was passed March 8th, 1869, and is entitled "An act to protect the health of the city of New Orleans, to locate the stock-landings and slaughter-houses, and to incorporate the Crescent City Live-Stock Landing and Slaughter-House Company."

The first section forbids the landing or slaughtering of animals whose flesh is intended for food, within the city of New Orleans and other parishes and boundaries named and defined, or the keeping or establishing any slaughter-houses or *abattoirs* within those limits except by the corporation thereby created, which is also limited to certain places afterwards mentioned. Suitable penalties are enacted for violations of this prohibition.

The second section designates the corporators, gives the name to the corporation, and confers on it the usual corporate powers.

The third and fourth sections authorize the company to establish and erect within certain territorial limits, therein defined, one or more stock-yards, stock-landings, and slaughter-houses, and imposes upon it the duty of erecting, on or before the first day of June, 1869, one grand slaughter-house of sufficient capacity for slaughtering five hundred animals per day.

It declares that the company, after it shall have prepared all the necessary buildings, yards, and other conveniences for that purpose, shall have the sole and exclusive privilege of conducting and carrying on the live-stock landing and slaughter-house business within the limits and privilege granted by the act, and that all such animals shall by landed at the stock-landings and slaughtered at the slaughter-houses of the company, and nowhere else. Penalties are enacted for infractions of this provision, and prices fixed for the maximum charges of the company for each steamboat and for each animal landed.

Section five orders the closing up of all other stock-landings and slaughter-houses after the first day of June, in the parishes of Orleans, Jefferson, and St. Bernard, and makes it the duty of the company to permit any person to slaughter animals in their slaughter-houses under a heavy penalty for each refusal. Another section fixes a limit to the charges to be made by the company for each animal so slaughtered in their building, and another provides for an inspection of all animals intended to be so slaughtered, by an officer appointed by the governor of the State for that purpose. . . .

This statute is denounced not only as creating a monopoly and conferring odious and exclusive privileges upon a small number of persons at the expense of the great body of the community of New Orleans, but it is asserted that it deprives a large and meritorious class of citizens—the whole of the butchers of the city—of the right to exercise their trade, the business to which they have been trained and on which they depend for the support of themselves and their families; and that the unrestricted exercise of the business of butchering is necessary to the daily subsistence of the population of the city.

But a critical examination of the act hardly justifies these assertions.

It is true that it grants, for a period of twenty-five years, exclusive privileges. . . . But it is not true that it deprives the butchers of the right to exercise their trade, or imposes upon them any restriction incompatible with its successful pursuit, or furnishing the people of the city with the necessary daily supply of animal food.

The act divides itself into two main grants of privilege,—the one in reference to stock-landings and stock-yards, and the other to slaughter-houses. That the landing of livestock in large droves, from steamboats on the bank of the river, and from railroad trains, should, for the safety and comfort of the people and the care of the animals, be limited to proper places, and those not numerous, it needs no argument to prove. Nor can it be injurious to the general community that while the duty of making ample preparation for this is imposed upon a few men, or a corporation, they should, to enable them to do it successfully, have the exclusive right of providing such landing-places, and receiving a fair compensation for the service.

It is, however, the slaughter-house privilege, which is mainly relied on to justify the charges of gross injustice to the public, and invasion of private right.

It is not, and cannot be successfully controverted, that it is both the right and the duty of the legislative body—the supreme power of the State or municipality—to prescribe and determine the localities where the business of slaughtering for a great city may be conducted. To do this effectively it is indispensable that all persons who slaughter animals for food shall do it in those places *and nowhere else.*

The statute under consideration defines these localities and forbids slaughtering in any other. It does not, as has been asserted, prevent the butcher from doing his own slaughtering. On the contrary, the Slaughter-House Company is required, under a heavy penalty, to permit any person who wishes to do so, to slaughter in their houses; and they are bound to make ample provision for the convenience of all the slaughtering for the entire city. The butcher then is still permitted to slaughter, to prepare, and to sell his own meats; but he is required to slaughter at a specified place and to pay a reasonable compensation for the use of the accommodations furnished him at that place.

The wisdom of the monopoly granted by the legislature may be open to question, but it is difficult to see a justification for the assertion that the butchers are deprived of the right to labor in their occupation, or the people of their daily service in preparing food, or how this statute, with the duties and guards imposed upon the company, can be said to destroy the business of the butcher, or seriously interfere with its pursuit.

The power here exercised by the legislature of Louisiana is, in its essential nature, one which has been, up to the present period in the constitutional history of this country, always conceded to belong to the States, however it may *now* be questioned in some of its details.

"Unwholesome trades, slaughter-houses, operations offensive to the senses, the deposit of powder, the application of steam power to propel cars, the building with combustible materials, and the burial of the dead, may all," says Chancellor Kent, "be interdicted by law, in the midst of dense masses of population, on the general and rational principle, that every person ought so to use his property as not to injure his neighbors; and that private interests must be made subservient to the general interests of the community." This is called the police power; and it is declared by Chief Justice Shaw that it is much easier to perceive and realize the existence and sources of it than to mark its boundaries, or prescribe limits to its exercise.

This power is, and must be from its very nature, incapable of any very exact definition or limitation. Upon it depends the security of social order, the life and health of the citizen, the comfort of an existence in a thickly populated community, the enjoyment of private and social life, and the beneficial use of property. . . .

The regulation of the place and manner of conducting the slaughtering of animals, and the business of butchering within a city, and the inspection of the animals to be killed for meat, and of the meat afterwards, are among the most necessary and frequent exercises of this power. It is not, therefore, needed that we should seek for a comprehensive definition, but rather look for the proper source of its exercise. . . .

It cannot be denied that the statute under consideration is aptly framed to remove from the more densely populated part of the city, the noxious slaughter-houses, and large and offensive collections of animals necessarily incident to the slaughtering business of a large city, and to locate them where the convenience, health, and comfort of the people require they shall be located. And it must be conceded that the means adopted by the act for this purpose are appropriate, are stringent, and effectual. But it is said that in creating a corporation for this purpose, and conferring upon it exclusive privileges—privileges which it is said constitute a monopoly—the legislature has exceeded its power. If this statute had imposed on the city of New Orleans precisely the same duties, accompanied by the same privileges, which it has on the corporation which it created, it is believed that no question would have been raised as to its constitutionality. In that case the effect on the butchers in pursuit of their occupation and on the public would have been the same as it is now. Why cannot the legislature confer the same powers on another corporation, created for a lawful and useful public object, that it can on the municipal corporation already existing? That wherever a legislature has the right to accomplish a certain result and that result is best attained by means of a corporation, it has the right to create such a corporation, and to endow it with the powers necessary to effect the desired and lawful purpose, seems hardly to admit of debate. The proposition is ably discussed and affirmed in the case of *McCulloch v. The State of Maryland*, in relation to the power of Congress to organize the Bank of the United States to aid in the fiscal operations of the government. . . .

Unless, therefore, it can be maintained that the exclusive privilege granted by this charter to the corporation, is beyond the power of the legislature of Louisiana, there can be no just exception to the validity of the statute. And in this respect we are not able to see that these privileges are especially odious or objectionable. The duty imposed as a consideration for the privilege is well defined, and its enforcement well guarded. The prices or charges to be made by the company are limited by the statute, and we are not advised that they are on the whole exorbitant or unjust. . . .

It may, therefore, be considered as established, that the authority of the legislature of Louisiana to pass the present statute is ample, unless some restraint in the exercise of that power be found in the constitution of that State or in the amendments to the Constitution of the United States. . . .

The plaintiffs in error . . . allege that the statute is a violation of the Constitution of the United States in these several particulars:

That it creates an involuntary servitude forbidden by the thirteenth article of amendment;

That it abridges the privileges and immunities of citizens of the United States;

That it denies to the plaintiffs the equal protection of the laws; and,

That it deprives them of their property without due process of law; contrary to the provisions of the first section of the fourteenth article of amendment. . . .

The most cursory glance at [the Civil War Amendments] discloses a unity of purpose, when taken in connection with the history of the times, which cannot fail to have an important bearing on any question of doubt concerning their true meaning. . . . Fortunately that history is fresh within the memory of us all, and its leading features, as they bear upon the matter before us, free from doubt.

The institution of African slavery, as it existed in about half the States of the Union, and the contests pervading the public mind for many years, between those who desired its curtailment and ultimate extinction and those who desired additional safeguards for its security and perpetuation, culminated in the effort, on the part of most of the States in which slavery existed, to separate from the Federal government, and to resist its authority. This constituted the war of the rebellion, and whatever auxiliary causes may have contributed to bring about this war, undoubtedly the overshadowing and efficient cause was African slavery.

In that struggle slavery, as a legalized social relation, perished. It perished as a necessity of the bitterness and force of the conflict. When the armies of freedom found themselves upon the soil of slavery they could do nothing less than free the poor victims whose enforced servitude was the foundation of the quarrel. And when hard pressed in the contest these men (for they proved themselves men in that terrible crisis) offered their services and were accepted by thousands to aid in suppressing the unlawful rebellion, slavery was at an end wherever the Federal government succeeded in that purpose. The proclamation of President Lincoln expressed an accomplished fact as to a large portion of the insurrectionary districts, when he declared slavery abolished in them all. But the war being over, those who had succeeded in re-establishing the authority of the Federal government were not content to permit this great act of emancipation to rest on the actual results of the contest or the proclamation of the Executive, both of which might have been questioned in after times, and they determined to place this main and most valuable result in the Constitution of the restored Union as one of its fundamental articles. Hence the thirteenth article of amendment of that instrument. Its two short sections seem hardly to admit of construction, so vigorous is their expression and so appropriate to the purpose we have indicated. . . .

The process of restoring to their proper relations with the Federal government and with the other States those which had sided with the rebellion, undertaken under the proclamation of President Johnson in 1865, and before the assembling of Congress, developed the fact that, notwithstanding the formal recognition by those States of the abolition of slavery, the condition of the slave race would, without further protection of the Federal government, be almost as bad as it was before. Among the first acts of legislation adopted by several of the States in the legislative bodies which claimed to be in their normal relations with the Federal government, were laws which imposed upon the colored race onerous disabilities and burdens, and curtailed their rights in the pursuit of life, liberty, and property to such an extent that their freedom was of little value, while they had lost the protection which they had received from their former owners from motives both of interest and humanity.

They were in some States forbidden to appear in the towns in any other character than menial servants. They were required to reside on and cultivate the soil without the right to purchase or own it. They were excluded from many occupations of gain, and were not permitted to give testimony in the courts in any case where a white man was a party. It was said that their lives were at the mercy of bad men, either because the laws for their protection were insufficient or were not enforced.

These circumstances . . . forced upon the statesmen who had conducted the Federal government in safety through the crisis of the rebellion, and who supposed that by the thirteenth article of amendment they had secured the result of their labors, the conviction that something more was necessary in the way of constitutional protection to the unfortunate race who had suffered so much. They accordingly passed through Congress the proposition for the fourteenth amendment[.] . . .

... A few years' experience satisfied the thoughtful men who had been the authors of the other two amendments that, notwithstanding the restraints of those articles on the States, and the laws passed under the additional powers granted to Congress, these were inadequate for the protection of life, liberty, and property, without which freedom to the slave was no boon. They were in all those States denied the right of suffrage. The laws were administered by the white man alone. It was urged that a race of men distinctively marked as was the negro, living in the midst of another and dominant race, could never be fully secured in their person and their property without the right of suffrage.

Hence the fifteenth amendment. . . . The negro having, by the fourteenth amendment, been declared to be a citizen of the United States, is thus made a voter in every State of the Union.

We repeat, then . . . no one can fail to be impressed with the one pervading purpose . . . lying at the foundation of each [of the Civil War Amendments], and without which none of them would have been even suggested; we mean the freedom of the slave race, the security and firm establishment of that freedom, and the protection of the newly-made freeman and citizen from the oppressions of those who had formerly exercised unlimited dominion over him. It is true that only the fifteenth amendment, in terms, mentions the negro by speaking of his color and his slavery. But it is just as true that each of the other articles was addressed to the grievances of that race, and designed to remedy them as the fifteenth.

We do not say that no one else but the negro can share in this protection. Both the language and spirit of these articles are to have their fair and just weight in any question of construction. Undoubtedly while negro slavery alone was in the mind of the Congress which proposed the thirteenth article, it forbids any other kind of slavery, now or hereafter. If Mexican peonage or the Chinese coolie labor system shall develop slavery of the Mexican or Chinese race within our territory, this amendment may safely be trusted to make it void. And so if other rights are assailed by the States which properly and necessarily fall within the protection of these articles, that protection will apply, though the party interested may not be of African descent. But what we do say, and what we wish to be understood is, that in any fair and just construction of any section or phrase of these amendments, it is necessary to look to the purpose which we have said was the pervading spirit of them all, the evil which they were designed to remedy, and the process of continued addition to the Constitution, until that purpose was supposed to be accomplished, as far as constitutional law can accomplish it.

The first section of the fourteenth article, to which our attention is more specially invited, opens with a definition of citizenship—not only citizenship of the United States, but citizenship of the States. No such definition was previously found in the Constitution, nor had any attempt been made to define it by act of Congress. . . .

To remove this difficulty primarily, and to establish a clear and comprehensive definition of citizenship which should declare what should constitute citizenship of the United States, and also citizenship of a State, the first clause of the first section was framed.

"All persons born or naturalized in the United States, and subject to the jurisdiction thereof, are citizens of the United States and of the State wherein they reside."

The first observation we have to make on this clause is, that it puts at rest both the questions which we stated to have been the subject of differences of opinion. It declares that persons may be citizens of the United States without regard to their citizenship of a particular State, and it overturns the Dred Scott decision by making *all persons* born within the United States and subject to its jurisdiction citizens of the United States. That its main purpose was to establish the citizenship of the negro can admit of no doubt. The phrase, "subject to its jurisdiction" was intended to exclude from its operation children of ministers, consuls, and citizens or subjects of foreign States born within the United States.

The next observation is more important in view of the arguments of counsel in the present case. It is, that the distinction between citizenship of the United States and citizenship of a State is clearly recognized and established. Not only may a man be a citizen of the United States without being a citizen of a State, but an important element is necessary to convert the former into the latter. He must reside within the State to make him a citizen of it, but it is only necessary that he should be born or naturalized in the United States to be a citizen of the Union.

It is quite clear, then, that there is a citizenship of the United States, and a citizenship of a State, which are distinct from each other, and which depend upon different characteristics or circumstances in the individual.

We think this distinction and its explicit recognition in this amendment of great weight in this argument, because the next paragraph of this same section, which is the one mainly relied on by the plaintiffs in error, speaks only of privileges and immunities of citizens of the United States, and does not speak of those of citizens of the several States. The argument, however, in favor of the plaintiffs rests wholly on the assumption that the citizenship is the same, and the privileges and immunities guaranteed by the clause are the same.

The language is, "No State shall make or enforce any law which shall abridge the privileges or immunities of citizens of *the United States*." It is a little remarkable, if this clause was intended as a protection to the citizen of a State against the legislative power of his own State, that the word citizen of the State should be left out when it is so carefully used, and used in contradistinction to citizens of the United States, in the very sentence which precedes it. It is too clear for argument that the change in phraseology was adopted understandingly and with a purpose.

Of the privileges and immunities of the citizen of the United States, and of the privileges and immunities of the citizen of the State, and what they respectively are, we will presently consider; but we wish to state here that it is only the former which are placed by this clause under the protection of the Federal Constitution, and that the latter, whatever they may be, are not intended to have any additional protection by this paragraph of the amendment.

If, then, there is a difference between the privileges and immunities belonging to a citizen of the United States as such, and those belonging to the citizen of the State as such[,] the latter must rest for their security and protection where they have heretofore rested; for they are not embraced by this paragraph of the amendment. . . .

It would be the vainest show of learning to attempt to prove by citations of authority, that up to the adoption of the recent amendments, no claim or pretence was set up that those rights depended on the Federal government for their existence or protection, beyond the very few express limitations which the Federal Constitution imposed upon the States—such, for instance, as the prohibition against ex post facto laws, bills of attainder, and laws impairing the obligation of contracts. But with the exception of these and a few other restrictions, the entire domain of the privileges and immunities of citizens of the States, as above defined, lay within the constitutional and legislative power of the States, and without that of the Federal government. Was it the purpose of the fourteenth amendment, by the simple declaration that no State should make or enforce any law which shall abridge the privileges and immunities of *citizens of the United States*, to transfer the security and protection of all the civil rights which we have mentioned, from the States to the Federal government? And where it is declared that Congress shall have the power to enforce that article, was it intended to bring within the power of Congress the entire domain of civil rights heretofore belonging exclusively to the States?

All this and more must follow, if the proposition of the plaintiffs in error be sound. For not only are these rights subject to the control of Congress whenever in its discretion any of them are supposed to be abridged by State legislation, but that body may also pass laws in advance, limiting and restricting the exercise of legislative power by the States, in their most ordinary and usual functions, as in its judgment it may think proper on all such subjects. And still further, such a construction followed by the reversal of the judgments of the Supreme Court of Louisiana in these cases, would constitute this court a perpetual censor upon all legislation of the States, on the civil rights of their own citizens, with authority to nullify such as it did not approve as consistent with those rights, as they existed at the time of the adoption of this amendment. The argument we admit is not always the most conclusive which is drawn from the consequences urged against the adoption of a particular construction of an instrument. But when, as in the case before us, these consequences are so serious, so far-reaching and pervading, so great a departure from the structure and spirit of our institutions; when the effect is to fetter and degrade the State governments by subjecting them to the control of Congress, in the exercise of powers heretofore universally conceded to them of the most ordinary and fundamental character; when in fact it radically changes the whole theory of the relations of the State and Federal governments to each other and of both these governments to the people; the argument has a force that is irresistible, in the absence of language which expresses such a purpose too clearly to admit of doubt.

We are convinced that no such results were intended by the Congress which proposed these amendments, nor by the legislatures of the States which ratified them.

Having shown that the privileges and immunities relied on in the argument are those which belong to citizens of the States as such, and that they are left to the State governments for security and protection, and not by this article placed under the special care of the Federal government, we may hold ourselves excused from defining the privileges and immunities of citizens of the United States which no State can abridge, until some case involving those privileges may make it necessary to do so.

But lest it should be said that no such privileges and immunities are to be found if those we have been considering are excluded, we venture to suggest some which owe their existence to the Federal government, its National character, its Constitution, or its laws.

One of these is . . . the right of the citizen of this great country, protected by implied guarantees of its Constitution, "to come to the seat of government to assert any claim he may have upon that government, to transact any business he may have with it, to seek its protection, to share its offices, to engage in administering its functions. He has the right of free access to its seaports, through which all operations of foreign commerce are conducted, to the subtreasuries, land offices, and courts of justice in the several States." . . .

Another privilege of a citizen of the United States is to demand the care and protection of the Federal government over his life, liberty, and property when on the high seas or within the jurisdiction of a foreign government. Of this there can be no doubt, nor that the right depends upon his character as a citizen of the United States. The right to peaceably assemble and petition for redress of grievances, the privilege of the writ of *habeas corpus*, are rights of the citizen guaranteed by the Federal Constitution. The right to use the navigable waters of the United States, however they may penetrate the territory of the several States, all rights secured to our citizens by treaties with foreign nations, are dependent upon citizenship of the United States, and not citizenship of a State. One of these privileges is conferred by the very article under consideration. It is that a citizen of the United States can, of his own volition, become a citizen of any State of the Union by a *bona fide* residence therein, with the same rights as other citizens of that State. To these may be added the rights secured by the thirteenth and fifteenth articles of amendment, and by the other clause of the fourteenth, next to be considered.

But it is useless to pursue this branch of the inquiry, since we are of opinion that the rights claimed by these plaintiffs in error, if they have any existence, are not privileges and immunities of citizens of the United States within the meaning of the clause of the fourteenth amendment under consideration. . . .

The argument has not been much pressed in these cases that the defendant's charter deprives the plaintiffs of their property without due process of law, or that it denies to them the equal protection of the law. . . .

. . . [I]t is sufficient to say that under no construction of that provision that we have ever seen, or any that we deem admissible, can the restraint imposed by the State of Louisiana upon the exercise of their trade by the butchers of New Orleans be held to be a deprivation of property within the meaning of that provision.

"Nor shall any State deny to any person within its jurisdiction the equal protection of the laws."

In the light of the history of these amendments, and the pervading purpose of them, which we have already discussed, it is not difficult to give a meaning to this clause. The existence of laws in the States where the newly emancipated negroes resided, which discriminated with gross injustice and hardship against them as a class, was the evil to be remedied by this clause, and by it such laws are forbidden.

If, however, the States did not conform their laws to its requirements, then by the fifth section of the article of amendment Congress was authorized to enforce it by suitable legislation. We doubt very much whether any action of a State not directed by way of discrimination against the negroes as a class, or on account of their race, will ever be held to come within the purview of this provision. It is so clearly a provision for that race and that emergency, that a strong case would be necessary for its application to any other. But as it is a State that is to be dealt with, and not alone the validity of its laws, we may safely leave that matter until Congress shall have exercised its power, or some case of State oppression, by denial of equal justice in its courts, shall have claimed a decision at our hands. We find no such case in the one before us, and do not deem it necessary to go over the argument again, as it may have relation to this particular clause of the amendment.

In the early history of the organization of the government, its statesmen seem to have divided on the line which should separate the powers of the National government from those of the State governments, and though this line has never been very well defined in public opinion, such a division has continued from that day to this.

The adoption of the first eleven amendments to the Constitution so soon after the original instrument was accepted, shows a prevailing sense of danger at that time from the Federal power. And it cannot be denied that such a jealousy continued to exist with many patriotic men until the breaking out of the late civil war. It was then discovered that the true danger to the perpetuity of the Union was in the capacity of the State organizations to combine and concentrate all the powers of the State, and of contiguous States, for a determined resistance to the General Government.

Unquestionably this has given great force to the argument, and added largely to the number of those who believe in the necessity of a strong National government.

But, however pervading this sentiment, and however it may have contributed to the adoption of the amendments we have been considering, we do not see in those amendments any purpose to destroy the main features of the general system. Under the pressure of all the excited feeling growing out of the war, our statesmen have still believed that the existence of the States with powers for domestic and local government, including the regulation of civil rights—the rights of person and of property—was essential to the perfect working of our complex form of government, though they have thought proper to impose additional limitations on the States, and to confer additional power on that of the Nation.

But whatever fluctuations may be seen in the history of public opinion on this subject during the period of our national existence, we think it will be found that this court, so far as its functions required, has always held with a steady and an even hand the balance between State and Federal power, and we trust that such may continue to be the history of its relation to that subject so long as it shall have duties to perform which demand of it a construction of the Constitution, or of any of its parts.

The judgments of the Supreme Court of Louisiana in these cases are

AFFIRMED.

2. *MINOR V. HAPPERSETT*, 88 U.S. 162 (1875)

Missouri's constitution mandated that "[e]very male citizen of the United States shall be entitled to vote." On October 15, 1872, Virginia Minor, a native-born white citizen of the United States and of Missouri, over the age of twenty-one years, applied to Reese Happersett, the registrar of voters, to be registered as a lawful voter for the general election to be held that November. Happersett refused to register Minor because she was not a "male citizen of the United States," and Minor sued Happersett for thus depriving her of the right to vote. The Missouri Supreme Court sustained the lower court's judgment in Happersett's favor, as did the United States Supreme Court. While acknowledging that native-born or naturalized women were

United States citizens, the Supreme Court also held that suffrage was not a right of citizenship and that not all citizens were voters.

The CHIEF JUSTICE [Morrison Waite] delivered the opinion of the court.

. . . It is contended that the provisions of the constitution and laws of the State of Missouri which confine the right of suffrage and registration therefor to men, are in violation of the Constitution of the United States, and therefore void. The argument is, that as a woman, born or naturalized in the United States and subject to the jurisdiction thereof, is a citizen of the United States and of the State in which she resides, she has the right of suffrage as one of the privileges and immunities of her citizenship, which the State cannot by its laws or constitution abridge.

There is no doubt that women may be citizens. They are persons, and by the fourteenth amendment "all persons born or naturalized in the United States and subject to the jurisdiction thereof" are expressly declared to be "citizens of the United States and of the State wherein they reside." But, in our opinion, it did not need this amendment to give them that position. Before its adoption the Constitution of the United States did not in terms prescribe who should be citizens of the United States or of the several States, yet there were necessarily such citizens without such provision. There cannot be a nation without a people. The very idea of a political community, such as a nation is, implies an association of persons for the promotion of their general welfare. Each one of the persons associated becomes a member of the nation formed by the association. He owes it allegiance and is entitled to its protection. Allegiance and protection are, in this connection, reciprocal obligations. The one is a compensation for the other; allegiance for protection and protection for allegiance. . . .

. . . [I]t is apparent that from the commencement of the legislation upon this subject alien women and alien minors could be made citizens by naturalization, and we think it will not be contended that this would have been done if it had not been supposed that native women and native minors were already citizens by birth.

. . . [T]he records of the courts are full of cases in which the jurisdiction depends upon the citizenship of women, and not one can be found, we think, in which objection was made on that account. Certainly none can be found in which it has been held that women could not sue or be sued in the courts of the United States. . . .

Other proof of like character might be found, but certainly more cannot be necessary to establish the fact that sex has never been made one of the elements of citizenship in the United States. In this respect men have never had an advantage over women. The same laws precisely apply to both. The fourteenth amendment did not affect the citizenship of women any more than it did of men. In this particular, therefore, the rights of Mrs. Minor do not depend upon the amendment. She has always been a citizen from her birth, and entitled to all the privileges and immunities of citizenship. The amendment prohibited the State, of which she is a citizen, from abridging any of her privileges and immunities as a citizen of the United States; but it did not confer citizenship on her. That she had before its adoption.

If the right of suffrage is one of the necessary privileges of a citizen of the United States, then the constitution and laws of Missouri confining it to men are in violation of the Constitution of the United States, as amended, and consequently void. The direct question is, therefore, presented whether all citizens are necessarily voters. . . .

It certainly is nowhere made so in express terms. The United States has no voters in the States of its own creation. The elective officers of the United States are all elected directly or indirectly by State voters. The members of the House of Representatives are to be chosen by the people of the States, and the electors in each State must have the qualifications requisite for electors of the most numerous branch of the State legislature. Senators are to be chosen by the legislatures of the States, and necessarily the members of the legislature required to make the choice are elected by the voters of the State. Each State must appoint in such manner, as the legislature thereof may direct, the electors to elect the President and Vice-President. The times, places, and manner of holding elections for Senators and Representatives are to be prescribed in each State by the legislature thereof; but Congress may at any time, by law, make or alter such regulations, except as to the place of choosing Senators. It is not necessary to inquire whether this power of supervision thus given to Congress is sufficient to authorize any interference with the State laws prescribing the qualifications of voters, for no such interference has ever been attempted. The power of the State in this particular is certainly supreme until Congress acts.

The amendment did not add to the privileges and immunities of a citizen. It simply furnished an additional guaranty for the protection of such as he already had. No new voters were necessarily made by it. Indirectly it may have had that effect, because it may have increased the number of citizens entitled to suffrage under the constitution and laws of the States, but it operates for this purpose, if at all, through the States and the State laws, and not directly upon the citizen.

It is clear, therefore, we think, that the Constitution has not added the right of suffrage to the privileges and immunities of citizenship as they existed at the time it was adopted. This makes it proper to inquire whether suffrage was coextensive with the citizenship of the States at the time of its adoption. If it was, then it may with force be argued that suffrage was one of the rights which belonged to citizenship, and in the enjoyment of which every citizen must be protected. But if it was not, the contrary may with propriety be assumed.

When the Federal Constitution was adopted, all the States, with the exception of Rhode Island and Connecticut, had constitutions of their own. These two continued to act under their charters from the Crown. Upon an examination of those constitutions we find that in no State were all citizens permitted to vote. Each State determined for itself who should have that power. . . .

In this condition of the law in respect to suffrage in the several States it cannot for a moment be doubted that if it had been intended to make all citizens of the United States voters, the framers of the Constitution would not have left it to implication. So important a change in the condition of citizenship as it actually existed, if intended, would have been expressly declared.

But if further proof is necessary to show that no such change was intended, it can easily be found both in and out of the Constitution. By Article 4, section 2, it is provided that "the citizens of each State shall be entitled to all the privileges and immunities of citizens in the several States." If suffrage is necessarily a part of citizenship, then the citizens of each State must be entitled to vote in the several States precisely as their citizens are. This is more than asserting that they may change their residence and become citizens of the State and thus be voters. It goes to the extent of insisting that while retaining their original citizenship they may vote in any State. This, we think, has never been claimed. And again, by the very terms of the amendment we have been considering (the fourteenth), "Representatives shall be apportioned among the several States according to their respective numbers, counting the whole number of persons in each State, excluding Indians not taxed. But when the right to vote at any election for the choice of electors for President and Vice-President of the United States, representatives in Congress, the executive and judicial officers of a State, or the members of the legislature thereof, is denied to any of the male inhabitants of such State, being twenty-one years of age and citizens of the United States, or in any way abridged, except for participation in the rebellion, or other crimes, the basis of representation therein shall be reduced in the proportion which the number of such male citizens shall bear to the whole number of male citizens twenty-one years of age in such State." Why this, if it was not in the power of the legislature to deny the right of suffrage to some male inhabitants? And if suffrage was necessarily one of the absolute rights of citizenship, why confine the operation of the limitation to male inhabitants? Women and children are, as we have seen, "persons." They are counted in the enumeration upon which the apportionment is to be made, but if they were necessarily voters because of their citizenship unless clearly excluded, why inflict the penalty for the exclusion of males alone? Clearly, no such form of words would have been selected to express the idea here indicated if suffrage was the absolute right of all citizens.

And still again, after the adoption of the fourteenth amendment, it was deemed necessary to adopt a fifteenth[.] . . . The fourteenth amendment had already provided that no State should make or enforce any law which should abridge the privileges or immunities of citizens of the United States. If suffrage was one of these privileges or immunities, why amend the Constitution to prevent its being denied on account of race, &c.? Nothing is more evident than that the greater must include the less, and if all were already protected why go through with the form of amending the Constitution to protect a part? . . .

The guaranty is of a republican form of government. No particular government is designated as republican, neither is the exact form to be guaranteed, in any manner especially designated. Here, as in other parts of the instrument, we are compelled to resort elsewhere to ascertain what was intended.

The guaranty necessarily implies a duty on the part of the States themselves to provide such a government. All the States had governments when the Constitution was adopted. In all the people participated to some extent, through their representatives elected in the manner specially provided. These governments the Constitution did not change. They were accepted precisely as they were, and it is, therefore, to be presumed that they were such as it was the duty of the States to provide. Thus we have unmistakable evidence of what was republican in form, within the meaning of that term as employed in the Constitution.

As has been seen, all the citizens of the States were not invested with the right of suffrage. In all, save perhaps New Jersey, this right was only bestowed upon men and not upon all of them. Under these circumstances it is certainly now too late to contend that a government is not republican, within the meaning of this guaranty in the Constitution, because women are not made voters.

. . . For nearly ninety years the people have acted upon the idea that the Constitution, when it conferred citizenship, did not necessarily confer the right of suffrage. If uniform practice long continued can settle the construction of so important an instrument as the Constitution of the United States confessedly is, most certainly it has been done here. Our province is to decide what the law is, not to declare what it should be.

We have given this case the careful consideration its importance demands. If the law is wrong, it ought to be changed; but the power for that is not with us. The arguments addressed to us bearing upon such a view of the subject may perhaps be sufficient to induce those having the power, to make the alteration, but they ought not to be permitted to influence our judgment in determining the present rights of the parties now litigating before us. No argument as to woman's need of suffrage can be considered. We can only act upon her rights as they exist. It is not for us to look at the hardship of withholding. Our duty is at an end if we find it is within the power of a State to withhold.

Being unanimously of the opinion that the Constitution of the United States does not confer the right of suffrage upon any one, and that the constitutions and laws of the several States which commit that important trust to men alone are not necessarily void, we

AFFIRM THE JUDGMENT.

3. *UNITED STATES V. REESE ET AL.*, 92 U.S. 214 (1876)

A federal grand jury indicted election officials in Lexington, Kentucky, for violation of sections 3 and 4 of the Enforcement Act of May 31, 1870, after they refused to accept the vote of African American William Garner because Garner allegedly had not paid a $1.50 capitation tax. The Supreme Court held that the Fifteenth Amendment to the Constitution did not confer a right of suffrage but only prohibited exclusion from voting on account of race, color, or previous condition of servitude and empowered Congress to enforce only that right by "appropriate legislation." Finding that portions of the Enforcement Act of May 31, 1870, exceeded the scope of the Fifteenth Amendment, the Supreme Court's ruling allowed states to disfranchise black voters as a practical matter by imposing literacy tests and poll taxes, which, while not racially based, had a disproportionate impact on African Americans.

MR. CHIEF JUSTICE [Morrison] WAITE delivered the opinion of the court.

This case . . . presents an indictment containing four counts, under sects. 3 and 4 of the act of May 31, 1870 (16 Stat. 140), against two of the inspectors of a municipal election in the State of Kentucky, for refusing to receive and count at such election the vote of William Garner, a citizen of the United States of African descent. . . .

In this court the United States abandon the first and third counts, and expressly waive the consideration of all claims not arising out of the enforcement of the Fifteenth Amendment of the Constitution.

. . . [T]he principal question left for consideration is, whether the act under which the indictment is found can be made effective for the punishment of inspectors of elections who refuse to receive and count the votes of citizens of the United States, having all the qualifications of voters, because of their race, color, or previous condition of servitude. . . .

The second count in the indictment is based upon the fourth section of this act, and the fourth upon the third section.

Rights and immunities created by or dependent upon the Constitution of the United States can be protected by Congress. The form and the manner of the protection may be such as Congress, in the legitimate exercise of its legislative discretion, shall provide. These may be varied to meet the necessities of the particular right to be protected.

The Fifteenth Amendment does not confer the right of suffrage upon any one. It prevents the States, or the United States, however, from giving preference, in this particular, to one citizen of the United States over another on account of race, color, or previous condition of servitude. Before its adoption, this could be done. It was as much within the power of a State to exclude citizens of the United States from voting on account of race, &c., as it was on account of age, property, or education. Now it is not. If citizens of one race having certain qualifications are permitted by law to vote, those of another having the same qualifications must be. Previous to this amendment, there was no constitutional guaranty against this discrimination: now there is. It follows that the amendment has invested the citizens of the United States with a new constitutional right which is within the protecting power of Congress. That right is exemption from discrimination in the exercise of the elective franchise on account of race, color, or previous condition of servitude. This, under the express provisions of the second section of the amendment, Congress may enforce by "appropriate legislation."

This leads us to inquire whether the act now under consideration is "appropriate legislation" for that purpose. The power of Congress to legislate at all upon the subject of voting at State elections rests upon this amendment. The effect of art. 1, sect. 4, of the Constitution, in respect to elections for senators and representatives, is not now under consideration. It has not been contended, nor can it be, that the amendment confers authority to impose penalties for every wrongful refusal to receive the vote of a qualified elector at State elections. It is only when the wrongful refusal at such an election is because of race, color, or previous condition of servitude, that Congress can interfere, and provide for its punishment. If, therefore, the third and fourth sections of the act are beyond that limit, they are unauthorized.

The third section does not in express terms limit the offence of an inspector of elections, for which the punishment is provided, to a wrongful discrimination on account of race, &c. This is conceded; but it is urged, that when this section is construed with those which precede it, and to which, as is claimed, it refers, it is so limited. The argument is, that the only wrongful act, on the part of the officer whose duty it is to receive or permit the requisite qualification, which can dispense with actual qualification under the State laws, and substitute the prescribed affidavit therefor, is that mentioned and prohibited in sect. 2,—to wit, discrimination on account of race, &c.; and that, consequently, sect. 3 is confined in its operation to the same wrongful discrimination.

This is a penal statute, and must be construed strictly; not so strictly, indeed, as to defeat the clear intention of Congress, but the words employed must be understood in the sense they were obviously used. . . . If, taking the whole statute together, it is apparent that it was not the intention of Congress thus to limit the operation of the act, we cannot give it that effect.

The statute contemplates a most important change in the election laws. Previous to its adoption, the States, as a general rule, regulated in their own way all the details of all elections. They prescribed the qualifications of voters, and the manner in which those offering to vote at an election should make known their qualifications to the officers in charge. This act interferes with this practice, and prescribes rules not provided by the laws of the States. It substitutes, under certain circumstances, performance wrongfully prevented for performance itself. If the elector makes and presents his affidavit in the form and to the effect prescribed, the inspectors are to treat this as the equivalent of the specified requirement of the State law. This is a radical change in the practice, and the statute which creates it should be explicit in its terms. Nothing should be left to construction, if it can be avoided. The law ought not to be in such a condition that the elector may act upon one idea of its meaning, and the inspector upon another. . . .

But when we go beyond the third section, and read the fourth, we find there no words of limitation, or reference even, that can be construed as manifesting any intention to confine its provisions to the terms of the Fifteenth Amendment. That section has for its object the punishment of all persons, who, by force, bribery, &c., hinder, delay, &c., any person from qualifying or voting. In view of all these facts, we feel compelled to say, that, in our opinion, the language of the third and fourth sections does not confine their operation to unlawful discriminations on account of race, &c. If Congress had the power to provide generally for the punishment of those who unlawfully interfere to prevent the exercise of the elective franchise without regard to such discrimination, the language of these sections would be broad enough for that purpose.

It remains now to consider whether a statute, so general as this in its provisions, can be made available for the punishment of those who may be guilty of unlawful discrimination against citizens of the United States, while exercising the elective franchise, on account of their race, &c.

There is no attempt in the sections now under consideration to provide specifically for such an offence. If the case is provided for at all, it is because it comes under the general prohibition against any wrongful act or unlawful obstruction in this particular. We are, therefore, directly called upon to decide whether a penal statute enacted by Congress, with its limited powers, which is in general language broad enough to cover wrongful acts without as well as within the constitutional jurisdiction, can be limited by judicial construction so as to make it operate only on that which Congress may rightfully prohibit and punish. For this purpose, we must take these sections of the statute as they are. We are not able to reject a part which is unconstitutional, and retain the remainder, because it is not possible to separate that which is unconstitutional, if there be any such, from that which is not. The proposed effect is not to be attained by striking out or disregarding words that are in the section, but by inserting those that are not now there. Each of the sections must stand as a whole, or fall altogether. The language is plain. . . . The question, then, to be determined, is, whether we can introduce words of limitation into a penal statute so as to make it specific, when, as expressed, it is general only.

It would certainly be dangerous if the legislature could set a net large enough to catch all possible offenders, and leave it to the courts to step inside and say who could be rightfully detained, and who should be set at large. This would, to some extent, substitute the judicial for the legislative department of the government. The courts enforce the legislative will when ascertained, if within the constitutional grant of power. Within its legitimate sphere, Congress is supreme, and beyond the control of the courts; but if it steps outside of its constitutional limitations, and attempts that which is beyond its reach, the courts are authorized to, and when called upon in due course of legal proceedings must, annul its encroachments upon the reserved power of the States and the people.

To limit this statute in the manner now asked for would be to make a new law, not to enforce an old one. This is no part of our duty.

We must, therefore, decide that Congress has not as yet provided by "appropriate legislation" for the punishment of the offence charged in the indictment; and that the Circuit Court properly sustained the demurrers, and gave judgment for the defendants. . . .

Judgment affirmed.

4. *UNITED STATES V. CRUIKSHANK ET AL.*, 92 U.S. 542 (1876)

After a disputed local election, the Republican governor of Louisiana declared African American R. C. Register the sheriff and white Daniel Shaw the judge of Grant Parish. Register, Shaw, and a group of blacks then occupied the courthouse at the parish seat, Colfax. On Easter Sunday, April 13, 1873, several hundred whites besieged the courthouse, and a firefight began when the occupants ignored their demand to vacate the building. A massacre ensued when the blacks inside tried to exit under a white flag after the courthouse was set on fire, including the mass execution of dozens of captured black prisoners. The following day, federal troops arrived in Grant Parish, but by that time well over a hundred blacks had been slaughtered. A grand jury indicted ninety-eight individuals for conspiring to prevent U.S. citizens from exercising their rights and privileges guaranteed under the Constitution and for committing murder, but only nine men were taken into custody and made to stand trial. Three of the individuals, including William Cruikshank, were convicted but later freed when the Supreme Court found their indictment defective and further ruled that the Fourteenth Amendment addressed only state action and left the acts of private individuals to the control of state law.

. . . MR. CHIEF JUSTICE [Morrison] WAITE delivered the opinion of the court.

This case comes here [from] the Circuit Court for the District of Louisiana[.] . . . It presents for our consideration an indictment containing sixteen counts, divided into two series of eight counts each, based upon sect. 6 of the Enforcement Act of May 31, 1870. . . .

The general charge in the first eight counts is that of "banding," and in the second eight, that of "conspiring" together to injure, oppress, threaten, and intimidate Levi Nelson and Alexander Tillman, citizens of the United States, of African descent and persons of color, with the intent thereby to hinder and prevent them in their free exercise and enjoyment of rights and privileges "granted and secured" to them "in common with all other good citizens of the United States by the constitution and laws of the United States."

The offences provided for by the statute in question do not consist in the mere "banding" or "conspiring" of two or more persons together, but in their banding or conspiring with the intent, or for any of the purposes, specified. To bring this case under the operation of the statute, therefore, it must appear that the right, the enjoyment of which the conspirators intended to hinder or prevent, was one granted or secured by the constitution or laws of the United States. If it does not so appear, the criminal matter charged has not been made indictable by any act of Congress. . . .

The people of the United States resident within any State are subject to two governments: one State, and the other National; but there need be no conflict between the two. The powers which one possesses, the other does not. They are established for different purposes, and have separate jurisdictions. To-gether they make one whole, and furnish the people of the United States with a complete government, ample for the protection of all their rights at home and abroad. True, it may sometimes happen that a person is amenable to both jurisdictions for one and the same act. Thus, if a marshal of the United States is unlawfully resisted while executing the process of the courts within a State, and the resistance is accompanied by an assault on the officer, the sovereignty of the United States is violated by the resistance, and that of the State by the breach of peace, in the assault. . . . This does not, however, necessarily imply that the two governments possess powers in common, or bring them into conflict with each other. . . . [The citizen] owes allegiance to the two departments, so to speak, and within their respective spheres must pay the penalties which each exacts for disobedience to its laws. In return, he can demand protection from each within its own jurisdiction.

The government of the United States is one of delegated powers alone. Its authority is defined and limited by the Constitution. All powers not granted to it by that instrument are reserved to the States or the people. No rights can be acquired under the constitution or laws of the United States, except such as the government of the United States has the authority to grant or secure. All that cannot be so granted or secured are left under the protection of the States. . . .

The first and ninth counts state the intent of the defendants to have been to hinder and prevent the citizens named in the free exercise and enjoyment of their "lawful right and privilege to peaceably assemble together with each other and with other citizens of the United States for a peaceful and lawful purpose." The right of the people peaceably to assemble for lawful purposes existed long before the adoption of the Constitution of the United States. In fact, it is, and always has been, one of the attributes of citizenship under a free government.... It is found wherever civilization exists. It was not, therefore, a right granted to the people by the Constitution. The government of the United States when established found it in existence, with the obligation on the part of the States to afford it protection. As no direct power over it was granted to Congress, it remains, according to the ruling in *Gibbons v. Ogden* . . . subject to State jurisdiction. Only such existing rights were committed by the people to the protection of Congress as came within the general scope of the authority granted to the national government.

The first amendment to the Constitution prohibits Congress from abridging "the right of the people to assemble and to petition the government for a redress of grievances." This, like the other amendments proposed and adopted at the same time, was not intended to limit the powers of the State governments in respect to their own citizens, but to operate upon the National government alone....

The particular amendment now under consideration assumes the existence of the right of the people to assemble for lawful purposes, and protects it against encroachment by Congress. The right was not created by the amendment; neither was its continuance guaranteed, except as against congressional interference. For their protection in its enjoyment, therefore, the people must look to the States. The power for that purpose was originally placed there, and it has never been surrendered to the United States.

The right of the people peaceably to assemble for the purpose of petitioning Congress for a redress of grievances, or for any thing else connected with the powers or the duties of the national government, is an attribute of national citizenship, and, as such, under the protection of, and guaranteed by, the United States.... If it had been alleged in these counts that the object of the defendants was to prevent a meeting for such a purpose, the case would have been within the statute, and within the scope of the sovereignty of the United States. Such, however, is not the case. The offence, as stated in the indictment, will be made out, if it be shown that the object of the conspiracy was to prevent a meeting for any lawful purpose whatever.

The second and tenth counts are equally defective. The right there specified is that of "bearing arms for a lawful purpose." This is not a right granted by the Constitution. Neither is it in any manner dependent upon that instrument for its existence. The second amendment declares that it shall not be infringed; but this, as has been seen, means no more than that it shall not be infringed by Congress. This is one of the amendments that has no other effect than to restrict the powers of the national government, leaving the people to look for their protection against any violation by their fellow-citizens of the rights it recognizes, to what is called . . . the "powers which relate to merely municipal legislation, or what was, perhaps, more properly called internal police," "not surrendered or restrained" by the Constitution of the United States.

The third and eleventh counts are even more objectionable. They charge the intent to have been to deprive the citizens named, they being in Louisiana, "of their respective several lives and liberty of person without due process of law." This is nothing else than alleging a conspiracy to falsely imprison or murder citizens of the United States, being within the territorial jurisdiction of the State of Louisiana. The rights of life and personal liberty are natural rights of man. . . . The very highest duty of the States . . . under the Constitution, was to protect all persons within their boundaries in the enjoyment of these "unalienable rights with which they were endowed by their Creator." Sovereignty, for this purpose, rests alone with the States. It is no more the duty or within the power of the United States to punish for a conspiracy to falsely imprison or murder within a State, than it would be to punish for false imprisonment or murder itself.

The fourteenth amendment prohibits a State from depriving any person of life, liberty, or property, without due process of law; but this adds nothing to the rights of one citizen as against another. It simply furnishes an additional guaranty against any encroachment by the States upon the fundamental rights which belong to every citizen as a member of society. . . . These counts in the indictment do not call for the exercise of any of the powers conferred by this provision in the amendment.

The fourth and twelfth counts charge the intent to have been to prevent and hinder the citizens named, who were of African descent and persons of color, in "the free exercise and enjoyment of their several right and privilege to the full and equal benefit of all laws and proceedings . . . enacted or ordained by the said State of Louisiana and by the United States; and . . . being in force in the said State and District of Louisiana aforesaid, for the security of their respective persons and property, then and there, at that time enjoyed at and within said State and District of Louisiana by white persons, being citizens of said State of Louisiana and the United States, for the protection of the persons and property of said white citizens." There is no allegation that this was done because of the race or color of the persons conspired against. When stripped of its verbiage, the case as presented amounts to nothing more than that the defendants conspired to prevent certain citizens of the United States, being within the State of Louisiana, from enjoying the equal protection of the laws of the State and of the United States.

The fourteenth amendment prohibits a State from denying to any person within its jurisdiction the equal protection of the laws; but this provision does not, any more than the one which precedes it, and which we have just considered, add any thing to the rights which one citizen has under the Constitution against another. The equality of the rights of citizens is a principle of republicanism. Every republican government is in duty bound to protect all its citizens in the enjoyment of this principle, if within its power. That duty was originally assumed by the States; and it still remains there. The only obligation resting upon the United States is to see that the States do not deny the right. This the amendment guarantees, but no more. The power of the national government is limited to the enforcement of this guaranty.

No question arises under the Civil Rights Act of April 9, 1866 . . . which is intended for the protection of citizens of the United States in the enjoyment of certain rights, without discrimination on account of race, color, or previous condition of servitude, because, as has already been stated, it is nowhere alleged in these counts that the wrong contemplated against the rights of these citizens was on account of their race or color. . . .

The sixth and fourteenth counts state the intent of the defendants to have been to hinder and prevent the citizens named, being of African descent, and colored, "in the free exercise and enjoyment of their several and respective right and privilege to vote at any election to be thereafter by law had and held by the people in and of the said State of Louisiana, or by the people of and in the parish of Grant aforesaid." In *Minor* v. *Happersett* . . . we decided that the Constitution of the United States has not conferred the right of suffrage upon any one, and that the United States have no voters of their own creation in the States. In *United States* v. *Reese* . . . we hold that the fifteenth amendment has invested the citizens of the United States with a new constitutional right, which is, exemption from discrimination in the exercise of the elective franchise on account of race, color, or previous condition of servitude. From this it appears that the right of suffrage is not a necessary attribute of national citizenship; but that exemption from discrimination in the exercise of that right on account of race, &c., is. The right to vote in the States comes from the States; but the right of exemption from the prohibited discrimination comes from the United States. The first has not been granted or secured by the Constitution of the United States; but the last has been.

Inasmuch, therefore, as it does not appear in these counts that the intent of the defendants was to prevent these parties from exercising their right to vote on account of their race, &c., it does not appear that it was their intent to interfere with any right granted or secured by the constitution or laws of the United States. We may suspect that race was the cause of the hostility; but it is not so averred. This is material to a description of the substance of the offence, and cannot be supplied by implication. Every thing essential must be charged positively, and not inferentially. The defect here is not in form, but in substance.

The seventh and fifteenth counts are no better than the sixth and fourteenth. The intent here charged is to put the parties named in great fear of bodily harm, and to injure and oppress them, because, being and having been in all things qualified, they had voted "at an election before that time had and held according to law by the people of the said State of Louisiana, in said State, to wit, on the fourth day of November, A.D. 1872, and at divers other elections by the people of the State, also before that time had and held according to law."

There is nothing to show that the elections voted at were any other than State elections, or that the conspiracy was formed on account of the race of the parties against whom the conspirators were to act. The charge as made is really of nothing more than a conspiracy to commit a breach of the peace within a State. Certainly it will not be claimed that the United States have the power or are required to do mere police duty in the States. If a State cannot protect itself against domestic violence, the United States may, upon the call of the executive, when the legislature cannot be convened, lend their assistance for that purpose. This is a guaranty of the Constitution (art. 4, sect. 4); but it applies to no case like this.

We are, therefore, of the opinion that the first, second, third, fourth, sixth, seventh, ninth, tenth, eleventh, twelfth, fourteenth, and fifteenth counts do not contain charges of a criminal nature made indictable under the laws of the United States, and that consequently they are not good and sufficient in law. They do not show that it was the intent of the defendants, by their conspiracy, to hinder or prevent the enjoyment of any right granted or secured by the Constitution.

We come now to consider the fifth and thirteenth and the eighth and sixteenth counts, which may be brought together for that purpose. The intent charged in the fifth and thirteenth is "to hinder and prevent the parties in their respective free exercise and enjoyment of the rights, privileges, immunities, and protection granted and secured to them respectively as citizens of the United States, and as citizens of said State of Louisiana," "for the reason that they, . . . being then and there citizens of said State and of the United States, were persons of African descent and race, and persons of color, and not white citizens thereof;" and in the eighth and sixteenth, to hinder and prevent them "in their several and respective free exercise and enjoyment of every, each, all, and singular the several rights and privileges granted and secured to them by the constitution and laws of the United States." The same general statement of the rights to be interfered with is found in the fifth and thirteenth counts.

. . . [T]hese counts are too vague and general. They lack the certainty and precision required by the established rules of criminal pleading. It follows that they are not good and sufficient in law. They are so defective that no judgment of conviction should be pronounced upon them.

The order of the Circuit Court arresting the judgment upon the verdict is, therefore, affirmed; and the cause remanded, with instructions to discharge the defendants.

5. *Hall v. DeCuir*, 95 U.S. 485 (1878)

The Louisiana Supreme Court affirmed an award of damages to Josephine DeCuir, an African American woman denied access to a cabin set aside for white passengers during her trip on a steamboat from New Orleans to Hermitage, Louisiana. The

Supreme Court overturned the Louisiana Supreme Court, and invalidated the Louisiana law on which the damages were based, by holding that the steamboat was involved in interstate commerce that could be regulated only by Congress and not the states.

... By the thirteenth article of the Constitution of Louisiana it is provided that "all persons shall enjoy equal rights and privileges upon any conveyance of a public character." By an act of the General Assembly ... approved Feb. 23, 1869, it was enacted as follows:—

"SECTION 1. All persons engaged within this State, in the business of common carriers of passengers, shall have the right to refuse to admit any person ... or to expel any person therefrom after admission, when such person shall, on demand, refuse or neglect to pay the customary fare, or when such person shall be of infamous character, or shall be guilty, after admission to the conveyance of the carrier, of gross, vulgar, or disorderly conduct, or who shall commit any act tending to injure the business of the carrier, prescribed for the management of his business, after such rules and regulations shall have been made known: *Provided*, said rules and regulations make no discrimination on account of race or color; and shall have the right to refuse any person admission to such conveyance where there is not room or suitable accommodations; and, except in cases above enumerated, all persons engaged in the business of common carriers of passengers are forbidden to refuse admission to their conveyance, or to expel therefrom any person whomsoever."[1]

"SECT. 4. For a violation of any of the provisions of the first and second sections of this act, the party injured shall have a right of action to recover any damage, exemplary as well as actual, which he may sustain, before any court of competent jurisdiction." ...

Benson, the defendant below, was the master and owner of the "Governor Allen," a steamboat enrolled and licensed under the laws of the United States for the coasting trade, and plying as a regular packet for the transportation of freight and passengers between New Orleans, in the State of Louisiana, and Vicksburg, in the State of Mississippi, touching at the intermediate landings both within and without Louisiana, as occasion required. The defendant in error, plaintiff below, a person of color, took passage upon the boat, on her trip up the river from New Orleans, for Hermitage, a landing-place within Louisiana, and being refused accommodations, on account of her color, in the cabin specially set apart for white persons, brought this action ... under the provisions of the act above recited, to recover damages for her mental and physical suffering on that account. Benson ... insisted ... that the statute was inoperative and void as to him, in respect to the matter complained of, because, as to his business, it was an attempt to "regulate commerce among the States," and, therefore, in conflict with art. 1, sect. 8, par. 3, of the Constitution of the

United States. The District Court of the parish held that the statute made it imperative upon Benson to admit Mrs. DeCuir to the privileges of the cabin for white persons, and that it was not a regulation of commerce among the States, and, therefore, not void. After trial, judgment was given against Benson for $1,000; from which he appealed to the Supreme Court of the State, where the rulings of the District Court were sustained. . . .

Benson having died, Hall, his administratrix, was substituted in this court.

MR. CHIEF JUSTICE [Morrison] WAITE delivered the opinion of the court.

For the purposes of this case, we must treat the act of Louisiana of Feb. 23, 1869, as requiring those engaged in inter-state commerce to give all persons travelling in that State, upon the public conveyances employed in such business, equal rights and privileges in all parts of the conveyance, without distinction or discrimination on account of race or color. Such was the construction given to that act in the courts below, and it is conclusive upon us as the construction of a State law by the State courts. It is with this provision of the statute alone that we have to deal. We have nothing whatever to do with it as a regulation of internal commerce, or as affecting any thing else than commerce among the States.

There can be no doubt but that exclusive power has been conferred upon Congress in respect to the regulation of commerce among the several States. . . . Thus, in *Munn v. Illinois* . . . it was decided that a State might regulate the charges of public warehouses, and in *Chicago, Burlington, & Quincy Railroad Co. v. Iowa,* . . . of railroads situate entirely within the State, even though those engaged in commerce among the States might sometimes use the warehouses or the railroads in the prosecution of their business. . . . By such statutes the States regulate, as a matter of domestic concern, the instruments of commerce situated wholly within their own jurisdictions, and over which they have exclusive governmental control, except when employed in foreign or inter-state commerce. As they can only be used in the State, their regulation for all purposes may properly be assumed by the State, until Congress acts in reference to their foreign or inter-state relations. When Congress does act, the State laws are superseded only to the extent that they affect commerce outside the State as it comes within the State. It has also been held that health and inspection laws may be passed by the States . . . ; and that Congress may permit the States to regulate pilots and pilotage until it shall itself legislate upon the subject[.] . . . The line which separates the powers of the States from this exclusive power of Congress is not always distinctly marked, and oftentimes it is not easy to determine on which side a particular case belongs. Judges not unfrequently differ in their reasons for a decision in which they concur. Under such circumstances it would be a useless task to undertake to fix an arbitrary rule by which the line must in all cases be located. It is far better to leave a matter of such delicacy to be settled in each case upon a view of the particular rights involved.

But we think it may safely be said that State legislation which seeks to impose a direct burden upon inter-state commerce, or to interfere directly with its freedom, does encroach upon the exclusive power of Congress. The statute now under consideration, in our opinion, occupies that position. It does not act upon the business through the local instruments to be employed after coming within the State, but directly upon the business as it comes into the State from without or goes out from within. While it purports only to control the carrier when engaged within the State, in must necessarily influence his conduct to some extent in the management of his business throughout his entire voyage. His disposition of passengers taken up and put down within the State, or taken up within to be carried without, cannot but affect in a greater or less degree those taken up without and brought within, and sometimes those taken up and put down without. A passenger in the cabin set apart for the use of whites without the State must, when the boat comes within, share the accommodations of that cabin with such colored persons as may come on board afterwards, if the law is enforced.

It was to meet just such a case that the commercial clause in the Constitution was adopted. . . . If each State was at liberty to regulate the conduct of carriers while within its jurisdiction, the confusion likely to follow could not but be productive of great inconvenience and unnecessary hardship. Each State could provide for its own passengers and regulate the transportation of its own freight, regardless of the interests of others. Nay more, it could prescribe rules by which the carrier must be governed within the State in respect to passengers and property brought from without. On one side of the river or its tributaries he might be required to observe one set of rules, and on the other another. Commerce cannot flourish in the midst of such embarrassments. No carrier of passengers can conduct his business with satisfaction to himself, or comfort to those employing him, if on one side of a State line his passengers, both white and colored, must be permitted to occupy the same cabin, and on the other be kept separate. Uniformity in the regulations by which he is to be governed from one end to the other of his route is a necessity in his business, and to secure it Congress, which is untrammelled by State lines, has been invested with the exclusive legislative power of determining what such regulations shall be. . . .

This power of regulation may be exercised without legislation as well as with it. By refraining from action, Congress, in effect, adopts as its own regulations those which the common law or the civil law, where that prevails, has provided . . . and those which the States, in the regulation of their domestic concerns, have established affecting commerce, but not regulating it within the meaning of the Constitution. In fact, congressional legislation is only necessary to cure defects in existing laws, as they are discovered, and to adapt such laws to new developments of trade. . . . Applying that principle to the circumstances of this case, congressional inaction left Benson at liberty to adopt such reasonable rules and regulations for the disposition of passengers upon his boat, while pursuing her voyage within Louisiana or without, as seemed to him most for the interest of all concerned. The statute under which this suit is brought, as construed by the State court, seeks to take away from him that power so long as he is within Louisiana; and while recognizing to the fullest extent the principle which sustains a statute, unless its unconstitutionality is clearly established, we think this statute, to the extent that it requires those engaged in the transportation of passengers among the States to carry colored passengers in Louisiana in the same cabin with whites, is unconstitutional and void. If the public good requires such legislation, it must come from Congress and not from the States.

We confine our decision to the statute in its effect upon foreign and inter-state commerce, expressing no opinion as to its validity in any other respect.

Judgment will be reversed and the cause remanded, with instructions to reverse the judgment of the District Court, and direct such further proceedings in conformity with this opinion as may appear to be necessary; and it is

So ordered.

6. *STRAUDER V. WEST VIRGINIA*, 100 U.S. 303 (1880)

A West Virginia law declared that only white men may serve on juries in that state. Taylor Strauder, a black man convicted by an all-white jury of murdering his wife, successfully appealed the verdict on the basis that excluding African Americans on racial grounds from participating in the administration of justice violated the Fourteenth Amendment.

MR. JUSTICE [William] STRONG delivered the opinion of the court.

The plaintiff in error, a colored man, was indicted for murder . . . in West Virginia, on the 20th of October, 1874, and upon trial was convicted and sentenced. The record was then removed to the Supreme Court of the State, and there the judgment . . . was affirmed. The present case is a writ of error to that court, and it is now, in substance, averred that at the trial in the State court the defendant (now plaintiff in error) was denied rights to which he was entitled under the Constitution and laws of the United States.

. . . [B]efore the trial of the indictment was commenced, the defendant presented his petition, verified by his oath, praying for a removal of the cause into the Circuit Court of the United States, assigning, as ground for the removal, that "by virtue of the laws of the State of West Virginia no colored man was eligible to be a member of the grand jury or to serve on a petit jury in the State; that white men are so eligible, and that by reason of his being a colored man and having been a slave, he had reason to believe, and did believe, he could not have the full and equal benefit of all laws and proceedings in the State of West Virginia for the security of his person as is enjoyed by white citizens, and that he had less chance of enforcing in the courts of the State his rights on the prosecution, as a citizen of the United States, and that the probabilities of a denial of them to him as such citizen on every trial which might take place on the indictment in the courts of the State were much more enhanced than if he was a white man." This petition was denied by the State court, and the cause was forced to trial. . . .

The law of the State to which reference was made in the petition for removal and in the several motions was enacted on the 12th of March, 1873 . . . and it is as follows: "All white male persons who are twenty-one years of age and who are citizens of this State shall be liable to serve as jurors, except as herein provided." The persons excepted are State officials.

In this court, several errors have been assigned, and the controlling questions underlying them all are, first, whether, by the Constitution and laws of the United States, every citizen of the United States has a right to a trial of an indictment against him by a jury selected and impanelled without discrimination against his race or color, because of race or color; and, second, if he has such a right, and is denied its enjoyment by the State in which he is indicted, may he cause the case to be removed into the Circuit Court of the United States?

It is to be observed that the first of these questions is not whether a colored man, when an indictment has been preferred against him, has a right to a grand or a petit jury composed in whole or in part of persons of his own race or color, but it is whether, in the composition or selection of jurors by whom he is to be indicted or tried, all persons of his race or color may be excluded by law, solely because of their race or color, so that by no possibility can any colored man sit upon the jury. . . .

[The Fourteenth Amendment] is one of a series of constitutional provisions having a common purpose; namely, securing to a race recently emancipated, a race that through many generations had been held in slavery, all the civil rights that the superior race enjoy. The true spirit and meaning of the amendments . . . cannot be understood without keeping in view the history of the times when they were adopted, and the general objects they plainly sought to accomplish. At the time when they were incorporated into the Constitution, it required little knowledge of human nature to anticipate that those who had long been regarded as an inferior and subject race would, when suddenly raised to the rank of citizenship, be looked upon with jealousy and positive dislike, and that State laws might be enacted or enforced to perpetuate the distinctions that had before existed. Discriminations against them had been habitual. It was well known that in some States laws making such discriminations then existed, and others might well be expected. The colored race, as a race, was abject and ignorant, and in that condition was unfitted to command the respect of those who had superior intelligence. Their training had left them mere children, and as such they needed the protection which a wise government extends to those who are unable to protect themselves. They especially needed protection against unfriendly action in the States where they were resident. It was in view of these considerations the Fourteenth Amendment was framed and adopted. It was designed to assure to the colored race the enjoyment of all the civil rights that under the law are enjoyed by white persons, and to give to that race the protection of the general government, in that enjoyment, whenever it should be denied by the States. It not only gave citizenship and the privileges of citizenship to persons of color, but it denied to any State the power to withhold from them the equal protection of the laws, and authorized Congress to enforce its provisions by appropriate legislation. . . .

If this is the spirit and meaning of the amendment, whether it means more or not, it is to be construed liberally, to carry out the purposes of its framers. It ordains that no State shall make or enforce any laws which shall abridge the privileges or immunities of citizens of the United States (evidently referring to the newly made citizens, who, being citizens of the United States, are declared to be also citizens of the State in which they reside). It ordains that no State shall deprive any person of life, liberty, or property, without due process of law, or deny to any person within its jurisdiction the equal protection of the laws. What is this but declaring that the law in the States shall be the same for the black as for the white; that all persons, whether colored or white, shall stand equal before the laws of the States, and, in regard to the colored race, for whose protection the amendment was primarily designed, that no discrimination shall be made against them by law because of their color? . . .

That the West Virginia statute respecting juries—the statute that controlled the selection of the grand and petit jury in the case of the plaintiff in error—is such a discrimination ought not to be doubted. Nor would it be if the persons excluded by it were white men. If in those States where the colored people constitute a majority of the entire population a law should be enacted excluding all white men from jury service, thus denying to them the privilege of participating equally with the blacks in the administration of justice, we apprehend no one would be heard to claim that it would not be a denial to white men of the equal protection of the laws. Nor if a law should be passed excluding all naturalized Celtic Irishmen, would there be any doubt of its inconsistency with the spirit of the amendment. The very fact that colored people are singled out and expressly denied by a statute all right to participate in the administration of the law, as jurors, because of their color, though they are citizens, and may be in other respects fully qualified, is practically a brand upon them, affixed by the law, an assertion of their inferiority, and a stimulant to that race prejudice which is an impediment to securing to individuals of the race that equal justice which the law aims to secure to all others.

The right to a trial by jury is guaranteed to every citizen of West Virginia by the Constitution of that State, and the constitution of juries is a very essential part of the protection such a mode of trial is intended to secure. The very idea of a jury is a body of men composed of the peers or equals of the person whose rights it is selected or summoned to determine; that is, of his neighbors, fellows, associates, persons having the same legal status in society as that which he holds. . . . It is well known that prejudices often exist against particular classes in the community, which sway the judgment of jurors, and which, therefore, operate in some cases to deny to persons of those classes the full enjoyment of that protection which others enjoy. Prejudice in a local community is held to be a reason for a change of venue. The framers of the constitutional amendment must have known full well the existence of such prejudice and its likelihood to continue against the manumitted slaves and their race, and that knowledge was doubtless a motive that led to the amendment. By their manumission and citizenship the colored race became entitled to the equal protection of the laws of the States in which they resided; and the apprehension that through prejudice they might be denied that equal protection, that is, that there might be discrimination against them, was the inducement to bestow upon the national government the power to enforce the provision that no State shall deny to them the equal protection of the laws. Without the apprehended existence of prejudice that portion of the amendment would have been unnecessary, and it might have been left to the States to extend equality of protection.

In view of these considerations, it is hard to see why the statute of West Virginia should not be regarded as discriminating against a colored man when he is put upon trial for an alleged criminal offence against the State. It is not easy to comprehend how it can be said that while every white man is entitled to a trial by a jury selected from persons of his own race or color, or, rather, selected without discrimination against his color, and a negro is not, the latter is equally protected by the law with the former. Is not protection of life and liberty against race or color prejudice, a right, a legal right, under the constitutional amendment? And how can it be maintained that compelling a colored man to submit to a trial for his life by a jury drawn from a panel from which the State has expressly excluded every man of his race, because of color alone, however well qualified in other respects, is not a denial to him of equal legal protection?

We do not say that within the limits from which it is not excluded by the amendment a State may not prescribe the qualifications of its jurors, and in so doing make discriminations. It may confine the selection to males, to freeholders, to citizens, to persons within certain ages, or to persons having educational qualifications. We do not believe the Fourteenth Amendment was ever intended to prohibit this. Looking at its history, it is clear it had no such purpose. Its aim was against discrimination because of race or color. As we have said more than once, its design was to protect an emancipated race, and to strike down all possible legal discriminations against those who belong to it. . . .

The Fourteenth Amendment makes no attempt to enumerate the rights it designed to protect. It speaks in general terms, and those are as comprehensive as possible. Its language is prohibitory; but every prohibition implies the existence of rights and immunities, prominent among which is an immunity from inequality of legal protection, either for life, liberty, or property. Any State action that denies this immunity to a colored man is in conflict with the Constitution. . . .

The judgment of the Supreme Court of West Virginia will be reversed, and the case remitted with instructions to reverse the judgment of the [trial court]; and it is

So ordered.

7. *UNITED STATES V. HARRIS*, 106 U.S. 629 (1883)

A grand jury returned an indictment containing four counts against R. G. Harris and nineteen others charging that on August 14, 1876, in Crockett County, Tennessee, Harris led an armed lynch mob into a Tennessee jail and captured four white prisoners. The deputy sheriff attempted to protect the prisoners, but he was not successful. The mob beat the four prisoners, and one of them died. The U.S. government brought criminal charges against Harris and the other defendants under section 2 of the Enforcement Act of April 20, 1871, which made it a crime for two or more persons to conspire for the purpose of depriving anyone of the equal protection of the laws. The Supreme Court ruled the law unconstitutional after holding that the Fourteenth Amendment authorized Congress to take steps only against state action that violated the amendment and thus applied only to the acts of states and not to the acts of individuals.

. . . Section 5519 of the Revised Statutes . . . was originally a part of sect. 2 of the act of April 20, 1871, c. 22. . . .

MR. JUSTICE [William] WOODS delivered the opinion of the court[.]

. . . Proper respect for a co-ordinate branch of the government requires the courts of the United States to give effect to the presumption that Congress will pass no act not within its constitutional power. This presumption should prevail unless the lack of constitutional authority to pass an act in question is clearly demonstrated. While conceding this, it must, nevertheless, be stated that the government of the United States is one of delegated, limited, and enumerated powers. . . . Therefore every valid act of Congress must find in the Constitution some warrant for its passage. . . .

There are only four paragraphs in the Constitution which can in the remotest degree have any reference to the question in hand. These are section 2 of article 4 of the original Constitution, and the Thirteenth, Fourteenth, and

Fifteenth Amendments. It will be convenient to consider these in the inverse of the order stated.

It is clear that the Fifteenth Amendment can have no application. . . .

Section 5519 . . . was framed to protect from invasion by private persons, the equal privileges and immunities under the laws, of all persons and classes of persons. It requires no argument to show that such a law cannot be founded on a clause of the Constitution whose sole object is to protect from denial or abridgment, by the United States or States, on account of race, color, or previous condition of servitude, the right of citizens of the United States to vote.

It is, however, strenuously insisted that the legislation under consideration finds its warrant in the first and fifth sections of the Fourteenth Amendment. . . .

It is perfectly clear from the language of the first section that its purpose also was to place a restraint upon the action of the States. In *Slaughter-House Cases* . . . it was held by the majority of the court . . . that the object of the second clause of the first section of the Fourteenth Amendment was to protect from the hostile legislation of the States the privileges and immunities of citizens of the United States; and this was conceded by Mr. Justice Field, who expressed the views of the dissenting justices in that case. In the same case the court, referring to the Fourteenth Amendment, said that "if the States do not conform their laws to its requirements, then by the fifth section of the article of amendment Congress was authorized to enforce it by suitable legislation."

The purpose and effect of the [first and fifth] sections of the Fourteenth Amendment . . . were clearly defined . . . in the case of *United States v. Cruikshank* . . . : "It is a guaranty of protection against the acts of the State government itself. It is a guaranty against the exertion of arbitrary and tyrannical power on the part of the government and legislature of the State, not a guaranty against the commission of individual offences; and the power of Congress, whether express or implied, to legislate for the enforcement of such a guaranty does not extend to the passage of laws for the suppression of crime within the States. The enforcement of the guaranty does not require or authorize Congress to perform "the duty that the guaranty itself supposes it to be the duty of the State to perform, and which it requires the State to perform."

When the case of *United States v. Cruikshank* came to this court, the same view was taken here. . . . : "The Fourteenth Amendment prohibits a State from depriving any person of life, liberty, or property without due process of law, or from denying to any person the equal protection of the laws; but this provision does not add anything to the rights of one citizen as against another. It simply furnishes an additional guarantee against any encroachment by the States upon the fundamental rights which belong to every citizen as a member of society. The duty of protecting all its citizens in the enjoyment of an equality of rights was originally assumed by the States, and it remains there. The only obligation resting upon the United States is to see that the States do not deny the right. This the amendment guarantees, and no more. The power of the national government is limited to this guaranty." . . .

These authorities show conclusively that the legislation under consideration finds no warrant for its enactment in the Fourteenth Amendment.

The language of the amendment does not leave this subject in doubt. When the State has been guilty of no violation of its provisions; when it has not made or enforced any law abridging the privileges or immunities of citizens of the United States; when no one of its departments has deprived any person of life, liberty, or property without due process of law, or denied to any person within its jurisdiction the equal protection of the laws; when, on the contrary, the laws of the State, as enacted by its legislative, and construed by its judicial, and administered by its executive departments, recognize and protect the rights of all persons, the amendment imposes no duty and confers no power upon Congress.

Section 5519 of the Revised Statutes is not limited to take effect only in case the State shall abridge the privileges or immunities of citizens of the United States, or deprive any person of life, liberty, or property without due process of law, or deny to any person the equal protection of the laws. It applies, no matter how well the State may have performed its duty. Under it private persons are liable to punishment for conspiring to deprive any one of the equal protection of the laws enacted by the State.

In the indictment in this case, for instance, which would be a good indictment under the law if the law itself were valid, there is no intimation that the State of Tennessee has passed any law or done any act forbidden by the Fourteenth Amendment. On the contrary, the *gravamen* of the charge against the accused is that they conspired to deprive certain citizens of the United States and of the State of Tennessee of the equal protection accorded them by the laws of Tennessee.

As, therefore, the section of the law under consideration is directed exclusively against the action of private persons, without reference to the laws of the State or their administration by her officers, we are clear in the opinion that it is not warranted by any clause in the Fourteenth Amendment to the Constitution.

We are next to consider whether the Thirteenth Amendment to the Constitution furnishes authority for the enactment of the section. . . .

It is clear that this amendment, besides abolishing forever slavery and involuntary servitude within the United States, gives power to Congress to protect all persons within the jurisdiction of the United States from being in any way subjected to slavery or involuntary servitude, except as a punishment for crime, and in the enjoyment of that freedom which it was the object of the amendment to secure. . . .

Congress has, by virtue of this amendment, declared, in sect. 1 of the [Civil Rights Act of 1866], that all persons within the jurisdiction of the United States shall have the same right in every State and Territory to make and enforce contracts, to sue, be parties, give evidence, and to the full and equal benefit of all laws and proceedings for the security of persons and property as is enjoyed by white citizens, and shall be subject to like punishment, pains, penalties, taxes, licenses, and exactions of every kind, and to none other.

But the question with which we have to deal is, does the Thirteenth Amendment warrant the enactment of sect. 5519 of the Revised Statutes. We are of opinion that it does not. Our conclusion is based on the fact that the provisions of that section are broader than the Thirteenth Amendment would justify. . . .

. . . If Congress has constitutional authority under the Thirteenth Amendment to punish a conspiracy between two persons to do an unlawful act, it can punish the act itself, whether done by one or more persons.

A private person cannot make constitutions or laws, nor can he with authority construe them, nor can he administer or execute them. The only way, therefore, in which one private person can deprive another of the equal protection of the laws is by the commission of some offence against the laws which protect the rights of persons, as by theft, burglary, arson, libel, assault, or murder. If, therefore, we hold that sect. 5519 is warranted by the Thirteenth Amendment, we should, by virtue of that amendment, accord to Congress the power to punish every crime by which the right of any person to life, property, or reputation is invaded. Thus, under a provision of the Constitution which simply abolished slavery and involuntary servitude, we should, with few exceptions, invest Congress with power over the whole catalogue of crimes. A construction of the amendment which leads to such a result is clearly unsound.

There is only one other clause in the Constitution of the United States which can, in any degree, be supposed to sustain the section under consideration; namely, the second section of article 4, which declares that "the citizens of each State shall be entitled to all the privileges and immunities of citizens of the several States." But this section, like the Fourteenth Amendment, is directed against State action. Its object is to place the citizens of each State upon the same footing with citizens of other States, and inhibit discriminative legislation against them by other States. . . .

It was never supposed that the section under consideration conferred on Congress the power to enact a law which would punish a private citizen for an invasion of the rights of his fellow citizen, conferred by the State of which they were both residents; on all its citizens alike. . . .

The point in reference to which the judges of the Circuit Court were divided in opinion must, therefore, be decided against the *constitutionality of the law*.

8. *CIVIL RIGHTS CASES: UNITED STATES V. STANLEY; UNITED STATES V. RYAN; UNITED STATES V. NICHOLS; UNITED STATES V. SINGLETON; ROBINSON & WIFE V. MEMPHIS AND CHARLESTON RAILROAD COMPANY,* 109 U.S. 3 (1883)

These cases were brought under the first and second sections of the Civil Rights Act passed on March 1, 1875. Two of the cases, those against Stanley and Nichols, were indictments for denying to blacks the accommodations and privileges of an inn or hotel in Kansas and Missouri, respectively; two of the cases, those against Ryan and Singleton, were for denying to individuals the privileges and accommodations of a theater in San Francisco and in New York, respectively; and the case against the Memphis and Charleston Railroad Company was brought in the Circuit Court of the United States for the western district of Tennessee. The Supreme Court ruled that the Fourteenth Amendment allowed Congress to address state action but that private acts of racial discrimination were wrongs governed by state law, and which the national government was without authority to prohibit.

MR. JUSTICE [Joseph] BRADLEY delivered the opinion of the court....

... Are these [first two] sections [of the Civil Rights Act of 1875] constitutional? The first section, which is the principal one, cannot be fairly understood without attending to the last clause, which qualifies the preceding part.

... [I]t is the purpose of the law to declare that, in the enjoyment of the accommodations and privileges of inns, public conveyances, theatres, and other places of public amusement, no distinction shall be made between citizens of different race or color, or between those who have, and those who have not, been slaves. Its effect is to declare, that in all inns, public conveyances, and places of amusement, colored citizens, whether formerly slaves or not, and citizens of other races, shall have the same accommodations and privileges in all inns, public conveyances, and places of amusement as are enjoyed by white citizens; and *vice versa.* The second section makes it a penal offence in any person to deny to any citizen of any race or color, regardless of previous servitude, any of the accommodations or privileges mentioned in the first section.

Has Congress constitutional power to make such a law? Of course, no one will contend that the power to pass it was contained in the Constitution before the adoption of the last three amendments. The power is sought, first, in the Fourteenth Amendment[.] ...

It is State action of a particular character that is prohibited. Individual invasion of individual rights is not the subject-matter of the amendment. It has a deeper and broader scope. It nullifies and makes void all State legislation, and State action of every kind, which impairs the privileges and immunities of citizens of the United States, or which injures them in life, liberty or property without due process of law, or which denies to any of them the equal protection of the laws. It not only does this, but ... the last section of the amendment invests

Congress with power to enforce it by appropriate legislation. To enforce what? To enforce the prohibition. To adopt appropriate legislation for correcting the effects of such prohibited State laws and State acts, and thus to render them effectually null, void, and innocuous. This is the legislative power conferred upon Congress, and this is the whole of it. It does not invest Congress with power to legislate upon subjects which are within the domain of State legislation; but to provide modes of relief against State legislation, or State action, of the kind referred to. It does not authorize Congress to create a code of municipal law for the regulation of private rights; but to provide modes of redress against the operation of State laws, and the action of State officers executive or judicial, when these are subversive of the fundamental rights specified in the amendment. Positive rights and privileges are undoubtedly secured by the Fourteenth Amendment; but they are secured by way of prohibition against State laws and State proceedings affecting those rights and privileges, and by power given to Congress to legislate for the purpose of carrying such prohibition into effect: and such legislation must necessarily be predicated upon such supposed State laws or State proceedings, and be directed to the correction of their operation and effect. . . .

And so in the present case, until some State law has been passed, or some State action through its officers or agents has been taken, adverse to the rights of citizens sought to be protected by the Fourteenth Amendment, no legislation of the United States under said amendment, nor any proceeding under such legislation, can be called into activity: for the prohibitions of the amendment are against State laws and acts done under State authority. Of course, legislation may, and should be, provided in advance to meet the exigency when it arises; but it should be adapted to the mischief and wrong which the amendment was intended to provide against; and that is, State laws, or State action of some kind, adverse to the rights of the citizen secured by the amendment. Such legislation cannot properly cover the whole domain of rights appertaining to life, liberty and property, defining them and providing for their vindication. That would be to establish a code of municipal law regulative of all private rights between man and man in society. It would be to make Congress take the place of the State legislatures and to supersede them. It is absurd to affirm that, because the rights of life, liberty and property (which include all civil rights that men have), are by the amendment sought to be protected against invasion on the part of the State without due process of law, Congress may therefore provide due process of law for their vindication in every case; and that, because the denial by a State to any persons, of the equal protection of the laws, is prohibited by the amendment, therefore Congress may establish laws for their equal protection. . . .

An inspection of the law shows that it makes no reference whatever to any supposed or apprehended violation of the Fourteenth Amendment on the part of the States. It is not predicated on any such view. It proceeds *ex directo* to declare that certain acts committed by individuals shall be deemed offences, and shall be prosecuted and punished by proceedings in the courts of the United States. . . . It applies equally to cases arising in States which have the justest laws respecting the personal rights of citizens, and whose authorities are ever ready to enforce such laws, as to those which arise in States that may have violated the prohibition of the amendment. In other words, it steps into the domain of local jurisprudence, and lays down rules for the conduct of individuals in society towards each other, and imposes sanctions for the enforcement of those rules, without referring in any manner to any supposed action of the State or its authorities.

If this legislation is appropriate for enforcing the prohibitions of the amendment, it is difficult to see where it is to stop. . . .

We have not overlooked the fact that the fourth section of the act now under consideration has been held by this court to be constitutional. That section declares "that no citizen, possessing all other qualifications which are or may be prescribed by law, shall be disqualified for service as grand or petit juror in any court of the United States, or of any State, on account of race, color, or previous condition of servitude; and any officer or other person charged with any duty in the selection or summoning of jurors who shall exclude or fail to summon any citizen for the cause aforesaid, shall, on conviction thereof, be deemed guilty of a misdemeanor, and be fined not more than five thousand dollars." . . . Disqualifications for service on juries are only created by the law. . . . In [*Ex parte Virginia*], the State, through its officer, enforced a rule of disqualification which the law was intended to abrogate and counteract. Whether the statute book of the State actually laid down any such rule of disqualification, or not, the State, through its officer, enforced such a rule: and it is against such State action, through its officers and agents, that the last clause of the section is directed. This aspect of the law was deemed sufficient to divest it of any unconstitutional character, and makes it differ widely from the first and second sections of the same act which we are now considering.

These sections, in the objectionable features before referred to, are different also from the law ordinarily called the "Civil Rights Bill," originally passed April 9th, 1866 . . . and re-enacted with some modifications in sections 16, 17, 18, of the Enforcement Act, passed May 31st, 1870[.] . . . This law is clearly corrective in its character, intended to counteract and furnish redress against State laws and proceedings, and customs having the force of law, which sanction the wrongful acts specified. In the Revised Statutes, it is true, a very important clause, to wit, the words "any law, statute, ordinance, regulation or custom to the contrary notwithstanding," which gave the declaratory section its point and effect, are omitted; but the penal part, by which the declaration is enforced, and which is really the effective part of the law, retains the reference to State laws, by making the penalty apply only to those who should subject parties to a deprivation of their rights under color of any statute, ordinance, custom, etc., of any State or Territory: thus preserving the corrective character of the legislation. . . .

In this connection it is proper to state that civil rights, such as are guaranteed by the Constitution against State aggression, cannot be impaired by the wrongful acts of individuals, unsupported by State authority in the shape of laws, customs, or judicial or executive proceedings. The wrongful act of an individual, unsupported by any such authority, is simply a private wrong, or a crime of that individual; an invasion of the rights of the injured party, it is true, whether they affect his person, his property, or his reputation; but if not sanctioned in some way by the State, or not done under State authority, his rights remain in full force, and may presumably be vindicated by resort to the laws of the State for redress. An individual cannot deprive a man of his right to vote, to hold property, to buy and sell, to sue in the courts, or to be a witness or a juror; he may, by force or fraud, interfere with the enjoyment of the right in a particular case; he may commit an assault against the person, or commit murder, or use ruffian violence at the polls, or slander the good name of a fellow citizen; but, unless protected in these wrongful acts by some shield of State law or State authority, he cannot destroy or injure the right; he will only render himself amenable to satisfaction or punishment; and amenable therefor to the laws of the State where the wrongful acts are committed. Hence, in all those cases where the Constitution seeks to protect the rights of the citizen against discriminative and unjust laws of the State by prohibiting such laws, it is not individual offences, but abrogation and denial of rights, which it denounces, and for which it clothes the Congress with power to provide a remedy. . . . It must assume that in the cases provided for, the evil or wrong actually committed rests upon some State law or State authority for its excuse and perpetration.

Of course, these remarks do not apply to those cases in which Congress is clothed with direct and plenary powers of legislation over the whole subject, accompanied with an express or implied denial of such power to the States, as in the regulation of commerce with foreign nations, among the several States, and with the Indian tribes, the coining of money, the establishment of post offices and post roads, the declaring of war, etc. . . . [W]here a subject is not submitted to the general legislative power of Congress, but is only submitted thereto for the purpose of rendering effective some prohibition against particular State legislation or State action in reference to that subject, the power given is limited by its object, and any legislation by Congress in the matter must necessarily be corrective in its character, adapted to counteract and redress the operation of such prohibited State laws or proceedings of State officers.

If the principles of interpretation which we have laid down are correct . . . it is clear that the law in question cannot be sustained by any grant of legislative power made to Congress by the Fourteenth Amendment. . . . The law in question, without any reference to adverse State legislation on the subject, declares that all persons shall be entitled to equal accommodations and privileges of inns, public conveyances, and places of public amusement, and imposes a penalty upon any individual who shall deny to any citizen such equal accommodations and privileges. This is not corrective legislation; it is primary and direct; it takes immediate and absolute possession of the subject of the right of admission to inns, public conveyances, and places of amusement. It supersedes and displaces State legislation on the same subject, or only allows it permissive force. It ignores such legislation, and assumes that the matter is one that belongs to the domain of national regulation. Whether it would not have been a more effective protection of the rights of citizens to have clothed Congress with plenary power over the whole subject, is not now the question. What we have to decide is, whether such plenary power has been conferred upon Congress by the Fourteenth Amendment; and, in our judgment, it has not. . . .

But the power of Congress to adopt direct and primary, as distinguished from corrective legislation, on the subject in hand, is sought, in the second place, from the Thirteenth Amendment, which abolishes slavery. . . .

It is true, that slavery cannot exist without law, any more than property in lands and goods can exist without law: and, therefore, the Thirteenth Amendment may be regarded as nullifying all State laws which establish or uphold slavery. But it has a reflex character also, establishing and decreeing universal civil and political freedom throughout the United States; and it is assumed, that the power vested in Congress to enforce the article by appropriate legislation, clothes Congress with power to pass all laws necessary and proper for abolishing all badges and incidents of slavery in the United States: and upon this assumption it is claimed, that this is sufficient authority for declaring by law that all persons shall have equal accommodations and privileges in all inns, public conveyances, and places of amusement; the argument being, that the denial of such equal accommodations and privileges is, in itself, a subjection to a species of servitude within the meaning of the amendment. Conceding the major proposition to be true, that Congress has a right to enact all necessary and proper laws for the obliteration and prevention of slavery with all its badges and incidents, is the minor proposition also true, that the denial to any person of admission to the accommodations and privileges of an inn, a public conveyance, or a theatre, does subject that person to any form of servitude, or tend to fasten upon him any badge of slavery? If it does not, then power to pass the law is not found in the Thirteenth Amendment. . . .

. . . Congress did not assume, under the authority given by the Thirteenth Amendment, to adjust what may be called the social rights of men and races in the community; but only to declare and vindicate those fundamental rights which appertain to the essence of citizenship, and the enjoyment or deprivation of which constitutes the essential distinction between freedom and slavery.

We must not forget that the province and scope of the Thirteenth and Fourteenth amendments are different[.] . . . What Congress has power to do under one, it may not have power to do under the other. Under the Thirteenth Amendment, it has only to do with slavery and its incidents. Under the Fourteenth Amendment, it has power to counteract and render nugatory all State laws and proceedings which have the effect to abridge any of the privileges or immunities of citizens of the United States, or to deprive them of life, liberty or property without due process of law, or to deny to any of them the equal protection of the laws. Under the Thirteenth Amendment, the legislation, so far as necessary or proper to eradicate all forms and incidents of slavery and involuntary servitude, may be direct and primary, operating upon the acts of individuals, whether sanctioned by State legislation or not; under the Fourteenth . . . it must necessarily be, and can only be, corrective in its character, addressed to counteract and afford relief against State regulations or proceedings.

The only question under the present head, therefore, is, whether the refusal to any persons of the accommodations of an inn, or a public conveyance, or a place of public amusement, by an individual, and without any sanction or support from any State law or regulation, does inflict upon such persons any manner of servitude, or form of slavery, as those terms are understood in this country? Many wrongs may be obnoxious to the prohibitions of the Fourteenth Amendment which are not, in any just sense, incidents or elements of slavery. Such, for example, would be the taking of private property without due process of law; or allowing persons who have committed certain crimes (horse stealing, for example) to be seized and hung by the *posse comitatus* without regular trial; or denying to any person, or class of persons, the right to pursue any peaceful avocations allowed to others. What is called class legislation would belong to this category, and would be obnoxious to the prohibitions of the Fourteenth Amendment, but would not necessarily be so to the Thirteenth, when not involving the idea of any subjection of one man to another. The Thirteenth Amendment has respect, not to distinctions of race, or class, or color, but to slavery. The Fourteenth Amendment extends its protection to races and classes, and prohibits any State legislation which has the effect of denying to any race or class, or to any individual, the equal protection of the laws.

. . . Can the act of a mere individual, the owner of the inn, the public conveyance or place of amusement, refusing the accommodation, be justly regarded as imposing any badge of slavery or servitude upon the applicant, or only as inflicting an ordinary civil injury, properly cognizable by the laws of the State, and presumably subject to redress by those laws until the contrary appears?

. . . [W]e are forced to the conclusion that such an act of refusal has nothing to do with slavery or involuntary servitude, and that if it is violative of any right of the party, his redress is to be sought under the laws of the State; or if those laws are adverse to his rights and do not protect him, his remedy will be found in the corrective legislation which Congress has adopted, or may adopt, for counteracting the effect of State laws, or State action, prohibited by the Fourteenth Amendment. It would be running the slavery argument into the ground to make it apply to every act of discrimination which a person may see fit to make as to the guests he will entertain, or as to the people he will take into his coach or cab or car, or admit to his concert or theatre, or deal with in other matters of intercourse or business. Innkeepers and public carriers, by the laws of all the States, so far as we are aware, are bound, to the extent of their facilities, to furnish proper accommodation to all unobjectionable persons who in good faith apply for them. If the laws themselves make any unjust discrimination, amenable to the prohibitions of the Fourteenth Amendment, Congress has full power to afford a remedy under that amendment and in accordance with it.

When a man has emerged from slavery, and by the aid of beneficent legislation has shaken off the inseparable concomitants of that state, there must be some stage in the progress of his elevation when he takes the rank of a mere citizen, and ceases to be the special favorite of the laws, and when his rights as a citizen, or a man, are to be protected in the ordinary modes by which other men's rights are protected. There were thousands of free colored people in this country before the abolition of slavery, enjoying all the essential rights of life, liberty and property the same as white citizens; yet no one, at that time, thought that it was any invasion of his personal status as a freeman because he was not admitted to all the privileges enjoyed by white citizens, or because he was subjected to discriminations in the enjoyment of accommodations in inns, public conveyances and places of amusement. Mere discriminations on account of race or color were not regarded as badges of slavery. If, since that time, the enjoyment of equal rights in all these respects has become established by constitutional enactment, it is not by force of the Thirteenth Amendment (which merely abolishes slavery), but by force of the Thirteenth and Fifteenth Amendments.

On the whole we are of opinion, that no countenance of authority for the passage of the law in question can be found in either the Thirteenth or Fourteenth Amendment of the Constitution; and no other ground of authority for its passage being suggested, it must necessarily be declared void, at least so far as its operation in the several States is concerned.

This conclusion disposes of the cases now under consideration. In the cases of the *United States* v. *Michael Ryan*, and of *Richard A. Robinson and Wife* v. *The Memphis & Charleston Railroad Company*, the judgments must be affirmed. In the other cases, the answer to be given will be that the first and second sections of the act of Congress of March 1st, 1875 . . . are unconstitutional and void, and that judgment should be rendered upon the several indictments in those cases accordingly.

And it is so ordered.

9. *EX PARTE YARBROUGH*, 110 U.S. 651 (1884) (THE KU KLUX CASES)

Jasper Yarbrough and seven other persons applied for a writ of habeas corpus and alleged that their trial, conviction, and sentence were illegal, null, and void. A grand jury indicted Yarbrough and the others on charges that on July 25, 1883, they "did, within the said Northern district of Georgia . . . combine, conspire, and confederate together, by force, to injure, oppress, threaten, and intimidate Berry Saunders, a person of color, and a citizen of the United States of America of African descent, on account of his race, color, and previous condition of servitude, in the full exercise and enjoyment of the right and privilege of suffrage in the election of a lawfully qualified person as a member of the congress of the United States of America, and because the said Berry Saunders had so exercised the same, and on account of such exercise, which said right and privilege of suffrage was secured to the said Berry Saunders by the constitution and laws of the United States of America . . . ; and, having so then and there conspired, the said [defendants] did unlawfully, feloniously, and willfully beat, bruise, wound, and maltreat the said Berry Saunders" and "did then and there unlawfully, willfully, and feloniously go in disguise on the highway, and on the premises of Berry Saunders, with the intent to prevent and hinder his free exercise and enjoyment of the right to vote at an election for a lawfully qualified person as a member of the congress of the United States of America[.]" The Supreme Court upheld Congress's authority to make it a crime for individuals to interfere with the right of a citizen to vote in a federal election.

MR. JUSTICE [Samuel] MILLER delivered the opinion of the court.

. . . This . . . leaves for consideration . . . whether the law of Congress, as found in the Revised Statutes of the United States, under which the prisoners are held, is warranted by the Constitution, or being without such warrant, is null and void.

If the law which defines the offence and prescribes its punishment is void, the court was without jurisdiction and the prisoners must be discharged.

Though several different sections of the Revised Statutes are brought into the discussion as the foundation of the indictments found in the record, we think only two of them demand our attention here, namely, sections 5508 and 5520. They are in the following language:

> "SEC. 5508. If two or more persons conspire to injure, oppress, threaten, or intimidate any citizen in the free exercise or enjoyment of any right or privilege secured to him by the Constitution or laws of the United States, or because of his having so exercised the same, or if two or more persons go in disguise on the highway, or on the premises of another, with intent to prevent or hinder his free exercise or enjoyment of any right or privilege so secured, they shall be fined not more than five thousand dollars and imprisoned not more than ten years; and

shall, moreover, be thereafter ineligible to any office or place of honor, profit, or trust created by the Constitution or laws of the United States.

"SEC. 5520. If two or more persons in any State or Territory conspire to prevent by force, intimidation, or threat, any citizen who is lawfully entitled to vote, from giving his support or advocacy, in a legal manner, toward or in favor of the election of any lawfully qualified person as an elector for President or Vice President, or as a member of the Congress of the United States; or to injure any citizen in person or property on account of such support or advocacy; each of such persons shall be punished by a fine of not less than five hundred nor more than five thousand dollars, or by imprisonment, with or without hard labor, not less than six months nor more than six years, or by both such fine and imprisonment."

. . . Stripped of its technical verbiage, the offence charged in this indictment is that the defendants conspired to intimidate Berry Saunders, a citizen of African descent, in the exercise of his right to vote for a member of the Congress of the United States, and in the execution of that conspiracy they beat, bruised, wounded, and otherwise maltreated him; and in the second count that they did this on account of his race, color, and previous condition of servitude, by going in disguise and assaulting him on the public highway and on his own premises.

. . . [W]e entertain no doubt that the conspiracy here described is one which is embraced within the provisions of the Revised Statutes which we have cited.

That a government whose essential character is republican, whose executive head and legislative body are both elective, whose most numerous and powerful branch of the legislature is elected by the people directly, has no power by appropriate laws to secure this election from the influence of violence, of corruption, and of fraud, is a proposition so startling as to arrest attention and demand the gravest consideration. . . .

If it has not this power, it is left helpless before the two great natural and historical enemies of all republics, open violence and insidious corruption.

The proposition that it has no such power is supported by the old argument often heard, often repeated, and in this court never assented to, that when a question of the power of Congress arises the advocate of the power must be able to place his finger on words which expressly grant it. The brief of counsel before us, though directed to the authority of that body to pass criminal laws, uses the same language. Because there is no *express* power to provide for preventing violence exercised on the voter as a means of controlling his vote, no such law can be enacted. It destroys at one blow, in construing the Constitution of the United States, the doctrine universally applied to all instruments of writing, that what is implied is as much a part of the instrument as what is expressed. This principle, in its application to the Constitution of the United

States, more than to almost any other writing, is a necessity, by reason of the inherent inability to put into words all derivative powers—a difficulty which the instrument itself recognizes by conferring on Congress the authority to pass all laws necessary and proper to carry into execution the powers expressly granted and all other powers vested in the government or any branch of it by the constitution. Article I, sec. 8, clause 18.

We know of no express authority to pass laws to punish theft or burglary of the treasury of the United States. Is there therefore no power in the Congress to protect the treasury by punishing such theft and burglary?

Are the mails of the United States and the money carried in them to be left to the mercy of robbers and of thieves who may handle the mail because the Constitution contains no express words of power in Congress to enact laws for the punishment of those offences? The principle, if sound, would abolish the entire criminal jurisdiction of the courts of the United States and the laws which confer that jurisdiction.

It is said that the States can pass the necessary law on this subject, and no necessity exists for such action by Congress. But the existence of State laws punishing the counterfeiting of the coin of the United States has never been held to supersede the acts of Congress passed for that purpose, or to justify the United States in failing to enforce its own laws to protect the circulation of the coin which it issues.

It is very true that while Congress at an early day passed criminal laws to punish piracy with death, and for punishing all ordinary offences against person and property committed within the District of Columbia, and in forts, arsenals, and other places within the exclusive jurisdiction of the United States, it was slow to pass laws protecting officers of the government from personal injuries inflicted while in discharge of their official duties within the States. This was not for want of power, but because no occasion had arisen which required such legislation, the remedies in the State courts for personal violence having proved sufficient. . . .

It is said that the parties assaulted in these cases are not officers of the United States, and their protection in exercising the right to vote by Congress does not stand on the same ground.

But the distinction is not well taken. The power in either case arises out of the circumstance that the function in which the party is engaged or the right which he is about to exercise is dependent on the laws of the United States.

In both cases it is the duty of that government to see that he may exercise this right freely, and to protect him from violence while so doing, or on account of so doing. This duty does not arise solely from the interest of the party concerned, but from the necessity of the government itself, that its service shall be free from the adverse influence of force and fraud practised on its agents, and that the votes by which its members of Congress and its President are elected shall be the *free* votes of the electors, and the officers thus chosen the free and uncorrupted choice of those who have the right to take part in that choice.

This proposition answers also another objection to the constitutionality of the laws under consideration, namely, that the right to vote for a member of Congress is not dependent upon the Constitution or laws of the United States, but is governed by the law of each State respectively.

If this were conceded, the importance to the general government of having the actual election—the voting for those members—free from force and fraud is not diminished by the circumstance that the qualification of the voter is determined by the law of the State where he votes. It equally affects the government, it is as indispensable to the proper discharge of the great function of legislating for that government, that those who are to control this legislation shall not owe their election to bribery or violence, whether the class of persons who shall vote is determined by the law of the State, or by the law of the United States, or by their united result.

But it is not correct to say that the right to vote for a member of Congress does not depend on the Constitution of the United States.

The office, if it be properly called an office, is created by that Constitution and by that alone. It also declares how it shall be filled, namely, by election. Its language is:

> "The House of Representatives shall be composed of members chosen every second year by the people of the several States, and the electors in each State shall have the same qualifications requisite for electors of the most numerous branch of the State legislature." Article I, section 2.

The States in prescribing the qualifications of voters for the most numerous branch of their own legislatures, do not do this with reference to the election for members of Congress. Nor can they prescribe the qualification for voters for those *eo nomine*. They define who are to vote for the popular branch of their own legislature, and the Constitution of the United States says the same persons shall vote for members of Congress in that State. It adopts the qualification thus furnished as the qualification of its own electors for members of Congress.

It is not true, therefore, that electors for members of Congress owe their right to vote to the State law in any sense which makes the exercise of the right to depend exclusively on the law of the State.

Counsel for petitioners, seizing upon the expression found in the opinion of the court in the case of *Minor* v. *Happersett* . . . that "the Constitution of the United States does not confer the right of suffrage upon any one," without reference to the connection in which it is used, insists that the voters in this case do not owe their right to vote in any sense to that instrument.

But the court was combating the argument that this right was conferred on all citizens, and therefore upon women as well as men.

In opposition to that idea, it was said the Constitution adopts as the qualification for voters of members of Congress that which prevails in the State where the voting is to be done; therefore, said the opinion, the right is not definitely conferred on any person or class of persons by the Constitution alone, because you have to look to the law of the State for the description of the class. But the court did not intend to say that when the class or the person is thus ascertained, his right to vote for a member of Congress was not fundamentally based upon the Constitution, which created the office of member of Congress, and declared it should be elective, and pointed to the means of ascertaining who should be electors.

The Fifteenth Amendment of the Constitution, by its limitation on the power of the States in the exercise of their right to prescribe the qualifications of voters in their own elections, and by its limitation of the power of the United States over that subject, clearly shows that the right of suffrage was considered to be of supreme importance to the national government, and was not intended to be left within the exclusive control of the States. It is in the following language:

> "SEC 1. The right of citizens of the United States to vote shall not be denied or abridged by the United States, or by any State, on account of race, color, or previous condition of servitude.
>
> "SEC. 2. The congress shall have power to enforce this article by appropriate legislation."

While it is quite true, as was said by this court in *United States* v. *Reese* . . . that this article gives no affirmative right to the colored man to vote, and is designed primarily to prevent discrimination against him whenever the right to vote may be granted to others, it is easy to see that under some circumstances it may operate as the immediate source of a right to vote. In all cases where the former slave-holding States had not removed from their Constitutions the words "white man" as a qualification for voting, this provision did, in effect, confer on him the right to vote, because, being paramount to the State law, and a part of the State law, it annulled the discriminating word "white," and thus left him in the enjoyment of the same right as white persons. . . .

In such cases this fifteenth article of amendment does . . . substantially confer on the negro the right to vote, and Congress has the power to protect and enforce that right.

In the case of *United States* v. *Reese* . . . this court said in regard to the Fifteenth Amendment, that "it has invested the citizens of the United States with a new constitutional right which is within the protecting power of Congress. That right is an exemption from discrimination in the exercise of the elective franchise on account of race, color, or previous condition of servitude." This new constitutional right was mainly designed for citizens of African descent.

The principle, however, that the protection of the exercise of this right is within the power of Congress, is as necessary to the right of other citizens to vote as to the colored citizen, and to the right to vote in general as to the right to be protected against discrimination.

The exercise of the right in both instances is guaranteed by the Constitution, and should be kept free and pure by congressional enactments whenever that is necessary.

The reference to cases in this court in which the power of Congress under the first section of the Fourteenth Amendment has been held to relate alone to acts done under State authority, can afford petitioners no aid in the present case. For, while it may be true that acts which are mere invasions of private rights, which acts have no sanction in the statutes of a State, or which are not committed by any one exercising its authority, are not within the scope of that amendment, it is quite a different matter when Congress undertakes to protect the citizen in the exercise of rights conferred by the Constitution of the United States essential to the healthy organization of the government itself. . . .

It is as essential to the successful working of this government that the great organisms of its executive and legislative branches should be the free choice of the people as that the original form of it should be so. In absolute governments, where the monarch is the source of all power, it is still held to be important that the exercise of that power shall be free from the influence of extraneous violence and internal corruption.

In a republican government, like ours, where political power is reposed in representatives of the entire body of the people, chosen at short intervals by popular elections, the temptations to control these elections by violence and by corruption is a constant source of danger.

Such has been the history of all republics, and, though ours has been comparatively free from both these evils in the past, no lover of his country can shut his eyes to the fear of future danger from both sources.

If the recurrence of such acts as these prisoners stand convicted of are too common in one quarter of the country, and give omen of danger from lawless violence, the free use of money in elections, arising from the vast growth of recent wealth in other quarters, presents equal cause for anxiety.

If the government of the United States has within its constitutional domain no authority to provide against these evils, if the very sources of power may be poisoned by corruption or controlled by violence and outrage, without legal restraint, then, indeed, is the country in danger, and its best powers, its highest purposes, the hopes which it inspires, and the love which enshrines it, are at the mercy of the combinations of those who respect no right but brute force, on the one hand, and unprincipled corruptionists on the other.

The . . . writ of habeas corpus denied.

10. *PLESSY V. FERGUSON*, 163 U.S. 537 (1896)

Louisiana in 1890 enacted a law requiring blacks and whites to use separate railway cars. Organized as a test case by citizens who sought to challenge the law, and with the cooperation of the railroad company, Homer Plessy, who was seven-eighths Caucasian, took a seat in a "white only" car of a Louisiana train, refused to vacate that seat, and was arrested. Radical Republican author, lawyer, and politician Albion Tourgée represented Plessy in the case. In its ruling, the Supreme Court gave sanction to the doctrine of "separate but equal" and held that a Louisiana law that required blacks and whites to use separate railroad cars did not deprive African Americans of equal protection under the Fourteenth Amendment. The ruling held that segregation, in and of itself, did not amount to unlawful discrimination, and it thus allowed for the imposition of laws that separated and restricted blacks from many areas of public life, including but not limited to restaurants, theaters, restrooms, and public schools. The lone dissenter, Justice John Harlan, issued a powerful opinion, also excerpted here.

. . . MR. JUSTICE [Henry] BROWN . . . delivered the opinion of the court.

This case turns upon the constitutionality of an act of the General Assembly of the State of Louisiana, passed in 1890, providing for separate railway carriages for the white and colored races. . . .

The first section of the statute enacts "that all railway companies carrying passengers in their coaches in this State, shall provide equal but separate accommodations for the white, and colored races, by providing two or more passenger coaches for each passenger train, or by dividing the passenger coaches by a partition so as to secure separate accommodations: *Provided*, That this section shall not be construed to apply to street railroads. No person or persons, shall be admitted to occupy seats in coaches, other than, the ones, assigned, to them on account of the race they belong to."[2]

By the second section it was enacted "that the officers of such passenger trains shall have power and are hereby required to assign each passenger to the coach or compartment used for the race to which such passenger belongs; any passenger insisting on going into a coach or compartment to which by race he does not belong, shall be liable to a fine of twenty-five dollars, or in lieu thereof to imprisonment for a period of not more than twenty days in the parish prison, and any officer of any railroad insisting on assigning a passenger to a coach or compartment other than the one set aside for the race to which said passenger belongs, shall be liable to a fine of twenty-five dollars, or in lieu thereof to imprisonment for a period of not more than twenty days in the parish prison; and should any passenger refuse to occupy the coach or compartment to which he or she is assigned by the officer of such railway, said officer shall have power to refuse to carry such passenger on his train, and for such refusal neither he nor the railway company which he represents shall be liable for damages in any of the courts of this State."

The third section provides penalties for the refusal or neglect of the officers, directors, conductors and employés of railway companies to comply with the act, with a proviso that "nothing in this act shall be construed as applying to nurses attending children of the other race." The fourth section is immaterial.

The information filed in the criminal District Court charged in substance that Plessy, being a passenger between two stations within the State of Louisiana, was assigned by officers of the company to the coach used for the race to which he belonged, but he insisted upon going into a coach used by the race to which he did not belong. Neither in the information nor plea was his particular race or color averred.

The petition for the writ of prohibition averred that petitioner was seven eighths Caucasian and one eighth African blood; that the mixture of colored blood was not discernible in him, and that he was entitled to every right, privilege and immunity secured to citizens of the United States of the white race; and that, upon such theory, he took possession of a vacant seat in a coach where passengers of the white race were accommodated, and was ordered by the conductor to vacate said coach and take a seat in another assigned to persons of the colored race, and having refused to comply with such demand he was forcibly ejected with the aid of a police officer, and imprisoned in the parish jail to answer a charge of having violated the above act.

The constitutionality of this act is attacked upon the ground that it conflicts both with the Thirteenth Amendment of the Constitution, abolishing slavery, and the Fourteenth Amendment, which prohibits certain restrictive legislation on the part of the States.

1. That it does not conflict with the Thirteenth Amendment, which abolished slavery and involuntary servitude, except as a punishment for crime, is too clear for argument. Slavery implies involuntary servitude—a state of bondage; the ownership of mankind as a chattel, or at least the control of the labor and services of one man for the benefit of another, and the absence of a legal right to the disposal of his own person, property and services. This amendment was said in the *Slaughter-house cases* to have been intended primarily to abolish slavery, as it had been previously known in this country, and that it equally forbade Mexican peonage or the Chinese coolie trade, when they amounted to slavery or involuntary servitude, and that the use of the word "servitude" was intended to prohibit the use of all forms of involuntary slavery, of whatever class or name. It was intimated, however, in that case that this amendment was regarded by the statesmen of that day as insufficient to protect the colored race from certain laws which had been enacted in the Southern States, imposing upon the colored race onerous disabilities and burdens, and curtailing their rights in the pursuit of life, liberty and property to such an extent that their

freedom was of little value; and that the Fourteenth Amendment was devised to meet this exigency.

So, too, in the *Civil Rights cases* . . . it was said that the act of a mere individual, the owner of an inn, a public conveyance or place of amusement, refusing accommodations to colored people, cannot be justly regarded as imposing any badge of slavery or servitude upon the applicant, but only as involving an ordinary civil injury, properly cognizable by the laws of the State, and presumably subject to redress by those laws until the contrary appears. . . .

A statute which implies merely a legal distinction between the white and colored races—a distinction which is founded in the color of the two races, and which must always exist so long as white men are distinguished from the other race by color—has no tendency to destroy the legal equality of the two races, or reestablish a state of involuntary servitude. Indeed, we do not understand that the Thirteenth Amendment is strenuously relied upon by the plaintiff in error in this connection.

2. . . . The proper construction of [the Fourteenth] amendment was first called to the attention of this court in the *Slaughter-house cases* . . . which involved, however, not a question of race, but one of exclusive privileges. The case did not call for any expression of opinion as to the exact rights it was intended to secure to the colored race, but it was said generally that its main purpose was to establish the citizenship of the negro; to give definitions of citizenship of the United States and of the States, and to protect from the hostile legislation of the States the privileges and immunities of citizens of the United States, as distinguished from those of citizens of the States.

The object of the amendment was undoubtedly to enforce the absolute equality of the two races before the law, but in the nature of things it could not have been intended to abolish distinctions based upon color, or to enforce social, as distinguished from political equality, or a commingling of the two races upon terms unsatisfactory to either. Laws permitting, and even requiring, their separation in places where they are liable to be brought into contact do not necessarily imply the inferiority of either race to the other, and have been generally, if not universally, recognized as within the competency of the state legislatures in the exercise of their police power. The most common instance of this is connected with the establishment of separate schools for white and colored children, which has been held to be a valid exercise of the legislative power even by courts of States where the political rights of the colored race have been longest and most earnestly enforced.

One of the earliest of these cases is that of *Roberts v. City of Boston* . . . in which the Supreme Judicial Court of Massachusetts held that the general school committee of Boston had power to make provision for the instruction of colored children in separate schools established exclusively for them, and to prohibit their attendance upon the other schools. . . . It was held that the powers of the committee extended to the establishment of separate schools for children of different ages, sexes and colors, and that they might also establish special schools for poor and neglected children, who have become too old to attend the primary school, and yet have not acquired the rudiments of learning, to enable them to enter the ordinary schools. Similar laws have been enacted by Congress under its general power of legislation over the District of Columbia . . . as well as by the legislatures of many of the States, and have been generally, if not uniformly, sustained by the courts. *State* v. *McCann*, 21 Ohio St. 198; *Lehew* v. *Brummell*, 15 S.W. Rep. 765; *Ward* v. *Flood*, 48 California, 36; *Bertonneau* v. *School Directors*, 3 Woods, 177; *People* v. *Gallagher*, 93 N.Y. 438; *Cory* v. *Carter*, 48 Indiana, 327; *Dawson* v. *Lee*, 83 Kentucky, 49.

Laws forbidding the intermarriage of the two races may be said in a technical sense to interfere with the freedom of contract, and yet have been universally recognized as within the police power of the State. *State* v. *Gibson*, 36 Indiana, 389.

The distinction between laws interfering with the political equality of the negro and those requiring the separation of the two races in schools, theatres and railway carriages has been frequently drawn by this court. Thus in *Strauder* v. *West Virginia* . . . it was held that a law of West Virginia limiting to white male persons, 21 years of age and citizens of the State, the right to sit upon juries, was a discrimination which implied a legal inferiority in civil society, which lessened the security of the right of the colored race, and was a step toward reducing them to a condition of servility. Indeed, the right of a colored man that, in the selection of jurors to pass upon his life, liberty and property, there shall be no exclusion of his race, and no discrimination against them because of color, has been asserted in a number of cases. *Virginia* v. *Rives*, 100 U.S. 313[.] . . . So, where the laws of a particular locality or the charter of a particular railway corporation has provided that no person shall be excluded from the cars on account of color, we have held that this meant that persons of color should travel in the same car as white ones, and that the enactment was not satisfied by the company's providing cars assigned exclusively to people of color, though they were as good as those which they assigned exclusively to white persons. *Railroad Company* v. *Brown*, 17 Wall. 445.

Upon the other hand, where a statute of Louisiana required those engaged in the transportation of passengers among the States to give to all persons travelling within that State, upon vessels employed in that business, equal rights and privileges in all parts of the vessel, without distinction on account of race or color, and subjected to an action for damages the owner of such a vessel, who excluded colored passengers on account of their color from the cabin set aside by him for the use of whites, it was held to be so far as it applied to interstate commerce, unconstitutional and void. *Hall* v. *De Cuir*, 95 U.S. 485. The court in this case, however, expressly disclaimed that it had anything whatever to do with the statute as a regulation of internal commerce, or affecting anything else than commerce among the States.

In the *Civil Rights case[s]*, 109 U.S. 3, it was held that an act of Congress, entitling all persons within the jurisdiction of the United States to the full and equal enjoyment of the accommodations, advantages, facilities and privileges of inns, public conveyances, on land or water, theatres and other places of public amusement, and made applicable to citizens of every race and color, regardless of any previous condition of servitude, was unconstitutional and void, upon the ground that the Fourteenth Amendment was prohibitory upon the States only, and the legislation authorized to be adopted by Congress for enforcing it was not direct legislation on matters respecting which the States were prohibited from making or enforcing certain laws, or doing certain acts, but was corrective legislation, such as might be necessary or proper for counteracting and redressing the effect of such laws or acts. . . .

Much nearer, and, indeed, almost directly in point, is the case of the *Louisville, New Orleans &c. Railway* v. *Mississippi*, 3 U.S. 587, wherein the railway company was indicted for a violation of a statute of Mississippi, enacting that all railroads carrying passengers should provide equal, but separate, accommodations for the white and colored races, by providing two or more passenger cars for each passenger train, or by dividing the passenger cars by a partition, so as to secure separate accommodations. The case was presented in a different aspect from the one under consideration, inasmuch as it was an indictment against the railway company for failing to provide the separate accommodations, but the question considered was the constitutionality of the law. In that case, the Supreme Court of Mississippi, 66 Mississippi 662, had held that the statute applied solely to commerce within the State, and, that being the construction of the state statute by its highest court, was accepted as conclusive. "If it be a matter," said the court, p. 591, "respecting commerce wholly within a State, and not interfering with commerce between the States, then, obviously, there is no violation of the commerce clause of the Federal Constitution. . . . No question arises under this section, as to the power of the State to separate in different compartments interstate passengers, or affect, in any manner, the privileges and rights of such passengers. All that we can consider is, whether the State has the power to require that railroad trains within her limits shall have separate accommodations for the two races; that affecting only commerce within the State is no invasion of the power given to Congress by the commerce clause."

A like course of reasoning applies to the case under consideration, since the Supreme Court of Louisiana in the case of the *State ex rel. Abbott* v. *Hicks, Judge, et al.*, 44 La. Ann. 770, held that the statute in question did not apply to interstate passengers, but was confined in its application to passengers travelling exclusively within the borders of the State. . . . In the present case no question of interference with interstate commerce can possibly arise, since the East Louisiana Railway appears to have been purely a local line, with both its termini within the State of Louisiana. Similar statutes for the separation of the two races upon public conveyances were held to be constitutional in [cases decided by the highest courts of Pennsylvania, Michigan, Illinois, and Tennessee, among others].

While we think the enforced separation of the races, as applied to the internal commerce of the State, neither abridges the privileges or immunities of the colored man, deprives him of his property without due process of law, nor denies him the equal protection of the laws, within the meaning of the Fourteenth Amendment, we are not prepared to say that the conductor, in assigning passengers to the coaches according to their race, does not act at his peril, or that the provision of the second section of the act, that denies to the passenger compensation in damages for a refusal to receive him into the coach in which he properly belongs, is a valid exercise of the legislative power. Indeed, we understand it to be conceded by the State's attorney, that such part of the act as exempts from liability the railway company and its officers is unconstitutional. The power to assign to a particular coach obviously implies the power to determine to which race the passenger belongs, as well as the power to determine who, under the laws of the particular State, is to be deemed a white, and who a colored person. This question, though indicated in the brief of the plaintiff in error, does not properly arise upon the record in this case, since the only issue made is as to the unconstitutionality of the act, so far as it requires the railway to provide separate accommodations, and the conductor to assign passengers according to their race.

It is claimed by the plaintiff in error that, in any mixed community, the reputation of belonging to the dominant race, in this instance the white race, is *property*, in the same sense that a right of action, or of inheritance, is property. Conceding this to be so, for the purposes of this case, we are unable to see how this statute deprives him of, or in any way affects his right to, such property. If he be a white man and assigned to a colored coach, he may have his action for damages against the company for being deprived of his so called property. Upon the other hand, if he be a colored man and be so assigned, he has been deprived of no property, since he is not lawfully entitled to the reputation of being a white man.

In this connection, it is also suggested by the learned counsel for the plaintiff in error that the same argument that will justify the state legislature in requiring railways to provide separate accommodations for the two races will also authorize them to require separate cars to be provided for people whose hair is of a certain color, or who are aliens, or who belong to certain nationalities, or to enact laws requiring colored people to walk upon one side of the street, and white people upon the other, or requiring white men's houses to be painted white, and colored men's black, or their vehicles or business signs to be of different colors, upon the theory that one side of the street is as good as the other, or that a house or vehicle of one color is as good as one of another color. The reply to all this is that every exercise of the police power must be reasonable, and extend only to such laws as are enacted in good faith for the promotion for the public good, and not for the annoyance or oppression of a particular class. Thus in *Yick Wo* v. *Hopkins*, 118 U.S. 356, it was held by this court that a municipal ordinance of the city of San Francisco, to regulate the carrying on of public laundries within the limits of the municipality, violated the provisions of the Constitution of the United States, if it conferred upon the municipal authorities arbitrary power, at their own will, and without regard to discretion, in the legal sense of the term, to give or withhold consent as to persons or places, without regard to the competency of the persons applying, or the propriety of the places selected for the carrying on of the business. It was held to be a covert attempt on the part of the municipality to make an arbitrary and unjust discrimination against the Chinese race. While this was the case of a municipal ordinance, a like principle has been held to apply to acts of a state legislature passed in the exercise of the police power. . . .

So far, then, as a conflict with the Fourteenth Amendment is concerned, the case reduces itself to the question whether the statute of Louisiana is a reasonable regulation, and with respect to this there must necessarily be a large discretion on the part of the legislature. In determining the question of reasonableness it is at liberty to act with reference to the established usages, customs and traditions of the people, and with a view to the promotion of their comfort, and the preservation of the public peace and good order. Gauged by this standard, we cannot say that a law which authorizes or even requires the separation of the two races in public conveyances is unreasonable, or more obnoxious to the Fourteenth Amendment than the acts of Congress requiring separate schools for colored children in the District of Columbia, the constitutionality of which does not seem to have been questioned, or the corresponding acts of state legislatures.

We consider the underlying fallacy of the plaintiff's argument to consist in the assumption that the enforced separation of the two races stamps the colored race with a badge of inferiority. If this be so, it is not by reason of anything found in the act, but solely because the colored race chooses to put that construction upon it. The argument necessarily assumes that if, as has been more than once the case, and is not unlikely to be so again, the colored race should become the dominant power in the state legislature, and should enact a law in precisely similar terms, it would thereby relegate the white race to an inferior position. We imagine that the white race, at least, would not acquiesce in this assumption. The argument also assumes that social prejudices may be overcome by legislation, and that equal rights cannot be secured to the negro except by an enforced commingling of the two races. We cannot accept this proposition. If the two races are to meet upon terms of social equality, it must be the result of natural affinities, a mutual appreciation of each other's merits and a voluntary consent of individuals. . . . Legislation is powerless to eradicate racial instincts or to abolish distinctions based upon physical differences, and the attempt to do so can only result in accentuating the difficulties of the present situation. If the civil and political rights of both races be equal one cannot be inferior to the other civilly or politically. If one race be inferior to the other socially, the Constitution of the United States cannot put them upon the same plane.

It is true that the question of the proportion of colored blood necessary to constitute a colored person, as distinguished from a white person, is one upon which there is a difference of opinion in the different States, some holding that any visible admixture of black blood stamps the person as belonging to the colored race . . . ; others that it depends upon the preponderance of blood . . . ; and still others that the predominance of white blood must only be in the proportion of three fourths. . . . But these are question to be determined under the laws of each State and are not properly put in issue in this case. Under the allegations of his petition it may undoubtedly become a question of importance whether, under the laws of Louisiana, the petitioner belongs to the white or colored race.

The judgment of the court below is, therefore,

Affirmed.

MR. JUSTICE [John M.] HARLAN dissenting.

. . . In respect of civil rights, common to all citizens, the Constitution of the United States does not, I think, permit any public authority to know the race of those entitled to be protected in the enjoyment of such rights. Every true man has pride of race, and under appropriate circumstances when the rights of others, his equals before the law, are not to be affected, it is his privilege to express such pride and to take such action based upon it as to him seems proper. But I deny that any legislative body or judicial tribunal may have regard to the race of citizens when the civil rights of those citizens are involved. Indeed, such legislation, as that here in question, is inconsistent not only with that equality of rights which pertains to citizenship, National and State, but with the personal liberty enjoyed by every one within the United States. . . .

. . . It was said in argument that the statute of Louisiana does not discriminate against either race, but prescribes a rule applicable alike to white and colored citizens. But this argument does not meet the difficulty. Every one knows that the statute in question had its origin in the purpose, not so much to exclude white persons from railroad cars occupied by blacks, as to exclude colored people from coaches occupied by or assigned to white persons. Railroad corporations of Louisiana did not make discrimination among whites in the matter of accommodation for travellers. The thing to accomplish was, under the guise of giving equal accommodation for whites and blacks, to compel the latter to keep to themselves while travelling in railroad passenger coaches. No one would be so wanting in candor as to assert the contrary. The fundamental objection, therefore, to the statute is that it interferes with the personal freedom of citizens. . . . If a white man and a black man choose to occupy the same public conveyance on a public highway, it is their right to do so, and no government, proceeding alone on grounds of race, can prevent it without infringing the personal liberty of each.

It is one thing for railroad carriers to furnish, or to be required by law to furnish, equal accommodations for all whom they are under a legal duty to carry. It is quite another thing for government to forbid citizens of the white and black races from travelling in the same public conveyance, and to punish officers of railroad companies for permitting persons of the two races to occupy the same passenger coach. If a State can prescribe, as a rule of civil conduct, that whites and blacks shall not travel as passengers in the same railroad coach, why may it not so regulate the use of the streets of its cities and towns as to compel white citizens to keep on one side of a street and black citizens to keep on the other? Why may it not, upon like grounds, punish whites and blacks who ride together in street cars or in open vehicles on a public road or street? Why may it not require sheriffs to assign whites to one side of a court-room and blacks to the other? And why may it not also prohibit the commingling of the two races in the galleries of legislative halls or in public assemblages convened for the consideration of the political questions of the day? Further, if this statute of Louisiana is consistent with the personal liberty of citizens, why may not the State require the separation in railroad coaches of native and naturalized citizens of the United States, or of Protestants and Roman Catholics?

The answer given at the argument to these questions was that regulations of the kind they suggest would be unreasonable, and could not, therefore, stand before the law. Is it meant that the determination of questions of legislative power depends upon the inquiry whether the statute whose validity is questioned is, in the judgment of the courts, a reasonable one, taking all the circumstances into consideration? A statute may be unreasonable merely because a sound public policy forbade its enactment. But I do not understand that the courts have anything to do with the policy or expediency of legislation. A statute may be valid, and yet, upon grounds of public policy, may well be characterized as unreasonable. . . . There is a dangerous tendency in these latter days to enlarge the functions of the courts, by means of judicial interference with the will of the people as expressed by the legislature. Our institutions have the distinguishing characteristic that the three departments of government are coördinate and separate. Each must keep within the limits defined by the Constitution. And the courts best discharge their duty by executing the will of the law-making power, constitutionally expressed, leaving the results of legislation to be dealt with by the people through their representatives. Statutes must always have a reasonable construction. Sometimes they are to be construed strictly; sometimes, liberally, in order to carry out the legislative will. But however construed, the intent of the legislature is to be respected, if the particular statute in question is valid, although the courts, looking at the public interests, may conceive the statute to be both unreasonable and impolitic. If the power exists to enact a statute, that ends the matter so far as the courts are concerned. The adjudged cases in which statutes have been held to be void, because unreasonable, are those in which the means employed by the legislature were not at all germane to the end to which the legislature was competent.

The white race deems itself to be the dominant race in this country. And so it is, in prestige, in achievements, in education, in wealth and in power. So, I doubt not, it will continue to be for all time, if it remains true to its great heritage and holds fast to the principles of constitutional liberty. But in view of the Constitution, in the eye of the law, there is in this country no superior, dominant, ruling class of citizens. There is no caste here. Our Constitution is color-blind, and neither knows nor tolerates classes among citizens. In respect of civil rights, all citizens are equal before the law. The humblest is the peer of the most powerful. The law regards man as man, and takes no account of his surroundings or of his color when his civil rights as guaranteed by the supreme law of the land are involved. It is, therefore, to be regretted that this high tribunal, the final expositor of the fundamental law of the land, has reached the conclusion that it is competent for a State to regulate the enjoyment by citizens of their civil rights solely upon the basis of race.

In my opinion, the judgment this day rendered will, in time, prove to be quite as pernicious as the decision made by this tribunal in the *Dred Scott case*. It was adjudged in that case that the descendants of Africans who were imported into this country and sold as slaves were not included nor intended to be included under the word "citizens" in the Constitution, and could not claim any of the rights and privileges which that instrument provided for and secured to citizens of the United States; that at the time of the adoption of the Constitution they were "considered as a subordinate and inferior class of beings, who had been subjugated by the dominant race, and, whether emancipated or not, yet remained subject to their authority, and had no rights or privileges but such as those who held the power and the government might choose to grant them." ... The recent amendments of the Constitution, it was supposed, had eradicated these principles from our institutions. But it seems that we have yet, in some of the States, a dominant race—a superior class of citizens, which assumes to regulate the enjoyment of civil rights, common to all citizens, upon the basis of race. The present decision, it may well be apprehended, will not only stimulate aggressions, more or less brutal and irritating, upon the admitted rights of colored citizens, but will encourage the belief that it is possible, by means of state enactments, to defeat the beneficent purposes which the people of the

United States had in view when they adopted the recent amendments of the Constitution, by one of which the blacks of this country were made citizens of the United States and of the States in which they respectively reside, and whose privileges and immunities, as citizens, the States are forbidden to abridge. Sixty millions of whites are in no danger from the presence here of eight millions of blacks. The destinies of the two races, in this country, are indissolubly linked together, and the interests of both require that the common government of all shall not permit the seeds of race hate to be planted under the sanction of law. What can more certainly arouse race hate, what more certainly create and perpetuate a feeling of distrust between these races, than state enactments, which, in fact, proceed on the ground that colored citizens are so inferior and degraded that they cannot be allowed to sit in public coaches occupied by white citizens? That, as all will admit, is the real meaning of such legislation as was enacted in Louisiana.

The sure guarantee of the peace and security of each race is the clear, distinct, unconditional recognition by our governments, National and State, of every right that inheres in civil freedom, and of the equality before the law of all citizens of the United States without regard to race. State enactments, regulating the enjoyment of civil rights, upon the basis of race, and cunningly devised to defeat legitimate results of the war, under the pretence of recognizing equality of rights, can have no other result than to render permanent peace impossible, and to keep alive a conflict of races, the continuance of which must do harm to all concerned. This question is not met by the suggestion that social equality cannot exist between the white and black races in this country. That argument, if it can be properly regarded as one, is scarcely worthy of consideration; for social equality no more exists between two races when travelling in a passenger coach or a public highway than when members of the same races sit by each other in a street car or in the jury box, or stand or sit with each other in a political assembly, or when they use in common the streets of a city or town, or when they are in the same room for the purpose of having their names placed on the registry of voters, or when they approach the ballot-box in order to exercise the high privilege of voting.

There is a race so different from our own that we do not permit those belonging to it to become citizens of the United States. Persons belonging to it are, with few exceptions, absolutely excluded from our country. I allude to the Chinese race. But by the statute in question, a Chinaman can ride in the same passenger coach with white citizens of the United States, while citizens of the black race in Louisiana, many of whom, perhaps, risked their lives for the preservation of the Union, who are entitled, by law, to participate in the political control of the State and nation, who are not excluded, by law or by reason of their race, from public stations of any kind, and who have all the legal rights that belong to white citizens, are yet declared to be criminals, liable to imprisonment, if they ride in a public coach occupied by citizens of the white race. It is scarcely just to say that a colored citizen should not object to occupying a public coach assigned to his own race. He does not object, nor, perhaps, would he object to separate coaches for his race, if his rights under the law were recognized. But he objects, and ought never to cease objecting to the proposition, that citizens of the white and black races can be adjudged criminals because they sit, or claim the right to sit, in the same public coach on a public highway.

The arbitrary separation of citizens, on the basis of race, while they are on a public highway, is a badge of servitude wholly inconsistent with the civil freedom and the equality before the law established by the Constitution. It cannot be justified upon any legal grounds.

. . . We boast of the freedom enjoyed by our people above all other peoples. But it is difficult to reconcile that boast with a state of the law which, practically, puts the brand of servitude and degradation upon a large class of our fellow-citizens, our equals before the law. The thin disguise of "equal" accommodations for passengers in railroad coaches will not mislead any one, nor atone for the wrong this day done. . . .

I am of opinion that the statute of Louisiana is inconsistent with the personal liberty of citizens, white and black, in that State, and hostile to both the spirit and letter of the Constitution of the United States. If laws of like character should be enacted in the several States of the Union, the effect would be in the highest degree mischievous. Slavery, as an institution tolerated by law would, it is true, have disappeared from our country, but there would remain a power in the States, by sinister legislation, to interfere with the full enjoyment of the blessings of freedom; to regulate civil rights, common to all citizens, upon the basis of race; and to place in a condition of legal inferiority a large body of American citizens, now constituting a part of the political community called the People of the United States, for whom, and by whom through representatives, our government is administered. Such a system is inconsistent with the guarantee given by the Constitution to each State of a republican form of government, and may be stricken down by Congressional action, or by the courts in the discharge of their solemn duty to maintain the supreme law of the land, anything in the constitution or laws of any State to the contrary notwithstanding.

For the reasons stated, I am constrained to withhold my assent from the opinion and judgment of the majority.

NOTES
FURTHER READING
INDEX

Introduction

1. *Congressional Globe,* 38th Cong., 1st sess. (May 31, 1864), 2615.

2. Wendell Phillips, "Under the Flag," in *Speeches, Lectures and Letters* (Boston: James Redpath, 1863), 414.

3. Henry Winter Davis, *Speech of Hon. Henry Winter Davis at Concert Hall, September 24, 1863* (Philadelphia, 1863), 12.

Chapter 1: The Status of African Americans before the Civil War

1. Leon Litwak, *North of Slavery: The Negro in the Free States, 1790–1860* (Chicago: University of Chicago Press, 1961), 279.

2. Paul Finkelman, "Prelude to the Fourteenth Amendment: Black Legal Rights in the Antebellum North," *Rutgers Law Journal* 17 (1986): 415–82.

3. *The Constitution of the American Anti-Slavery Society, with the Declaration of the National Anti-Slavery Convention at Philadelphia, December, 1833, and the Address to the Public, Issued by the Executive Committee of the Society, in September, 1835* (New York: American Anti-Slavery Society, 1833), 6–8.

4. All quotes in this paragraph and the next are from *Sarah C. Roberts v. The City of Boston,* 59 Mass. 198 (Massachusetts Supreme Judicial Court, 1850).

5. Brackets appear in original.

6. "Sanford" is the correct spelling of the name, but because of a court clerk error, the title of the case is officially *Dred Scott v. Sandford.*

7. Roy P. Basler, ed., *The Collected Works of Abraham Lincoln,* 9 vols. (New Brunswick, N.J.: Rutgers University Press, 1953), 2:494–502.

8. Basler's *Collected Works* has this as "in" but notes that in the *Chicago Daily Press and Tribune* of July 12, 1858, it is "it."

9. The brackets in this sentence and two paragraphs below appear in the original.

Chapter 2: The Expansion of Governmental Power and the Nationalization of the Union

1. Roy P. Basler, ed., *The Collected Works of Abraham Lincoln,* 9 vols. (New Brunswick, N.J.: Rutgers University Press, 1953), 4:419.

2. See document 8 in this chapter.

3. *Ex parte Vallandingham,* 68 U.S. 243, 249 (1863).

4. An Act donating Public Lands to the several States and Territories which may provide Colleges for the Benefit of Agriculture and the Mechanic Arts, 12 Stat. 503 (July 2, 1862).

5. Basler, *Collected Works,* 4:331–32.

6. Ibid., 5:436–37.

7. The original uses both the "Lamdin" and "Lambdin" spellings.

Chapter 3: African Americans, Emancipation, and Military Service

1. See document 7 in this chapter.

2. Ira Berlin, Joseph P. Reidy, and Leslie S. Rowland, eds., *The Black Military Experience* (Cambridge: Cambridge University Press, 1982), 1–2.

3. Again, both "Sandford" and "Sanford" are found in the original.

4. Roy P. Basler, ed., *The Collected Works of Abraham Lincoln*, 9 vols. (New Brunswick, N.J.: Rutgers University Press, 1953), 6:406–10.

5. In this section, brackets that were found in the original have been replaced with parentheses, and my interpolations are now in brackets.

6. The transcripts, written quickly during trial, are also marked by a great deal of irregularity in terms of spelling and formatting. The transcripts that follow in this section retain these irregularities and inconsistencies; any changes or interpolations are enclosed in brackets. In addition, speakers' names are italicized for clarity.

7. A roundabout was a shorter uniform jacket, more suitable for the summer months or duty in warmer climates.

8. In this transcript, most of the questions and answers were originally enclosed in quotation marks, which I have omitted here.

Chapter 4: Rights during the Civil War and Reconstruction: Potential, Change, and Opposition

1. *Proceedings of the Southern States Convention of Colored Men, Held in Columbia, S.C., Commencing October 18, Ending October 25, 1871* (Columbia, S.C.: Carolina Printing Company, 1871), 39.

2. Frederick Douglass, "At Last, at Last, the Black Man Has a Future: An Address Delivered in Albany, New York, on 22 April, 1870," in *The Frederick Douglass Papers*, series 1, ed. John W. Blassingame and John R. McKivigan (New Haven: Yale University Press, 1979), 4:265–72, 266–67, 270–71.

3. *Congressional Globe*, 39th Cong., 1st sess. (December 21, 1865), 107–8.

4. Ibid., 127–28.

5. In this section, brackets that were found in the original have been replaced with parentheses, and my interpolations are now in brackets.

6. *Congressional Globe*, 39th Cong., 1st sess. (January 29, 1866), 474.

7. Ibid., 477.

8. Ibid. (January 31, 1866), 528.

9. Ibid. (January 30, 1866), 504.

10. Ibid. (January 31, 1866), 561 (Davis); ibid. (February 1, 1866), 570 (Morrill).

11. Ibid. (February 2, 1866), 603.

Chapter 5: Judicial Interpretation and Limitation of the Civil War Amendments and Civil Rights Legislation

1. The original skips from Section 1 to Section 4.

2. The strange comma usage in this sentence appears in the original.

Further Reading

H. Robert Baker, *The Rescue of Joshua Glover: A Fugitive Slave, the Constitution, and the Coming of the Civil War* (Athens: Ohio University Press, 2006).

Herman Belz, *Abraham Lincoln, Constitutionalism, and Equal Rights in the Civil War Era* (New York: Fordham University Press, 1998).

———, *A New Birth of Freedom: The Republican Party and Freedmen's Rights, 1861–1866*, 2nd ed. (New York: Fordham University Press, 2000).

Michael Les Benedict, *A Compromise of Principle: Congressional Republicans and Reconstruction, 1863–1869* (New York: W. W. Norton, 1974).

———, *Preserving the Constitution: Essays on Politics and the Constitution in the Reconstruction Era* (New York: Fordham University Press, 2006).

Ira Berlin, *Many Thousands Gone: The First Two Centuries of Slavery in North America* (Cambridge: Harvard University Press, 1998).

Paul A. Cimbala and Randall M. Miller, eds., *The Freedmen's Bureau and Reconstruction: Reconsiderations* (New York: Fordham University Press, 1999).

Michael Kent Curtis, *No State Shall Abridge: The Fourteenth Amendment and the Bill of Rights* (Durham, N.C.: Duke University Press, 1986).

Nicole Etcheson, *Bleeding Kansas: Contested Liberty in the Civil War Era* (Lawrence: University Press of Kansas, 2004).

Daniel Farber, *Lincoln's Constitution* (Chicago: University of Chicago Press, 2003).

Don E. Fehrenbacher, *The Dred Scott Case: Its Significance in American Law and Politics* (New York: Oxford University Press, 1978).

Paul Finkelman, "Prelude to the Fourteenth Amendment: Black Legal Rights in the Antebellum North," *Rutgers Law Journal* 17 (1986): 415–82.

———, ed., *Slavery and the Law* (Madison, Wis.: Madison House Publishers, 1997).

Eric Foner, *Reconstruction: America's Unfinished Revolution 1863–1877* (New York: Harper and Row, 1988).

Philip S. Foner and George E. Walker, eds., *Proceedings of the Black National and State Conventions, 1865–1900* (Philadelphia: Temple University Press, 1986).

———, *Proceedings of the Black State Conventions, 1840–1865*, 2 vols. (Philadelphia: Temple University Press, 1979–80).

George M. Fredrickson, *Big Enough to Be Inconsistent: Abraham Lincoln Confronts Slavery and Race* (Cambridge: Harvard University Press, 2008).

Allen C. Guelzo, *Lincoln and Douglas: The Debates That Defined America* (New York: Simon and Schuster, 2008).

———, *Lincoln's Emancipation Proclamation: The End of Slavery in America* (New York: Simon and Schuster, 2004).

Sally E. Hadden, *Slave Patrols: Law and Violence in Virginia and the Carolinas* (Cambridge: Harvard University Press, 2001).

Harold Holzer, ed., *The Lincoln-Douglas Debates: The First Complete, Unexpurgated Text* (New York: Fordham University Press, 2004).

Harold Holzer and Sara Vaughn Gabbard, eds., *Lincoln and Freedom: Slavery, Emancipation, and the Thirteenth Amendment* (Carbondale: Southern Illinois University Press, 2007).

Harold Holzer, Edna Greene Medford, and Frank J. Williams, *The Emancipation Proclamation: Three Views* (Baton Rouge: Louisiana State University Press, 2006).

James Oliver Horton and Lois E. Horton, *In Hope of Liberty: Culture, Community and Protest among Northern Free Blacks, 1700–1860* (New York: Oxford University Press, 1997).

Harold M. Hyman, *A More Perfect Union: The Impact of the Civil War and Reconstruction on the Constitution* (New York: Alfred A. Knopf, 1973).

Robert J. Kaczorowski, *The Politics of Judicial Interpretation: The Federal Courts, Department of Justice, and Civil Rights, 1866–1876*, 2nd ed. (New York: Fordham University Press, 2005).

———, "Revolutionary Constitutionalism in the Era of the Civil War and Reconstruction," *New York University Law Review* 61 (1986): 863–940.

———, "To Begin the Nation Anew: Congress, Citizenship, and Civil Rights after the Civil War," *American Historical Review* 92 (1987): 45–68.

Bruce Laurie, *Beyond Garrison: Antislavery and Social Reform* (New York: Cambridge University Press, 2005).

Nicholas Lemann, *Redemption: The Last Battle of the Civil War* (New York: Farrar, Straus and Giroux, 2006).

Charles A. Lofgren, *The Plessy Case: A Legal-Historical Interpretation* (New York: Oxford University Press, 1988).

Earl M. Maltz, *Civil Rights, the Constitution, and Congress, 1863–1869* (Lawrence: University Press of Kansas, 1990).

Matthew Mason, *Slavery and Politics in the Early American Republic* (Chapel Hill: University of North Carolina Press, 2006).

Brian McGinty, *Lincoln and the Court* (Cambridge: Harvard University Press, 2008).

Thomas D. Morris, *Southern Slavery and the Law: 1619–1860* (Chapel Hill: University of North Carolina Press, 1996).

Mark E. Neely Jr., *The Fate of Liberty: Abraham Lincoln and Civil Liberties* (New York: Oxford University Press, 1991).

William E. Nelson, *The Fourteenth Amendment: From Political Principle to Judicial Doctrine* (Cambridge: Harvard University Press, 1988).

William J. Novak, "The Legal Transformation of Citizenship in Nineteenth-Century America," in *The Democratic Experiment*, ed. Meg Jacobs et al., 84–119 (Princeton, N.J.: Princeton University Press, 2003).

James Oakes, *The Radical and the Republican: Frederick Douglass, Abraham Lincoln, and the Triumph of Antislavery Politics* (New York: W. W. Norton, 2007).

Patrick Rael, *Black Identity and Black Protest in the Antebellum North* (Chapel Hill: University of North Carolina Press, 2002).

Elizabeth Regosin, *Freedom's Promise: Ex-Slave Families and Citizenship in the Age of Emancipation* (Charlottesville: University Press of Virginia, 2002).

David A. J. Richards, *Conscience and the Constitution: History, Theory, and Law of the Reconstruction Amendments* (Princeton, N.J.: Princeton University Press, 1993).

Heather Cox Richardson, *The Death of Reconstruction: Race, Labor, and Politics in the Post–Civil War North, 1865–1901* (Cambridge: Harvard University Press, 2001).

———, *The Greatest Nation of the Earth: Republican Economic Policies during the Civil War* (Cambridge: Harvard University Press, 1997).

Michael Ross, *Justice of Shattered Dreams: Samuel Freeman Miller and the Supreme Court during the Civil War Era* (Baton Rouge: Louisiana State University Press, 2003).

Christian G. Samito, *Becoming American Under Fire: Irish Americans, African Americans, and the Politics of Citizenship during the Civil War Era* (Ithaca, N.Y.: Cornell University Press, 2009).

———, "The Intersection between Military Justice and Equal Rights: Mutinies, Courts-Martial, and Black Civil War Soldiers," *Civil War History* (June 2007): 170–202.

Donald R. Shaffer, *After the Glory: The Struggles of Black Civil War Veterans* (Lawrence: University Press of Kansas, 2004).

Silvana R. Siddali, *From Property to Person: Slavery and the Confiscation Acts, 1861–1862* (Baton Rouge: Louisiana State University Press, 2005).

Amy Dru Stanley, *From Bondage to Contract: Wage Labor, Marriage, and the Market in the Age of Slave Emancipation* (New York: Cambridge University Press, 1998).

John Stauffer, *The Black Hearts of Men: Radical Abolitionists and the Transformation of Race* (Cambridge: Harvard University Press, 2002).

Albert J. Von Frank, *The Trials of Anthony Burns: Freedom and Slavery in Emerson's Boston* (Cambridge: Harvard University Press, 1998).

Michael Vorenberg, *Final Freedom: The Civil War, the Abolition of Slavery, and the Thirteenth Amendment* (New York: Cambridge University Press, 2001).

Christopher Waldrep, *Roots of Disorder: Race and Criminal Justice in the American South, 1817–80* (Urbana: University of Illinois Press, 1998).

Xi Wang, "The Making of Federal Enforcement Laws, 1870–1872," *Chicago-Kent Law Review* 70 (1995): 1013–58.

———, *The Trial of Democracy: Black Suffrage and Northern Republicans 1860–1910* (Athens: University of Georgia Press, 1997).

Frank J. Williams, *Judging Lincoln* (Carbondale: Southern Illinois University Press, 2002).

Keith P. Wilson, *Campfires of Freedom: The Camp Life of Black Soldiers during the Civil War* (Kent, Ohio: Kent State University Press, 2002).

C. Vann Woodward, *The Strange Career of Jim Crow* (1955; New York: Oxford University Press, 2001).

INDEX

I have generally not listed documents except where they are discussed in text written by the editor other than the introductory note for each document. Illustrations are italicized.

abolitionism, 6, 7–8

Act of July 27, 1868, 220–22

African Americans, 1; activism, 6–7, 21–24, 28, 30–33, 33, 35, 115–23, 127–56, 157, 159–63, 166, 168–83, 236–56, 260–61, 285–89; African American interpretation of military service, 30–33, 100, 115–19, 120–22, 159–63, 170–71, 173–75, 177–83; and the American Revolution, 6–7, 30–33, 171; convention movement, 7, 164, 166 168–83; emigrationism, 7, 173; integrationism, 7; military service, 30–33, 100–101, 103, 110–11, 115–56, 157, 159, 160, 164; military service and freedom from slavery, 103, 157–59; rights before the war, 5–6, 21–24, 42–52; violence against, 2, 165–68 (*see also* Ku Klux Klan; White Line; white supremacism); white interpretation of military service, 123–27, 182, 188–89, 197, 212, 213, 223–26, 265–66. *See also* Black Codes; citizenship; Civil Rights Act of 1866; Civil Rights Act of 1875; courts-martial; Emancipation Proclamation; Enforcement Acts; Fifteenth Amendment; Fourteenth Amendment; Fugitive Slave Act of 1793; Fugitive Slave Act of 1850; fugitive slaves; Reconstruction Acts; slavery; segregation; suffrage; Thirteenth Amendment; unequal pay

Alabama, 62, 67, 164, 166, 169, 190–92

Albany, New York, 6

American Anti-Slavery Society, 6, 227

American Freemen's Inquiry Commission, 183

Ames, Adelbert, 254

Antietam, 103

Arkansas, 164, 166

Aves, Thomas, 11

Banks, Robert, 247

Baker, Wallace, 140–48

Baltimore, Maryland, 59–60

Bangor, Maine, 60

Barron v. Baltimore, 261

Bates, Edward, 72, 105, 117, 164

Bean, Jacob A., 130–38

Beck, Joseph M., 236

Bellow, Frank, 231

Belmont, August, 213

Benét, Stephen, 139

Bidderman, Tom, 247

Black Codes, 165, 189–96, 198–99

blockade, 60, 67

Blythe, David G., 111

Boston, Massachusetts, 21–24. *See also* Burns affair

Boutwell, George S., 164, 169, 185–88

Bowser, David Bustill, 119

Bradley, Joseph, 297

branches of government, 59–60, 63–79

Breckinridge, John C., 85

Brockway, Charles B., 188–89

Brown, Henry, 310

Brown, John, 112

Buchanan, Franklin, 85

Buchanan, James, 111

Buckner, Simon B., 85

A graduate of the College of the Holy Cross, **Christian G. Samito** earned a law degree from Harvard Law School and a doctorate in American history from Boston College. He edited for publication the Civil War letters of Colonel Patrick R. Guiney and Major General Francis C. Barlow and published an article about courts-martial and black Civil War soldiers. His book about citizenship during the era of the Civil War and Reconstruction is forthcoming. In addition to teaching at Boston College and Boston University Law School, he practices law in Boston.